Matrimonial Consent Orders and Agreements

FITZPATRICK DRUMMOND
12/14 KING STREET
WAKEFIELD
WF1 2SQ
TELEPHONE: (01924) 369916

To Anne, Robin, William and Alice
Emma, Patrick, Dominic and Zoe

Matrimonial Consent Orders and Agreements

Third Edition

David Salter, MA, LLM (Cantab)
Solicitor
Partner in Booth & Co, Leeds
Vice-Chairman of Solicitors' Family Law Association
Member of Family Proceedings Rules Committee
Recorder of the Crown Court

Simon Bruce, MA (Oxon)
Solicitor
Partner in Farrer & Co, London
Member of the Solicitors' Family Law
Association Procedure Committee

LAW & TAX

© Pearson Professional Ltd 1996

ISBN 0 85121 971 3

Published by
FT Law & Tax
21–27 Lamb's Conduit Street
London WC1N 3NJ

Associated Offices
Australia, Belgium, Canada, Hong Kong, India, Japan, Luxembourg, Singapore, Spain, USA

First published 1986
Third edition 1996

All rights reserved. No part of this publication may be reproduced stored in a retrieval system, or transmitted, in any form or by any means, electronic, mechanical, photocopying recording or otherwise, without the prior written permission of the publishers.

No responsibility for loss occasioned to any person acting or refraining from action as a result of the material in this publication can be accepted by the author[s] or publishers

A CIP catalogue record for this book is available from the British Library

Typeset by Servis Filmsetting Ltd
Printed in Great Britain by
Biddles Ltd

Contents

Preface		ix
Table of Cases		xi
Table of Statutes		xxi
Table of Statutory Instruments		xxv

1	Introduction	1
	1 History	1
	2 The choice: agreement or consent order?	7
	3 The path of law reform	8

2	Agreements	12
	1 Contractual requirements	12
	2 Classification	14
	(a) Oral or written	14
	(b) Maintenance or separation agreements	15
	(c) Reconciliation agreements	16
	(d) Cohabitation contracts	16
	(e) Pre-marital contracts	20
	(f) Mediated agreements	21
	3 Content and construction of maintenance or separation agreements	22
	(a) Recitals	22
	(b) Agreement to live apart	22
	(c) Non-molestation clause	22
	(d) Future proceedings	23
	(e) Maintenance	23
	(f) Indemnity and covenant not to apply for ancillary relief	24
	(g) Property	25
	(h) Residence and contact	25
	(i) Taxation	26
	(j) Agreement to leave by will	26
	(k) Relevant law	26
	(l) Costs	26

	4	Discharge of maintenance or separation agreements	26
		(a) By agreement	26
		(b) By breach	26
		(c) By operation of law	27
	5	The rule in *Hyman v Hyman*	27
		(a) The decision	27
		(b) Matrimonial Causes Act 1973	28
	6	The court's approach to agreements	29
		(a) Background	29
		(b) *Edgar v Edgar*	30
		(c) *Edgar* applied	32
		(d) Other approaches to agreements	38
		(e) Conclusion	39
3	Consent orders		41
	1	Agreements subject to the approval of the court	41
	2	Agreements made rules of court	43
	3	*Tomlin* orders	48
	4	Consent orders	48
		(a) The background	48
		(b) Matrimonial Causes Act 1973, s 33A	51
		(c) Family Proceedings Rules 1991, r 2.61	51
		(d) Procedure	58
		(e) Inquiry by the court	61
	5	The duty to disclose	63
		(a) The facts	64
		(b) The decision	64
	6	Drafting the consent order	67
4	The clean break		78
	1	Origins	78
	2	Concept	80
		(a) The decision in *Minton*	80
		(b) Matrimonial Causes Act 1973, s 25A	81
		(c) Types of clean break	82
		(d) Methods of effecting a clean break	83
		(e) Interpretation by the courts	93
	3	Suitability	101
		(a) Advantages	101
		(b) Children	103
		(c) Insufficient resources	106
		(d) Short marriages	107
		(e) Long separations	108
		(f) Need	108
		(g) Conduct	109

	(h) Difficulties of enforcement	109
	(i) Removal of bitterness	109
	4 Calculation	110

5 Consensus and the Child Support Act — 116
  1 Introduction — 116
  2 Agreements relating to child maintenance — 117
  3 Written agreements and consent orders — 119
  4 Old agreements and order — 121
    (a) Pending applications — 121
    (b) Old agreements and orders — 121
    (c) Benefit recipients — 122
  5 Relationship between child maintenance assessments and agreements/court orders — 123
  6 A new approach — 124
    (a) Family orders — 125
    (b) The clean break — 125

6 Challenging consent orders and agreements — 128
  1 Introduction — 128
  2 Setting aside — 129
    (a) Grounds — 129
    (b) Procedure — 162
  3 Matrimonial Causes Act 1973, ss 23 and 24 — 176
  4 Liberty to apply — 178
  5 Resist specific performance of an agreement — 179

7 Variation — 182
  1 Agreements — 183
  During the lives of the parties — 183
    (a) Variation of an agreement as a post-nuptial settlement under the Matrimonial Causes Act 1973, s 24(1)(c) — 183
    (b) Application for ancillary relief under the Matrimonial Causes Act 1973, ss 22–24 — 184
    (c) Alteration of agreements during the lives of the parties under the Matrimonial Causes Act 1973, s 35 — 184
    (d) Alteration of maintenance agreements for children during the lives of the parties under the Children Act 1989, Sched 1, para 10 (formerly the Family Law Reform Act 1987, s 15) — 189
  After the death of one party — 191
    (a) Alteration of agreements after the death of one party under s 36 — 191

		(b) Alteration of maintenance agreements for children after the death of one party under the Children Act 1989, Sched 1, para 11 (formerly the Family Law Reform Act 1987, s 16)	193
		(c) Inheritance (Provision for Family and Dependants) Act 1975, ss 17 and 18	193
	2	Consent orders	195
		(a) When and how may an order be varied?	195
		(b) Principles governing the exercise of the court's powers	206
		(c) Procedure	213
	3	Agreements made rules of court	213
	4	Undertakings	214
8	Enforcement		215
	1	Agreements	216
	2	Consent orders	216
	3	Enforcement procedures	217
	4	Recitals incorporated in a consent order	220
	5	Agreements made rules of court	220
	6	Undertakings	221

Appendices

1	Pre-marital contract	222
2	Cohabitation contract	225
3	Reconciliation agreement	229
4	Separation deed	231
5	Draft consent order	233
6	Property adjustment order with Child Support Act charge back	237
7	Application to make a rule of court into a consent order	239
8	Affidavit in support of application for leave to appeal out of time	241
9	Application to show cause why an order should not be made in agreed terms	246
10	Affidavit in support of an application to show cause why an order should not be made in agreed terms	248
11	Family Proceedings Rules 1991, r 2.61 (as amended)	251
12	Statement of information pursuant to the Family Proceedings Rules 1991, r 2.61	253

Addendum

The decision in *Harris (formerly Manahan) v Manahan*   257

Index   259

Preface

Agreements are not just 'flavour of the month'. Agreement is now the name of the game. Practitioners are getting this message from every quarter and every litigation process is being geared towards expeditious dispute resolution—whether by agreement or otherwise: Family Law Act 1996, Lord Woolf's Final Report to the Lord Chancellor on the Civil Justice System, the Lord Chancellor's Ancillary Relief Pilot Project the Code of Conduct of the Solicitors' Family Law Association; the list goes on.

That is where this book comes in. Its primary purpose is to provide a practitioner's guide to an important area of family law described by Professor Cretney as the private ordering of financial matters. The first edition of this book appeared in March 1986. In its preface, there appears this comment:

> It is paradoxical that as much of the relevant law remains shrouded in confusion and procedural entanglement as is still the case, despite the vast number of applications for ancillary relief which are ultimately dealt with by way of a consent order.

The shroud was lifted in many respects because Ward J (as he then was) saw fit to succumb to what he described as the 'siren call' of the profession to elucidate the procedures on setting aside a consent order in *B-T v B-T* [1990] 2 FLR 1. Since 1986, much else has, of course, changed in the fast-moving field of family law and the line of cases since *B-T v B-T*, which we analyse in this book, has shown that the area remains something of a minefield. Our hope remains, however, that the busy practitioner will find this book of some use whether it be in alleviating the frustration of having a consent order returned by the court or resolving the complex situation which arises when it is necessary to set aside a consent order.

We are particularly grateful to our colleagues in our respective firms for the help that they have given along the way. Our thanks must also go to our publishers, F T Law & Tax, for their patience and their help. We hope that the law is accurately stated on the basis of the sources available to us in July 1996.

David Salter and Simon Bruce
July 1996

Table of Cases

A v A [1994] 1 FLR 657; [1995] 1 FCR 309; [1994] Fam Law 368, Fam Div............104
A v A [1995] 1 FLR 345; [1995] 2 FCR 137; [1995] Fam Law 242, Fam Div............109
A v A [1996] 1 FLR 14...4
Adams v Adams [1941] 1 All ER 334 24
Allsop v Allsop (1980) 11 Fam Law 18, CA; (1980) 124 SJ 710 134
Alonso v Alonso (1974) 4 Fam Law 164; (1974) 118 SJ 660 ....178, 220
Amey v Amey [1992] 2 FLR 89; [1992] FCR 289 ....43, 154
Annandale v Harris (1729) 2 P Wms 432...17
Ashley v Blackman [1988] 2 FLR 278; [1988] Fam 85; (1988) 18 Fam Law 430........98, 106, 211
Aspden v Hildesley [1982] 2 All ER 53; [1982] 1 WLR 264; [1982] STC 206 46–8
Atkinson v Atkinson [1984] FLR 524..177
Atkinson v Atkinson [1988] 2 FLR 353; [1988] Ch 93; [1988] 2 WLR 204 ......110, 211
Atkinson v Atkinson [1995] 2 FLR 356; [1995] Fam Law 604, Fam Div....75, 100, 110
Atkinson and Caston (1991) *The Times*, 17 April, CA 220
Attar v Attar (No 1) [1985] FLR 649; (1984) 15 Fam Law 252.................................111
Attar v Attar (No 2) [1985] FLR 653; (1984) 15 Fam Law 252.................................108
B (A Minor) (Supervision Order: Parental Undertaking), *Re*, (1996) *The Times*, 12 January 71
B v B [1982] 3 FLR 298; (1982) 12 Fam Law 92, CA *affming*; (1982) 12 Fam Law 28 5
B v B [1990] 1 FLR 20 ....111, 113–15
B v B [1994] 1 FLR 219; [1994] 1 FCR 885; (1994) Fam Law 187, Fam Div 160
B v B [1995] 2 FLR 813 110
B v B (Consent Order: Variation) [1995] 1 FLR 9; [1995] Fam Law 70, Fam Div 58, 91, 196, 206
B (GC) v B (BA) [1970] 1 All ER 913 *sub nom* Brister v Brister [1970] 1 WLR 664..133, 169, 209
B v M [1994] 1 FLR 342; [1994] 1 FCR 769; [1994] Fam Law 370, County Court.....122
B v Miller & Co. [1996] 2 FLR 23 ....58, 131
B (MAL) v B (NE) [1968] 1 WLR 1109; [1968] 112 SJ 520 210
B-T v B-T [1990] 2 FLR 1..7, 129, 137, 163–4, 166, 169–71
Backhouse v Backhouse [1978] 1 All ER 1158; [1978] 1 WLR 243; [1977] 7 Fam Law 212..34, 140, 142–3
Balfour v Balfour [1919] 2 KB 571 12
Bank of Montreal v Stuart [1911] AC 120 140
Banyard v Banyard [1984] FLR 64; (1985) 15 Fam Law 120, CA 84
Barber v Barber [1987] Fam Law 125 ....67, 136, 174
Barber v Barber [1993] 1 FLR 476; [1992] Fam Law 436; [1993] 1 FCR 65, CA 155

TABLE OF CASES

Barclays Bank plc v O'Brien [1994] 1 FLR 1; (1994) 26 HLR 75; [1994] Fam Law 78 140
Barder v Barder [1987] 2 All ER 440, CA; [1987] 2 FLR 480; [1988] AC 20 .... 7, 103, 125, 128–9, 138, 145, 147–9, 151–60, 168–9, 171, 174–7, 180, 182, 198, 245
Barnes v Barnes [1972] 3 All ER 872; [1972] 1 WLR 1381; 116 SJ 801, CA 98
Barrett v Barrett [1988] 2 FLR 516; [1988] FCR 707, CA 91, 96, 206
Barry v Barry [1992] 2 FLR 233; [1992] Fam 140; [1992] 2 WLR 799 .... 44, 84, 203
Bateman v Bateman [1979] 2 WLR 377; [1979] Fam 25; (1979) 9 Fam Law 86 210
Beach v Beach [1995] 2 FLR 160; [1995] 2 FCR 526; [1995] Fam Law 545, Fam Div 36
Beales v Beales [1972] 2 All ER 667; [1972] Fam 210; [1972] 2 WLR 972 23
Beighton v Beighton (1974) 4 Fam Law 119, CA 206, 210
Belcher v Belcher [1995] 1 FLR 916; [1995] 2 FCR 143; [1995] Fam Law 408, CA 72
Bellenden v Bellenden, Bellenden v Salterthwaite [1948] 1 All ER 343, CA 97, 211
Bennett v Bennett [1952] 1 All ER 413; [1952] 1 KB 249; [1952] TLR 400 29
Bennett v Bennett (1976) *The Times*, 24 March 103
Benson v Benson (Deceased) [1996] 1 FLR 692 ..... 38, 129, 161, 163–4, 167–71, 257–8
Benyon v Nettlefold (1850) 3 Mac & G 94 17
Bernard v Josephs [1982] 2 WLR 1052; [1982] Ch 391; (1983) 4 FLR 178 19
Bernstein v O'Neill [1989] 2 FLR 1; (1989) 19 Fam Law 175 218
Board v Checkland [1987] 2 FLR 257 .... 44, 73
Bolsom v Bolsom (1983) FLR 21; (1982) 12 Fam Law 143, CA 203
Bosley v Bosley [1958] 2 All ER 167; [1958] 1 WLR 645; 102 SJ 437, CA 15
Boylan v Boylan [1988] 1 FLR 282; [1988] FCR 689; (1988) 18 Fam Law 62 ..... 72, 86, 96, 198, 209, 212
Bradley-Hale Re [1995] 4 All ER 865; [1995] 1 WLR 1097; [1995] 2 FLR 838 218
Brent v Brent (1978) 9 Fam Law 59, CA 76
Brister v Brister [1970] 1 WLR 664; *see* B (GC) v B (BA) 133, 169, 209
Brockwell v Brockwell (1975) 6 Fam Law 46 .... 36, 39, 41, 42
Brodie v Brodie [1917] P 271 13
Brown v Brown [1959] 2 All ER 266; [1959] P 86; [1959] 2 WLR 776 183
Brown v Brown (1978) 9 Fam Law 216, CA 35
Brown v Brown (1980) FLR 322; (1978) 9 Fam Law 216, CA 96
Brown v Kirrage (1980) 11 Fam Law 141 .... 69, 93
Bryant v Bryant (1976) 120 SJ 165 109
Bullock v Bullock [1986] 1 FLR 372; (1985) 16 Fam Law 129, CA 111
Burrows v Burrows (1981) *The Times*, 10 March, CA 199
Burton v Burton [1986] 2 FLR 419; (1986) 16 Fam Law 330 72
Butlin-Sanders v Butlin [1985] FLR 204; (1985) 15 Fam Law 126 .... 142, 176
C, Re [1993] 2 FLR 799 .... 129–30, 164–5, 169–70, 177, 257–8
C v C [1989] 1 FLR 11; [1989] FCR 558 .... 105, 109, 196
C v C [1994] 2 FLR 272; [1995] 1 FCR 75; [1994] Fam Law 561, Fam Div 165
C v C [1995] 2 FLR 171; [1995] Fam Law 605, Fam Div 107
Calderbank v Calderbank [1975] 3 WLR 586; (1975) 5 Fam Law 190, CA 4–5
Camm v Camm [1983] 4 FLR 577; (1983) 13 Fam Law 112, CA 32–3, 35, 141, 177, 197
Carson v Carson (1981) 2 FLR 352, CA; [1983] 1 WLR 285 68
Carson v Carson [1983] 1 All ER 478; [1983] 1 WLR 285; (1981) 2 FLR 352, CA 85, 93
Carter v Carter [1980] 1 All ER 827; [1980] 1 WLR 390; (1980) 10 Fam Law 117, CA 89, 93
Chandler v Kerley [1978] 2 All ER 492; [1978] 1 WLR 693; (1978) 8 Fam Law 108, CA 17

TABLE OF CASES

Chandless-Chandless v Nicholson [1942] 2 KB 321...70
Chaterjee v Chaterjee [1976] 1 All ER 719 ....86, 197
Chaudhuri v Chaudhuri [1992] 2 FLR 73; [1992] Fam Law 385; [1992] 2 FCR
  426, CA...102, 138
Clark v Clark [1989] 1 FLR 174; (1989) 19 Fam Law 111 218
Clark v Clark (No 2) [1939] 2 All ER 392..27
Clothier v Clothier (1980) *unreported*, CA Transcript No 392 209
Clutton v Clutton [1991] 1 FLR 242; [1991] 1 WLR 359; [1991] 1 All ER 340..........83
C M Van Stillevoldt BV v El Carriers Inc [1983] 1 WLR 297 174
Coleman v Coleman [1972] 3 All ER 886; [1973] Fam 10; [1972] 3 WLR 681 84
Combe v Combe [1951] 2 All ER 767; [1951] 2 KB 215; 95 SJ 317, CA...................29
Cook v Cook [1984] FLR 446; (1984) 14 Fam Law 121, CA 33–4, 43
Cook v Cook [1988] 1 FLR 521; (1988) 18 Fam Law 163, CA 102, 133, 138, 151
Cornick v Cornick [1994] 2 FLR 530; [1994] 2 FCR 1189; [1994] Fam Law
  617, Fam Div...130, 146–9, 151, 153–4, 156, 158–9, 198
Cornick v Cornick (No 2) [1995] 2 FLR 490; CA...209
Covell v Sweetland [1968] 2 All ER 1016; [1968] 1 WLR 1466; 112 SJ 821 24
Cowie v Cowie [1983] Fam Law 250 211
Crabtree v Crabtree [1953] 2 All ER 56; [1953] 1 WLR 708; 119 SJ 711, CA 15
Cresswell v Patter [1978] 1 WLR 255n 142, 163, 176
Cristel v Cristel [1951] 2 All ER 574; [1951] 2 KB 725; 95 SJ 561, CA 179
Cross v Cross (1983) 4 FLR 235; (1982) 12 Fam Law 182 ...36, 133, 140, 176, 180, 216
Crozier v Crozier [1994] 1 FLR 126; [1994] Fam 114; [1994] 2 WLR 444 ....11, 104,
  125–6, 138, 159–60, 168, 209
Curtis v Curtis [1969] 2 All ER 207; [1969] 1 WLR 422; 113 SJ 242, CA 218
Cutts v Head [1984] Ch 290; [1984] 2 WLR 349; 128 SJ 117.....................................4
D v D (1974) 5 Fam Law 61 185
Dackham v Dackham [1987] 2 FLR 358; (1987) 17 Fam Law 345, CA 73
Dart v Dart [1996] 2 FLR 286...111–12
Dean v Dean [1978] 3 All ER 758; [1978] 3 WLR 288; (1978) 8 Fam Law 171 ..39, 220
Delaney v Delaney [1990] 2 FLR 457; [1991] Fam Law 22 [1991];
  FCR 161, CA..106, 211
De Lasala v De Lasala [1979] 2 All ER 1146; [1980] AC 546; [1979] 3 WLR 390 47,
  83–4, 94–5, 131–2, 134, 142, 164–6, 169, 185, 213–15, 220
Dinch v Dinch [1987] 1 All ER 818; [1987] 1 WLR 252; [1987] 2 FLR 162 ....7, 67, 86,
  88, 198, 204
Dipper v Dipper [1980] 2 All ER 722; [1981] Fam 31; [1980] 3 WLR 626 93
Diwell v Farnes [1959] 2 All ER 379; [1959] 1 WLR 624; 103 SJ 431, CA................17
Dunford v Dunford [1980] 1 All ER 122; [1980] 1 WLR 5; (1979) 10 Fam Law
  76, CA 89, 93
Dutfield v Gilbert H Stephens & Sons [1988] Fam Law 473 3
Duxbury v Duxbury [1987] 1 FLR 7; (1987) 17 Fam Law 13, CA 110, 113–15, 211
E v C [1990] 1 FLR 412 107
E v C [1996] 1 FLR 472 124
E v E [1990] 2 FLR 233; [1989] FCR 591; (1989) 153 JPN 722 ....4, 183
Edgar v Edgar [1980] 3 All ER 887; [1980] 1 WLR 1410; (1980) 11 Fam Law
  20, CA 21, 29–33, 37–8, 127, 140, 143, 162, 176, 196, 236
Edmonds v Edmonds [1990] 2 FLR 202; [1990] FCR 856, CA 153, 156
Empson v Empson (1979) 10 Fam Law 209..93
Evans v Evans [1981] 2 FLR 33 ....35, 140
Evans v Evans [1989] 1 FLR 351...109, 211
Evans v Evans [1990] 1 FLR 319...4, 5
F (A Minor), Re [1992] 1 FLR 561; [1992] Fam Law 330, CA...............................131

TABLE OF CASES

F v F (Ancillary Relief: Substantial Assets) [1995] 2 FLR 45; [1995] Fam Law 546, Fam Div 21, 44, 66, 84, 111, 203
F v F (Duxbury Calculation: Rate of Return) [1996] 1 FLR 833 ....5, 114
Fender v St John-Mildmay [1938] AC 1 18
Fisher v Fisher [1989] 1 FLR 423; (1989) 19 Fam Law 269, CA 100
Foot v Foot [1986] Fam Law 13 211
Foster v Foster [1964] 3 All ER 541, CA; [1964] 1 WLR 1155n 207
Fawke v Fawke [1938] 2 All ER 638 24
Frary v Frary [1993] 2 FLR 696, CA; [1994] 1 FCR 595; [1993] Fam Law 628, CA 20
Fry v Lane (1888) 40 Ch D 312 142
Fullard (deceased), Re [1981] 2 All ER 796; [1981] 3 WLR 743; (1981) 11 Fam Law 92
Fuller v Fuller [1973] 2 All ER 650 22
Furlong-Taylor v Furlong-Taylor (1982) 13 Fam Law 143, CA 209
Furneaux v Furneaux (1974) 118 SJ 204 187
Furniss v Furniss (1982) 3 FLR 46; (1982) 12 Fam Law 30, CA 56
G v G (1979) *The Times*, 12 November 59
G v G [1985] FLR 894; (1985) 15 Fam Law 321, HL 97
Gaisberg v Storr [1949] 2 All ER 411, CA; [1949] WN 337 29
Galloway v Galloway (1914) 30 TLR 531 13
Gammans v Ekins [1950] 2 All ER 140; [1950] 2 KB 328; 94 SJ 435, CA 17
Gandolfo v Gandolfo [1980] 1 All ER 833; [1981] QB 359; [1980] 2 WLR 680 221
Garcia v Garcia [1992] 1 FLR 256, CA; [1992] Fam 83; [1992] 2 WLR 347 38
Garner v Garner [1992] 1 FLR 573; [1992] Fam Law 331; (1992) 156 JPN 202, CA 182, 207–8, 210
Gengler v Gengler [1976] 2 All ER 81 55
Gojkovic v Gojkovic [1990] 1 FLR 140; [1990] 2 All ER 84; [1990] FCR 119 ..112, 114
Gojkovic v Gojkovic (No 2) [1991] 2 FLR 233; [1992] Fam 40; [1991] 3 WLR 621 4
Goodinson v Goodinson [1954] 2 All ER 255; [1954] 2 QB; 98 SJ 369, CA 29
Gorman v Gorman [1964] 3 All ER 739; [1964] 1 WLR 1440; 108 SJ 878, CA ..30, 186
Gould v Gould [1969] 3 All ER 728; [1969] 3 WLR 490; 113 SJ 508, CA 12
Grainger v Grainger [1954] 2 All ER 665; [1954] 1 WLR 1270; 98 SJ 700, DC 211
Graves v Graves (1893) 69 LT 420 45
Green v Green [1993] 1 FLR 326; [1993] Fam Law 119 43
Green v Rozen [1955] 2 All ER 797 221
Gregory v Wainwright (1984) 14 Fam Law 86 ....195, 201, 203, 208
Griffiths v Griffiths [1974] 1 All ER 932; [1974] 1 WLR 1350; (1973) 5 Fam Law 59, CA 109
Griffiths v Griffiths [1985] Fam Law 88 104
Guerrera v Guerrera [1974] 3 All ER 460; [1974] 1 WLR 1542; (1974) 5 Fam Law 28, CA 178
Gurney v Gurney (1989) *unreported* 67, 136
H v H (1983) 13 Fam Law 180 13
H v H [1988] 2 FLR 114; (1988) 18 Fam Law 293 ....25, 89, 92
H v H [1993] 2 FLR 35; [1993] 2 FCR 357 ....99, 218, 220
H v H (Clean Break: Non-Disclosure: Costs) [1994] 2 FLR 309; [1994] Fam Law 15, Fam Div 4
H v H (Financial Relief: Non-Disclosure: Costs) [1994] 2 FLR 94; [1994] 2 FCR 301; [1994] Fam Law 497, Fam Div 37
Hadkinson v Hadkinson [1952] 2 All ER 567; [1952] 2 TLR 416 62
Hall v Hall (1972) *The Times*, 30 June 45

TABLE OF CASES

Hammond v Mitchell, *sub nom* H v M (Property: Beneficial Interest) [1992] 1
  FLR 229; [1991] Fam Law 473; [1991] FCR 938...20
Hanlon v The Law Society [1980] 2 All ER 199; [1980] 2 WLR 756; 124 SJ 360.....102
Harman v Glencross [1986] 2 FLR 241; [1986] 1 All ER 545; (1986) 16 Fam
  Law 215, CA 96
Harris (formerly Manahan) v Manahan [1996] All ER 454 257–8
Harrison v Harrison (1983) 13 Fam Law 20 ....93, 134, 174
Hayfield v Hayfield [1957] 1 All ER 598; [1957] 1 WLR 473; 101 SJ 249 206
H v B [1987] 1 All ER 766; [1987] 1 FLR 405 ....66, 140
Heard v Heard [1995] 1 FLR 970; [1995] Fam Law 477, CA....................146, 158, 245
Hedges v Hedges [1991] 1 FLR 196; [1991] Fam Law 267; [1990] FCR 952, DC 108
Hendrix v Hendrix (1981) *unreported*, CA...110
Hepburn v Hepburn [1989] 1 FLR 373; (1989) 19 Fam Law 271, CA; [1989]
  FCR 618 ....96, 97, 99, 100, 211
Herbert v Herbert (1978) 122 SJ 826 221
Hewitson v Hewitson [1995] 1 FLR 241; [1995] 2 FCR 588; [1995] Fam Law 129.....159
Hill v Hill [1984] Fam Law 83, CA 136
Hope-Smith v Hope-Smith [1989] 2 FLR 56; (1989) 19 Fam Law 268, CA 102, 146,
  152, 175
Horrocks v Forray [1976] 1 All ER 737 17
Howes v Bishop [1909] 2 KB 390...140
Huddersfield Banking Co Ltd v Henry Lister & Son Ltd [1895] 2 Ch 273;
  [1895–9] All ER Rep 868 ....48, 130–1
Hughes v Singh (1989) *The Times*, 21 April 144–5
Hulley v Thompson [1981] 1 All ER 1128; [1981] 1 WLR 159; (1981) 2 FLR 53.......62
Hyman v Hyman [1929] AC 601 ....15, 27–9, 32, 79, 94
Isaacs v Robertson [1984] 3 All ER 140; [1985] AC 97...62
Iskin v Aktar (1994) *The Times*, 20 October, CA..48
J (HD) v J (AM) [1980] 1 All ER 156 211
James v James [1963] 2 All ER 465; [1963] 3 WLR 331; 107 SJ 116, DC 218
Jeavons v Jeavons (1983) *unreported*, CA Transcript No 240....................................174
Jeffrey v Jeffrey (No 2) [1952] P 122; [1952] 1 All ER 790, CA...............................183
Jenkins v Livesey [1984] FLR 452 ....7, 49–50
Jenkins v Livesey [1985] AC 424; [1985] 2 WLR 47; (1985) 15 Fam Law 310, HL
  rvsg (1984) 14 Fam Law 180, CA...72
Jessel v Jessel [1979] 3 All ER 645; [1979] 1 WLR 1148............................40, 93–4, 206
Johnson v Johnson [1980] FLR 331 174
Jones v Jones [1971] 3 All ER 1201 197
Jones v Maynard [1951] Ch 572; [1951] 1 All ER 802 19
Jones v Padavatton [1969] 2 All ER 616, CA 12
K v K [1961] 2 All ER 266; [1961] 1 WLR 802 186
K v K (Financial Provision) [1992] 2 FCR 265..35
Kent-Jones v Kent (1985) *unreported*, CA Transcript No 373 185
Kern v Kern (1988) 39
Kiely v Kiely [1988] 1 FLR 248; (1988) 18 Fam Law 51, CA 104
Kirk v Eustace [1937] 2 All ER 715..24
Knibb v Knibb [1987] 2 FLR 396; (1987) 17 Fam Law 346, CA 86, 201, 203
Kyte v Kyte [1988] Fam Law 145; [1987] 3 WLR 1114; [1987] 3 All ER 1041, CA 211
L v L [1961] 3 All ER 834; CA; [1961] 3 WLR 1182..........................49, 79, 80, 88, 89
L v L (1980) *The Times*, 13 November..199
L v L (1981) 11 Fam Law 57; 124 SJ 828 149
L v L [1994] 2 FLR 234...199–200
Ladbroke v Ladbroke (1977) 7 Fam Law 213...36, 197

TABLE OF CASES

Ladd v Marshall [1954] 3 All ER 745; [1954] 1 WLR 1489; 96 SJ 870...144–5, 148, 173
Lane, Re [1986] 1 FLR 283; (1984) 16 Fam Law 74 150
Langstone v Hayes [1946] 1 All ER 114..24
Law v Harragin (1917) 33 TLR 381...13
Layton v Martin [1986] 2 FLR 227; (1986) 16 Fam Law 212 ....17, 18
Lewis v Lewis [1977] 3 All ER 992; [1977] 1 WLR 409; 121 SJ 271, CA..........207, 208
Lidington Re [1940] 3 All ER 600 24
Livesey v Jenkins [1985] 1 All ER 106; see Jenkins v Livesey 6–8, 14, 45, 53–5, 63,
 64, 66, 67, 70, 71, 135–36, 138, 141, 151, 152, 214
Lloyds Bank Ltd v Bundy [1974] 2 All ER 757..34, 35, 143
Lyle v Lyle [1972] 117 SJ 70..142
M, Re (1990) *The Times*, 31 March...133
M v M [1987] 2 FLR 1; (1987) 17 Fam Law 195 ....96, 109
M v M [1993] 2 FLR 723...112
MH v MH [1982] 3 FLR 429..46, 178, 185, 211, 213, 214, 221
MacDonald v MacDonald [1963] 2 All ER 857...205
McC (RD) v McC (JA) [1971] 2 All ER 1097 174
McKenzie v Royal Bank of Canada [1934] AC 468 140
McQuiban v McQuiban [1913] P 208..27, 216
Marsden v Marsden [1972] 2 All ER 1162; [1972] Fam 280; [1972] 3 WLR 136......131
Marsh v Marsh [1993] 2 All ER 794; [1993] 1 WLR 744; [1993] 1 FLR 467....145, 170
Masefield v Alexander [1995] 1 FLR 100; [1995] 2 FCR 663; [1995] Fam Law
 130 ....84, 86, 89, 178, 203, 205
Mawson v Mawson [1994] 2 FLR 985; [1994] 2 FCR 852; [1995] Fam Law 9,
 Fam Div 124
May v May [1929] All ER Rep 484..24
Merritt v Merritt [1970] 2 All ER 760; [1970] 1 WLR 1211; 114 SJ 455, CA 12
Meyrick's, Settlement Re [1921] 1 CH 311..16
Mills v Mills [1940] 2 All ER 254; [1940] P 124 ....78, 80, 88
Milne v Milne (1981) FLR 286; 125 SJ 375, CA...72
Minton v Minton [1979] 1 All ER 79; [1979] AC 593; [1979] 2 WLR 31 .....2, 6, 78–80,
 83, 84, 88, 89, 94, 95, 103, 141, 177
Moisi v Moisi (1984) 5 Fam Law 26 109
Moore v Moore (1981) 11 Fam Law 109, CA 105–6
Moorish v Moorish (1984) 14 Fam Law 26, CA...4, 5
Morley-Clarke v Jones [1985] 3 WLR 749, CA; [1986] 1 WLR 978; [1985] 3 All
 ER 193...187, 205
Morris v Morris [1985] FLR 1176; (1985) 16 Fam Law 24, CA 98, 109, 212
Mouncer v Mouncer [1972] 1 All ER 289...22
Mullins v Howell (1879) 11 Ch D 763 ....132, 179
Munks v Munks [1985] FLR 576...44, 62
Munks v Munks [1985] FLR 345; (1985) 15 Fam Law 131, CA 73
N v N (Divorce: Agreement Not to Defend) [1992] 1 FLR 266...........................13, 16
N v N (Consent Order: Variation) [1993] 2 FLR 868 ....40, 60, 61, 69, 71, 81, 82, 90,
 91, 94, 102, 181, 196
N v N (Valuation: Charge-back Order) [1996] 1 FLR 361 ....76, 196, 205, 206
National Westminster Bank plc v Morgan [1985] AC 686 ....35, 141, 143
Negus v Forster (1882) 46 LT 675 ....24, 26
Nicol v Nicol (1886) 31 Ch D 524 26
Niebor v Niebor (1993) *The Independent*, 23 August, CA..40
Nikoloff v Nikoloff (1977) *The Times*, 28 March (1977) 7 Fam Law 129 ....179, 198
Norman v Norman [1983] 1 All ER 486; [1983] 1 WLR 295; (1983) 13 Fam Law
 17 85
O'Dougherty v O'Dougherty (1983) 4 FLR 407; (1982) 12 Fam Law 248 150
Omielan v Omielan [1996] 2 FLR 306 ....85, 86, 179

TABLE OF CASES

Orton v Orton (1959) 109 SJ 50 184
P v P (Financial Relief: Non-Disclosure) [1994] 2 FLR 381; [1994] 1 FCR 293; [1994] Fam Law 498, Fam Div 4, 110
Pace v Doe [1977] 1 All ER 176; [1977] Fam 18; 120 SJ 818 .... 185, 187
Page v Page (1981) 2 FLR 198 111–12
Pao On v Lau Yiu Long [1980] AC 614 143
Pardy v Pardy [1939] 3 All ER 779; [1939] P 288 27
Parker v Clark [1960] 1 WLR 286 .... 12, 19
Parkes v Parkes [1971] 3 All ER 870; [1971] 1 WLR 1481 131–2
Pasley v Pasley (1964) 108 SJ 383 221
Passmore v Gill [1987] 1 FLR 441; (1987) 17 Fam Law 195, CA 150, 174
Payne v Payne [1968] 1 All ER 1113; [1968] 1 WLR 390; 112 SJ 110, CA 207
Peacock v Peacock [1984] 1 All ER 1069 53
Peacock v Peacock [1991] Fam Law 139; [1991] 1 FLR 324 .... 88, 198
Pearce v Pearce (1980) 1 FLR 261; (1979) 10 Fam Law 209, CA 105
Penrose v Penrose [1994] 2 FLR 621; [1994] 2 FCR 1167; [1994] Fam Law 618, CA 145, 148, 151, 204
Popat v Popat [1991] 2 FLR 163; [1991] Fam Law 100 203–4
Potter v Potter [1982] 2 All ER 321; [1982] 1 WLR 1255; (1982) 12 Fam Law 208, CA 111
Potter v Potter [1990] 2 FLR 27 202
Potts v Potts [1976] 6 Fam Law 217, CA 179
Pounds v Pounds [1994] 1 FLR 775; [1994] 1 WLR 1535; [1994] 4 All ER 777 ... 42, 44, 63, 73, 162
Powys v Powys [1971] 3 All ER 116; [1971] 3 WLR 154; 115 SJ 347 .... 86, 101, 197
Practice Direction: Ancillary Relief Procedure: Pilot Scheme [1996] 2 FLR 368 .... 3, 213
Practice Direction, 26 September 1972 [1972] 3 All ER 704 .... 42, 45, 59
Practice Direction [1975] 3 All ER 403 191–2
Practice Direction, 7 March 1977 [1977] 1 WLR 320 59
Practice Direction, 4 March 1980 [1980] 1 All ER 1008 179
Practice Direction, 13 April 1984 [1984] 2 All ER 256 .... 49, 50, 61, 62, 65
Practice Direction, 17 February 1986 [1986] 1 FLR 337 .... 56, 57
Practice Direction, 28 July 1986 [1986] 2 FLR 171 3
Practice Direction, 13 February 1989 [1989] 1 FLR 307 217
Practice Direction, 5 January 1990 [1990] 1 FLR 234 57
Practice Direction, 19 August 1991 [1991] 3 All ER 896 236
Practice Direction, 18 October 1991 [1992] 1 All ER 421 3
President's Practice Direction, 31 January 1995 [1995] 1 FLR 456 6
Preston v Preston [1981] FLR 331 113
Preston v Preston [1982] 1 All ER 41; (1981) 125 SJ 496, CA 105, 111–12
Primavera v Primavera [1991] 1 FLR 16; [1991] Farm Law 471; [1992] FRC 77, CA 209, 211
Prow v Brown (1982) 12 Fam Law 214; (1983) FLR 352 .... 135–6, 176
Purcell v FC Trigell Ltd [1971] 1 QB 358; [1970] 3 All ER 671; 114 SJ 668, CA .. 48, 179
R, Re [1995] 1 FLR 123 131
Radziej v Radziej [1968] 3 All ER 624n; [1968] 1 WLR 1928n; 112 SJ 822 183
Ratcliffe v Ratcliffe [1962] 3 All ER 993; [1962] 1 WLR 1455, 106 SJ 900, CA ... 30, 186
Redmond v Redmond [1986] 2 FLR 173 .... 133–4, 144
Registrar's Direction, 10 April 1974 [1974] 2 All ER 1120; [1974] 1 WLR 937 50
Richardson v Richardson [1993] 4 All ER 673; [1994] 2 WLR 241; [1994] 1 FLR 286 .... 40, 88, 90–93, 206
Richardson v Richardson (No 2) [1994] 2 FLR 1051; [1994] 2 FCR 826; [1995] Fam Law 14, Fam Div 83, 97, 102, 196, 206
Ritchie v Ritchie [1996] 1 FLR 898 .... 167–9, 171, 174

TABLE OF CASES

Roberts v Roberts [1969] 3 All ER 479 211
Robinson v Robinson [1982] 2 All ER 699n; (1983) 4 FLR 102; 126 SJ 36, CA.......64, 67, 128, 136, 144, 164–7, 171, 182
Rodewald v Rodewald [1977] 2 All ER 609; [1977] Fam 192..55
Rooker v Rooker [1988] 1 FLR 219; (1988) 18 Fam Law 55 ....144, 151, 153, 220
Roots v Roots [1987] 17 Fam Law 397; [1987] 1 FLR 89 211
Rose v Laskington Ltd [1989] 3 All ER 306; [1989] 3 WLR 873; 133 SJ 1033, DC 219
Rose v Rose (1883) 8 PD 98...23
Ross v Pearson [1976] 1 All ER 790; [1976] 1 WLR 224; (1975) 6 Fam Law 9, DC 218
Ross v Ross [1989] 2 FLR 257 175
Rundle v Rundle [1992] 2 FLR 80; [1992] Fam Law 388; [1992] 2 FCR 361, CA.....157
Russell v Russell [1956] 1 All ER 466...94
Russell v Russell [1986] 1 FLR 465 218
S v S (1980) *The Times*, 10 May..112
S v S [1986] 3 All ER 566..72, 86
S v S [1987] 1 FLR 71; [1986] Fam Law 364, CA; [1987] 1 WLR 382; [1987] 2 All ER 312, CA..105, 109, 198, 205
S v S [1990] 2 FLR 252; [1989] FCR 582, CA..4, 5
S v S [1994] 2 FLR 228; [1994] 2 FCR 1225; [1994] Fam Law 438, Fam Div..........146, 159, 177
S v S (Reserved Costs Order) [1995] 1 FLR 739; [1995] 2 FCR 402; [1995] Fam Law 409..76
Sabbagh v Sabbagh [1985] FLR 29; (1984) 15 Fam Law 187 ....21, 32, 176
Salter (1989) *Law Society's Gazette*, 5 July 20 199
Sandford v Sandford [1986] 1 FLR 412; [1985] 16 Fam Law 104, CA 68, 69, 87, 93, 196, 198
Sansom v Sansom [1966] 2 All ER 396 211
Scallon v Scallon [1990] 1 FLR 194...77
Schaefer v Schuhmann [1972] 1 All ER 621..26
Scott v Scott [1959] 1 All ER 531; [1959] 2 WLR 497n 13
Seaton v Seaton [1986] 2 FLR 398; (1986) 16 Fam Law 267; 130 SJ 242..................109
Senior Registrar's Statement, 20 August 1975 (1975) 119 SJ 596................................59
Sharp v Sharp [1984] FLR 752..212
Shaw v Fitzgerald [1992] 1 FLR 357; [1992] FCR 162...18
Shaw, Smith v Shaw, *Re* [1918] P47; [1918] 87 LJP 49; [1918] 118 LT 334 CA...........47
Sherdley v Sherdley [1988] AC 213; [1987] 2 WLR 1071; [1987] 2 All ER, HL 7
Simister v Simister (No 2) [1987] 1 FLR 194; [1987] 17 Fam Law 50..........30, 36, 182, 184, 186, 187, 191
Singer (formerly Sharegin) v Sharegin [1984] FLR 114; (1984) 14 Fam Law 58, CA 5
Skone v Skone [1971] 2 All ER 582; [1971] 1 WLR 812; 115 SJ 424, CA 144
Slater v Slater (1982) 3 FLR 364; (1982) 12 Fam Law 153, CA 56
Smallman v Smallman [1971] 3 All ER 717; [1971] 3 WLR 588; 115 SJ 527, CA ..33, 43
Smethurst v Smethurst [1977] 3 All ER 1110; [1977] 3 WLR 472; (1977) 7 Fam Law 177, DC 209
Smith v McInerney [1994] 2 FLR 1077; [1994] 2 FCR 1086; [1995] Fam Law 10, Fam Div...29, 38, 74, 105, 127, 155, 238
Smith v Smith [1970] 1 All ER 244; [1970] 1 WLR 155; 113 SJ 920, CA..................109
Smith v Smith [1991] 2 All ER 306, CA..153
Springette v Defoe [1992] 2 FLR 388; (1992) 24 HLR 552; [1992] Fam Law 489 19
Staerck v Staerck, *unreported*, Court of Appeal, 20 July 1987 16
Starkey v Starkey [1938] 3 All ER 773..16

TABLE OF CASES

Steadman v Steadman [1974] 2 All ER 977; [1974] 3 WLR 56; 118 SJ 480, CA 14
Stephens v Avery [1988] 2 All ER 477; [1988] 2 WLR 1280; (1988) 132 SJ 822 17
Stewart v The Law Society [1987] 1 FLR 223; [1987] 17 Fam Law 52 .... 87, 102
Stockford v Stockford (1982) 3 FLR 58; [1982] 12 Fam Law 30, CA 56,106
Suter v Suter and Jones [1987] 2 FLR 232; [1987] Fam 111; [1987] 2 All ER 336, CA 91, 105
Sutton v Sutton [1984] 1 All ER 168; [1984] Ch 184; [1984] 2 WLR 116 ..... 14, 33, 176, 180, 216
Symmons v Symmons [1993] 1 FLR 317 221
T v S [1994] 2 FLR 883; [1994] 1 FCR 743; [1995] Fam Law 11, Fam Div 104
T v T [1988] 1 FLR 480 .... 91, 196
Tandy v Tandy (1986) unreported CA Transcript No 929 106
Tanner v Tanner [1975] 1 WLR 1346; [1975] 3 All ER 776; (1975) 5 Fam Law 193, CA 17
Taylor v Harman and Warners, unreported, 21 July 1986 19
Taylor v Taylor [1987] 1 FLR 142; (1986) 16 Fam Law 366, CA 86, 179
Thwaite v Thwaite [1981] 2 All ER 789; [1982] Fam 1; [1981] 3 WLR 96 .. 1, 46, 47, 48
Thompson v Thompson [1985] 2 All ER 243; [1986] Fam 38; [1985] 3 WLR 17 ...... 85, 204
Thompson v Thompson [1988] 2 FLR 170; [1988] 1 WLR 562; (1988) 18 Fam Law 289 .... 83, 93, 146
Thompson v Thompson [1991] 2 FLR 530; [1992] Fam Law 18; [1992] 1 FCR 368, CA 155, 157, 158, 245
Thwaite v Thwaite [1981] 2 All ER 789; [1982] Fam 1; [1981] 3 WLR 96 .... 83, 130–131, 131, 139, 144, 169, 177, 179, 185, 218
Thyssen-Bornemisza v Thyssen-Bornemisza [1985] FLR 670; [1985] Fam 1; [1985] 1 All ER 328, CA 111–12
Tilley v Tilley (1979) 10 Fam Law 89 203
Toleman v Toleman [1985] FLR 62; (1984) 14 Fam Law 316, CA 137
Tommey v Tommey [1982] 3 All ER 385; [1982] Fam 15; [1983] 4 FLR 159 .... 48, 63, 65, 130, 134, 141
Twiname v Twiname [1992] 1 FLR 29; [1991] Fam Law 520; [1992] FCR 185, CA 108
Upfill v Wright [1911] 1 KB 506 17
Van G v Van G (Financial Provision: Millionaire's Reference) [1985] 1 FLR 328 66
Stillevoldt (Van) (CM) BV v El Carriers Inc [1983] 1 WLR 207; [1983] 1 All ER 699, CA 175
Vicary v Vicary [1992] 2 FLR 271; [1992] Fam Law 428; [1993] 1 FCR 533, CA 114
Victor v Victor [1911–13] All ER Rep 959; [1912] 1 KB 247 .... 27, 216
W v W [1995] 2 FLR 259; [1995] Fam Law 548, Fam Div 111, 112
Wachtel v Wachtel [1973] 1 All ER 829; [1973] Fam 72; [1973] 2 WLR 366 .... 35, 56, 96, 109
Wales v Wadham [1977] 2 All ER 125; (1976) The Times, 26 June; [1977] 1 WLR 199 .... 14, 65, 66, 132, 135, 136
Walker v Hall [1984] FLR 126 19
Walker v Perkins (1764) 1 Wm Bl 517 17
Walsh v Walsh [1989] Fam Law 158–9 96
Warden v Warden [1981] 3 All ER 193; [1982] Fam 10; [1981] 3 WLR 435 187
Warren v Warren [1983] FLR 529, CA; (1983) 13 Fam Law 49 .... 149, 153, 157
Waterman v Waterman [1989] 1 FLR 380; (1989) 19 Fam Law 227, CA ... 90, 105, 196
Watkin v Watson-Smith (1986) The Times, 3 July; [1986] CLY 1282 142
Watkinson v Legal Aid Board [1991] 2 FLR 26; [1991] 1 WLR 419; [1991] 2 All ER 953 .... 87, 102
Watson v Lucas [1980] 3 All ER 647; [1980] 1 WLR 1493; 124 SJ 513, CA 18

Wells v Wells [1992] 2 FLR 66; [1992] Fam Law 386; [1992] 2 FCR 368, CA..138, 139, 146, 151, 160
Weston, Davies v Tagart, Re [1900] 2 Ch 164..12
Whitfield v Whitfield [1985] FLR 955; (1985) 15 Fam Law 329, CA 195, 214
Whiting v Whiting (1988) 2 FLR 189; [1988] 2 All ER 275; (1988) 18 Fam Law 429, CA 56, 91, 92, 97, 98, 99
Windeler v Whitehall [1990] 2 FLR 505; (1990) 154 JPN 29; [1990] FCR 268 19
Wilkins v Wilkins [1969] 2 All ER 463; [1969] 1 WLR 922; 113 SJ 226...................207
Williams v Williams [1957] 1 All ER 305; [1957] 1 WLR 148; 101 SJ 108, CA..........29
Williams v Williams [1971] 2 All ER 764; [1971] 3 WLR 92; 114 SJ 826, CA ..109, 197
Williams v Williams [1980] FLR 157; (1980) 11 Fam Law 23, CA 174
Wilson v Wilson (1848) 1 HL Cas 538..13
Woodley v Woodley [1992] 2 FLR 417; [1993] 1 FCR 701; [1993] Fam Law 24, CA..218
Woodley v Woodley (No 2) [1993] 2 FLR 477; [1994] 1 WLR 1167; [1993] 4 All ER 1010..218
Worlock v Worlock [1994] 2 FLR 689; [1994] 2 FCR 1157; [1994] Fam Law 619, CA 139, 159
Wright v Wright [1970] 3 All ER 209; [1970] 1 WLR 1219; 114 SJ 619, CA........31, 93
Zamet v Hyman [1961] 1 WLR 1442; 105 SJ 911; [1961] 3 All ER 933, CA........17, 21

Table of Statutes

Attachment of Earnings Act 1971—
  s 3(3A) 7
Administration of Justice Act 1970—
  s 11(*b*) 221
  s 28(1) 221
  Sched 8, para 2A 221
Affiliation Proceedings Act 1957 123
Children Act 1989 .... 11, 19, 25, 232
  s 1(5) 25
  s 2(9)–(11) 25
  s 4 19
  s 31 72
  Sched 1 .... 104, 123, 237
    para 2(1) 104
    para 3(1),(2) 190
    para 10 .... 189–91, 228
      (1) ... 15, 20, 30, 189, 193
      (3) 190–1
      (4),(5) 190
      (6) 190–1
      (7) 191
    para 11 .... 20, 30, 193
      (1), (3)–(6), (27) 193
Child Support Act 1991 .... 8, 11, 13,
      15, 19, 20, 29, 30, 38, 62,
      82, 101, 103–6, 116–126,
      139, 188–9, 210, 232, 237
  s 4 122
    (10) 117–18, 118–22
  s 6 .... 8, 24, 117–18
  s 8 .... 118–20, 123, 217
    (1)–(3) 119
    (3) 124
    (4) 122
    (5) 8, 118–21, 124–5
      (*a*) 117, 120
      (*b*) 120
    (6) 122, 217

Child Support Act 1991—*contd*
  s 8(7),(8) 122–3, 217
  s 9 .... 24, 117, 124
    (1) 15, 29, 117, 123
    (2),(3) 29, 117
    (4) 13, 29, 117
    (5) 118
      (*b*) 119
    (6) 118
  s 10(1) 123
    (2) 29, 123
  s 18(6) 122
    (8) 121
  ss 28A–28I 116
  s 28A 126
  ss 35, 36 15
  Sched 4B, Part I, paras 3, 4 126
Child Support Act 1995 232
  s 1 116
  s 8 117
  s 18 118
    (1) 118, 122
    (3) 119
    (5) 118
    (9) 119, 121
County Court Act 1994—
  s 23(*g*) 175
  s 39 219
  s 76 167
Divorce Reform Act 1969 2
  s 7 43
Domestic Proceedings and Magistrates'
  Courts Act 1978 237
  s 6 .... 2, 7
Domestic Proceedings and Magistrates'
  Courts Act 1978 123
Domestic Violence and Matrimonial
  Proceedings Act 1976, s 1(2) 18

TABLE OF STATUTES

Family Income Supplements Act 1970,
  s 1 18
Family Law Act 1996 ....4, 10, 11, 21,
                                           23, 42
  Part II 4
  s 3 23
  s 7(11),(13) 10
  s 9 10
  Part III 4
  Sched 1 10
  Sched 2 201
  Sched 8, s 16(7) 199
  Sched 9 23
Family Law Reform Act 1987—
  s 15 189
  s 16 193
Family Law (Scotland) Act 1985 123
Finance Act 1988 ....7, 14, 15, 56,
                                         205, 210
  s 36 23
    (1) 15
    (4) 14
Housing Act 1985, s 58(2) 18
Income and Corporation and Taxes Act
  1988—
  s 347B 8, 23
    (1) 15
Inheritance (Provision for Family and
  Dependants) Act 1975 ....25, 91–2, 196
  s 1(1),(1A) 18
  s 2 ....25, 91, 191, 229
  s 3 92
  s 15 ....25, 56, 75, 82, 91–2, 113
    (1) 91
  s 21 ....25, 92
Inheritance Tax Act 1984, ss 10, 11 59
Insolvency Act 1986 218
  Part VIII 218
  s 281(5)(*b*) 218
  s 339 87
Justice (Provision for Family and
  Dependants) Act 1975—
  s 2 193–4
  s 5 194
  s 15(1) 194
  s 17 193–4
    (1)–(4) 194
  s 18 193
    (1)(*b*) 194–5
    (2) 194
    (3) 195
  s 25(1) 193
Law of Property Act 1925, s 40 ....14, 180

Law of Property (Miscellaneous
  Provisions) Act 1989—
  s 1 12
    (3) 13
  s 2 216
    (1),(5),(8) 14
Law Reform (Succession) Act 1995—
  s 2 18
Maintenance Agreements Act 1957 ...181
Maintenance Enforcement Act
  1991 217
  s 1(2) 217
    (4) 219
      (*b*) 217
    (5) 217, 219
    (6),(10) 217
Married Women's Property Act
  1882—
  s 1 13
  s 17 ....38, 68
Matrimonial and Family Proceedings
  Act 1984 ....40, 49, 79, 81, 96,
                          100, 176, 206–7, 211
  s 3 ....34, 61, 79
  s 5 79
  s 6 ....79, 205–6
  s 7 ....2, 7, 51
  Part III 123
  s 35 42
  s 39 170
Matrimonial Causes Act 1923 27
Matrimonial Causes Act 1963 2
  s 4(3) 41
Matrimonial Causes Act 1965 41
Matrimonial Causes Act 1973 ......36, 39,
                            45, 47, 104, 122,
                           128, 201, 237
  s 1 (2)(*d*) 23, 180, 229, 231
  s 5 132
  s 7 41–43
  s 10 (2),(3) 38
  Part II 123, 221
  ss 22–24 71
  s 22 53
  s 22A (7),(8) 201
  ss 23–25 ....137, 163
  s 23 ......8, 30, 31, 35, 39, 42, 45, 48, 64,
              176, 177, 179, 181, 184, 214
    (1) 30, 79, 84, 89
      (*a*),(*b*) 81, 88, 93, 229
      (*c*) 81, 89, 93
    (4) 89, 104
    (5) 44, 47, 73

Matrimonial Causes Act 1973—*contd*
s 23(6) 199–200
s 24 .... 8, 30, 31, 35, 39, 42, 45, 48,
 64, 68, 81, 93, 176, 177,
 179, 181, 183–4, 214
 (1)(*c*) 15, 21, 183–4
 (2) 183
 (3) 44, 47, 73
s 24A 81, 85–6, 93, 179
 (1) 205
 (2) 90–1
 (3) 88–9
s 25 .... 21, 30–32, 35, 39, 50, 53, 61,
 62, 64, 65, 81, 91, 104, 110–12,
 114, 125, 136, 148, 176, 180,
 183–4, 207–11
 (1) 65, 66, 81–2, 103
 (2) 52, 56, 62, 153
 (*a*) 84
 (*f*) 112
 (*g*) 109
 (3) 52, 56, 62
 (4) 186
s 25A 34, 61, 79, 81–2, 93,
 96, 99, 101, 105–9
 (1) 81, 195
 (1A) 79
 (2) 81, 108
 (3) 81, 97
s 25B 54
 (1)–(7) 84
 (4) 83, 195, 234
s 25C 54, 83–4, 195
s 27 .... 24, 56, 186
 (5) 195
s 28(1) 205
 (1A) 75, 90–2, 97, 102,
 108, 195–6, 234, 236
 (2) 205
 (3) 176
s 29(1) 104
 (2) 188
 (3) 104, 188
s 30 .... 44, 219
 (1) (*a*)–(*c*) 44
s 31 .... 36, 46, 83, 86, 88, 90,
 93, 96–7, 109, 122, 179, 182,
 184, 195–6, 202, 204–6, 214
 (1) 83, 97
 (2) 83, 195
 (*d*) 204
 (*f*) 86
 (2A) 197

Matrimonial Causes Act 1973—*contd*
s 31(2B) 84
 (4) 83
 (5) 86, 187, 197–9
 (6) 205
 (7) 71, 79, 97–9, 100–101,
 198, 206–8, 210–11, 236
 (*a*) 97, 212
 (9) 191, 205
 (10) 97, 205
s 32 217
 (2) 216, 218
s 33 172
s 33A 7, 9, 42, 50, 51, 65
 (1) 50, 61–2, 63
 (3) 52
ss 34–36 .... 15, 30
s 34 .... 34, 94, 181
 (1) 15, 28, 40, 117
 (*a*) 94, 181
 (*b*) 28
 (2) 15, 28, 35, 117, 183,
 187, 191, 194
s 35–36 36
s 35 .... 30, 35, 46, 83, 95, 118–19,
 182–5, 187–8, 191,
 213, 214
 (1) 185
 (2) 185–6
 (*b*)(i) 35, 184
 (3)–(5) 188
 (6) 176, 184
s 36 191–4
 (2)–(4) 191
 (5) 191, 205
 (6) 191
s 37 215
Matrimonial Causes (Property and
 Maintenance) Act 1958, s 1(1) 79
Matrimonial Homes Act 1983 71
Matrimonial Proceedings and Property
 Act 1970 197
Pensions Act 1995 84
 s 166 83–4
 (3) 83, 86
 (6) 84
Rent Act 1977 18
Settled Land Act 1925 75
Social Security Act 1986—
 s 24 .... 62, 126, 159
Social Security Administration Act
 1992 105
 s 100 101

Social Security Administration Act
  1992—*contd*
  ss 106–108 ....11, 237
  s 106 ....62, 125
  s 107 ....62, 101, 125
Supreme Court Act 1981—
  s 17(2) 172
  s 39 219
Supreme Court of Judicature
  (Consolidation) Act 1925, s 190 79
Taxation of Chargeable Gains Act
  1992—
  s 58 58
    (1) 7
Trustees of Land and Appointment of
  Trustees Act 1996 75

Table of Statutory Instruments

Child Maintenance (Written Agreements) Order 1993 (SI No 620) 120
Child Support Act 1991 (Commencement No 3 and Transitional Provisions) Order 1992 (SI No 2644)—
    Sched, Part I...................................121
                para 5(2)...........119, 121
Child Support Act 1991 (Commencement No 3 and Transitional Provisions) Amendment Order 1993 (SI No 966)...................121
Child Support and Income Support (Amendment) Regulations 1995 (SI No 1045)...................................116
    reg 27(1),(2)...................................123
    reg 57 126
Child Support Departure Direction (Anticipatory Application) Regulations 1996 (SI No 635)........126
Child Support (Maintenance Arrangements and Jurisdiction) Regulations 1992 (SI No 2645)—
    reg 3(1) 123
        (2) 123–4
        (3),(5).....................................123
    reg 4 29
        (1),(2)......................................123
        (3) 124
    reg 9 ....118, 121–2
    Sched, Part I, para 5(2)..................121
Child Support (Maintenance Assessment and Special Cases) Regulations 1992 (SI No 1815)—
    Sched 3A 126
Child Support (Miscellaneous Amendments) (No 2) Regulations 1995 (SI No 3261).......118, 121–2, 124
Child Support (Miscellaneous Amendments and Transitional Provisions) Regulations 1994 (SI No 227), Part III......................122
Civil Legal Aid (General) Regulations 1989 (SI No 339) 235
    regs 96, 97.................................76, 77
    reg 107..235
County Court (Amendment) Rules 1991 (SI No 525) 23
County Court (Forms Amendment) Rules 1991 (SI No 526).....................23
County Court (Interest on Judgment Debts) Order 1991 (SI No 1184)......74
County Court Rules 1981 (SI No 1687) 192
    Ord 11, r 10 4
    Ord 13, r 4..................................86, 145
        (1),(2).............167, 174, 201
    Ord 22, r 10 202
    Ord 25, r 3 217
    Ords 26–32 219
    Ord 37.....................................137, 172
        r 1....................129, 167–9, 171, 172, 176
        (1) 163, 165
        (5)....................................176
        r 6 ....129, 170, 173
        (1)....................................170
    Ord 48, r 3(1) 192
        rr 7, 9 193
        r 9 189
Family Proceedings (Amendment) (No 2) Rules 1996 (SI No 1674),
    r 4(1)..54
Family Proceedings Courts (Children Act 1989) Rules (SI No 1395)—
    r 4 191

Family Proceedings Rules 1991 (SI No 1247)..................52, 121, 164, 192
  r 1.2 52
    (1) 213
  r 2.6(6) 192
  r 2.10(2) 23
  r 2.42 172
  rr 2.53–2.68 213
  r 2.53(2) 198
    (3) 213
  r 2.58(2) 213
  r 2.59(4) 54, 55
  r 2.61 ....46, 50–63, 65–67, 110, 120, 137–8, 207, 213, 251–3
    (1) 56, 70
    (dd) 54
    (2) 52, 213
    (3) 55, 57, 60
  r 2.63 ....66, 140, 143, 171, 189
  r 2.64(2) 213
  r 3.1(10) 56
  rr 3.2 189
  rr 3.3(2) 192
    (3) 192–3
  r 3.4 192
    (3), (4), (6) 192
  r 3.5 ....189, 192
    (2) 192
  r 4.4 191
  r 7.1 219
    (1),(5) 217
  rr 7.2, 7.4–7.6, 7.22–9 219
  r 8.1 ....129, 257–8
    (2) 170
  r 10.9 220
  r 10.10 189
  Appendix I 57, 88, 92, 189, 192, 253–5
High Court and County Courts Jurisdiction Order 1991 (SI No 724) 175–6
  art 2 191
Insolvency Rules 1986 (SI No 1925), r 12.3 218

Magistrates' Courts Rules 1981 (SI No 552)—
  r 105 188
Matrimonial Causes (Amendment) Rules 1984 (SI No 1511) 51
Matrimonial Causes (Amendment No 2) Rules 1985 (SI No 1315), r 9 52
Matrimonial Causes Rules 1971 (SI No 953), r 6 42
Matrimonial Causes Rules 1973 (SI No 2016) 42
Matrimonial Causes Rules 1977 (SI No 344)—
  r 54 172
  rr 73–75 52
  r 76A 46, 50–52, 56–58, 65, 67, 138
    (5) 53
  r 124(1) 145
Parental Responsibility Agreement (Amendment) Regulations 1994 (SI No 3157) 20
Parental Responsibility Agreement Regulations 1991 (SI No 1478) 20
Rules of the Supreme Court 1965 (SI No 1776)—
  Ord 3, r 5(1) 201
  Ord 22, r 14 4
  Ord 30 219
  Ord 31, r 1 43
  Ord 37(1) 144
  Ord 45, rr 3, 4 219
  Ord 46, r 5 219
  Ord 47 219
  Ord 48 217
  Ords 49–52 219
  Ord 58 173
  Ord 59 ....129, 173
    r 1A(6)(z) 173
    r 1B(1)(b) 169, 173
      (f) 173
    r 4 174
    r 10(2) 143, 145
    r 14(2) 174
      (a) 175
  Ord 62, r 9(d) 4

Chapter 1

Introduction

> The facts of the case are as simple as the procedural tangle is formidable, reflecting, as counsel for the husband says, the confusion prevailing in the profession about consent orders in the matrimonial jurisdiction (*Thwaite* v *Thwaite* [1981] 2 All ER 789, at 792 per Ormrod LJ).

It is the purpose of this book to examine the law and procedure relating not only to consent orders in the matrimonial jurisdiction of the High Court and the divorce county counts, but also to agreements between spouses and cohabitees, in the hope that at least part of that confusion, which the authors suspect may have persisted notwithstanding developments since 1981, may be dispelled.

1 History

It is readily understandable why the parties to a matrimonial dispute should wish to resolve their differences by an agreement or consent order, which offers them both the flexibility and the certainty that an externally imposed solution cannot. A considerable saving may be made in costs and the necessity for enforcement action may be avoided where obligations are voluntarily assumed.

The desirability of placing the decision-making responsibility upon the parties was amply demonstrated by the definition of 'conciliation' put forward by the Finer Committee:

> ... assisting the parties to deal with the consequences of established breakdown of their marriage, whether resulting in a divorce or a separation, by reaching agreements or giving consents or reducing the area of conflict upon custody, support, access to and education of the children, financial provision, the disposition of the matrimonial home, lawyers' fees and every other matter arising from the breakdown which calls for a decision on future arrangements (Report of the Committee on One-Parent Families (1974) Cmnd 5629, para 4.288).

The concept of the matrimonial consent order, however, only received statutory recognition in the High Court and the divorce county courts in the Matrimonial and Family Proceedings Act 1984, s 7, which came into force on 12 October 1984. In this respect, it could be said that the magistrates' courts stole the thunder of the superior courts in that they already had the power to make orders in terms agreed between the parties without proof of formal grounds under the Domestic Proceedings and Magistrates' Courts Act 1978, s 6. It is therefore remarkable to consider that just over two decades before in 1963 an agreement providing for the conduct of a divorce suit was collusive and thus unlawful. The court had to be satisfied not only that the guilty spouse had committed a matrimonial offence but also as to the absence of collusion, condonation and connivance. The Matrimonial Causes Act 1963 reduced collusion from an absolute to a discretionary bar to divorce and was hailed in *Minton* v *Minton* ([1979] 1 All ER 79, at 86 per Lord Scarman) as 'a major step forward towards the promotion of conciliation and harmony between people whose marriages had foundered, and the elimination of marital bitterness'. Only upon the implementation of the Divorce Reform Act 1969 on 1 January 1971 was the concept of the matrimonial offence swept away and with it the need for the court to satisfy itself as to the absence of any of the statutory bars to the grant of a decree.

In the short space of two decades or so, a full circle had been turned. 'Far from being a bar to the grant of a decree, agreement between the parties as to the manner in which their marriage should be terminated and as to all other aspects of their affairs is now positively encouraged' (Report of the Matrimonial Causes Procedure Committee (the Booth Report) (1985), para 2.3).

Long before formal statutory recognition was given to consent orders, their importance was highlighted by the very high proportion of orders made by consent either before a hearing or at the door of the court. A survey carried out by the Solicitors' Family Law Association of its members in March 1994 covering 14,447 cases revealed that 85.6 per cent of cases resulted in a court order being obtained by agreement. This increasing trend reflects a number of factors. One of these has been the continued growth of the mediation movement. Formerly, it was thought that there was a clear distinction between conciliation and mediation services. However, the two terms are now interchangeable; mediation is regarded as the preferred term. This is reflected in the fact that the umbrella organisation to which independent services have been affiliated has changed its name from the initial National Family Conciliation Council (NFCC) to the National Association of

Family Mediation and Conciliation Services (NAFMCS) and ultimately in 1992 to National Family Mediation (NFM). Mediation is a form of alternative dispute resolution. It can be broadly divided into property mediation, child mediation and comprehensive mediation.

Comprehensive mediation was first offered by the Family Mediators' Association (FMA), which was set up in December 1988 following a pilot project 'Solicitors in Mediation' which had operated on a small scale in London since February 1986. Mediation by FMA mediators is comprehensive, encompassing all issues connected with divorce or separation, including finance and property, on an inter-disciplinary basis by two co-mediators: a lawyer-mediator working jointly with another mediator from a different professional background, such as counselling, psychology, family therapy or social work. FMA is also developing a mediation model involving sole mediators.

Court-based schemes have been available in some areas for some time. The scheme set up at Bristol County Court in 1976 was an early example. A scheme has operated in the Principal Registry since 1 January 1993 (see *Practice Direction 18 October 1991* [1992] 1 All ER 421). There has been further encouragement by the *Practice Direction 28 July 1986* [1986] 2 FLR 171, which instructs judges or district judges, before ordering a court welfare report to be prepared, to consider referring a dispute relating to children to any local (mediation) service.

Out-of-court, comprehensive mediation is now offered both by services affiliated to NFM and by FMA mediators. There is also a scheme operated by the Family Law Bar Association (FLBA), which enables solicitors to submit agreed facts to a member of the FLBA for an opinion. Recent developments have included the establishment of the UK College of Mediation in 1996 by NFM, FMA and Family Mediation Scotland as a training and regulatory body. 1996 also saw the setting up of a training scheme for solicitor mediators by the Solicitors' Family Law Association as well as the establishment of the British Association of Lawyer Mediators (BALM) and the Ancillary Relief Pilot Project.

The Solicitors' Family Law Association has seen a rapid expansion of its membership since its formation in 1982. The need for a conciliatory approach is the main platform of the Association's Code of Practice, which received judicial approval in *Dutfield* v *Gilbert H Stephens & Sons* [1988] Fam Law 473. The Code, which was republished in a new edition in 1994, recommends that solicitors should advise, negotiate and conduct matters so as to encourage and assist the parties to achieve a constructive settlement of their differences as quickly as may be reasonable whilst recognising that they may need time to come to terms with their new situation. As the Code emphasises, a family dispute is not a contest in which there is one winner and one loser, but rather a search for fair solutions.

The desirability of a conciliatory approach to the resolution of the issues in a divorce is now enshrined in statute. Under the Family Law Act 1996, s 1 the court and any person, in exercising functions under or in consequence of Pts II and III of the Act (including, therefore, the lawyers) are to have regard to general principles that, *inter alia*, the parties are to be encouraged to take all practicable steps to save the marriage; that a marriage being brought to an end should be brought to an end with minimum distress to the parties and to the children affected; and with questions dealt with in a manner designed to promote as good a continuing relationship between the parties and any children affected as is possible in the circumstances. Perhaps reflecting these general principles, the Courts and Legal Services Committee of the Law Society has recommended, in the developing debate about accreditation of family lawyers, that family lawyers should adopt a non-adversarial approach, which would be a condition of accreditation (see, for example, para 28 of the consultation document published by the Law Society in May 1996).

The principle enshrined in the decision of *Calderbank* v *Calderbank* [1975] 3 WLR 586 has served to underline the importance of the need for negotiations which might lead to a settlement which can then be reflected in a consent order (see also *Cutts* v *Head* [1984] Ch 290). This practice has now been provided for in RSC Ord 22, r 14 and Ord 62, r 9(*d*) and CCR Ord 11, r 10. Indeed, it has been held that an obligation does exist to make a *Calderbank* offer or, put another way, there is a duty to negotiate (*Moorish* v *Moorish* (1984) 14 Fam Law 26; *Evans* v *Evans* [1990] 1 FLR 319; *E* v *E* [1990] 2 FLR 233; *S* v *S* [1990] 2 FLR 252; *A* v *A* (Costs Appeal) [1996] 1 FLR 14). The Court of Appeal held in *Gojkovic* v *Gojkovic* (No 2) [1991] 2 FLR 233 that the concept of no order for costs where both parties had been reasonable in their approach to a dispute was not one of general application in the Family Division, save in children cases, and was certainly not one of general application in *Calderbank* offers. Butler-Sloss LJ held that there was a wide discretion in the court in awarding costs and a *Calderbank* offer should influence but ought not to govern the exercise of that discretion. There were many reasons which might affect the court in considering costs, such as culpability in the conduct of litigation, delay or excessive zeal in seeking disclosure (*H* v *H* (Clean Break: Non-Disclosure: Costs) [1994] 2 FLR 309; *P* v *P* (Financial Relief: Non-Disclosure) [1994] 2 FLR

381); *F* v *F* (Duxbury Calculation: Rate of Return) [1996] 1 FLR 833). But it was inappropriate and unhelpful to enumerate those reasons or to constrain in any way the wide exercise of that discretion. The starting point in a case where there had been an offer was that *prima facie*, if the applicant received no more or less than the offer made, he was at risk not only of not being awarded costs but also of paying the costs of the other party after communication of the offer and a reasonable time to consider it. There was no difference in principle between the position of a party who had failed to obtain an order equal to the offer made and who had paid the costs and a party who failed by the offer to meet the award made by the court, in which case *prima facie* costs should follow the event, with the proviso that other factors in the Family Division might alter that *prima facie* position.

These comments echoed the thinking expressed by Cumming-Bruce LJ in *Singer (formerly Sharegin)* v *Sharegin* [1984] FLR 114, at 119–120:

> The judge . . . can proceed on the basis that the party costs will be paid by the respondent unless the respondent has protected himself or herself by a Calderbank offer.

The question of costs remains in the discretion of the court (per Purchas LJ, *S* v *S* [1990] 2 FLR 252). In that instance, the offeree had simply rejected an offer without making any attempt to negotiate.

The point was made in *Moorish* v *Moorish* (above) that the onus was upon the respondent to the application to make the *Calderbank* offer. Whilst it has been recognised for some time that it is possible to make a reverse *Calderbank* offer (*B* v *B* [1982] 3 FLR 298), it is now clear that it is incumbent upon both parties to negotiate to deal with the concerns expressed by Booth J in *Evans* v *Evans* (above).

In this decision, Booth J expressed (at 320) her anxiety at:

> the enormity of the costs which have been incurred in comparison with the assets which are available to meet the needs of the parties.

She continued (at 321):

> The situation recurs again and again when the court finds itself unable to make appropriate provision for the parties and their children because of their liability for legal costs and it is a matter of the gravest concern to all judges.

As a result, Booth J issued general guidelines to the profession with the concurrence of the President of the Family Division. Guideline 11 (at 322) lays further stress on the duty to negotiate:

(11) The desirability of reaching a settlement should be borne in mind throughout the proceedings. While it is necessary for the legal advisers to have sufficient knowledge of the financial situation of both parties before advising their client on a proposed settlement, the necessity to make further inquiries must always be balanced by consideration of what they are realistically likely to achieve and the increased costs which are likely to be incurred by making them.

The potential cost of matrimonial litigation is therefore such that it, or the effect of the Legal Aid Board's statutory charge, can act as a constraint upon the parties to settle their differences. Judicial concern about this issue was highlighted by the *President's Practice Direction 31 January 1995* [1995] 1 FLR 456 and is the focus of the Ancillary Relief Pilot Project which is to operate in certain courts with effect from 1 October 1996.

Following the decision of the House of Lords in *Minton* v *Minton* [1979] 1 All ER 79, it had become fashionable to talk in terms of a particular type of consent order: the 'clean break'. As Lord Scarman said in his opinion in *Minton* (at 87–88):

> There are two principles which inform the modern legislation. One is the public interest that spouses, to the extent that their means permit, should provide for themselves and their children. But the other—of equal importance—is the principle of 'the clean break'. The law now encourages spouses to avoid bitterness after family break-down and to settle their money and property problems. An object of the modern law is to encourage each to put the past behind them and to begin a new life which is not overshadowed by the relationship which has broken down. It would be inconsistent with this principle if the court could not make, as between the spouses, a genuinely final order unless it was prepared to dismiss the application.

The principle of the clean break has been buttressed by the important decision of the House of Lords in *Livesey* v *Jenkins* [1985] 1 All ER 106. In the words of Lord Hailsham (at 108):

> Consent orders which effect a clean break between former spouses are, when there has been full relevant disclosure, much to be encouraged, and, properly negotiated, greatly reduce the pain and trauma of divorce. They are, therefore, not lightly to be overthrown.

The impact of the decision in *Livesey* v *Jenkins*, not only in the House of Lords but in the Court of Appeal, has, as will be seen, been fundamental to the development of consent orders. The decision makes clear the basis upon which a consent order will be set aside as well as establishing the principle of full and frank disclosure. It should also be remembered that the Matrimonial and Family

Proceedings Act 1984, s 7, which inserted a new s 33A into the Matrimonial Causes Act 1973, was a direct reaction to the decision of the Court of Appeal in *Jenkins* v *Livesey* [1984] FLR 452.

The continuing importance of this branch of family law can be further underlined by the fact that it has, since the decision in *Livesey* v *Jenkins*, occupied the time of the House of Lords in *Dinch* v *Dinch* [1987] 1 All ER 818, *Sherdley* v *Sherdley* [1988] AC 213 and *Barder* v *Barder* [1987] 2 All ER 440 and that Ward J considered it appropriate in *B–T* v *B–T* [1990] 2 FLR 1 to give lengthy general guidance to the profession on the procedure relating to setting aside consent orders.

2 The choice: agreement or consent order?

Much will depend upon whether proceedings are envisaged in the short term. Divorce proceedings may not be possible because of the absolute one year bar. Whilst the possibility of an order under s 6 of the Domestic Proceedings and Magistrates' Courts Act 1978, as mentioned above, or judicial separation proceedings should be borne in mind, an agreement may reflect arrangements made for maintenance, residence and contact or the transfer of assets from one party to another, where no proceedings are immediately envisaged. In such circumstances, an agreement may bring about a speedier conclusion and represent a saving in costs. An agreement may be appropriate where the parties have agreed that a divorce will in due course be based upon two years' separation and consent. The agreement will also serve to record the fact and date of separation. Where proceedings have been issued, an agreement which is concluded at an early stage, before the court's powers to make a lump sum or property adjustment order arise and which do not take effect until decree absolute, can ensure that a transfer between the husband and wife will be an exempt transfer for inheritance tax purposes (see p 59 as to the position under a court order). For the purposes of capital gains tax, relief will only apply to disposals between spouses occurring no later than the end of the year of assessment in which they were last living together (Taxation of Chargeable Gains Act 1992, s 58(1)).

Following the Finance Act 1988, passed in the wake of *Sherdley* v *Sherdley* [1988] AC 213, there is no longer any distinction to be drawn as to the tax relief obtainable on maintenance payments payable under new written agreements and court orders (ie all orders applied for or agreements made on or after 15 March 1988, all orders made after 30 June 1988 (other than orders varying an existing obligation) and agreements made before 15 March 1988 written particulars of which had not been received by the Inland Revenue before 1 July 1988). On such agreements or orders, the maintenance is no longer treated as a charge on the income of the payer with consequent tax relief. However, in the case of 'qualifying maintenance payments' (as defined by the Income and Corporation Taxes Act 1988, s 347B), the payer may make a deduction in arriving at his taxable income limited in 1996/97 to £1,720 restricted to relief at the lower rate of income tax of 15 per cent. The particular considerations affecting child maintenance are discussed on pp 23–24.

The contents of an agreement and a consent order may be very similar in scope given the use of suitably worded undertakings in a consent order to deal with matters outside the court's powers under the Matrimonial Causes Act 1973, ss 23, 24 (*Livesey* v *Jenkins* [1985] 1 All ER 106, at 118–119).

Enforcement (discussed further in Chapter 8) of an agreement involves one party suing upon the contract and then enforcing the judgment obtained, whereas enforcement of a consent order involves invoking the enforcement weaponry of the court on the order already in existence. Variation of agreements and consent orders is discussed in Chapter 7; if all other factors are equal, the procedure relating to the variation of consent orders may be preferred.

By far the greatest advantage of a consent order made on divorce is its power to achieve complete finality. Neither an agreement nor capital provision ordered by the court on the grant of a decree of judicial separation can offer any foolproof guarantee that a spouse cannot successfully make a subsequent application for ancillary relief on divorce.

The choice between an agreement or a consent order has not been made simpler by the Child Support Act 1991. However, if an agreement can be reached over child maintenance which is to be incorporated either in an agreement or a consent order under the Child Support Act 1991, s 8(5), the residual risk that the payee may ultimately be obliged to apply to the Child Support Agency under the Child Support Act 1991, s 6 upon claiming state benefits is one which must be faced in either event.

3 The path of law reform

July 1985 saw the publication of the Booth Report. Its terms of reference included the recommendation of reforms which might be made to mitigate the intensity of disputes and encourage settlements. Its recommendations included at para 4.66 the use of an initial hearing to 'provide a convenient opportunity for the court to make consent orders. This the court could do on the basis of the parties' written statements as to the children and finance. It would, of course, be open to the court to ask questions of the parties and to refuse to make the order in the agreed terms if it required further information or was not satisfied that the parties fully understood the legal effect of what was proposed. The financial statement, properly completed, should provide sufficient information for the court to make consent orders for financial relief under s 33A of the Matrimonial Causes Act 1973'. It was recommended that claims for ancillary relief should be made in a separate composite application for financial provision and financial statement which should accompany the (joint) application for divorce. This procedure was seen as assisting 'the parties in identifying and understanding the specific issues. It would also focus the minds of the parties on the financial consequences of divorce for them and for their children' (para 4.30). It was recommended that the parties should attend the informal initial hearing, together with their legal advisers if they wish. The report recommended that conciliation should form a recognised part of the legal procedure, which should be generally available early in the proceedings. Conciliation should be available at court on the same day as the initial hearing and should not be confined to custodial issues. Potential for conciliation was seen in respect of financial issues alongside the need for professional advice.

The Booth Report recognised recognised conciliation as 'a most positive and potentially valuable response' to recent developments in family law (para 3.10).

Many had high hopes that this value would be reflected in the results of the work of a Project Unit set up at Newcastle University by the Lord Chancellor following the Report of the Inter-Departmental Committee on Conciliation (1983) to monitor and assess the costs and effectiveness of the different types of conciliation schemes. The work of the Unit commenced in September 1985 for a three-year period with a view to submitting a report to the Lord Chancellor based on its research, enabling him to decide whether a publicly-funded National Family Conciliation Service should be established and, if so, how such a service might best be organised and funded. In April 1989, the report was published by the Lord Chancellor's Department. It indicated that conciliation provided an additional cost and concluded:

> Whether a national conciliation service should be established (and, if so, on what basis) is a matter for political judgment since conciliation involves positive resource costs. Our research indicates that conciliation,

particularly of certain categories, generates important social benefits. We have been able to identify the factors which, on our understanding, contribute most to the effectiveness of conciliation and have provided in outline a model which attempts to integrate those factors into a set of coherent arrangements. Whether or not this, or any other model for a national conciliation service, proves to be politically acceptable, we are of the opinion, shared by many others, that some rationalisation of the confusing network of services currently available is a priority need.

As a continuation of its work, the Project Unit began research into various models suggested by the then National Family Conciliation Council for comprehensive mediation encompassing financial issues. The result of its research was published by the Joseph Rowntree Foundation in 1994. It was demonstrated that, during comprehensive mediation, 80 per cent of couples reached some agreement.

The Law Commission's Report: The Ground for Divorce (1990) Law Com No 192 recommended that divorce should be proved by the expiry of a minimum period of one year. In December 1993 the Government published its Consultation Paper 'Looking to the Future: Mediation and the Ground for Divorce'. The paper canvassed a number of options for reform of divorce law (including the recommendations put forward by the Law Commission in its 1990 Report) and the greater use of family mediation. There followed a Government White Paper published in April 1995, a Bill and ultimately the Family Law Act 1996 itself, which is due to come into effect not before 1998. The Act provides for a period for reflection and consideration, which is an ideal context for mediation (upon which the Act places heavy reliance) alongside independent legal advice. This period of nine months is the minimum period before which a divorce order may be granted (and the period may be extended, for example, if there is a child of the family under the age of sixteen when the application is made (FLA 1996 s 7(11) and (13)). The parties have first to satisfy the court that they have settled their future arrangements in accordance with s 9 and Sched 1 of the Act. It is to be noted that the settling of arrangements does not necessarily involve the making of a consent order by the court, but also embraces, for example, nothing more than a declaration by both parties that they have made their financial arrangements.

It remains to be seen whether these provisions will in fact serve only to fuel further litigation as parties hasten to achieve an ill-conceived solution, which may be difficult or impossible to enforce, simply so that the divorce order may be granted.

The Government's White Paper on the maintenance of children 'Children Come First' (Cm 1263), published in October 1990 in the same week as the Law Commission's recommendations on the ground for divorce, was followed by the Child Support Act 1991, which came into force subject to transitional provisions on 5 April 1993. The Act enables child maintenance to be assessed by the Child Support Agency as opposed to the courts on the basis of mathematical formulae. The full impact of these changes on consent orders (particularly those involving a clean break) and agreements still remains to be fully explored. As has already been seen with the changes brought about by the Social Security Administration Act 1992, ss 106–108 and *Crozier v Crozier* [1994] 1 FLR 126 (see Chapter 5), the popularity of clean break consent orders may decline at least where there is any likelihood of either party claiming income support now or in the future. The prospect of a fully unified Family Court, with adequate provision for mediation, remains as far off as when this work was first published in 1986 particularly in view of the creation of the Child Support Agency.

The underlying philosophy of the Children Act 1989 is the private ordering of arrangements for children on the basis that the court will only intervene and make an order where parents cannot make their own arrangements. The jurisdictional changes contained in the Act and regulations and rules made under it, making remedies for children available in all civil courts and all care cases beginning in the magistrates' court subject to a power to transfer, gave rise to speculation as to whether such changes would be a prelude to a new Family Court or a substitute for it. The Lord Chancellor's response to this speculation was that they should be regarded as neither. The Lord Chancellor, however, indicated in the debates on the Act in the House of Lords that with the Act the Government had put in hand a programme of work which would extend step by step to all aspects of family law and business, looking at the matching of judicial resources to cases, the matching of procedure to substantive law, the organisation and function of welfare services and the appropriate balance between formal adjudication and conciliation. This programme has now continued with the Family Law Act 1996.

The path of law reform may by common accord lead inevitably towards the ultimate destination of a Family Court with provision for mediation; however, the journey remains an arduous one with many obstacles in its course.

Chapter 2

Agreements

1 Contractual requirements

The first requirement with which any matrimonial agreement must conform is the basic law of contract.

(*a*) It must be established that there was an intention to create a legal relationship (*Balfour v Balfour* [1919] 2 KB 571; *Gould* v *Gould* [1969] 3 All ER 728). A family arrangement depending on the good faith of the parties in keeping the promises made and not intended to be a rigid binding agreement will not be enforceable as a contract (*Jones* v *Padavatton* [1969] 2 All ER 616, CA). The Court of Appeal here considered the arrangement between mother and daughter as far too vague and uncertain to be enforceable. However, Fenton Atkinson, LJ indicated (at 624H) that he did not think that lack of formality and precision in expressing the arrangement is necessarily an indication that no contract was intended having regard to what the court knows of the parties and their relationship. Indeed, in *Parker* v *Clark* [1960] 1 WLR 286, an exchange of letters, taken with the surrounding circumstances, was sufficient to show that the parties intended to enter into an agreement which was binding in law and not a mere unenforceable family arrangement. If the parties are living apart or are about to separate, the court will be more likely to presume that such an intention exists than if they are living together or are to separate for a short period only (*Merritt* v *Merritt* [1970] 2 All ER 760).

(*b*) Good consideration must be shown by the party seeking to enforce the agreement. Mutual agreements to live apart constitute valuable consideration (*Re Weston, Davies* v *Tagart* [1900] 2 Ch 164). It is usual, however, for matrimonial agreements to be made as deeds under seal, thereby avoiding any possible pitfalls regarding consideration. It is recommended that, notwithstanding the Law of Property

(Miscellaneous Provisions) Act 1989, s 1, where there is any doubt as to whether consideration has passed, the agreement should still be executed under seal. Attestation is now a formal legal requirement (Law of Property (Miscellaneous Provisions) Act 1989, s 1(3)). An agreement by a party not to apply to the court for further financial provision cannot oust the jurisdiction of the court and thus cannot constitute good consideration. (See below section 5*a*.)

(*c*) There must be reality of consent, in the absence of which the agreement is voidable and may be set aside at the instigation of the innocent party. This is further discussed in Chapter 6.

(*d*) A wife now, of course, has full capacity to enter into a contractual relationship without the joining of trustees as a result of the Married Women's Property Act 1882, s 1.

(*e*) The object of the agreement must be lawful. An agreement to separate in the future has been treated as contrary to public policy and thus void. To be valid it has been held that the agreement must have been made after the separation has occurred or when it was imminent (*Wilson* v *Wilson* (1848) 1 HL Cas 538). An agreement by the parties before marriage to separate after marriage has been treated as *a fortiori* void as being against public policy (*Brodie* v *Brodie* [1917] P 271; *Scott* v *Scott* [1959] 1 All ER 531). However, decisions declaring the invalidity of agreements on public policy grounds must be treated with caution. Apart from *H* v *H* (1983) 13 Fam Law 180 discussed below and *N* v *N* (Divorce: Agreement Not to Defend) [1992] 1 FLR 266 (see p 16), there have been no reported decisions since the introduction of the current divorce legislation. Given the emergence of cohabitation contracts and pre-marital contracts, judicial reaction may now be very different from that reflected in the above cases. An agreement may be void for mistake where, for example, the parties believe themselves to be validly married when in fact the marriage was bigamous (*Galloway* v *Galloway* (1914) 30 TLR 531; *Law* v *Harragin* (1917) 33 TLR 381). The extent to which an agreement may be void insofar as it prevents a wife from applying to the court for ancillary relief is discussed below on pp 27 *et seq*. A provision in an agreement which purports to restrict any person's right to apply for a maintenance assessment under the Child Support Act 1991 will be void (Child Support Act 1991, s 9(4)) (see p 117). A 'wife-swopping' agreement, under the terms of which each husband undertook to support his new partner, was deemed to be 'clearly unenforceable in law' (*H* v *H* (1983) 13 Fam Law 180).

(f) There is no general duty of full and frank disclosure. Matrimonial agreements are not subject to the common law doctrine of *uberrima fides*, since they are not agreements where only one party possesses knowledge of all the material facts (*Wales* v *Wadham* [1977] 2 All ER 125, at 139–142, confirmed on this ground by *Livesey* v *Jenkins* [1985] 1 All ER 106, at 115). It is, of course, still open to the parties to agree that negotiations shall proceed on the basis of full and frank disclosure and to state in the agreement that it has been arrived at on the basis that there has been full and frank disclosure. The agreement is less likely to be displaced in subsequent proceedings, if full and frank disclosure has been provided.

2 Classification

(a) Oral or written

A matrimonial agreement may be entered into orally, in writing or by deed. As has been seen, a deed avoids the need to show good consideration. The principal difficulty of an oral agreement is that its existence and terms may be difficult to prove in the absence of some form of written document.

Formerly, if an oral agreement amounted to a 'contract for the sale or other disposition of land or any other interest in the land', it was unenforceable unless there was a sufficient written note or memorandum to satisfy the Law of Property Act 1925, s 40 or an act of part performance (*Steadman* v *Steadman* [1974] 2 All ER 977; *Sutton* v *Sutton* [1984] 1 All ER 168). However, the Law of Property Act 1925, s 40 has been repealed by the Law of Property (Miscellaneous Provisions) Act 1989, s 2(8). Although the equitable doctrine of part performance is not expressly mentioned by the 1989 Act, the basis of its jurisdiction has been removed, as it is no longer possible to use the remedy of specific performance to enforce an oral contract which was valid but unenforceable. Now, all contracts for the sale or other disposition of 'an interest in land' can only be made in writing (Law of Property (Miscellaneous Provisions) 1989, s 2(1)) subject to the three exceptions found in s 2(5) of the Act.

For the purposes of securing tax relief on maintenance payments, an agreement made before 15 March 1988 will be subject to the 'old rules' under the Finance Act 1988 and will qualify for full tax relief, provided that the written agreement (or written particulars of the terms of an oral agreement) were sent to the payer's Inspector of Taxes before the end of June 1988 (Finance Act 1988, s 36(4)). If, however, the agreement was made on or after 15 March 1988, it will only qualify under the 'new rules' introduced by the Finance Act 1988 for limited tax relief if it is a *written* agreement (Income and Corporation Taxes Act 1988, s 347B(1) inserted by the Finance Act 1988, s 36(1)).

It is, however, safer from every viewpoint to rely on a written agreement or deed. In the simplest of cases (particularly where costs may be an overriding consideration because of the use of the Green Form Scheme), an exchange of correspondence between solicitors on all outstanding matters should suffice. An oral agreement cannot be altered by the court under the provisions of the Matrimonial Causes Act 1973, ss 34–36: the power to alter maintenance agreements contained in the Matrimonial Causes Act 1973 only applies to maintenance agreements made in writing (Matrimonial Causes Act 1973, s 34(2)). It follows that an oral agreement may only be varied by subsequent agreement between the parties (unless it qualifies as an ante-nuptial or post-nuptial settlement under the Matrimonial Causes Act 1973, s 24(1)(c)). Alternatively, an application could be made to the court for ancillary relief. If a written maintenance agreement includes a provision which purports to restrict any right to apply to a court for an order containing financial arrangements, then that provision is void as is any provision purporting to restrict the right to apply for a maintenance assessment under the Child Support Act 1991. However, any other financial arrangement is not thereby rendered void or unenforceable and is (unless they are void or unenforceable for any other reason and subject to ss 35 and 36 of the Act) binding on the parties to the agreement (Matrimonial Causes Act 1973, s 34(1)). Whilst such an agreement is, therefore, not rendered totally void, it will still, when it falls to be considered by the court, be subject to the rule in *Hyman* v *Hyman* [1929] AC 601 as discussed below.

(b) Maintenance or separation agreements
A maintenance agreement is an agreement where one party agrees to pay maintenance to the other or for a child while the parties live apart. Statutory definitions are to be found in the Matrimonial Causes Act 1973, s 34(2), the Child Support Act 1991, s 9(1), and the Children Act 1989, Sched 1, para 10(1), s 15(1), which are discussed on pp 28, 117 and 189 respectively. By contrast, a separation agreement, which will usually make provision for maintenance, is an agreement under which the parties agree to live separately. Whether a particular agreement or deed will amount to a separation agreement is a question of construction (*Crabtree* v *Crabtree* [1953] 2 All ER 56; *Bosley* v *Bosley* [1958] 2 All ER 167). The essence of the distinction is that under a

separation agreement neither party can be in desertion, unless the agreement has been treated by one party as a nullity (*Starkey* v *Starkey* [1938] 3 All ER 773).

(c) Reconciliation agreements
As has been seen, an agreement providing for a future separation may be void as being contrary to public policy. Parties who are living apart may wish to effect a reconciliation secure in the knowledge that, should the reconciliation prove unsuccessful, their respective financial positions will have been previously agreed. In such circumstances, public policy is not contravened where a reconciliation agreement on a resumption of cohabitation provides for a possible future separation, as this promotes rather than hinders reconciliation (*Re Meyrick's Settlement* [1921] 1 Ch 311). However, such an agreement should not contain unreasonable conditions attaching to the resumption of cohabitation as opposed to a future separation (*Staerck* v *Staerck*, unreported, Court of Appeal, 20 July 1987).

In *N* v *N* (Divorce: Agreement Not to Defend) [1992] 1 FLR 266, the husband and the wife entered into what was described as a comprehensive agreement for a possible reconciliation in the following terms:

> W undertakes not to proceed with the divorce suit for at least five months, in order that the parties can examine the possibility of reconciliation. H agrees that, if at the end of the five month period W does not withdraw her petition but intends to proceed with the divorce suit, he will not defend the petition.

Ewbank J held that, since collusion as a bar to divorce had been abolished, the agreement not to defend was not against public policy and was perfectly proper. The husband was debarred from defending the divorce because of the reconciliation agreement and, in any event, the court would not in the circumstances grant him leave to file an answer out of time.

A precedent for a reconciliation agreement is to be found at Appendix 3.

(d) Cohabitation contracts
Whilst this work is directly concerned with the private ordering of the obligations of spouses towards each other under family law, attempts by parties to relationships outside marriage to regulate their affairs cannot be ignored. They enjoy a freedom of contract unavailable to married couples. Thus, the frequency of relationships outside mar-

riage has seen the emergence of the cohabitation contract—an agreement entered into either at the inception of or during the subsistence of cohabitation, which governs both the parties' continuing relationship and their rights on the breakdown of that relationship.

Any attempt to establish a legally enforceable agreement out of the type of informal arrangements encountered in cohabitation may founder because the presumption that in agreements of a domestic nature parties do not intend to create a legally binding relationship will not have been rebutted. For example, in *Layton* v *Martin* [1986] 2 FLR 227, Scott J declined to accept that a letter offering 'financial security' followed by cohabitation could lead to contractual enforceability. Scott J put the matter in this way (at 239):

> . . . in family or quasi-family situations there is always the question whether the parties intended to create a legally binding contract between them. The more general and less precise the language of the so-called contract, the more difficult it will be to infer that intention.

However, the court was prepared to infer a contractual licence in *Tanner* v *Tanner* [1975] 1 WLR 1346; *Chandler* v *Kerley* [1978] 2 All ER 492; cf *Horrocks* v *Forray* [1976] 1 All ER 737.

Where it is established that a cohabitation contract was intended to create a legal relationship and the other relevant contractual requirements discussed on pp 12 *et seq* have been met, there remains the risk that the court will refuse to enforce the contract as being founded on an immoral consideration (*Diwell* v *Farnes* [1959] 2 All ER 379, at 384). It is doubted whether the body of case law (eg *Walker* v *Perkins* (1764) 1 Wm B1 517; *Benyon* v *Nettlefold* (1850) 3 Mac & G 94; *Upfill* v *Wright* [1911] 1 KB 506; *Gammans* v *Ekins* [1950] 2 All ER 140), which casts doubts upon the enforceability of cohabitation contracts on public policy considerations, would still be held to be valid today having regard to the marked shift in contemporary values. Sir Nicholas Browne-Wilkinson V-C held in *Stephens* v *Avery* [1988] 2 All ER 477 at 481:

> The court's function is to apply the law, not personal prejudice. Only in a case where there is still a generally accepted moral code can the court refuse to enforce rights in such a way as to offend that generally accepted code.

A distinction may in any event be drawn where the contract is entered into when the parties are already cohabiting (*Annandale* v *Harris* (1729) 2 P Wms 432). Duress or coercion may also vitiate the contract (*Zamet* v *Hyman* [1961] 1 WLR 1442).

Some statutory recognition has gradually been given to the status of cohabitation by eg the Family Income Supplements Act 1970, s 1, the Inheritance (Provision for Family and Dependants) Act 1975, s 1(1) and (1A) (as amended by the Law Reform (Succession) Act 1995, s 2), the Domestic Violence and Matrimonial Proceedings Act 1976, s 1(2) and the Housing Act 1985, s 58(2). Significantly, Scott J did not suggest in *Layton* v *Martin* that, had there been an intention to create a legally binding relationship, the contract would have been unenforceable on the public policy grounds of immorality. Rather, he held at 238:

> An agreement by one party to pay to the other, say £5,000 a year, or a lump sum of £15,000 is enforceable, if it complies with the requirements of contracts, as a contract.

A contract may well be void on public policy grounds if either of the parties is married at the time the agreement is entered into (cf *Fender* v *St John-Mildmay* [1938] AC 1, where a promise made by a spouse after decree nisi of divorce to marry a third party after the decree had been made absolute was held not to be void as against public policy, and *Watson* v *Lucas* [1980] 3 All ER 647, where a man who remained married to another woman throughout the time he lived with a protected tenant was not barred from becoming a member of the tenant's 'family' for the purposes of the Rent Act 1977; see also *Shaw* v *Fitzgerald* [1992] 1 FLR 357).

Given the changing social and legal attitudes towards cohabitation—a change described as the privatisation of marriage—a wide diversity of individual contracts is possible. However, until such contracts are fully endorsed by the courts, the following cautionary note may be sounded:

- *Careful drafting* is vital.
- The *essential elements* of any legally binding contract must be present. These have already been reviewed in relation to matrimonial agreements on pp 12–14. In particular, an intention to create legally binding relations must be shown.
- The *form* of the contract is important: a formal written contract executed as a deed is to be preferred if only to show that the agreement is not simply of a domestic nature and that there was an intention to create a binding legal relationship. Express oral or implied contracts should be avoided.
- The *purpose* of the contract should be to regulate a relationship between unmarried parties rather than to provide for a sexual relationship so as to minimise the risk of the contract being tainted with immorality (*Fender* v *St John-Mildmay* [1938] AC 1, at 42).

- The *content* of the contract should concentrate upon terms which have a bearing upon practical issues of the continuing relationship and those which have relevance on the breakdown of the relationship rather than matters of a personal or sexual nature. This may help to ensure that there is an identifiable valid consideration standing apart from any sexual relationship (*Parker* v *Clark* [1960] 1 WLR 286). Since an agreement to live together will not itself be enforceable (and may indeed taint the whole contract with immorality unless the particular covenant is severable, see p 29), the agreement to cohabit should appear as a recital rather than as part of the operative clauses of the contract. In this way the agreement can focus upon financial issues such as ownership of property acquired before the inception of the relationship and during its subsistence. Other matters which are commonly dealt with include the right of the parties to occupy the home, provision as to savings and financial obligations as between the parties and (subject to the Child Support Act 1991) towards any children, both during the relationship and in the event of its breakdown. It must always be borne in mind that any support obligation between cohabitees can only arise out of an agreement; there is no duty on the part of one partner to support the other. As Millett J put it in *Windeler* v *Whitehall* [1990] 2 FLR 505 at 506: 'If this were California, this would be a claim for palimony, but it is England and it is not.' In most instances, the home will not only be dealt with in the cohabitation contract but in a separate deed of trust, which sets out the parties' respective beneficial interests. This will be essential if the beneficial interests are to be varied from those contained in the conveyance or transfer on purchase. The importance of such action has been stressed by the Court of Appeal in *Bernard* v *Josephs* [1982] 2 WLR 1052 and *Walker* v *Hall* [1984] FLR 126 at 129E; and by the potential liability in negligence of the solicitor who fails to advise clients about the relative merits of joint tenancies and tenancies in common (*Taylor* v *Harman and Warners* Warner J, unreported, 21 July 1986 (1988) 85 *Law Society's Gazette* 26 and *Springette* v *Defoe* [1992] 2 FLR 388 at 390P). It must be remembered that, where personal property is concerned, it will belong to the party who acquired it, unless there is evidence of a contrary agreement. In the case of joint bank or building society accounts, a 'common pool' may be established—as in the case of married couples (see *Jones* v *Maynard* [1951] Ch 572)—with the result that the parties will be joint tenants of the contents of the account until severance.
- Any provision relating to *children* must be seen in the context of the Children Act 1989 and in particular s 4. As the unmarried father

acquires no parental responsibilities automatically, it will be possible for unmarried parents to agree to share parental responsibility by a 'parental responsibility agreement'. Such an agreement will be valid even whilst the parties are living together, but to be effective it must be in a prescribed form and be recorded as provided for by the Parental Responsibility Agreement Regulations 1991 (SI No 1478) and the Parental Responsibility Agreement (Amendment) Regulations 1994 (SI 1994 No 3157).

The Children Act 1989, Sched 1, para 10 provides for the alteration of 'maintenance agreements' relating to children during the lifetime of the parties, whereas para 11 provides for alteration following the death of one of the parties (see, further, pp 189 and 193).

Any financial provision relating to children must also be seen in the context of the Child Support Act 1991 (see chapter 5).

- Ultimately, the agreement will be subject to the *court's discretion* as to whether or not to give effect to it. It will not do so, for example, where there is evidence of undue influence or duress. Further, where changed circumstances brought about perhaps by the passage of time render the contract unworkable, the court may vary or override it.

Equally, it must be borne in mind that a cohabitation contract may have certain advantages:

- A cohabitation contract may provide some element of *certainty* which can overcome the procedural wrangles and costs otherwise involved in unmarried property disputes (eg *Hammond* v *Mitchell*, *sub nom H* v *M* (Property: Beneficial Interest) [1992] 1 FLR 229).
- Where one cohabitee is a party to *divorce proceedings*, a cohabitation agreement may be of evidential value in establishing whether there is any financial dependancy and, if so, the extent of that dependancy (*Frary* v *Frary* [1993] 2 FLR 696, CA).

A precedent for a cohabitation contract is found at Appendix 2.

(e) Pre-marital contracts
Given the high incidence of divorce, it is not surprising that those contemplating marriage may consider a pre-marital contract even if this smacks of a somewhat cynical approach. It may be significant that pre-marital contracts may be considered more frequently in second marriages. Such a contract will commonly attempt to regulate what is to happen on the breakdown of the marriage to assets acquired before and during the marriage. The parties may also wish to deal with a wide range of matters of a non-financial nature: for example, the timing and frequency of the arrival of children or their

personal and sexual relations. Such provisions can do no more than record the parties' expectations and will not be of any binding legal effect. Whilst such contracts may be of assistance in the event of an amicable breakdown, the court will not be bound by such contracts for the reasons explained on pp 27 *et seq*. The court will retain its overall discretionary powers under the Matrimonial Causes Act 1973, s 25. It would appear that the principle in *Edgar* v *Edgar* [1980] 3 All ER 887 applies to pre-marital contracts just as to post-marital arrangements (*Sabbagh* v *Sabbagh* [1985] FLR 29). A contract will not, however, be binding where there is evidence of undue influence (*Zamet* v *Hyman* [1961] 1 WLR 1442, CA). Further, the most recent judicial pronouncement on the effect of pre-marital contracts suggests that they are of very limited significance in this jurisdiction. Thorpe J held in *F* v *F* (Ancillary Relief: Substantial Assets [1995] 2 FLR 45 at 66 that the rights and responsibilities of those whose financial affairs are regulated by statute cannot be much influenced by contractual terms which were devised for the control and limitation of standards that are intended to be of universal application. The court also has the power to vary a pre-marital contract as an ante-nuptial settlement under s 24(1)(*c*) of the 1973 Act. Where the parties' concern relates solely to the matrimonial home, a specific agreement as to the beneficial interests can be dealt with by means of a separate declaration of trust. But again, such a declaration could be overridden by the court, for example, in the context of an ancillary relief application upon divorce.

A precedent for a pre-marital contract is to be found at Appendix 1.

(f) Mediated agreements

The Family Law Act 1996 will place mediation at the forefront of the means by which the various issues arising on family breakdown may be resolved. The types of agreements which may arise within mediation and their precise legal status remain to be refined. However, the following four mediation summaries—not all of which amount to an agreement—may be identified. First an interim summary, which is legally privileged, will be maintained on file by the mediators throughout the mediation. It should not use the word 'agreement' or be signed by the parties. Secondly, there may be an interim agreement, which is not legally privileged, in limited circumstances, for example, to record interim contact or financial arrangements. Thirdly, a final mediation summary, which is still legally privileged, will summarise mutually acceptable proposals for settlement following a [partially] successful mediation subject to each party receiving independent legal advice. The summary should not use the words 'agreement' or 'agree' and should be signed by the mediators but not by the parties. Such a summary should give a concise neutral statement of each party's position in relation to any unresolved issues. Finally, there is an open summary of financial information, which is not legally privileged, which records the disclosure made by each of the parties attaching any supporting documents.

3 Content and construction of maintenance or separation agreements

Agreements or deeds are as simple or complex as the affairs of the parties themselves. They do, however, in general have certain clauses in common as discussed below. An agreement or deed will usually begin with short historical or narrative recitals leading to the operative clauses in the body of the agreement. A modern style precedent of a separation deed is to be found in Appendix 4.

(a) Recitals

Recitals will customarily give information as to the date of marriage, details of the children and the date of the existing or imminent future separation. It may also be considered prudent to include recitals indicating that the parties intend to create legal relations, that they have each taken independent legal advice and that there has been full and frank financial disclosure. Such recitals may be viewed as narrative recitals. Historical recitals may record, for example, a prior capital payment or prior transfer of the family home.

(b) Agreement to live apart

If the agreement is to be a separation agreement, the parties agree to live separate and apart, thereby releasing each other from the duty to cohabit and placing neither party in desertion. The formal record of the fact and date of separation is of evidential value in any subsequent proceedings. In dealing with the separation in the recitals and in the operative clauses of the deed, it should be borne in mind that a separation may occur even when the parties are living under the same roof providing there are two separate households (see, eg *Mouncer* v *Mouncer* [1972] 1 All ER 289; *Fuller* v *Fuller* [1973] 2 All ER 650).

(c) Non-molestation clause

A clause has been traditionally included in agreements that neither party shall 'molest, annoy or interfere with the other'. However, the use of the word 'molest' now runs contrary to the move towards plain

English represented by the County Court (Amendment) Rules 1991 (SI 1991 No 525) and the County Court (Forms Amendment) Rules 1991 (SI 1991 No 526).

(d) Future proceedings

The purpose of an agreement may be to regulate the position of the parties during a period of separation prior to a divorce based upon two years' separation and consent under the Matrimonial Causes Act 1973, s 1(2)(*d*). In such circumstances, it is common to agree who is to petition for a divorce on this basis, indicating the court out of which proceedings are to issue and any agreement reached over the question of costs. Whilst it is also common for an agreement to record the consent of one party to a decree being granted along with agreements to do all that is necessary to provide evidence of such consent and not to withdraw such consent, it should be borne in mind that consent once given may be withdrawn (FPR 1991, r 2.10(2); *Beales* v *Beales* [1972] 2 All ER 667). It is also usual for such an agreement to deal with ancillary financial matters, as indicated below. Agreements have in the past included a *Rose* v *Rose* clause whereby each party agrees not to base any subsequent proceedings on previous conduct (*Rose* v *Rose* (1883) 8 PD 98). It is doubted whether future proceedings can still be regulated in this way following the abolition of the doctrine of the matrimonial offence. However, such a clause may, depending on its construction, act as an estoppel.

Any agreement as to future proceedings will now have to have regard to the operation of the Family Law Act 1996 and its revisions to divorce procedures. Schedule 9 of the Act enables the Lord Chancellor by order to provide transitional arrangements for those who have been living apart when s 3 of the Act is brought into force.

(e) Maintenance

An agreement will normally make provision for the payment of maintenance to the wife and any children. A limited degree of tax relief is available not only for spousal maintenance but also where the child maintenance is expressed to be payable to the spouse or former spouse for the benefit of the child. Where this is done, the payer can claim a deduction from his total taxable income of the total amount of maintenance paid as spousal maintenance and for all relevant children or £1,790 (in 1996/97 at 15 per cent), whichever is the lesser (Income and Corporation Taxes Act 1988, s 347B inserted by the Finance Act 1988, s 36). Clearly, this device will only be of use where no maintenance for the wife is contemplated or where that maintenance alone does not exceed £1,790 (in 1996/97). If the spouse through whom the payments are being channelled remarries, the payer will lose the extra tax allowance even though the payments are still being made for the benefit of a child or children. In order to secure this limited tax relief, the agreement must be in writing (see p 15). Quite apart from the Child Support Act 1991, s 9 (see p 117), under which any agreement purporting to restrict the right to apply for a maintenance assessment under the 1991 Act is void, little will be achieved by incorporating any provision for child maintenance in an agreement where the wife is in receipt of or is claiming income support, family credit or disability working allowance, as the Department of Social Security will seek authority from her to carry out an assessment and recover child support maintenance under the Child Support Act 1991, s 6.

The extent of the husband's obligation to maintain must be carefully defined, as in the absence of such definition, the covenant to maintain may survive independently of the agreement to separate and thereby continue after a resumption of cohabitation (*Negus* v *Forster* (1882) 46 LT 675), divorce (*May* v *May* [1929] All ER Rep 484; cf *Covell* v *Sweetland* [1968] 2 All ER 1016) and even after a decree of nullity in the case of a voidable marriage (*Adams* v *Adams* [1941] 1 All ER 334). A covenant to pay maintenance to the wife during her lifetime is binding on the husband's executors after his death (*Kirk* v *Eustace* [1937] 2 All ER 715) and even after a decree of nullity (*Fowke* v *Fowke* [1938] 2 All ER 638). Whether a particular covenant will cease on the death of the husband is a matter of construction depending upon what was intended (*Re Lidington* [1940] 3 All ER 600; *Langstone* v *Hayes* [1946] 1 All ER 114). It is now no longer customary to include in an agreement a *dum casta* clause whereby the husband would no longer remain under a duty to maintain the wife in the event of subsequent adultery because of the abolition of the doctrine of the matrimonial offence, although a *dum sola* clause whereby maintenance would terminate upon cohabitation or remarriage will normally be included. If the husband complies with the provisions of the agreement as to maintenance, it is *prima facie* evidence that he is providing reasonable maintenance, should the wife commence proceedings, eg under the Matrimonial Causes Act 1973, s 27 claiming failure to provide reasonable maintenance.

(f) Indemnity and covenant not to apply for ancillary relief
An indemnity may afford a husband some limited form of protection against debts contracted by the wife after separation. The husband

may still be liable on contracts made by her if estopped from denying that she had his authority to pledge his credit. The effect of a covenant not to take proceedings for ancillary relief is discussed in detail on pp 27 *et seq*. If the agreement provides for a clean break settlement, it is customary for the agreement to provide that the parties will invite the court in subsequent divorce proceedings to dismiss their respective claims for ancillary relief and to make an order under the Inheritance (Provision for Family and Dependants) Act 1975, s 15, that neither party will on the death of the other seek an order under s 2 of that Act against the deceased's estate. A covenant of this latter type might be used as a defence by the personal representatives of the deceased to proceedings brought by the survivor under the 1975 Act. The agreement would be admissible in evidence under s 21 of the 1975 Act. Where the agreement provides for continuing maintenance, it may nonetheless be appropriate to provide for a clean break on death limited to capital only (see *H* v *H* [1988] 2 FLR 114). It might still be argued that a wife could seek a capital order under s 2 of the 1975 Act representing the capitalisation of her maintenance claims against the estate. A form of consent order incorporating such terms may be agreed in advance and annexed to the deed with a view to being filed subsequently in the divorce proceedings.

(g) Property
The parties will wish to make provision for the ownership and occupation of the matrimonial home and the distribution of their other capital assets.

(h) Residence and contact
There is a 'no order presumption', ie an order should only be made where it is considered better than no order at all under the Children Act 1989, s 1(5). This non-intervention principle places the responsibility on parents to agree arrangements for their children on separation. In this context, reference should be made to s 2(9)–(11) of the 1989 Act. The underlying philosophy of the 1989 Act is therefore to encourage parents to reach their own arrangements with regard to residence and contact. It is not suggested that it will usually be necessary for detailed contact arrangements to be recorded in an agreement. However, it may be useful to record, for example, holiday arrangements. A record of the broad agreement reached in a separation agreement does not in any way undermine the philosophy of the 1989 Act.

(i) Taxation

It may be necessary to make provision that one party will be responsible for the fiscal consequences of a specified transaction and to give the other party an indemnity in relation to this from a specified date.

(j) Agreement to leave by will

The husband may covenant with his wife, such covenant to be binding upon his executors, to make provision for her by will. The wife's remedy in the event of the husband's non-compliance would be to sue the husband's estate under the covenant (see *Schaefer* v *Schuhmann* [1972] 1 All ER 621).

(k) Relevant law

It is usual for the parties not only to agree that the relevant law applicable to a separation agreement will be that of England and Wales, but also that, where there is a conflict of jurisdictions, the parties wish any application to the court to be dealt with in England and Wales. This may be of some evidential value to enable a party to obtain a stay of proceedings issued later in breach of the agreement.

(l) Costs

The agreement should deal with the question of liability for the costs of its preparation.

4 Discharge of maintenance or separation agreements

(a) By agreement

An agreement may be discharged under its own terms or by a subsequent agreement between the parties. A resumption of cohabitation may terminate all the obligations in an agreement and not simply the agreement to separate depending upon the construction of the individual agreement (*Negus* v *Forster* (1882) 46 LT 675; *Nicol* v *Nicol* (1886) 31 Ch D 524).

(b) By breach

An agreement may be repudiated by one party giving the other party a right to treat it as discharged. The party in breach does not have to be informed by the other party that the repudiation has been accepted. It is sufficient to show that there was no intention to rely on the agreement and that the agreement was a 'dead letter'. It is a question of fact whether a particular breach will amount to repudiation. Failure to pay maintenance may not of itself amount to repudiation but a persistent failure may do so (*Pardy* v *Pardy* [1939] 3 All ER 779). If the party not in breach affirms the validity of the agreement, eg by suing for maintenance under it, that party thereby refuses to accept the repudiation and desertion will not begin (*Clark* v *Clark* (No 2) [1939] 2 All ER 392).

(c) By operation of law
An agreement to separate will be discharged by subsequent matrimonial proceedings, but it is a question of construction whether a husband's obligation to maintain a wife under the agreement will continue thereafter, as already discussed above in section 3(*e*). On a husband's bankruptcy, a wife is entitled to prove in the bankruptcy for future maintenance with the result that no action will lie for maintenance payable after the commencement of the bankruptcy. The wife is therefore entitled to treat the agreement as discharged (*Victor* v *Victor* [1912] 1 KB 247; *McQuiban* v *McQuiban* [1913] P 208).

5 The rule in *Hyman* v *Hyman*

(a) The decision
The House of Lords decided in *Hyman* v *Hyman* [1929] AC 601 that a wife could not enter into a valid agreement with a husband not to apply for maintenance on a divorce and that it is open to the court to entertain an application for ancillary relief notwithstanding the existence of such an agreement. The facts of the case were, briefly:

> On 20 September 1919 the parties entered into a separation deed, under the terms of which H made financial provision for W and W agreed not to seek further maintenance beyond that provided in the deed. At the date of the deed, H was living in adultery with another woman, which adultery continued after the date of the deed. On 18 July 1923, the Matrimonial Causes Act 1923 became law whereby for the first time a wife was given the right to obtain a divorce solely on the ground of adultery by her husband. On 11 January 1926, W filed a petition for divorce on the ground of H's adultery during the two preceding years. W subsequently applied for maintenance and H in opposition to the application sought to rely on the provisions of the separation deed.

Lord Hailsham LC held in his opinion at 608:

> I am prepared to hold that the parties cannot validly make an agreement either (1) not to invoke the jurisdiction of the Court, or (2) to control the powers of the Court when its jurisdiction is invoked.

and at 614:

It is sufficient for the decision of the present case to hold, as I do, that the power of the Court to make provision for a wife on the dissolution of her marriage is a necessary incident of the power to decree such a dissolution, conferred not merely in the interests of the wife, but of the public, and that the wife cannot by her own covenant preclude herself from invoking the jurisdiction of the Court or preclude the Court from the exercise of that jurisdiction.

(b) *Matrimonial Causes Act 1973*

The rule in *Hyman* v *Hyman*, as it relates to written agreements, is embodied in the Matrimonial Causes Act 1973, s 34(1) which provides:

> (1) If a maintenance agreement includes a provision purporting to restrict any right to apply to a court for an order containing financial arrangements then:
> (*a*) that provision shall be void; but
> (*b*) any other financial arrangements contained in the agreement shall not thereby be rendered void or unenforceable, and shall, unless they are void or unenforceable for any other reason (and subject to ss 35 and 36 below), be binding on the parties to the agreement.

A 'maintenance agreement' means (s 34(2)):

> . . . any agreement in writing made, whether before or after the commencement of this Act, between the parties to a marriage, being:
>
> (*a*) an agreement containing financial arrangements, whether made during the continuance or after the dissolution or annulment of the marriage; or
> (*b*) a separation agreement which contains no financial arrangements in a case where no other agreement in writing between the same parties contains such arrangements.

'Financial arrangements' mean (s 34(2)):

> Provisions governing the rights and liabilities towards one another when living separately of the parties to a marriage (including a marriage which has been dissolved or annulled) in respect of the making or securing of payments or the disposition or use of any property, including such rights and liabilities with respect to the maintenance or education of any child, whether or not a child of the family.

As has already been seen when distinguishing between oral and written agreements, the saving provisions of s 34(1)(*b*) do not protect an oral agreement from being rendered totally void, insofar as it purports to restrict the right of a party to apply to the court for ancillary relief.

(c) Child Support Act 1991

The effect of the 1991 Act upon agreements is discussed in detail in Chapter 5. It is sufficient to mention here that s 9(2) of the 1991 Act provides that nothing in the Act is to be taken to prevent any person from entering into a maintenance agreement. A 'maintenance agreement' for this purpose means any agreement for the making, or for securing the making, of periodical payments by way of maintenance ... to or for the benefit of any child (s 9(1)). However, the existence of a maintenance agreement does not prevent any party to the agreement, or any other person, from applying to the Child Support Agency for a maintenance assessment with respect to any child to or for whose benefit periodical payments are to be made or secured under the agreement (s 9(3)). A provision in any agreement which purports to restrict the right of any person to apply for a maintenance assessment is void (s 9(4)). Nonetheless, the court has used the principle in *Edgar* v *Edgar* [1980] 3 All ER 887, discussed below, to ensure that the terms of a previous separation agreement are upheld (*Smith* v *McInerney* [1994] 2 FLR 1077; see p 127).

The effect of a maintenance assessment under the 1991 Act upon an existing agreement is dealt with in s 10(2) of the 1991 Act and the Child Support (Maintenance Arrangements and Jurisdiction) Regulations 1992 (SI 1992 No 2645), reg 4. Briefly, a maintenance agreement within the meaning of s 9(1) of the 1991 Act will become unenforceable from the effective date of the maintenance assessment under the 1991 Act, so far as it relates to children dealt with under the agreement. Where a maintenance assessment is made with respect to one or more but not all of the children covered by the agreement, the agreement will only be unenforceable where the amount payable under the agreement to or for the benefit of each child is separately specified.

6 The court's approach to agreements

(a) Background

The effect of the rule in *Hyman* v *Hyman* is that, because an agreement restricting the right of a party to apply to the court is void, the whole agreement will be void if such a covenant constitutes the whole or main consideration (*Gaisberg* v *Storr* [1949] 2 All ER 411; *Combe* v *Combe* [1951] 2 All ER 767; *Bennett* v *Bennett* [1952] 1 All ER 413). The position would be otherwise if other consideration existed or if the offending covenant were severable (*Goodinson* v *Goodinson* [1954] 2 All ER 255; *Williams* v *Williams* [1957] 1 All ER 305). These decisions must now be seen against the background of the Matrimonial Causes Act 1973, ss 34–36, the Children Act 1989, Sched 1, paras 10 and 11 (see pp 189 and 193) and the Child Support Act 1991 (see Chapter 5).

Despite the fact that the court is therefore able to entertain a wife's application for ancillary relief, the court will not be inclined to alter an agreement under the Matrimonial Causes Act 1973, s 35, unless the change in circumstances is such that the agreement has become unjust (*Ratcliffe* v *Ratcliffe* [1962] 3 All ER 993; *Gorman* v *Gorman* [1964] 3 All ER 739; *Simister* v *Simister* (No 2) [1987] 1 FLR 194).

(b) Edgar v *Edgar*

Where the court is asked to consider an application for ancillary relief under the Matrimonial Causes Act 1973, ss 23 or 24, the court will have regard to the agreement within the meaning of conduct for the purposes of the Matrimonial Causes Act 1973, s 25. The leading decision in this context is that of the Court of Appeal in *Edgar* v *Edgar* [1980] 3 All ER 887, the facts of which were:

> W entered into a separation deed on 1 April 1976 with H against the advice of those representing her. Under the terms of the deed, W received capital provision and maintenance for herself and the children. W agreed under the deed not to claim a lump sum or a transfer of property order in subsequent divorce proceedings. No pressure was applied by H on W to accept the terms of the deed. H carried out his obligations under the deed. On 3 November 1978, W issued a petition for divorce, upon which a decree nisi was pronounced on 24 January 1979. Subsequently, W proceeded with an application for ancillary relief including an application for a lump sum order.

The Court of Appeal held that, in exercising its discretion whether or not to order a lump sum payment under the Matrimonial Causes Act 1973, s 23(1), the court was required to give effect to a prior agreement by the wife not to claim a lump sum by treating that agreement as conduct of the parties which fell to be taken into account under the Matrimonial Causes Act 1973, s 25.

Ormrod LJ put forward this proposition in *Edgar* (at 893):

> To decide what weight should be given, in order to reach a just result, to a prior agreement not to claim a lump sum, regard must be had to the conduct of both parties leading up to the prior agreement, and to their subsequent conduct in consequence of it. It is not necessary in this connection to think in formal legal terms, such as misrepresentation or estoppel; *all* the circumstances as they affect each of two human beings must be considered in the complex relationship of marriage. So the

circumstances surrounding the making of the agreement are relevant. Undue pressure by one side, exploitation of a dominant position to secure an unreasonable advantage, inadequate knowledge, possibly bad legal advice, an important change of circumstances, unforeseen or overlooked at the time of making the agreement, are all relevant to the question of justice between the parties. Important too is the general proposition that, formal agreements, properly and fairly arrived at with competent legal advice, should not be displaced unless there are good and substantial grounds for concluding that an injustice will be done by holding the parties to the terms of their agreement. There may well be other considerations which affect the justice of this case; the above list is not intended to be an exclusive catalogue.

The mere fact that there was disparity of bargaining power between the parties is not of itself a ground for ignoring an agreement, unless there is evidence that a husband has exploited that disparity in a way which was unfair to the wife, so as to induce her to act to her disadvantage. The Court of Appeal in *Edgar* applied the test in *Wright* v *Wright* [1970] 3 All ER 209 that it was incumbent upon the wife in seeking to justify an award of further provision to offer *prima facie* evidence that justice required that she be relieved from the effect of the agreement.

The position can thus be summarised in the propositions put forward by Eastham J in the first instance decision in *Edgar* with the gloss placed upon them by Ormrod LJ in the Court of Appeal (at 893–894):

> (1) Notwithstanding an agreement, a wife is entitled to pursue a claim for ancillary relief under the Matrimonial Causes Act 1973, ss 23 and 24;

> (2) If she does pursue such a claim, the court not only has jurisdiction to entertain it, but is bound to take into account all the considerations listed in the Matrimonial Causes Act 1973, s 25;

> (3) The existence of an agreement is a very relevant circumstance under s 25 and, in the case of an arm's length agreement based on legal advice between parties of equal bargaining power, is a most important piece of conduct to be considered under s 25;

> (4) Providing there is such equality, the mere fact that the wife would have done better by going to court will not generally be a ground for giving her more;

> (5) If the court, on the evidence, takes the view that having regard to the exploitation of the disparity of bargaining power, it would be unjust not to exercise its powers under ss 23 or 24 (having regard to the considerations under s 25), it should exercise such powers even if no ground is established which would have entitled the wife to avoid the deed at common law.

The decision in *Edgar* v *Edgar* has its origins in the opinion of Lord Hailsham LC in *Hyman* v *Hyman* [1929] AC 601 (at 609), where he held:

> ... the fact that the deed of separation has been entered into by both parties, the fact that it was executed by the wife voluntarily and upon independent legal advice, the fact that the wife was prepared to accept the provision then made as adequate at the time, the benefits which she obtains in the shape of the guarantee by Mr Walter Hyman and in the continuance of the weekly payments after her husband's death, all form part of that conduct of the parties which by the express terms of the statute is to be taken into account by the Court in determining what it thinks reasonable . . . The only question which the order appealed against determines is that the existence of the covenant in the deed of separation does not preclude the wife from making an application to the Court; this by no means implies that, when the application is made, the existence of the deed or its terms are not most relevant factors for consideration by the Court in reaching a decision.

As has been seen on p 21, Balcombe J took the view in *Sabbagh* v *Sabbagh* [1985] FLR 29, at 37 that a pre-marital contract should be included in all the circumstances of the case that the court has to consider under the Matrimonial Causes Act 1973, s 25.

(c) Edgar applied

Attention has already been drawn to the circumstances surrounding the making of an agreement which Ormrod LJ in *Edgar* considered the court should have regard in deciding the weight to be attached to it. These merit individual consideration:

(i) Bad legal advice

A decision which contrasts with *Edgar* in relation to *bad legal advice* is that of the Court of Appeal in *Camm* v *Camm* [1983] 4 FLR 577. The Court of Appeal held in the latter that a wife should not be bound by an agreement which was 'most disadvantageous' to her despite a delay of some seven years in applying for periodical payments for herself. The court took into account not only the fact that she was under extreme pressure, coming partly from herself and partly from the fact that the husband refused to concede anything about periodical payments, but also the standard of legal advice which the wife received. After referring to the passage from *Edgar* quoted above, Ormrod LJ held (at 580):

> And I made it clear that [that referring to *Edgar*] was not, of course, an exclusive list. I still think it was right to refer to bad legal advice, although in that passage I was not thinking in terms of negligence by the

solicitor . . . I was thinking in terms of exactly what I said, 'bad legal advice', and we are all familiar with cases in which parties are badly advised. That is to say, it is not necessarily negligent advice to take a course or permit a client to take a course which a more experienced, or stronger minded legal adviser would have discouraged. It seems to me plain if one compares the facts of this case with the facts in *Edgar* v *Edgar* that the quality of legal advice on which parties act is of some relevance to the justice of the case. In *Edgar* v *Edgar* the wife was fully legally advised, and strongly advised not to enter into the deed of separation containing a particular clause which limited her capital thereafter; but nonetheless, she went ahead. In this case there was very much less clear legal advice by her solicitor and the whole matter was dealt with, obviously, on quite a different level. In *Edgar* v *Edgar* the whole thing was formally negotiated between solicitors for a period of months, and there could have been no possible misunderstanding or shadow of a doubt in the mind of the wife when she elected to ignore the legal advice she had been given. In this case there is no question, I think, of the wife ignoring any legal advice. It is said that she was told, somehow, that the effect of entering into this agreement might deprive her of all future maintenance but . . . I would have expected that at least she would have been required by her solicitor to sign a document which would make it absolutely clear that she knew what she was doing. I think the quality of legal advice is relevant on the issue of justice, but not in terms of negligence actions.

It should be noted that in *Camm* the agreement had been incorporated into an order made on the decree nisi (see Ormrod LJ, at 582). The effect of the order was that no order for periodical payments was made for the wife and hence it was necessary to return to the agreement. There was neither a clean break order dismissing the wife's claim for periodical payments nor an order for nominal periodical payments.

In further contrast to the decision in *Camm* is the decision of the Court of Appeal in *Cook* v *Cook* [1984] FLR 446. Here, it was held that a separation deed, entered into by a wife against the advice of her solicitors and made subject to the approval of the court and which included a provision that all her claims for financial provision should be dismissed, was a sufficient consent by the wife to the dismissal of her claims. As to the fact that the consent was given at the date of the agreement rather than at the date of the hearing, it was held in *Cook* that where an agreement is subject to the approval of the court it was binding upon the parties until it was brought to the court for approval (applying *Smallman* v *Smallman* [1971] 3 All ER 717). However, in *Sutton* v *Sutton* [1984] 1 All ER 168 it was held that an oral agreement made without legal advice being taken by either party, which had not been made subject to the court's approval, would not be enforced as it purported to oust the court's jurisdiction and was accordingly contrary to public policy. An illuminating discussion of this decision by Dr Ines Weyland is to be found at [1985] Fam Law 114–115. Whilst the court now has the power under the Matrimonial Causes Act 1973, s 25A (added by the Matrimonial and Family Proceedings Act 1984, s 3) to impose a clean break without the consent of a wife to the dismissal of her claims, the decision in *Cook* is still of relevance in that a court may well be more inclined to order a clean break where evidence of consent exists.

(ii) Undue pressure and exploitation of a dominant position
It was held in *Backhouse* v *Backhouse* [1978] 1 All ER 1158 that a wife's application for a lump sum order and a transfer of property order in relation to the matrimonial home should be approached on the basis that a previous transfer by the wife of her interest to the husband had not been made. Although the husband did not use duress in the sense of threats to secure the wife's signature to the transfer, the wife felt a sense of guilt at the breakdown of the marriage and was not advised by the husband to take independent legal advice. She received no consideration for the transfer except a release from her liability under the mortgage. Balcombe J made these *obiter* comments (at 1166):

> When a marriage has broken down, both parties are liable to be in an emotional state. The party remaining in the matrimonial home, as the husband did in this case, has an advantage. The wife is no doubt in circumstances of great emotional strain. It seems to me that she should at least be encouraged to take independent advice so that she may know whether or not it is right for her, whatever the circumstances of the breakdown of the marriage may be, to transfer away what is her only substantial capital asset. It is possible that this is something which may come under the general heading which Lord Denning MR referred to in *Lloyds Bank Ltd* v *Bundy* ([1974] 3 All ER 757, at 763) as 'inequality of bargaining power' where he summarised the various categories in which transactions can be set aside: duress, unconscionable transactions and so on, and suggested that through all these instances runs a single thread, that they rest on inequality of bargaining power. If that be right then it seems to me that this transaction is an example of something which is done where the parties did not have equal bargaining power and should not be at any rate encouraged by the courts. I consider too that counsel for the wife had a valid point when she said that by analogy with s 34 of the Matrimonial Causes Act 1973, which precludes parties from contracting out of their right to apply to the court for an order containing financial arrangements, the court should not look with favour on

assignments of proprietary interests in the matrimonial home made without the benefit of legal advice.

The comments of Lord Denning MR in *Lloyds Bank Ltd* v *Bundy* were disapproved by the House of Lords in *National Westminster Bank plc* v *Morgan* [1985] AC 686 (see p 143). In *Evans* v *Evans* (1981) 2 FLR 33 no weight was attached to an agreement entered into by a wife without the benefit of legal advice at the office of her husband's solicitors giving up her rights to financial provision at a time when she was subject to emotional stress.

A decision which in many senses is similar to that of *Camm* is that of Thorpe J in *K* v *K* (Financial Provision) [1992] 2 FCR 265. Whilst the wife in *Camm* was under extreme pressure, the decision was also concerned with bad legal advice. In *K* v *K*, the wife entered an agreement against her solicitor's advice. Whilst the wife had not been directly pressurised to enter into the agreement, she was pressurised to do so by the surrounding circumstances. The agreement resulted in her accepting less than had been originally offered without any change in circumstances. Thorpe J concluded that the wife was not to be held to the terms of the agreement and proceeded to carry out the exercise required by the Matrimonial Causes Act 1973, s 25 on her application for ancillary relief. It is perhaps to be noted that the agreement in question had been incorporated into a draft consent order, which the wife had signed. However, the husband's solicitors had negligently failed to proceed with the consent application over a period of eighteen months. It was during this period that the wife discovered that the consequences of the agreement were far from satisfactory for her and in consequence issued an application for ancillary relief.

(iii) An important change in circumstances and inadequate knowledge

It is significant to note that the Court of Appeal held in *Brown* v *Brown* (1978) 9 Fam Law 216 that an agreement concluded on competent legal advice in 1972 would be upheld notwithstanding the fact that different legal advice would have been given following the decision in *Wachtel* v *Wachtel* [1973] 1 All ER 829. Where there is a change of circumstances, a maintenance agreement within the meaning of the Matrimonial Causes Act 1973, s 34(2) (see p 28) can only be varied by the court under s 35 of the 1973 Act. It cannot be discharged under the court's jurisdiction in ancillary relief without regard to s 35 of the 1973 Act. However, the provisions of such an agreement may be revoked under s 35(2)(*b*)(*i*) of the 1973 Act and fresh orders made under ss 23 and 24 of the 1973 Act, enabling all future variations of maintenance to be dealt with under s 31 of the 1973 Act (*Simister* v *Simister* (No 2) [1987] 1 FLR 194). The purpose of the Matrimonial Causes Act 1973, ss 35–36 is not to encourage applications to vary an agreement; there should be some degree of permanence about any order made under that jurisdiction (*Orton* v *Orton* (1959) 109 Sol Jo 50).

In *Cross* v *Cross* (1983) FLR 235, the wife entered into an agreement with the husband whereby he agreed to transfer his half-share in the matrimonial home to her. The wife did not, however, disclose that at the time of the agreement she had moved out of the property to live with her new husband. The husband subsequently learned of the wife's departure and rescinded the agreement. His solicitors made a new offer that the property should be sold and the proceeds be divided two-thirds to the wife and one-third to the husband. The wife refused the offer and applied for specific performance of the agreement or alternatively a transfer of property order. Wood J held that in considering the wife's application under the 1973 Act the existence of the original agreement was a material circumstance to be taken into account and given due weight (*Brockwell* v *Brockwell* (1975) 6 Fam Law 46; *Ladbrooke* v *Ladbrooke* (1977) 7 Fam Law 213). In deciding whether to grant a decree of specific performance, it was held that this was a discretionary remedy and the court should refuse an order upon the grounds of mistake or where it would be highly unreasonable or cause an injustice. The court applied the equitable maxim that 'he who comes to equity must come with a clean hand' in relation to the conduct of the wife in failing to disclose her change of circumstances and future plans before and after the agreement. The court refused a decree of specific performance and ordered the sale of the matrimonial home with a lump sum payable to the husband.

In *Beach* v *Beach* [1995] 2 FLR 160, a decision of Thorpe J, a husband applied in the financial relief proceedings consequent upon the divorce for a lump sum payment. At the time of the application, he was living with his parents and was in receipt of income support. During the marriage, the wife had invested substantial sums in the husband's farming business. Following a series of financial mishaps, classified by the judge as conduct which it would be inequitable to disregard, the parties reached an agreement in February 1990 (some four and a half years before the final hearing) under which the wife should receive £450,000 net from the proceeds of sale of the farming business in full and final settlement of any claims by either party under the Matrimonial Causes Act 1973. However, the husband failed to sell the farm, he was declared bankrupt in December 1990 and, in

March 1992, the farm was sold by the trustee in bankruptcy for such a sum as realised for the wife capital and real property together worth £405,000. It had been envisaged under the February 1990 agreement, drawing upon a valuation of the business at that time, that the husband would himself receive a substantial capital payment. In the event, he received nothing.

Before Thorpe J (as he then was), the husband applied for a lump sum which he would use, *inter alia*, to finance a new business. The wife contended, on the other hand, that the husband should be constrained by the agreement and the *Edgar* principles.

The judge decided that the case did not fall properly within the *Edgar* classification, stating at 168A-C and F:

> The classic *Edgar* case contains a litigant who seeks to depart unreasonably or capriciously from a fairly negotiated formal settlement . . . Here I contemplate circumstances which are totally different from the circumstances contemplated by the contracting parties . . . My conclusion, therefore, is that although the agreement of 20 February 1990 is of importance, it is only of importance as part of the developing history. My essential duty is to determine this application upon the criteria contained in s 25, as amended.

The judge concluded that the disparity between the present position of the husband and wife was so great that in all the circumstances the wife should pay a lump sum to the husband of £60,000.

(iv) Other applications of the Edgar principle

In *H* v *H* (Financial Relief: Non-Disclosure: Costs) [1994] 2 FLR 94, the parties entered into a separation agreement which provided, *inter alia*, that the former matrimonial home should be sold. The wife was to receive not less than one-half of the gross proceeds of sale, but the husband was given the right to purchase the wife's interest. The husband exercised this right and the wife transferred her interest in the property in consideration of the husband purchasing a separate property for her. The purchase was funded by a mortgage taken out in the wife's name guaranteed by the husband, who was to pay the instalments. The value of the property purchased for the wife was less than one-half of the gross value of the former matrimonial home. In subsequent divorce proceedings, both parties made cross-applications for ancillary relief and the husband informed the wife that he would not make any further payments in respect of the mortgage. The husband was found by the district judge to have failed to disclose his true financial position and to have been spending money recklessly. He was ordered to be responsible for five-ninths of the mortgage repayments relating to the wife's property. On appeal, Thorpe J found that the district judge had given too little weight on the *Edgar* principle to the pre-existing contractual agreement and too much attention to the asserted impecuniosity of the husband at the date of the hearing. The only basis suggested for departing from the contractual obligation was that the husband had not received independent legal advice. He had, however, been employed for many years in solicitors' offices.

Smith v *McInerney* [1994] 2 FLR 1077, which is also a decision of Thorpe J, provides an interesting example of the interaction of the Child Support Act 1991 with the *Edgar* principle. The decision is discussed fully on p 127.

A further recent application of the *Edgar* principle is *Benson* v *Benson (Deceased)* [1996] 1 FLR 692 (which contained an application for leave to appeal out of time against a consent order and which is therefore examined in detail on pp 163 below). Bracewell J held that an agreement by the relevant parties as to the non-enforcement of the order was binding upon them; each party had been fully and appropriately advised on the terms of the agreement; and there was adequate consideration (in this instance forbearance by one of the parties to enforce a term in the order).

(d) Other approaches to agreements

Where a party is in breach of an obligation under a separation agreement, it may be possible to apply under the Matrimonial Causes Act 1973, s 10(2) for the decree absolute of divorce to be delayed pending payment of what is due under the agreement (*Garcia* v *Garcia* [1992] 1 FLR 256, CA). This particular form of protection is only available to a respondent after the granting of a decree nisi of divorce based upon two years' separation with consent or five years' separation. In *Garcia*, the parties had entered into an agreement which had been ratified by a Spanish court, under which the husband had agreed to pay to the wife *inter alia* a monthly sum for the maintenance of their son. The husband stopped the maintenance payments in breach of the agreement. He then came to live in England where he issued a divorce petition based upon five years' separation. The wife made an application under the Matrimonial Causes Act 1973, s 10(2) to delay the decree absolute on the ground that the husband had failed to keep up the maintenance payments. It was the duty of the court under the Matrimonial Causes Act 1973, s 10(3) in considering the wife's application to have regard to 'all the circumstances including the age, health, conduct, earning capacity, financial resources and financial obligations of each of the parties'. The Court of Appeal held that this provision was not intended to be restricted to financial needs or obligations arising *after* divorce, but could also refer as here to *past* obligations which had not been fulfilled.

(e) Conclusion

Nothing in the Matrimonial Causes Act 1973 enables the parties to contract out of the provisions of ss 23 or 24 of the Act or to preclude the court from performing the duties imposed upon it under s 25. Where there is an agreement entered into with full knowledge and with the advantage of legal advice, it is something to which considerable attention should be paid by the court in considering whether to exercise its discretion to award a lump sum. An agreement may, however, preclude a claim under the Married Women's Act 1882, s 17 (*Brockwell* v *Brockwell* (1975) 6 Fam Law 46).

The court retains jurisdiction over the award of ancillary relief and a discretion as to whether to make an order under the Matrimonial Causes Act 1973, ss 23 or 24 in the terms of the agreement. Where an agreement has been arrived at by parties who are both legally represented and who have conducted their negotiations at arm's length, the agreement itself will provide *prima facie* evidence of the reasonableness of its provisions (*Dean* v *Dean* [1978] 3 All ER 758). In *Dean*, it was held that the agreement made reasonable provision for the wife and the agreement was incorporated as an order of the court. Bush J held (at 767):

> The court must, in performing its duty under s 25 in circumstances where there is an agreement between the parties, adopt the broad rather than the particular approach. On the one hand, the court has a duty under s 25, but at the same time the court owes a duty to uphold agreements validly arrived at and which are not on the face of them, or in fact, against public policy. In general terms also, it is wrong for the court to stir up problems with parties who have come to an agreement.

In *Kern* v *Kern* (1988), Thorpe J adopted a two-stage approach. First, it was necessary to ascertain whether there was a binding agreement between the parties disposing of the wife's outstanding claims for ancillary relief. In *Kern*, leading counsel with authority to contract had announced in the face of the court that a contractual bargain had been completed between the litigants; that, as a matter of law, is conclusive of the contractual state. Secondly, if there is a binding agreement, the court should then proceed to consider whether it should make an order that gives effect to the agreement. On the facts before him, Thorpe J held that, if the respondent was not prepared to consent to an order in the terms of the agreement, he would immediately impose such an order on the basis that that was what had seemed fair to the parties.

An undertaking by a wife in an agreement not to apply for a variation of her periodical payments order is void under the Matrimonial Causes Act 1973, s 34(1) (*Jessel* v *Jessel* [1979] 3 All ER 645). However, a side letter containing an agreement that a wife does not intend to apply for an extension of a term maintenance order except in unforeseen circumstances was highly relevant and could not be disregarded. Although the side letter was strictly void, the agreement should be upheld on the *Edgar* principle. This approach was in line with the effect of the amendments made by the Matrimonial and Family Proceedings Act 1984 to encourage clean breaks between spouses (*N* v *N* (Consent Order: Variation) [1993] 2 FLR 868, *sub nom Niebor* v *Niebor* (1993) *The Independent*, 23 August, CA; cf *Richardson* v *Richardson* [1993] 4 All ER 673 (see p 90).

Chapter 3

Consent orders

1 Agreements subject to the approval of the court

Matrimonial Causes Act 1973, s 7 provides:

> Provision may be made by rules of court for enabling the parties to a marriage, or either of them, on application made either before or after the presentation of a petition for divorce, to refer to the court any agreement or arrangement made or proposed to be made between them, being an agreement or arrangement which relates to, arises out of, or is connected with, the proceedings for divorce which are contemplated or, as the case may be, have begun, and for enabling the court to express an opinion, should it think it desirable to do so, as to the reasonableness of the agreement or arrangement and to give such directions, if any, in the matter as it thinks fit.

No rules have in fact been made pursuant to the Matrimonial Causes Act 1973, s 7 and the description given to the section in *Brockwell* v *Brockwell* (1975) 6 Fam Law 46 as being 'an almost vestigial provision, not unlike the human appendix' is entirely appropriate. Its origins lay in the Matrimonial Causes Act 1963, s 4(3) which reduced collusion from an absolute to a discretionary bar to divorce. The parties were permitted to make bargains relating to the conduct of divorce proceedings, provided that they were disclosed to the court and approved of by the court as being reasonable. This provision was carried through into the Matrimonial Causes Act 1965. However, when collusion as a bar to divorce was abolished by the Divorce Reform Act 1969, there was no longer any necessity to approve agreements in order to avoid the risk that the court would decide that an agreement was collusive. Nonetheless, Parliament carried through something approaching s 4(3) of the 1963 Act into what is now s 7 of the 1973 Act. The section was, however, altered so that the court was no longer even obliged to make any comment at all on an agreement if it did not wish to do so. Provision by rules of court was made by the

Matrimonial Causes Rules 1971, r 6. These rules were repealed by the Matrimonial Causes Rules 1973 on 11 January 1974; even while they were extant the procedure of referring an agreement to a judge under these rules was disapproved, not least because of the costs involved (para 3 of *Practice Direction 26 September 1972* (Decrees and Orders: Agreed Terms) [1972] 1 WLR 1313). There is therefore no current provision by rules to enable an application to be made under s 7. Enigmatically, the Matrimonial and Family Proceedings Act 1984, s 35 directs that any provision to be made by rules of court for the purposes of s 7 of the 1973 Act with respect to any power exercisable by the court on an application made before the presentation of a petition must confer jurisdiction to exercise the power on divorce county courts. Perhaps s 7 is not therefore quite such a 'vestigial appendix' at least in the mind of the Parliamentary draftsman as recently as 1984.

In *Brockwell* (at 47), Ormrod LJ observed that the only function of s 7 was that:

> ... it did provide a means by which parties could take an agreement or a proposed arrangement to the Court at an early stage for approval, and thus insure against a subsequent application, under sections 23 or 24, after the granting of a divorce, in order to avoid or modify the agreement that they had reached. Clearly, if the Court before the hearing of the petition came to the conclusion that the agreement proposed was a reasonable one, it would be impossible to contend under sections 23 or 24 that it should be varied, unless in the meanwhile an entirely new situation had arisen.

It should be noted that s 33(A) of the 1973 Act, which provides that 'notwithstanding anything in the previous provisions of this part of this Act, the Court may ... make an order in the terms agreed' does *not* validate the s 7 procedure. It was argued by Counsel in *Pounds* v *Pounds* [1994] 1 FLR 780 that this section modified the provisos that orders for lump sum and property adjustment cannot be effective until decree absolute, but this proposition was rejected by the Court of Appeal.

The more common practice is for the agreement reached between the parties to be made a rule of court or be incorporated into a consent order, as discussed below. Section 7 can therefore largely be regarded as being obsolete, although it is conceivable that it may stage a come-back. It is provided in the Family Law Act 1996 that the court will have power to make orders relating to children, financial provision and property adjustment orders at any time during the period of reflection and consideration following the filing of the 'Statement of Marital Breakdown' and before a divorce order.

The effect of agreements made subject to the approval of the court was usefully summarised by Lord Denning MR in *Smallman* v *Smallman* [1971] 3 All ER 717, at 720:

> In my opinion, if the parties have reached an agreement on all essential matters, then the clause 'subject to the approval of the court' does not mean there is no agreement at all. There is an agreement, but the operation of it is suspended until the court approves it. It is the duty of one party or the other to bring the agreement before the court for approval. If the court approves, it is binding on the parties. If the court does not approve, it is not binding. But, pending the application to the court, it remains a binding agreement which neither party can disavow.

It should be noted that this was a case where the opinion of the court had been sought as to the reasonableness of an agreement made 'subject to the approval of the court' under what was then the Divorce Reform Act 1969, s 7 (now the Matrimonial Causes Act 1973, s 7) but the principle could equally apply to any agreement between the parties, including minutes of consent order filed at the same time as the application for special procedure divorce. The moral of this is that the practitioner must ensure that he specifies (if this is what is intended) that the agreement is subject to the court's approval. *Smallman* was applied in *Amey* v *Amey* [1992] 2 FLR 89, where it was agreed following the divorce of the parties that the wife was to receive £120,000 from the husband by way of clean break settlement. The lump sum was paid and the minutes of order were drafted by the wife's counsel, but she died before the minutes were approved by the husband's solicitors and the court. It was held by Scott Baker J that this stood as an agreement at common law, which did not depend at all, for its validity, on being made into a consent order.

The case of *Cook* v *Cook* [1984] FLR 446, referred to above on p 33, is a more recent example of an agreement made subject to the approval of the court, where on the facts the Court of Appeal found that there was no ground for refusing to approve the agreement.

2 Agreements made rules of court

Whilst an agreement may be reached at an early stage in the proceedings, the court does not have power to make a consent order until the granting of the decree nisi to take effect on decree absolute, except for interim relief such as maintenance pending suit for a spouse, a financial provision order benefiting a child of the family, orders for the sale of land pursuant to RSC Order 31, r 1 (following the decision in *Green* v *Green* [1993] 1 FLR 326) or orders permitting the release or appropriation of monies following the principles established in *Barry* v *Barry* [1992] 2 FLR 233 and *F* v *F* (Ancillary Relief: Substantial Assets) [1995] 2 FLR 45. This is because of the effect of the Matrimonial Causes Act 1973, ss 23(5) and 24(3). If a financial provision order in favour of a party or a property adjustment order is made before decree nisi, the order is without jurisdiction and can be set aside. Jurisdiction cannot be conferred by consent or estoppel. In *Munks* v *Munks* [1985] FLR 576 and *Board* v *Checkland* [1987] 2 FLR 257 it was held that jurisdiction cannot be saved by the 'slip rule' or the inherent jurisdiction. The slip rule was, however, effectively used by the Court of Appeal in *Pounds* v *Pounds* [1994] 1 FLR 780 to correct the dating of a consent order; the court staff had erroneously dated the order with the date of the appointment before the district judge who approved its terms before decree nisi when granting a special procedure certificate rather than the date (post decree nisi) when the order was actually sealed and made. In the words of Waite LJ:

> Such orders should be drawn up and dated with the utmost care ... A putting together of heads by chief clerks and district judges ought to make it possible, for those who have not done so already, to devise for their court files and computers a suitable warning system to prevent any financial consent order being inadvertently allocated a date antecedent to the decree nisi.

It is important to check the dates supplied on sealed court orders as soon as you receive them back from court.

For a further discussion of the problems surrounding agreements made at an early stage, the reader is referred to (1988) 85 *Law Society's Gazette*, 21 September, 34.

Section 23(5) provides:

> Without prejudice to the power to give a direction under s 30 below for the settlement of an instrument by conveyancing counsel, where an order is made under subs (1)(*a*), (*b*) or (*c*) above on or after granting a decree of divorce or nullity of marriage, neither the order nor any settlement made in pursuance of the order shall take effect unless the decree has been made absolute.

Section 23(5) deals with orders for periodical payments and lump sum payments, secured or unsecured. Section 24(3) makes similar provision for property adjustment orders.

Where ss 23(5) or 24(3) preclude a consent order being made immediately, it will therefore be convenient for the agreement reached to be made a rule of court. This is a grossly under-used procedure.

The agreement must contain a specific provision that it is to be filed and made a rule of court (*Practice Direction 26 September 1972* [1972] 3 All ER 704, para 2—it is an indication of the paucity of rules of court that this paragraph of the *Practice Direction* has actually been deleted from the *Compendium of Practice Directions* circulated among the judges at the courts (see, for example, the amended text of the *Practice Direction* in *The Family Court Practice* (Jordans, 1996)) albeit that the provision has not been formally cancelled and so still applies. If some of the terms of the agreement fall outside the powers of the court conferred by the Matrimonial Causes Act 1973, ss 23 and 24, such terms should be expressed as undertakings (see p 71 as to the comments of Lord Brandon in *Livesey* v *Jenkins* [1985] 1 All ER 106, at 118–119 on the general use of undertakings). The terms of the agreement to be made a rule of court may, where appropriate, include a provision that the terms be made an order of the court at the appropriate time (*Graves* v *Graves* (1893) 69 LT 420). The precedent for such an application is to be found at Appendix 7. It is therefore possible to obtain an order whereby specified provision is made a rule of court, and whereby (for instance) the parties' claims under the Matrimonial Causes Act 1973 are to be dismissed upon implementation of the clauses in the rule of court.

The desirability of the use of this practice was emphasised by Ormrod J (as he then was) in *Hall* v *Hall* (1972) *The Times*, 30 June, where he commented that:

> . . . in divorce suits where terms of compromise were reached or an involved order—not a simple order—would be made, there was a good deal to be said for using the old probate practice, which would simplify any subsequent proceedings. The parties should agree that the terms be made rules of court and both parties should sign them. The practice should be followed as a routine measure. Though the problem of enforcing settlements could be acute, fortunately it did not often arise.

The procedural requirements relating to the filing of a rule of court are governed by a paragraph of the *Practice Direction 26 September 1972* [1972] 3 All ER 704 which (as explained above) has been deleted. It is submitted that the correct procedure is to file the document signed by the parties and their solicitors at the Principal Registry or court at which the petition or other originating process has been filed. However, the subsequent phasing in of the special procedure has restricted adherence to the terms of the *Practice Direction* to suits which are to be heard in open court eg a suit for nullity, a suit to be heard in the ordinary undefended list or any defended suit as well as to cases where an agreement is reached after the district judge's certificate has been granted but before decree nisi. Where the special procedure does apply, there does not appear to be any formal procedure laid down. However, it is submitted that the correct course is for the petitioner in the affidavit in support of his or her petition to ask for the agreed terms to be made a rule of court, lodging the agreed terms signed by or on behalf of both parties with the request for directions. Alternatively, if the application to make the terms of agreement a rule of court is made before special procedure directions are sought, the agreed terms should be lodged *ex parte* signed by or on behalf of both parties. (It is submitted by Duckworth on p 320 of volume I of *Matrimonial Property and Finance*, 5th ed (FT Law & Tax) that the rule of court should not ante-date decree nisi, but there is no authority for this proposition, which should be treated with caution as one of the main functions of making an agreement a rule of court is that this may be done before decree nisi.) The Family Proceedings Rules 1991, r 2.61 (formerly MCR 1977, r 76A; see section 4(*c*) below) does not apply to an application to make an agreement a rule of court, but this does not obviate the need for full and frank disclosure on normal principles.

The effect of making an agreement a rule of court can be demonstrated by reference to *MH* v *MH* [1982] 3 FLR 429 and *Aspden (Inspector of Taxes)* v *Hildesley* [1982] 2 All ER 53. In *MH*, a deed of separation was made a rule of court on the granting of the decree nisi on 24 April 1974, which was made absolute on 27 June 1974. On 17 July 1974, a registrar made a consent order for periodical payments and secured provision for the wife and for maintenance of the children to give effect to some of the clauses in the deed of separation. Certain other matters contained in the deed of separation could not, however, be the subject of a court order eg payment of the children's educational expenses, payment of life insurance premiums for the benefit of the wife and children, payment of the outgoings and maintenance on the wife's home and provision of a domestic servant. Wood J held that, when the deed of separation was made a rule of court, it became a final court order for the purposes of enforcement and thus ceased to be a subsisting maintenance agreement capable of variation under the Matrimonial Causes Act 1973, s 35 (applying *De Lasala* v *De Lasala* [1979] 2 All ER 1146). So far as the consent order of 17 July 1974 was concerned, this was an order capable of variation under the Matrimonial Causes Act 1973, s 31, as its legal effect was derived from the court order and not from the preceding agreement (applying *Thwaite* v *Thwaite* [1981] 2 All ER 789; see p 47 and pp 130–131). The advantage of having an agreement made into a rule of court is therefore related to the ease of enforcement of the obligation. A rule of court can be enforced as a court order, rather than having to initiate a fresh action. Doubtless because the rule of court is a protective weapon used before orders become operative on decree absolute there is no case law which illustrates whether obligations contained in rules of court are variable, and, if they are, what the appropriate procedure for variation would be. It is submitted that if variation was required, the appropriate relief under the Matrimonial Courts Act 1973 should be sought (see p 184).

Aspen v *Hildesley* [1982] 2 All ER 53 was a decision of Nourse J in the Chancery Division in a tax case. Terms of compromise in the form of cross-undertakings followed by a consent order were filed and made a rule of court on the making of the decree nisi granted to the taxpayer. Paragraph 1 ordered the taxpayer to transfer forthwith his interest in the former matrimonial home to his wife. Paragraph 2 ordered the taxpayer to make periodical payments to the wife from decree absolute. Paragraph 3 ordered that the foregoing financial provision was in satisfaction of all the wife's claims for ancillary relief and against the taxpayer's estate. The question was whether a disposal for capital gains tax purposes had taken place on the making of the order on the decree nisi.

Nourse J held (at 58):

> Counsel for the Crown referred me to the recent case in the Court of Appeal of *Thwaite* v *Thwaite* [1981] 2 All ER 789, [1981] 3 WLR 96, in which it was held that where parties to matrimonial proceedings agreed terms, and by consent those terms were embodied in an order of the court, the legal effect of their agreement derived from the court's order and not from contract. However, it is clear that the consent order there in question had been made after decree absolute, and in the light of ss 23(5) and 24(3) of the Matrimonial Causes Act 1973 I do not think that either that case or *De Lasala* v *De Lasala* [1979] 2 All ER 1146, [1980] AC 546, a decision of the Privy Council on which the Court of Appeal based itself, is to be taken as a decision on the effect of a consent order made before decree absolute. In such a case the matter would appear to rest on contract in accordance with the normal rule which was recognised by the Court of Appeal in *Thwaite* v *Thwaite*. Moreover, in this case the order was not a full consent order but an order that the agreed terms 'be filed and made a Rule of Court'. That is a very familiar formula in the Family Division. It seems from the decision of the Court of Appeal in *Re Shaw, Smith* v *Shaw* [1918] P 47, and in particular from the judgment of Warrington LJ (at 53–54), that the effect of an order in that form is that the obligation remains contractual.

The 'normal rule' referred to by Nourse J was described by Ormrod LJ in *Thwaite* at 794 as 'the general principle frequently stated in cases arising in other divisions of the High Court, that the force and effect of consent orders derives from the contract between the parties leading to, or evidenced by, or incorporated in, the consent order (see, for example, *Huddersfield Banking Co Ltd* v *Henry Lister & Son Ltd* [1895] 2 Ch 273, [1895–9] All ER Rep 868, and *Purcell* v *F C Trigell Ltd* [1970] 3 All ER 671, at 676–677, [1971] 1 QB 358, at 366–367 per Buckley LJ)'.

In *Tommey* v *Tommey* [1982] 3 All ER 385, Balcombe J distinguished the order before him for consideration and that in *Aspden* v *Hildesley* on the grounds that the order before him was an order dismissing all further financial claims and not a positive order under ss 23 or 24 and that it was a consent order as opposed to being terms which had been filed and made a rule of court.

Balcombe J in *Tommey* (at 391) explained the decision in *Aspden* v *Hildesley* in this way:

> If [Nourse J] was intending to say no more than this, that as at [the date of the order] (12 February 1976) and pending decree absolute the order was contractual in effect, I would respectfully agree with him. But, if he is intending to say that after the decree had been made absolute the order still remains contractual, then I would, respectfully, disagree, because it seems to me that a decision in those terms would be inconsistent with the decision of the Court of Appeal in *Thwaite* v *Thwaite* [1981] 2 All ER 789, which is binding on both of us.

3 *Tomlin* orders

A *Tomlin* order is a procedural device similar in purpose to making an agreement a rule of court. Such an order directs that all further proceedings on an application for ancillary relief be stayed on terms set out in the schedule to the order with liberty to the parties to apply for the purpose of carrying the terms into effect. Where necessary, the terms will be enforced by an order for specific performance.

As with a rule of court, the *Tomlin* order can incorporate terms which the court does not have jurisdiction to order, and a *Tomlin* order can similarly be made at any stage after the filing of the petition or other initiating process. In *Iskim* v *Aktar* (1994) *The Times*, 20 October, CA it was held that the court has an inherent power to rectify a *Tomlin* order where the order mistakenly does not reflect the agreement correctly.

4 Consent orders

(a) The background

Some of the historical background to consent orders has already been discussed in Chapter 1. The process of evolution of the matrimonial consent order, in a form eventually given statutory recognition in the Matrimonial and Family Proceedings Act 1984, began to gather momentum following the decision of the Court of Appeal in *Jenkins* v *Livesey* [1984] FLR 452, the facts of which are set out on p 64. The Court of Appeal, where the judgment was delivered by Arnold P, was critical of the practice of registrars in making consent orders (at 455–456):

> We have referred above to it being unrealistic to regard the question whether the wife would remarry as having been before the registrar by reason of his duty to consider whether to give or withhold his sanction and approval of the agreement. The reason why we made this observation was that it emerged in the course of the argument that in the case of this particular agreement, the registrar had embodied it in the consent order and thereby given his sanction and approval to it with no representation whatsoever before him and no knowledge whatsoever of the facts beyond what appeared in the application dated 19 August 1982, which simply set out the terms intended to be embodied in the consent order and included nothing else whatsoever. The result was that the registrar knew nothing whatsoever about the circumstances of the parties or their respective fortunes or anything else concerning them except the minimal amount of information which could be inferred from the contents of the application.
>
> We were further informed that this was a common state of affairs, and that in exercising their functions to give or withhold sanction and approval in such circumstances, registrars were accustomed to rely simply on the circumstances that the joint application was made by firms of solicitors with whom they were well acquainted and where this was so give their sanction and approval simply because of the conviction that such firms of solicitors would not put forward agreed terms unless they were fit to be approved by the court. We do not of course know how far this practice extends, but we are bound to say that we regard it as a very slender basis for the discharge of the jurisdiction established by *L* v *L* [1961] 3 All ER 834, and that in any ordinary circumstances we should regard an attendance before the registrar as necessary to enable answers to be given to any queries that he might have in the course of the exercise of the jurisdiction.

As a direct result of this decision, a *Practice Direction 13 April 1984* [1984] 2 All ER 256 was issued by the Senior Registrar of the Family Division:

> The decision of the Court of Appeal in *Jenkins* v *Livesey* (formerly Jenkins) (1983) *The Times*, 22 December is a reminder that in all cases where application is made for financial provision or property adjustment order the court is required to have before it an agreed statement of the general nature of the means of each party signed by the parties or their

solicitors. If affidavits of means have been filed it will be sufficient if the statement is in the form of a certificate that there has been no change of substance since the date of the affidavit or, if there has, what changes there have been. If no such evidence has been filed the statement should include a summary of the amount or value of the capital and income resources of each of the spouses (and, if relevant, of any minor child) and any special features which require to be considered under s 25 of the Matrimonial Causes Act 1973.

Where a spouse's claim for periodical payments is being dismissed the registrar will need to be satisfied that it is appropriate that the parties should be financially independent and that the claimant consents to dismissal. In all cases where a wife is acting in person and her claim for periodical payments is being dismissed, the wife's attendance before the registrar is required save in exceptional circumstances.

This direction should be read in conjunction with the *Registrar's Direction* of 10 April 1974 ([1974] 2 All ER 1120, [1974] 1 WLR 937).

The direction caused some consternation within the profession. It was seen as something of a slur on the profession's ability to deal adequately with freely negotiated matrimonial settlements. Some took exception to the additional work and the attendant increase in costs to the client or the legal aid fund created by the preparation of statements of means and appearances before (at that time) a registrar, which were not previously required. The direction has not been formally cancelled, but the first paragraph is clearly superseded by the Matrimonial Causes Rules 1977, r 76A (now the Family Proceedings Rules 1991, r 2.61). It is arguable that the second paragraph of the direction does still survive. This part of the direction is more restrictive in requiring attendances before a (at that time) registrar than the comments of the Court of Appeal in *Jenkins* v *Livesey*, thus reflecting some acceptance of the reality of the additional workload which would otherwise have been imposed on registrars. It is, however, submitted that the second paragraph of the direction has been superseded by s 33A(1) of the 1973 Act, which allows a consent order to be made on the basis only of the prescribed information, notwithstanding the fact that a party may be acting in person and/or a clean break order be involved. Such circumstances may, of course, merit the court exercising its supervisory jurisdiction by making further inquiries, as discussed on pp 61–63. This submission is supported by the fact that the *Practice Direction 13 April 1984* [1984] 2 All ER 256 is not even included in the *Compendium of Practice Directions* annually updated and distributed to the courts and is, although not yet formally cancelled, procedurally a dead letter.

(b) Matrimonial Causes Act 1973, s 33A

The Matrimonial and Family Proceedings Act 1984, s 7 became law on 12 October 1984 and gave statutory recognition to the concept of a matrimonial consent order by adding s 33A to the Matrimonial Causes Act 1973. Section 33A provides:

> 33A—(1) Notwithstanding anything in the preceding provisions of this Part of the Act, on an application for a consent order for financial relief the court may, unless it has reason to think that there are other circumstances into which it ought to inquire, make an order in the terms agreed on the basis only of the prescribed information furnished with the application.
>
> (2) Subsection (1) above applies to an application for a consent order varying or discharging an order for financial relief as it applies to an application for an order for financial relief.
>
> (3) In this section—
> 'consent order', in relation to an application for an order, means an order in the terms applied for to which the respondent agrees;
> 'order for financial relief' means an order under any of ss 23, 24, 24A or 27 above; and
> 'prescribed' means prescribed by rules of court.

(c) Family Proceedings Rules 1991, r 2.61 (formerly MCR 1977, r 76A)

The information prescribed by rules of court referred to in s 33A was provided by MCR 1977, r 76A, which was hurriedly added by the Matrimonial Causes (Amendment) Rules 1984 (SI 1984 No 1511) in time for 12 October 1984. Rule 76A in its original form was not without its problems. The old rule provided:

> 76A *Information on application for consent order for financial relief*
>
> (1) Subject to para (2), there shall be lodged with every application for a consent order for financial relief or for a consent order varying or discharging an order for financial relief, a statement of information relied on in support of the application which shall include:
> (*a*) the date of the marriage and the respective ages of the parties and of any minor child of the family;
> (*b*) an estimate in summary form of the approximate amount or value of the capital and income resources of each of the parties and, where relevant, of any minor child of the family;
> (*c*) what is intended with regard to the occupation or disposal of the matrimonial home;
> (*d*) what arrangements are intended for the accommodation of each of the parties and, where relevant, or any minor child of the family; and
> (*e*) any especially significant circumstances from amongst those

matters listed in s 25(2) and (3) of the Act of 1973, and in particular the value of any benefit (for example, a pension or a death benefit) which by reason of dissolution or annulment of the marriage either party will lose the chance of acquiring upon the death of the other.

(2) Where an application is made for a consent order for maintenance pending suit or for an interim order pending the final determination of an applicatin for ancillary relief, or for a consent order varying an order for periodical payments, para (1) shall be sufficiently complied with if the statement of information required to be lodged with the application includes the information mentioned in para (1)(*a*) and (*b*) but omits information about capital resources.

(3) Where a relevant affidavit has been filed for use on an application under rr 73, 74 or 75 paras (*b*) and (*c*) of para (1) shall be sufficiently complied with if a reference is made to the relevant affidavit and it is stated that there has been no material change in the matters mentioned in the affidavit or, if there has been such a change, what has changed is stated.

(4) The statement lodged under para (1) may be made in more than one document provided that each document in respect of each party shall be signed:
   (*a*) where a solicitor is acting for that party by that solicitor; and
   (*b*) where no solicitor is acting for that party by that party.

(5) Where the statement is signed by a solicitor in accordance with para (4) the solicitor shall certify that his client has been advised whether it would be in the interest of the client to agree to the proposed order.

The difficulties surrounding the old r 76A led to it being amended with comparative speed. The Matrimonial Causes (Amendment No 2) Rules 1985 (SI 1985 No 1315), r 9 substituted a revised r 76A, which came into operation on 16 September 1985. The Matrimonial Causes Rules 1977 have now been replaced with effect from 14 October 1991 by the Family Proceedings Rules 1991 and the revised rule is reproduced in almost identical terms in r 2.61 of the 1991 Rules (see Appendix 11).

The 1985 revision brought about a number of significant changes:

(i) Rule 2.61 no longer applies to an application for a consent order for maintenance pending suit. Section 33A(3) of the 1973 Act defines 'financial relief' so as to exclude an order for maintenance pending suit in contrast to the definition contained in the Family Proceedings Rules 1991, r 1.2. Despite the definition in s 33A(3), the old r 76A did apply to a consent order for maintenance pending suit (r 2.61(2)). It is difficult to see why the procedure should not continue to apply, subject to the omission of information about capital resources allowed for in the old rule. Rule 2.61 does somewhat illogically apply to a consent order for interim periodical payments. The basis of the duty to make full and frank disclosure is to be found in the requirement imposed upon the court by s 25 of the 1973 Act to exercise its discretion according to the criteria contained in that section, as the House of Lords indicated in *Livesey* v *Jenkins*. In a statutory sense, s 25 only applies to applications under ss 23 and 24 and not to maintenance pending suit (s 22). Whilst this could explain this particular amendment in the revised rule, it has been held in *Peacock* v *Peacock* [1984] 1 All ER 1069 that the principles governing an application for maintenance pending suit are the same as those governing an application for a final order. One can only conclude that no statement of information is required on a consent application for maintenance pending suit.

(ii) A more detailed procedure is laid down for obtaining the consent order. This procedure is discussed in detail below in section 4(*d*).

(iii) No certificate is required, as was formerly the case under the old r 76A(5), that the solicitor had advised his client whether it would be in the interest of the client to agree to the proposed order. It was in any event unnecessary for the solicitor to state the nature of the advice which he had given.

(iv) The revised rule still provides that the statement of information may be made in more than one document. It is, therefore, perhaps the most unsatisfactory feature of the revised rule that it still does not provide that, where separate statements of information are filed, copies must be served on the other party. This obvious lacuna has led to local Practice Directions being made by some courts that a consent order will not be made, unless the parties certify that the other party has been served. It is hardly satisfactory that, in the absence of such a local direction, the access of each party to the court file may technically be the only means which a party has of seeing the other party's statement of information, when the decision of the House of Lords in *Livesey* v *Jenkins* has underlined the duty to make full and frank disclosure both to the court and to the other party so clearly. There are, of course, cases where the parties come to solicitors having already reached a financial agreement or where an agreement is achieved at a very early stage after the involvement of solicitors and before any in-depth investigation of the financial position has taken place. In such circumstances, it may not be the wish of the parties to disclose their financial circumstances. They may be reluctant to incur the costs involved. They may feel that embarking upon this procedure would only prolong bitterness and conceivably overturn the agreement reached. It is submitted that even in such cases, as in the case of all consent orders to which r 2.61 applies, the service of the statement of information on the other party to the application before the making of the order, where the statement is contained in more than one document, is essential. There is clearly a greater risk of an order being set aside for non-disclosure, if the r 2.61 statement is not copied to the other party. The same principle will also apply where one party adds financial information to a statement already partly completed by the other before filing it at court. It should be remembered that the duty to make full and frank disclosure, as explained by the House of Lords in *Livesey* v *Jenkins*, is more extensive than the obligations imposed by r 2.61.

(v) The revised rule makes specific provision that the statement should indicate whether either party has remarried or has any present intention to marry or cohabit with another person, thereby reflecting the facts of *Livesey* v *Jenkins* itself.

(vi) The statement must also indicate, where a consent transfer of property order is sought, that any mortgagee has been served with notice of the application and that no objection to the transfer has been made by the mortgagee within fourteen days of service. This ensures compliance with the Family Proceedings Rules 1991, r 2.59(4). It should be noted that the hearing will be adjourned and appropriate costs (including perhaps wasted costs) orders will be made if the r 2.59(4) requirements have not been carried out by the time of the hearing.

The statement must also indicate, where the order (including an order for variation) imposes any requirement on the trustees or managers of a pension scheme by virtue of MCA s 25B or s 25C, that those trustees or managers have been served with the notice of application and that no objection to such an order has been made by them within 14 days of service (the new r 2.61(*dd*), inserted by The Family Proceedings (Amendment) (No 2) Rules 1996, r 4(1), and applying only to proceedings commenced by petition presented on or after 1 July 1996).

(vii) Rule 2.61 is no longer sufficiently complied with by reference to a relevant affidavit which has already been filed together with a statement that there has been no material change in the matters mentioned in the affidavit or, if there has been such a change, a statement as to what change has occurred. As indicated below, affidavits may be relied upon under r 2.61(3) if the parties attend the hearing. Whilst it may be that it is easier for district judges to refer to a summary of the parties' financial positions rather than to sometimes copious affidavits of means, it is regrettable that in such circumstances the additional costs of r 2.61 statements should have to be incurred.

(viii) Rule 2.61 still does not impose any positive duty to reveal any changes which occur after the preparation of the statement of information, although it is submitted that such a duty does exist up to the making of the order under the rule in *Livesey* v *Jenkins*.

(ix) The revised rule now specifically deals with the position where a consent order is agreed immediately before or at some time during the hearing. In such circumstances, the court may under r 2.61(3) dispense with the lodging of a statement of information and give directions for the information which would otherwise be required to be given in the normal statement of information to be given in such manner as the court sees fit. This means that the court can dispense altogether with the lodging of a statement of information, relying upon oral evidence, affidavits of means already filed or, presumably, information obtained from the parties' legal representatives. However, r 2.61(3) no longer permits the court to dispense with the lodging of the consent order as was the case under the revised r 76A. It is submitted that the court should only use the dispensing procedure in r 2.61(3) so long as r 2.59(4) has been complied with. It is best practice, however, always to attend at any final hearing with a blank r 2.61 statement which can be filled in appropriately if required, where settlement is reached at the hearing.

(x) The nature of 'estimate in summary form' of the parties' financial resources differs in r 2.61 insofar as income resources are concerned. The revised rule refers to the 'net income of each party and of any minor child of the family' as compared with the simple reference to 'income resources of each of the parties and, where relevant, of any minor child of the family' in the old rule. When the revised rule was introduced in September 1985, it was difficult to understand why this terminology had been used. It had long been established that the courts should approach the calculation of maintenance by reference to the *gross* incomes of the parties (*Gengler* v *Gengler* [1976] 2 All ER 81; cf *Rodewald* v *Rodewald* [1977] 2 All ER 609). It was necessary when using the one-third approach propounded in *Wachtel* v *Wachtel*

[1973] 1 All ER 829 as a starting point in calculating maintenance on the basis of the parties' gross incomes then to have regard to the *net effect* of the proposed order and then make any necessary adjustments (*Furniss* v *Furniss* (1982) 3 FLR 46; *Stockford* v *Stockford* (1982) 3 FLR 58; as explained by *Slater* v *Slater* (1982) 3 FLR 364). However, the changes brought about by the Finance Act 1988 (see p 7 and pp 23–24) have given the use of net figures meaningful significance.

(xi) A statement of information under the revised rule is still required to draw attention to 'any other especially significant matters' but there is no longer any direction that in particular regard should be had to s 25(2) and (3) of the 1973 Act and the value of any benefit such as a pension or death benefit which would be lost on the divorce or annulment of the marriage. The practitioner should not therefore be diffident at using this opportunity to justify any particular features of the order which may seem questionable to the district judge. In particular, r 2.61 does not contain any requirement to give any supporting information where an order is sought under the Inheritance (Provision for Family and Dependants) Act 1975, s 15. However, following the decision of the Court of Appeal in *Whiting* v *Whiting* (1988) 2 FLR 189, it may be considered appropriate as a 'belt and braces' approach to include in the r 2.61 statement information which satisfies the requirements of *Whiting* depending on local practice (see p 92).

Rule 2.61 itself brought about with effect from 14 October 1991 four amendments to the 1985 revision of r 76A:

- Rule 2.61(1) no longer contains any specific reference to the Matrimonial Causes Act 1973, s 27. However, r 2.61 applies to applications for consent orders under s 27 by virtue of the Family Proceedings Rules 1991, r 3.1(10).
- Rule 2.61(1) no longer refers to the lodging of minutes of the order in the terms sought but rather to two copies of a draft of the order in the terms sought. One of the two copies must be indorsed with a statement signed by the respondent to the application signifying his agreement. It is presumed that in view of the clarification given to the revised r 76A by the *Practice Direction 17 February 1986* [1986] 1 FLR 337 that the signature of the solicitor on record as acting for the respondent will suffice. The purpose of requiring two copies of the draft order to be lodged is presumably to enable one copy to be sealed by the court and sent out to the parties without the necessity of retyping in the court office with attendant delay.

- The dispensation procedure in r 2.61(3) may be invoked where all or any of the parties attend the hearing, whereas the revised r 76A required the parties (presumably all parties) to attend.
- Rule 2.61(3) no longer permits the court to dispense with the lodging of minutes of the order but only the statement of information.

The revisions of 1985 and 1991 have brought about some welcome changes, although some earlier problems remain unresolved and certain parts of the original r 76A which were of benefit remain revoked. The purpose of r 2.61 must, however, be seen as striking a balance between providing the court with no background information on a consent application and providing all that would be required on a contested application.

A form of statement of information was suggested in the *Practice Direction 17 February 1986* [1986] 1 FLR 337. This Practice Direction clarified two issues. First, despite the strict wording of r 76A(1), it was considered that the rule was properly complied with if the minute of consent order was signed by the solicitors on record as acting for the respondent. Secondly, whilst r 76A did not require the statement of information to be signed by either party, the Practice Direction suggested that practitioners may consider it appropriate for the statement to be signed by or on behalf of both parties as a means of establishing the accuracy of the information relating to their respective clients. These two areas of clarification still hold good notwithstanding the revision of the form of statement of information by the *Practice Direction 5 January 1990* [1990] 1 FLR 234, which has now become Form M1 in Appendix 1 to the Family Proceedings Rules 1991. Form M1 appears in Appendix 12. The revisions which have taken place make it clear that the details of capital and net incomes should be stated as at the date of the statement (and not as they will be following the implementation of the order). Additionally, the statement should give the net equity of any property concerned and the effect of its proposed distribution.

It would be a mistake to suppose that the practitioner has to follow rigidly the exact format and size of the r 2.61 statements produced by the various law stationers, which provide very limited space for explanation of the capital positions of the parties. The various headings can be typed out to provide as much space as is required for proper completion of the form.

(xii) It would also be a mistake to 'dash off' a r 2.61 statement, thinking that it is of minimal importance; it is in fact a critically important document, even in a case where affidavits of means have been filed. First, the practitioner will actually be risking increasing costs by such an approach, because it is possible that the judge will query the contents of the statement and refer the draft consent order back to the parties for further comment. (The authors know of one case where the draft order obliged the husband to pay by way of lump sum to the wife more than he disclosed as his total assets on the r 2.61 statement).

Secondly, slipshod or faulty completion of the r 2.61 statement could strengthen the judge's arm in any subsequent application in the cause, for instance, by way of variation or appeal out of time. *B v B* (Consent Order: Variation) [1995] 1 FLR 9 is a case in point. The judge found that a component of the bad advice/negligence of the wife's solicitor (subsequently sued by the wife) was the completion of the statement. 'The r 76(A) statement is slipshod in the extreme, and probably led the district judge into making the order without inquiry.' The full indictment reads as follows:

> The duration of the marriage is recorded as three years and six months; not a word about the preceding years of cohabitation. The age of the wife is omitted. Against the entry 'minor children' is typed the ambiguous figure '11'. The capital resources and income position is stated for the wife making no reference at all to her joint interest [in the house]. The box that is provided to enable the parties to put before the court the significant additional circumstances is simply left blank.

It is a salutary lesson to take away from this decision that the parties' agreement relating to maintenance was set aside on the basis of the bad advice given to the wife. The headnote records that it was held *per curiam* that:

> where the financial affairs of a family were complex or substantial, it was vital that the spouses received professional services from specialist practitioners in the field. Where the solicitor instructed was not experienced in family work, the specialist Bar was always available.

Criticism of a r 2.61 statement was also a feature of *B v Miller & Co* [1996] 2 FLR 23.

(d) Procedure

The first question which must be asked is whether it is appropriate for the agreement reached to be made into a consent order or whether it should be made a rule of court for the reasons discussed on pp 43 *et seq*. Tax considerations may in certain circumstances dictate that the agreement should be made a rule of court because a property adjustment order or a lump sum order does not take effect until decree absolute. For capital gains tax purposes, the relief provided by Taxation of Chargeable Gains Act 1992, s 58 applies only to disposals up to the date of decree absolute or (if earlier) 5 April in the year of separation. The matrimonial home is treated more generously under extra-statutory concession D6. The position with regard to inheritance tax is more liberal and in general, in the absence of any element of gratuitous benefit, transfers made under a court order (Inheritance Tax Act 1984, s 10) or variation (s 11) may be exempt even if made after decree absolute; see also *Senior Registrar's Statement 20 August 1975* (1975) 119 SJ 596; *G* v *G* (1979) *The Times*, 12 November).

If a consent order is appropriate, the exact procedure will depend upon the stage at which the agreement is reached. If an agreement is reached before a district judge's certificate under the special procedure is applied for, there should be lodged at court in the case of an application by a petitioner, when requesting directions under the special procedure (according to the procedure set out at para 11 of the *Practice Direction 7 March 1977* [1977] 1 WLR 320:

(1) notice of intention to proceed with the application already made in the petition in Form M13 (or otherwise Form M11 or Form A in the courts where the Ancillary Relief Procedure Pilot scheme is in force;—see [1996] 2 FLR 368);
(2) two copies of the draft of the order in the terms sought, one of which is indorsed with a statement signed by the respondent to the application (or the solicitor on record as acting for him) signifying his agreement;
(3) statement(s) of information under r 2.61 signed by or on behalf of the parties.

This will enable the consent order to be made (subject to decree absolute) on the pronouncement of the decree nisi. Upon receipt of the district judge's certificate, the practitioner should check that it recites that the draft consent order has been approved and will be made into an order on the date when the decree nisi is pronounced.

Where the application is by a petitioner and is one to which the special procedure does not apply or the district judge's certificate has already been granted, the above documents should simply be lodged at court as soon as the agreement has been reached (following the requirements of *Practice Direction 26 September 1972* [1972] 3 All ER 704 insofar as they are extant (see p 45)).

An application by a respondent for a consent order would require:
(1) notice of application in Form M13 (where an answer has been filed which incorporated all relevant financial claims or otherwise in Form M11 (or Form A where appropriate) praying for the financial relief which is dealt with in the consent order; district judges take the view that they do not have jurisdiction to make orders in respect of which applications have not been made;

(2) two copies of the draft order in the terms sought, one indorsed with a statement signed by the respondent to the application (or the solicitor on record as acting for him) signifying his agreement;
(3) statement(s) of information under r 2.61 signed by or on behalf of the parties.

A consent application by a petitioner or a respondent for an order solely for maintenance pending suit is not governed by r 2.61 and can be dealt with by lodging at court an appropriate notice of application (in Form M11, M13 or A) incorporating the terms of the agreed order indorsed with the consent of the respondent to the application.

If the consent order is to take the form of a mutual clean break, the respondent to the application should lodge a notice of application in the appropriate form for dismissal purposes only. The principle of the clean break is discussed in Chapter 4.

No fee is payable when lodging an application for a consent order, unless the appropriate notice of application has already been filed.

The wording of r 2.61 is such as to suggest that the application and the draft order should be contained in separate documents. In practice, the two copies of the draft order and statement(s) of information under r 2.61 will often suffice.

If the agreement is reached at the door of the court or, if for any other reason all or any of the parties attend the hearing, the court may dispense with the lodging of statement(s) of information and deal with the application as indicated above in section (*c*)(ix)(r 2.61(3)).

Side letters
It may also be necessary to file a 'side letter' at the court if the consent order refers to a side letter, or if there is a side letter containing subsidiary terms agreed by the parties which are not set out in the consent order. It is a widespread practice amongst practitioners to put such (usually minor) subsidiary terms in an agreed side letter, rather than to incorporate them into the consent order. Sometimes, however, they do contain items of significance, and the Court of Appeal has in effect directed that such side letters should be filed at the court together with the consent order so that the judge can be alerted to the salient points of the overall agreement contained not only in the consent order but also in the side letter. In *N* v *N* [1993] 2 FLR 868 the wife had agreed in a consent order to fixed-term maintenance for five years, and had agreed in a side letter not to apply for an extension save in exceptional circumstances. The parties had a child who, at the time of the appeal, was aged 11. Butler-Sloss LJ, giving the judgment of the court, commented:

I am not happy that the side letter was not shown to the district judge in a case where, albeit it was a consent order, none the less he had to have regard to the child as the first consideration. He should have had an opportunity to consider it.

Another point to take away is that it is not good practice to relegate significant aspects of consent orders to side letters rather than putting them in the consent order itself. As Butler-Sloss LJ said in *N* v *N*:

> I question the suitability of a side letter in a child case where the child will still only be ten or so when the five year period has passed.

It is better practice, not least for enforcement reasons to put significant terms in the order itself rather than in side letters.

(e) Inquiry by the court

As has been seen, s 33A(1) of the 1973 Act enables the court to make a consent order in the terms agreed on the basis of prescribed information, *unless it has reason to think that there are other circumstances into which it ought to inquire.*

The scant information available to district judges in the form of copies of the draft order and statement(s) of information under r 2.61 coupled with the pressure on district judges' time does not readily assist in identifying cases where an appointment should be given for the parties and their legal representatives to attend before the district judge. As a result of the substitution of the revised s 25 in the Matrimonial Causes Act 1973 by the Matrimonial and Family Proceedings Act 1984, s 3, it is reasonable to assume the court will intervene where it is clear that the first consideration is not being given to the welfare of minor children of the family, for example, because the order makes no provision for accomodation for the children without any explanation being given in the accompanying r 2.61 statement. Section 3 of the 1984 Act also inserted s 25A into the 1973 Act, which imposes upon the court the duty to consider whether it would be appropriate to terminate the financial obligations of each party towards the other. It is submitted that it is expecting too much by way of judicial intervention under the procedure provided for by s 33A(1) for the duty imposed by s 25A to be fully complied with. If, however, the submitted order itself provides for a clean break, the district judge may be inclined to direct that an appointment be given for the attendance of the parties, particularly if one party is acting in person. It is submitted that despite the non-cancellation of the *Practice Direction 13 April 1984* [1984] 2 All ER 256 an attendance before the district judge is not an essential requirement, since the *Practice Direction* has been superseded by s 33A(1) of the 1973 Act.

The court's supervisory jurisdiction may be exercised where there are any unusual features, for example, the payment of a lump sum to a husband. The court may feel inclined to intervene to protect the interests of the state, if an unfair burden is being placed upon the welfare benefit system (see eg *Hulley* v *Thompson* [1981] 1 All ER 1128, where it was held that a wife's consent to an order under which no provision would be made for the children in consideration of a capital payment did not on the facts preclude the Department of Social Security proceeding against the husband under the then applicable statutory provisions, namely the Social Security Act 1986, s 24 (and now ss 106 and 107 of the Social Security Administration Act 1992, which enables the Secretary of State to pursue a liable parent through the Magistrates' Court in order to recoup means-tested state benefits) for provision for the children—any such scheme would of course now fall foul of the Child Support Act 1991). Courts on the other hand are usually happy to ensure that, as far as still possible, an order is tax-effective for the family as a whole. Whilst the extent of the court's inquisitorial role is unclear, it would seem that 'other circumstances' are not limited to matters listed in s 25(2) and (3) of the 1973 Act. It will be noted that r 2.61 specifically omits any referene to s 25.

The supervisory jurisdiction exercised by the court should be distinguished from the making of a selective order, that is, where the district judge makes a consent order in some but not all of the terms agreed. It is submitted that the parties must always be given an opportunity to renegotiate where a district judge feels inclined to pursue such a course. A selective order made without reference back to the parties is made without jurisdiction and is irregular. Such an order can be set aside by the court which made it (*Hadkinson* v *Hadkinson* [1952] 2 All ER 567; *Isaacs* v *Robertson* [1984] 3 All ER 140; *Munks* v *Munks* [1985] FLR 576). Lord Diplock summarised the position in *Isaacs* v *Robertson* at 143:

> The contrasting legal concepts of voidness and voidability form part of the English law of contract. They are inapplicable to orders made by a court of unlimited jurisdiction in the course of contentious litigation. Such an order is either irregular or regular. If it is irregular it can be set aside by the court that made it on application to that court; if it is regular it can only be set aside by an appellate court on appeal if there is one to which an appeal lies.

The courses open to a district judge when considering an application for the consent order are:

- to approve the order providing that the draft is properly prepared and all the necessary information under r 2.61 has been provided;
- to list the application for a short appointment where the court thinks 'that there are other circumstances into which it ought to inquire' under s 33A(1);
- to refuse to approve the order and usually return the draft to the parties for the terms to be renegotiated with an indication of the parts which the district judge finds objectionable.

The exact supervisory role of the court is still in the process of evolution. A fundamental part of this process is what can realistically be expected of district judges within the available time constraints. The situation, unsatisfactory though it may be, was summarised by Balcombe J in *Tommey* v *Tommey* [1982] 3 All ER 385, at 390 (although this passage must now to some extent be read in the light of the comments of Lord Brandon in *Livesey* v *Jenkins* [1985] 1 All ER 106, at 116):

> A judge who is asked to make a consent order cannot be compelled to do so: he is no mere rubber stamp. If he thinks there are matters about which he needs to be more fully informed before he makes the order, he is entitled to make such inquiries and require such evidence to be put before him, as he considers necessary. But, *per contra*, he is under no obligation to make inquiries or require evidence. He is entitled to assume that parties of full age and capacity know what is in their own best interests, more especially when they are represented before him by counsel or solicitors.

The scope of the judicial supervisory role was similarly summarised by Waite LJ in *Pounds* v *Pounds* [1994] 1 FLR 775 (in a judgment which described the steps leading up to the making of the order and the judicial functions within that) as follows (at 780, paras A–B):

> The effect of s 33A and the rules and directions made under it is thus to confine the paternal function of the court when approving final consent orders to a broad appraisal of the parties' financial circumstances as disclosed in summary form, without descent into the valley of detail. It is only if this survey puts Court on inquiry as to whether there are other circumstances into which it ought to probe more deeply that any further investigation is required of the judge before approving the bargain that the parties made for themselves.

5 The duty to disclose

As will be seen from Chapter 6, a consent order may be set aside for material non-disclosure. What therefore is the nature and extent of the duty to disclose? This question is answered by the decision of the House of Lords in *Livesey* v *Jenkins* [1985] 1 All ER 106.

(a) The facts
The parties were married in 1957 and separated in 1981. It was agreed that W would seek a divorce on the basis of H's adultery and be entitled to custody of the two children. The marriage was dissolved on W's petition on 14 April 1982. After negotiation, the parties' solicitors reached a final agreement on 12 August 1982 with regard to ancillary relief. It was agreed that there should be a consent order under the terms of which H should transfer to W his half-share in the matrimonial home, subject to the mortgage on it, for the express purpose of providing a home for W and the children, and that by consent all W's claims for financial provision for herself should be dismissed. On 18 August 1982 W became engaged to L, but failed to disclose this fact either to her own solicitors or to H or to his solicitors. On 19 August 1982, the parties' solicitors made a joint application to the registrar for a consent order in the agreed terms. The consent order was made on 2 September 1982. W married L on 24 September 1982 and two months later advertised the matrimonial home for sale.

(b) The decision
The decision in *Livesey* v *Jenkins* has had wide implications covering, as will be seen, the form of consent orders and, as discussed on p 135, the basis upon which a consent order will be set aside for material non-disclosure. The decision insofar as it relates to the duty to disclose establishes the following propositions:

(i) The House of Lords relied on the decision of the Court of Appeal in *Robinson* v *Robinson* [1982] 2 All ER 699n, itself based upon long established authority, in ruling that *the parties were under a duty before an order for ancillary relief, including a consent order, is made under ss 23 or 24 of the 1973 Act to make full and frank disclosure to the court and the other party of 'all the circumstances of the case, including, inter alia, the particular matters' specified in s 25 of the 1973 Act* (Lord Brandon, at 113).

The basis of the duty to make full and frank disclosure is the statutory requirement imposed by s 25 that the court must exercise its discretion to make orders under ss 23 and 24 in accordance with the criteria prescribed by that section and that, unless the parties make full and frank disclosure of all material matters, the court cannot lawfully or properly exercise such jurisdiction. Applying this principle to consent orders, Lord Brandon commented (at 114):

... once it is accepted that this principle of full and frank disclosure exists, it is obvious that it must apply not only to contested proceedings heard with full evidence adduced before the court, but also to exchanges of information between parties and their solicitors leading to the making of consent orders without further inquiry by the court. If that were not so, it would be impossible for a court to have any assurance that the requirements of s 25(1) [*as it then was*] were complied with before it made such consent orders.

(ii) *The parties will not have discharged the duty to make full and frank disclosure merely by complying with the requirements of r 2.61.* Lord Brandon emphasised this at 118:

It must not be thought however that these further provisions [*Practice Direction 13 April 1984 and r 2.61*] alter in any way at all the basic principle of the need for full and frank disclosure by the parties before a consent order is made.

Rather, Lord Brandon regarded the Practice Direction and the introduction of r 2.61 (then r 76A) as being 'steps in the right direction'.

It is submitted that there is a distinction between:

(1) the rigorous duty to disclose one's financial position fully which is a duty owed by a spouse to the court and to the other party (which Lord Brandon highlights); and

(2) the threshold to be surmounted by a party in fulfilling the elementary disclosure exercise provided by s 33A: a step can be taken in the right direction by completing the r 2.61 statement, but the acid test of whether or not a proper disclosure has been made will be if/when an application to set aside the consent order is made as a result of non-disclosure.

(iii) *The duty of full and frank disclosure is general in its nature.* Questions of remarriage and cohabitation are expressly covered by r 2.61. There may, however, be other less obvious matters which should be disclosed, for example, an inheritance, which is about to be received, or any significant change in a party's terms of employment, which may shortly occur.

Given the nature of the duty to disclose every matter (including matters outside the scope of s 25), it is safer to resolve any doubt by disclosure rather than risk a consent order being set aside.

(iv) The duty to make full and frank disclosure exists *at all times* up to the making of the order. *Wales* v *Wadham* [1977] 2 All ER 125 and *Tommey* v *Tommey* [1982] 3 All ER 385 are wrongly decided insofar as they suggest that the duty to disclose arises only if there is a duty to file an affidavit of means when the jurisdiction of the court has been invoked by filing a notice of application in Form M11 or M13. In *Wales* v *Wadham*, which also involved the non-disclosure by a wife of her intention to remarry, it had been held that the agreement reached was not a contract requiring *uberrima fides* nor did the law and practice of the Family Division require a wife to disclose her intention to remarry when she was not under a duty to file an affidavit of means. This was rejected in *Livesey* v *Jenkins*.

The duty continues after initial disclosure has been made. As Lord Brandon put it (at 113), the parties must 'ensure that the information provided is correct, complete and up to date'. This does not, however, extend beyond the consent order to enable a wife to invoke the questionnaire procedure under FPR, r 2.63, where there are no subsisting ancillary proceedings nor pending proceedings either to appeal out of time or to set aside the consent order. To do so would be to permit a fishing expedition, for example, to found a variation application (*H* v *B* [1987] 1 All ER 766).

(v) The duty to disclose applies to *both contested and consent proceedings*, as indicated by the comments of Lord Brandon (at 114) quoted above.

(vi) The duty to disclose applies *whether or not the parties are legally represented*. Lord Brandon (at 116) put the matter in this way:

> [*The requirement of full and frank disclosure*] is, as I have sought to stress, a requirement founded on the terms of s 25(1) [*as it then was*] of the 1973 Act, and, for reasons of public policy, it is not open to parties, whether represented by lawyers or not, to disregard, or contract out of, such requirement.

(vii) The *parties cannot contract out* of the duty to disclose, as indicated by the dictum of Lord Brandon above. There is, however, anecdotal evidence that district judges may be prepared to accept a 'sketchy' disclosure in a r 2.61 statement in appropriate cases; in a big-money case, for example, it is conceivable that a statement could repeat the 'millionaire's defence' along the lines of a spouse having capital above £x and therefore being able to fund the proposed settlement (notwithstanding the court's willingness, in contested applications under r 2.63, to require a breakdown in approximate terms of the overall financial resources—see for example *Van G* v *Van G* (Financial Provision: Millionaire's Defence) [1995] 1 FLR 328 and *F* v *F* (Ancillary Relief: Substantial Awards) [1995] 2 FLR 45).

(viii) The duty is owed *both to the court and to the other party*, as Lord Brandon made clear at 113. It is unsafe to rely on knowledge which the other party may, albeit indirectly, have as to the existence of a particular asset: the duty to disclose is also owed to the court. The decision of the Court of Appeal in *Barber* v *Barber* [1987] Fam Law 125 can be regarded as being decided on its own particular facts. There, the wife sought leave to appeal out of time against an order of a circuit judge restoring a consent order originally made on 15 December 1981. The wife alleged only partial disclosure by the husband of a pension scheme. She knew of the existence of the scheme, but not of its complex mechanics. MCR 1977, r 76A (now FPR 1991, r 2.61) was not in operation in 1981 and no other documentary evidence of means had been filed at court. The scheme was not raised in any contemporaneous correspondence. Stephen Brown LJ refused leave to appeal, finding that there was no non-disclosure by the husband because the wife had acknowledged that she was aware of the pension scheme at the time of the consent order. The decision is difficult, if not impossible, to reconcile with *Robinson* v *Robinson* (Disclosure) (1983) 4 FLR 102, at 109 and *Livesey* v *Jenkins* [1985] 1 All ER 106, at 114, both of which were cited in argument. It is submitted that the decision must now be treated with caution, if only because the introduction of r 76A would require the disclosure of the pension scheme to the court. *Barber* was not followed by Jupp J in *Gurney* v *Gurney* (1989), unreported.

6 Drafting the consent order

Given the amount of time spent by matrimonial practitioners drafting and by district judges in considering consent orders, it is not perhaps a matter of great surprise that the construction of consent orders should become an issue to occupy the House of Lords in *Dinch* v *Dinch* [1987] 2 FLR 162. The facts in *Dinch* were:

> W applied in divorce proceedings for ancillary relief, *inter alia*, by way of a periodical payments order, a lump sum order and a property adjustment order. H applied under the Married Women's Property Act 1882, s 17 for an order for the immediate sale of the matrimonial home. The two applications were consolidated and an order made by consent on 26 November 1980. The consent order contained periodical payments orders in favour of W and a child of the family. The matrimonial home and jointly owned contents were to be sold and the proceeds to be divided equally between H and W, subject to certain deductions from H's share, the sale not to be effected until the child reached the age of seventeen or ceased full-time education. We was to receive from H's share of the net proceeds a sum plus interest in full and final settlement of all sums due to her and the child under an earlier interim

maintenance order. At the end of 1981, H accepted voluntary redundancy and thus disabled himself from complying with the periodical payments orders. On 21 June 1983, H applied to the court for an order varying the periodical payments to a nominal sum, an order remitting the arrears and an order for the immediate sale of the matrimonial home, the son by then having ceased full-time education. The registrar made an order for immediate sale from which W appealed. We then gave notice of her intention to proceed with an application for a secured provision order and subsequently gave notice of the restoration of applications for a lump sum order, a transfer of property order and an order further postponing the sale. Her appeal and these further applications were heard together by a circuit judge who reduced the periodical payments to a nominal sum, remitted all arrears not already secured by charging order and made an order for the immediate sale of the matrimonial home. Her further applications were dismissed on the ground that the original consent order was an order made under the Matrimonial Causes Act 1973, s 24 and accordingly the court had no jurisdiction to make any further order which would constitute a variation of that order. W appealed to the Court of Appeal which allowed her appeal from the judge's dismissal of her applications, holding *inter alia* that the consent order did not constitute an exercise of the court's powers to make a property adjustment order under the Matrimonial Causes Act 1973, s 24 but was an order declaring the interests of the parties under the Married Women's Property Act 1882, s 17. The Court of Appeal ordered the transfer of H's interest in the matrimonial home to W, subject to a charge in favour of H not enforceable until W died, remarried or left voluntarily. H's appeal to the House of Lords was allowed.

Insofar as the consent order had the effect of reducing the husband's beneficial entitlement to the property, it amounted to a property adjustment order under s 24 of the 1973 Act, as a result of which no further order in relation to the same property could be obtained. In any event, whether or not the consent order had been made pursuant to s 24 of the 1973 Act, where the order was intended to represent a final and conclusive one-for-all financial settlement, either overall or in relation to a particular property, that precluded any further claim to relief in relation to that property.

It is discernible therefore that the House of Lords approved the test for construing consent orders adopted in *Carson* v *Carson* (1981) FLR 352 and *Sandford* v *Sandford* [1986] 1 FLR 412. As Lord Oliver put it at 173:

> One has, as it seems to me, simply to look at the order and any admissible material available for its construction, and determine what the court intended—or, in the case of the consent order, what the parties intended—to effect by the order.

This approach is in notable contrast to that adopted in *Brown* v *Kirrage* (1980) 11 Fam Law 141, where Brandon LJ regarded the dismissal of a wife's claim for ancillary relief as a matter of such seriousness that the court ought to be extremely cautious about implying a dismissal where none is actually expressed in the order. (Refer to our comments on the case of *N* v *N* on p 81 in this connection.) The *Dinch* test does not, however, mean that, where an order is silent as to a particular claim, the order should always be construed as containing a dismissal of that claim. It is a question of construction in each case.

Lord Oliver sounded the following warning to the profession:

> The appeal is yet another example of the unhappy results flowing from the failure to which I ventured to draw attention in *Sandford* v *Sandford* [1986] 1 FLR 412, to take sufficient care in the drafting of consent orders in matrimonial proceedings to define with precision exactly what the parties were intending to do in relation to the disposal of the petitioner's claims for ancillary relief so as to avoid any future misunderstanding as to whether those claims, or any of them, were or were not to be kept alive. The hardship and injustice that such failure inevitably causes, particularly in cases where one or both parties are legally aided and the only substantial family asset consists of the matrimonial home, are so glaring in the instant case that I feel impelled once again to stress in the most emphatic terms that it is in all cases the imperative professional duty of those invested with the task of advising the parties to these unfortunate disputes to consider with due care the impact which any terms that they agree on behalf of their clients has, and is intended to have, upon any outstanding application for ancillary relief, and to ensure that such appropriate provision is inserted in any consent order made as will leave no room for any future doubt or misunderstanding, or saddle the parties with the wasteful burden of wholly unnecessary costs. It is, of course, also the duty of any court called upon to make such a consent order to consider for itself, before the order is drawn up and entered, the jurisdiction which it is being called upon to exercise and to make clear what claims for ancillary relief are being finally disposed of. I would, however, like to emphasise that the primary duty in this regard must lie upon those concerned with the negotiation and the drafting of the terms of the order and that any failure to fulfil such duty occurring hereafter cannot be excused simply by reference to some inadvertent lack of vigilance on the part of the court or its officers in passing the order in a form which the parties have approved.

Prevention is better than cure. A well-drawn order is to be preferred to reliance upon aids to construction. The following guidelines are offered in an attempt to summarise good practice in relation to the preparation of consent orders:

What is the purpose of the consent order?

A consent order is a legal document recording the agreement reached between the parties. It is not therefore to be expected that every consent order will be immediately understood by every lay client. A surplusage of recitals is not the key to breaking down the communication barrier: there can be no substitute for explaining to the client by letter the meaning and effect of an order. It is good practice for the practitioner to send a letter to the client containing an explanation of the draft consent order, and, when it has been approved and engrossed, to have the client sign it (regardless of any obligation or otherwise to obtain your client's signature on the document pursuant to r 2.61(1)).

Is the order clearly marked 'BY CONSENT'?

If an order is made by consent, the practice should invariably be that that fact is clearly expressed on the face of the order. The court will not treat an order as a consent order, unless it is satisfied that it was in fact made by consent. A consent order in the technical sense is not one which embodies provisions to which neither party objects (*Chandless-Chandless* v *Nicholson* [1942] 2 KB 321). An order marked 'BY CONSENT' cannot be appealed on its merits as there has been no adjudication on the merits. As was said by Nourse LJ in the Court of Appeal in *Re F (A Minor)* (Custody: Consent Order: Procedure) [1992] 1 FLR 561:

> The Court cannot entertain an appeal against a perfected and subsisting order by a party who is expressed to have consented to it. While the order stands, the party who seeks to appeal is estopped by the record from saying that he did not give his consent and thus from re-opening the subject matter of the dispute. Moreover, the Lower Court has *ex hypothesi* not adjudicated on the validity of its own order, so that there is nothing to be brought up for question in a Court of Appeal.

However, an appeal can lie against a consent order if there has been non-disclosure following the principle established in *Livesey* v *Jenkins* (see further p 135).

How is the order constructed?

It is usual to find that the constituent elements of an order are recitals, which may include agreements, undertakings and the orders of the court themselves. The recitals and undertakings form the preamble to the order; the orders are contained in the operative part of the order. It is critical that each term is placed in the correct part of the minute. As will be seen, this is a decision which is circumscribed by the jurisdiction of the court. The practitioner must also have in mind the enforceability of the obligations which he seeks to impose. There is no purpose, for example, in incorporating in an order an undertaking not to seek a variation order, as the court should not accept an undertaking to oust its own jurisdiction. There is, however, no reason why this term should not be dealt with by means of a recited agreement. It may still be of dubious enforceability but will be of some evidential value, to which the court might have regard as a matter of conduct under the Matrimonial Causes Act 1973, s 31(7). It may also be upheld as an agreement between the parties (see, for example, *N* v *N* [1993] 2 FLR 868, where the court upheld the agreement between parties in a side letter to the consent order that the wife should not be allowed to apply for an extension of her maintenance payments).

Can the court make this order?
The court only has jurisdiction to make orders which come within the powers conferred by the Matrimonial Causes Act 1973, ss 22–24 and other statutory provisions such as, for instance, pursuant to the Matrimonial Homes Act 1983. Terms which fall outside these powers should be dealt with either by undertakings or as agreements. The fact that the parties have agreed that an order should be made does not confer jurisdiction on the court to make an order in terms where jurisdiction would otherwise not exist. In *Livesey* v *Jenkins* [1985] 1 All ER 106, Lord Brandon put the matter in this way (at 118–119):

> The third matter relates to the form of the consent order made in this case. I said earlier that its form was open to a number of criticisms, and it is right that I should now indicate what these criticisms are. When a consent order is drafted it is essential that all its terms should come clearly within the court's powers conferred on it by ss 23 and 24 of the 1973 Act. In the present case there are several terms which are not within those powers. These are para 2, which directs that the wife shall be solely responsible, after the transfer to her of the husband's half share in the matrimonial home, for the mortgage on it and all other outgoings relating to it, and paras 4, 5 and 6, which direct that the husband and the wife are to be solely responsible for certain specified bank overdrafts and loan accounts. There is nothing in s 23 or s 24 of the 1973 Act which directly empowers the court to make orders of these kinds. That being so, the proper procedure for incorporating the obligations concerned into a consent order is by formulating them as undertakings given to the court. Such undertakings are, needless to say, enforceable as effectively as direct orders.

(In *Re B (A Minor)* (Supervision Order: Parental Undertaking) (1996) *The Times*, 12 January, which related to a supervision order made under Children Act 1989 s 31, it was held that, as the county court had no inherent jurisdiction to grant injunctions, it could have no inherent jurisdiction to accept undertakings in the care proceedings. Some practitioners, and apparently some county courts, have used this division as authority for the proposition that the court should not accept an undertaking to perform an obligation (including a financial obligation) which cannot be ordered. The authors respectfully disagree with any such proposition, the dicta of Lord Brandon in *Jenkins* v *Livesey* [1985] AC 424 being binding House of Lords authority in relation to the drafting of matrimonial consent orders to the effect that a party could undertake to perform an obligation which he cannot be ordered to do.)

The court has no power to order a husband to take out an insurance policy to compensate a wife for loss of pension rights (*Milne* v *Milne* (1981) FLR 286). There is no jurisdiction to order one party to pay the debts of either party, which are not connected to an interest in the property (eg a hire purchase liability), out of the proceeds of sale of the matrimonial home (*Burton* v *Burton* [1986] 2 FLR 419). Nor may a party be ordered to indemnify the other party (whether in relation to businesses or bank overdrafts—see *Belcher* v *Belcher* [1995] 1 FLR 916—or otherwise). Matters outside the court's jurisdiction can also include, for example, a lump sum to discharge a wife's entitlement to periodical payments where a lump sum has already been ordered. In such circumstances, the second lump sum should be dealt with by way of an undertaking (*S* v *S* [1986] 3 All ER 566; *Boylan* v *Boylan* [1988] 1 FLR 282).

What is the function of a recital?
Recitals may be historical or narrative. For example, a recital may be used to record an agreement to sell the matrimonial home, where no order for sale can be made because no decree nisi has been pronounced, or completion of the sale is envisaged before decree absolute. There is certainly no need to introduce a minute at great length by way of recital. An introductory recital—for example, of a clean break nature—may prove to be an aid to construction if there is some later ambiguity in the operative part of the order.

Is the term in the correct part of the order?
It is not difficult inadvertently to incorporate an agreement in the operative part of the order. Bearing in mind the above guidelines, each term will have its proper place in the minute. Having determined

this, care should be taken to ensure that there are no unnecessary duplications as a result of which recitals or undertakings repeat matters referred to in the operative part of the order.

Has a decree nisi been pronounced?
The court does not have power to make a consent order until the granting of a decree nisi to take effect on decree absolute, except for maintenance pending suit for a spouse or a financial provision order benefiting a child of the family (Matrimonial Causes Act 1973, ss 23(5) and 24(3); *Munks* v *Munks* [1985] FLR 345; *Board* v *Checkland* [1987] 2 FLR 257; *Pounds* v *Pounds* [1994] 1 FLR 775; see p 44 for a fuller commentary on this). Where an agreement is reached before special procedure directions are requested, the application for a consent order may be lodged at court when requesting special procedure directions (see p 59). There is a school of thought that one should apply for the consent order after pronouncement of the decree nisi so as to avoid any delay in the pronouncement of the decree nisi in case the application for the consent order has to be referred back to the parties. However, that could involve significant delay in the making of the order, and it therefore may be better practice to apply for the consent order at the same time as applying for the decree nisi under the special procedure; if there are any points which the district judge has on the wording of the draft order, he could raise them with the parties without delaying the date of the decree nisi.

Is the order intended to come into effect before decree absolute?
The Matrimonial Causes Act 1973, ss 23(5) and 24(3) not only preclude the making of a consent order until after the granting of a decree nisi—except as mentioned above—but also preclude the order taking effect until the decree nisi has been made absolute. If therefore the order is to be made before decree absolute, the time for compliance with obligations set out in the order eg in the case of a lump sum order, must run from the date of decree absolute, or the order must be made 'subject to decree absolute'. If it is intended to implement an agreement, eg relating to the sale of the matrimonial home, prior to decree absolute, the agreement could either be made a rule of court (see p 43) or dealt with in the preamble to the minute (see p 72). However, these restrictions do not mean that a district judge may not even hear an application until after decree absolute as the registrar thought in *Dackham* v *Dackham* [1987] 2 FLR 358.

Has every claim, which is to be dismissed or made the subject of an order, already been made either in the petition or answer or in Form M11?
A consent order cannot be made, unless the relief has already been sought. In the case of a respondent who has not filed an answer, Form M11 marked 'for dismissal purposes only' should be filed where appropriate. It is insufficient to include in the order a recital 'all such claims being deemed to have been made'.

Is the order precise?
Common drafting errors include:

- *Have all relevant dates been stated in the order?* For example, omissions which can occur include the commencement date for periodical payments and the period within which a lump sum is to be paid. When drafting an order for periodical payments in favour of a child which is to continue beyond the age of seventeen years, and the child is to continue in full-time education beyond that age, it should be made clear that it is the later date, if the order is expressed in the alternative, which is the operative date on which the order will cease (*Practice Direction 10 July 1987* [1987] 2 All ER 1084).
- *Has provision for interest been included in a lump sum order of less than £5,000?* The court cannot later insert a provision for interest, if this has been overlooked originally. For a full discussion of this topic, the reader is referred to (1989) *Law Society's Gazette*, 5 July, 20, which must now be read in the light of County Court (Interest on Judgment Debts) Order 1991 (SI 1991 No 1184) which provides for automatic interest on county court lump sum orders over £5,000 made on or after 1 July 1991.
- *Is the order complete?* It is very easy to prepare an order which does not provide for a complete clean break because, for example, a husband's application for a lump sum order has not been dismissed. On the other hand, the intention may be to leave a husband's claim for lump sum or property adjustment orders alive for the express purpose of enabling him to recoup monies from his wife in future (see *Smith* v *McInerney* [1994] 2 FLR 1077, where the court kept open the husbands's property adjustment claims to allow him to recover from the wife the excess of the child support payments assessed by the Child Support Agency over the amount of maintenance payments which he had contracted with the wife to pay for their benefit; a similar preservation of a party's lump sum claims was made in the order made

at first instance in *Atkinson* v *Atkinson* reported within the judgment of Thorpe J at [1995] 2 FLR 356). Care should be taken to ensure that all interim orders are discharged and thereafter final orders made or claims dismissed as appropriate. It may be that a party has provided undertakings in the course of the suit (for example, not to dispose of any capital assets) and these may need to be discharged. Do not forget to include an order under the Inheritance (Provision for Family and Dependants) Act 1975, s 15 or agreements relating to it (for instance, an agreement by a wife not to make any claim of a capital nature pursuant to that Act), where appropriate.

- *Is the term of any periodical payments order intended to be extendable?* If it is not, it is critical that the order contains a direction pursuant to the Matrimonial Causes Act 1973, s 28(1A). See, for instance, *Richardson* v *Richardson* [1994] 1 FLR 286, where the omission of this direction was fatal to the husband's case that the parties had agreed to limit the wife's maintenance to a term.
- *Does it make sense?* It is as well to read through a long and complex order, particularly when it has served its time on the word processor, to ensure that it is not self-contradictory. For example, if a lump sum order has been included in a clean break order, one should not then proceed to dismiss all claims without adding words such as 'save as aforesaid'. Further, where compliance with undertakings are made a condition precedent of a clean break, care should be taken to ensure that the undertakings are not of a continuing nature. Where undertakings in this way do postpone a clean break, consider restricting the undertaker's right to apply for financial relief to recovery of what is due under the undertaking, by means of a supplementary agreement in the preamble to the order.
- *Have you inadvertently created a strict settlement?* Until the coming into force of the Trusts of Land and Appointment of Trustees Act 1996, the spectre of the Settled Land Act 1925 will appear if an 'immediate, binding trust for sale' has not been imposed by the order. For this reason, it may be a good idea to draft a deed of trust at the same time as the consent order, and to attach it to the order. For a further discussion of this topic, the reader is referred to [1987] Fam Law 43.

Are you satisfied that the consent order in the form in which it has been prepared can be enforced?
The order must clearly indicate the person upon whom the obligation is imposed. It is insufficient, for example, to ask for an order that 'the

matrimonial home known as ——————— be transferred into the name of the petitioner'. Problems of enforcement are discussed fully in Chapter 8.

Are you satisfied by the enforcement mechanisms which you have put into the consent order itself?
The wording of the order itself will be determinative of the way in which the order will be enforced. In *N* v *N* (Valuation: Charge-back Order) [1996] 1 FLR 361, Singer J considered the wording of an order made in contested ancillary relief proceedings in 1982. In the 1982 order, provision had been made to enable the wife to purchase a flat for herself subject to a charge in favour of the husband of one-fifth of the net proceeds of sale. The order provided a mechanism whereby a surveyor would be nominated by the President of the Royal Institute of Chartered Surveyors to establish the market value in the event that the wife wished to redeem the charge. The order provided that both parties were at liberty to apply generally.

In 1992, chartered surveyors were appointed to value the wife's flat in accordance with the provisions of the order, to compute the value of the husband's one-fifth charge. The husband did not accept that valuation and instructed independent surveyors. He then issued a summons seeking a ruling as to the value of the property. The district judge heard evidence as to the value of the property, determined the application, and the husband appealed her order. It was held by Singer J that the court did not have jurisdiction to consider the alternative valuations relied upon by the husband and the wife; the parties should have accepted the valuation of the surveyor appointed under the machinery provided for by the original order. The judge cast some doubt on the broad interpretation which has been put on a Court of Appeal decision in *Brent* v *Brent* (1978) 9 Fam Law 59 to the effect that there is no jurisdiction in the court to bind parties in advance to the valuation of a particular expert, as being out of tune with the strong move towards greater court intervention in ancillary relief proceedings in recent times.

Does the order for costs reflect the agreement reached?
In particular, have any orders for reserved costs been picked up. In *S* v *S* (Reserved Costs Order) [1995] 1 FLR 739, the court allowed the wife's free-standing application, following the making of a final order, that the indemnity costs order made in the final order should be extended to include the reserved costs orders made in the interlocutory stages of the case; and, in addition, that (since there had been an

oversight) the order would be amended under the slip rule to include the reserved costs. If the client is legally aided, one should not overlook the Civil Legal Aid (General) Regulations 1989, regs 96 and 97, which concern the postponement of the enforcement of the legal aid charge over money and land, where a lump sum ordered to be paid or a property ordered to be transferred is to be used for the purpose of purchasing a home for the assisted person or his dependants (*Scallon v Scallon* [1990] 1 FLR 194). The wording of the appropriate certificate is to be found in the *Practice Direction 19 August 1991* [1991] 3 All ER 896.

Has 'liberty to apply' been included in the order?
See, further, p 178.

Do you need to file a notice of acting before signing the consent order?
It is not possible to include in a work of this size precedents of all of the many types of consent orders which are commonly found in practice. A very useful set of precedents for consent orders (4th ed) is published by the Solicitors' Family Law Association and can be obtained from the Permanent Secretary, Solicitors' Family Law Association, PO Box 302, Keston, Kent, BR2 6EZ (£35 to members and £45 to non-members). These precedents were prepared following discussions with representatives of the Principal Registry and the Association of District Judges. A general purpose form of consent order is set out in Appendix 5. It is normally a good idea to check through the precedent book before completing any draft minutes, as an aide-mémoire of clauses which could conveniently be inserted in the draft.

Chapter 4

The clean break

1 Origins

The origins of the principle of the clean break can be traced back to *Mills* v *Mills* [1940] 2 All ER 254, described by the House of Lords in *Minton* v *Minton* [1979] 1 All ER 79, at 84 per Lord Scarman as 'a decision of the Court of Appeal which established the practice of the court in making consent orders'. The brief facts in *Mills* were:

> W had obtained a consent order for maintenance on 29 December 1932. H fell into arrears under the order and the parties came to terms, under which W agreed to accept a capital sum in satisfaction of all past and future claims. As a result, a further consent order was made on 9 October 1933 that H pay the agreed capital sum, that the existing consent order for maintenance be discharged and that the maintenance petition [application] be dismissed. It was a term of the order that the matter should not be reopened without the leave of the court. H's financial position subsequently improved and on 31 January 1940 W asked for leave to apply for maintenance.

Sir Wilfrid Greene MR held at 259–260:

> The original order went when it was discharged by the order of 9 October 1933. The maintenance petition was dismissed, and, from 9 October 1933, onwards, there was not in existence any order for maintenance, or any petition asking for maintenance. The slate was clean. Neither the order nor the petition remained in a state of suspended animation. They were gone. In that state of affairs, the present application, not linked up to some existing order of the court, or to some pending application made in due time, it would be hopelessly out of time under the section.

The court rejected the view that the inclusion of the words 'this matter not to be reopened without the leave of the court' merely suspended the operation of the original order of December 1932. As Sir Wilfrid Greene MR put it (at 261): 'Once the order is discharged, the jurisdiction of the court disappears'.

The Court of Appeal in *Mills* (at 259) also rejected the view that the rule in *Hyman* v *Hyman* (see pp 27 *et seq*) does not allow the parties by consent to terminate an order of the court.

The power of the court to order maintenance at the time Mills was decided was contained in the Supreme Court of Judicature (Consolidation) Act 1925, s 190, which enabled the court to exercise its powers solely 'on any decree for divorce or nullity of marriage'. By judicial interpretation 'on' was gradually extended to mean 'on or within a reasonable time thereafter'. The court's powers were, however, enlarged by the Matrimonial Causes (Property and Maintenance) Act 1958, s 1(1) which enabled the court to make maintenance orders after a decree of divorce, nullity or judicial separation 'either on pronouncing such a decree or at any time thereafter'. In reviewing the background to the clean break after the 1958 Act, Lord Scarman commented in *Minton* (at 84):

> ... once there was a decree, the jurisdiction was now without a time limit. The passage of time might influence the exercise of the court's discretion, but it could not destroy the jurisdiction.

The Court of Appeal in *L* v *L* [1961] 3 All ER 834 held that the change in the law brought about by the 1958 Act did not alter the principle established in *Mills* so as to give the court jurisdiction to entertain a fresh application by a wife who had, in pursuance of an agreement sanctioned by the court, received an agreed sum and had her application dismissed. *L* v *L* was described in *Minton* as remaining 'a decision of critical importance' as s 23(1) of the 1973 Act repeats broadly the provisions of s 1(1) of the 1958 Act. *L* v *L* was expressly approved in *Minton*.

The principle of the clean break was, as will be seen, carried forward by case law until the enactment of the Matrimonial and Family Proceedings Act 1984: the then Solicitor General, Sir Patrick Mayhew, described the object of the Act as being 'to reflect and affirm the principles which have been worked out in the courts over the last 13 years' (para 21 of his Memorandum to the House of Commons Special Standing Committee, Official Report, second sitting, Tuesday 20 March 1984). Sections 3, 5 and 6 of the 1984 Act inserted new sections 25A, 25(1A) and 31(7) respectively into the Matrimonial Causes Act 1973: all of these new provisions bear upon the clean break.

The Act was passed in the teeth of vociferous opposition from pressure groups which highlighted, for instance that

> the only protection for women is the minimum and highly subjective requirement that there be no undue hardship. The proposals assume that

men and women have equal opportunities in relation to education, training and employment' (Rights of Women);

'putting a time limit on maintenance for a spouse puts the lone parent under considerable pressure when he/she should be concentrating on bringing up children—if the clean break provision is not supposed to apply to parents with dependent children, the [Act] should say so' (Gingerbread).

2 Concept

(a) The decision in Minton

The concept of the clean break has been enshrined in modern common law in the decision of the House of Lords in *Minton* v *Minton* [1979] 1 All ER 79. The words of Lord Scarman which underline the importance of this concept have already been quoted above on p 6.

The facts of *Minton* were:

W obtained a decree of divorce in November 1971 which was made absolute in December 1972. Following negotiations, W and H reached a settlement of financial and property issues in January 1973 which was recorded in three agreements, the first two of which were embodied in consent orders made on 22 January 1973. Under the first agreement, the matrimonial home was to be conveyed to W in consideration of the payment by W to H of £10,000, H was to pay W maintenance at the rate of 5p per year 'until the matrimonial home is conveyed to [W] such payments to cease on completion of the conveyance' and no lump sum order was to be made in favour of W. The second agreement was not relevant to the appeal. Under the third agreement, which was not referred to in the consent orders but which was expressed to be 'collateral to and conditional upon the necessary court orders being made as per draft "consent orders"', W was to hand to H on completion a document stating that she waived and relinquished any or all claims in respect of maintenance in the future. The conveyance of the matrimonial home was completed and the nominal order for periodical payments came to an end. On 10 November 1976, W applied to the court to vary the order for periodical payments made under the order of 22 January 1973 by increasing the amount payable in respect of herself and the children. The judge varied the order in respect of the children but dismissed W's application in respect of herself for want of jurisdiction. The judge's decision was upheld by the Court of Appeal and the House of Lords.

The essential feature of *Minton* is that there had been no formal dismissal of the wife's claims, as had been the case in *Mills* and *L* v *L*. The broader principle was put by Lord Scarman (at 87) in this way:

Once an application has been dealt with upon its merits, the court has no future jurisdiction save where there is a continuing order capable of variation or discharge under s 31 of the Act.

(b) Matrimonial Causes Act 1973, s 25A

The statutory basis of the clean break principle is now found in s 25A (and, on variation applications, in the provisions of s 31). Section 25A(1) imposes a mandatory duty on the court, on granting a decree of divorce or nullity, to consider whether it would be appropriate to exercise its powers under ss 23(1)(*a*), (*b*) or (*c*), 24 or 24A so as to terminate the parties' financial obligations to each other as soon after the grant of decree as is just and reasonable. In similar vein, s 25A(2) imposes a duty on the court to consider limiting the term of any order for periodical payments or secured periodical payments 'for such term as would in the opinion of the court be sufficient to enable the party in whose favour the order is made to adjust without undue hardship to the termination of his or her financial dependence upon the other party'. Section 25A(3) contains the court's power to impose a clean break. It enables the court to dismiss an application for periodical payments or secured periodical payment with a direction that there shall be no further application in relation to the marriage under the Matrimonial Causes Act 1973, s 23(1)(*a*) or (*b*), if it considers that no continuing obligation should be imposed on either party to make or secure periodical payments.

There was a tendency, corrected by the Court of Appeal in the cases which we go on to consider, to elevate the s 25A considerations into 'pre-eminent' provisions of more weight than the other factors to be borne in the judicial mind pursuant to s 25. Two particular matters have therefore been stressed by the Court of Appeal:

(1) Consideration of s 25A is only *part* of the judicial function. The most significant factor in the overall equation is a further provision contained in s 25(1) (also introduced by the 1984 Act), namely the requirement that 'first consideration [be] given to the welfare while a minor or any child of the family who has not attained the age of eighteen'. Roch LJ put it in this way in *N* v *N* [1993] 2 FLR 868 at 881 E–F:

> ... where there is a child of the family who has not attained the age of eighteen, the court must consider the welfare of such a child first before any other relevant matter and the welfare of such a child will be the most important consideration, more important than any other single factor, but it will not be paramount in the sense that it can be overridden by a combination of other relevant and applicable factors.

We observe, in our analyses of the cases, how there is a tension between s 25(1) and s 25A, which has not always been easy to resolve. Indeed Butler-Sloss LJ remarked in the leading judgment in *N* v *N* that nothing that she had said about

> questions over term orders in child cases is in any way to be taken as an encouragement to wives with children not to go out and stand on their own two feet and bring to an end their financial dependency upon their former husband as soon as possible. The termination of financial dependency upon the husband is an important message from the amendments to the 1973 Act.

(2) Section 25A imposes on the court the duty to *consider* termination of financial dependency. 'Consider' is the vital word: it should not be taken to imply that a clean break should be strived for regardless of all circumstances.

The way in which the courts have interpreted these provisions is discussed on pp 93 *et seq.*

(c) Types of clean break

The term 'clean break' is used to describe a varying degree of separation of the parties' affairs. The term is generally used in the context of financial matters, although it was applied in the personal relationship between parents by Roskill LJ in *Dipper* v *Dipper* [1980] 2 All ER 722.

When financial matters are under consideration, a distinction should be made between a clean break between the parties in respect of payments for their own financial needs and between them as regards payments for the benefit of the children of the family (which actually has always as a matter of law been impossible; note in particular the provisions of the Child Support Act 1991, and see further p 103 below).

What then is meant by a clean break? There is no one exhaustive definition and the answer will depend upon how clean a clean break can be achieved in the particular circumstances. It is hoped that the following general observations may assist:

- The classic clean break is where all outstanding claims for ancillary relief of both parties are dismissed and an order made under the Inheritance (Provision for Family and Dependants) Act 1975, s 15 (see p 91).
- Care should be taken to avoid an order indicating that 'no order' has been made on the application or one omitting a formal dismissal where no substantive order has been made of a non-variable nature (see p 91).
- A *Mesher* or *Martin* order, whereby the former matrimonial home

THE CLEAN BREAK

is to be sold at some defined point in the future, does not offend against the clean break principle providing the parties' maintenance claims are dismissed (*Clutton* v *Clutton* [1991] 1 FLR 242).
- A 'postponed clean break' is achievable (see p 91).
- A clean break is possible where children are involved (see p 103).
- There can be a 'one-sided' clean break ie the claims of one party may be dismissed irrespective of whether there is a dismissal of the other party's claims (*Thompson* v *Thompson* [1988] 2 FLR 170).
- It appears to be accepted—at least at appellate level—that a nominal order is not necessarily always inconsistent with the clean break principle (see pp 96–101).

(d) Methods of effecting a clean break

The concept of the clean break depends, adopting the dictum of Lord Scarman in *Minton* referred to above, on achieving a final order which is not 'capable of variation or discharge under s 31'. As has been seen in Chapter 2, an agreement of itself cannot prevent a subsequent application to the court, especially where there are minor children involved (see, for example *Richardson* v *Richardson* (No 2) [1994] 2 FLR 1051, upheld on appeal by Balcombe LJ and May LJ on 8 December 1994, unreported). However, once a consent order has been made embodying the terms of the agreement its legal effect derives from the order and not the antecedent agreement. In this way, the policy of the clean break cannot be defeated by an application to vary a 'subsisting maintenance agreement' under the Matrimonial Causes Act 1973, s 35 (*De Lasala* v *De Lasala* [1979] 2 All ER 1146; *Thwaite* v *Thwaite* [1981] 2 All ER 789).

- *Non-variable orders*

Under s 31(1) of the 1973 Act, the court has power, *inter alia*, to vary, discharge or suspend the types of orders referred to in s 31(2). Certain orders are not mentioned in s 31(2), ie a property adjustment order (except a settlement of property or variation of settlement order following a decree of judicial separation and subject to the provisions of s 31(4)) and a lump sum order (except as to any provision for payment by instalments), and are not therefore capable of variation under s 31(1). These are final orders. However, s 31 of the 1973 Act has been prospectively amended by the Pensions Act 1995, s 166(3). These amendments came into force on 1 July 1996. A deferred lump sum order which includes provision made by virtue of s 25B(4) or s 25C of the 1973 Act (which are also inserted by the Pensions Act 1995, s 166) are included in the types of orders referred to in s 31(2). Section 25B(4) of the 1973 Act enables, *inter alia*, a deferred lump sum order to be made against the trustees or managers of a pension scheme. Section 25C of the 1973 Act deals with lump sums payable in respect of death. However, the power to vary a deferred lump sum order made under s 25C of the 1973 Act ceases to apply on the death of either of the parties to the marriage (s 31(2B) of the 1973 Act). The extension to the court's power to vary introduced by the Pensions Act 1995 enables the types of lump sum orders referred to above to be varied in any way even as to quantum. However, s 25B(3)–(7) and s 25C of the 1973 Act do not affect the powers of the court under s 31 in relation to any order made before the Pensions Act 1995, s 166 came into force on 1 July 1996 (Pensions Act 1995, s 166(6)). It is implicit therefore that s 25B(1) and (2) would affect any such order: these subsections relate to the heightened consideration to be given to pensions and the removal of the foreseeability test currently found in s 25(2)(*a*) of the 1973 Act.

The words 'lump sum or sums' used in s 23(1) of the 1973 Act do not enable the court to make successive lump sum orders (*Coleman* v *Coleman* [1972] 3 All ER 886; *Minton* v *Minton* [1979] 1 All ER 79; *Banyard* v *Banyard* [1984] FLR 64); an order relating to an interim capital payment (as in *Barry* v *Barry* [1992] 2 FLR 233 and as referred to in *F* v *F* (Ancillary Relief: Substantial Assets) [1995] 2 FLR 45 does not count as a lump sum order for this purpose; care should be taken in the drafting of a *Barry*-type order so as to avoid the lump sum claims being dismissed prematurely. The subsection 'permits only a single order which may, where appropriate, include a provision for the payment of more than one lump sum as, for instance, where one sum is paid immediately and the further sum contingently on the happening of a future event such as the falling in of a reversionary interest in an estate to which one of the parties to the marriage is entitled' (*De Lasala* v *De Lasala* [1979] 2 All ER 1146, at 1154).

In *Masefield* v *Alexander* (Lump Sum: Extension of Time) [1995] 1 FLR 100 a husband succeeded in his application on appeal that the-court had jurisdiction to extend time for the payment of a lump sum:

> A consent order had been made, by virtue of which H was to pay to W a lump sum of £100,000 on or before 1 January 1994 to enable her to purchase a property. It was agreed that if H failed to pay the lump sum on or before 1 January 1994, the former matrimonial home would be sold forthwith with the net sale proceeds being divided between the parties in certain proportions. On 31 December 1993, H applied to extend time. His application was dismissed by the district judge on 12 January 1994. On 3 February 1994 the sum of £100,000 became available and that sum together with interest was tendered to W, but was rejected. H's appeal to the High Court Judge was refused in July 1994.

Butler-Sloss LJ, giving the leading judgment, held that the court could under its inherent jurisdiction allow time to be extended for the payment of a lump sum, provided that the failure to make the lump sum payment did not strike at the heart of the order; she distinguished the cases, including *Knibb* (see below), in which a party had a 'proprietorial interest' in property as a direct result of the failure to comply with the order. In the present case, time was held not to be of the essence, and the wife was not prejudiced by the slight delay in her receipt of the lump sum.

The case is especially significant because it is authority that the court will be prepared to extend time (provided that time is not of the essence and especially where a paying party is not to blame for the delay) in consent orders just as a court would be prepared to do in an order made after a contested hearing. A court had jurisdiction by virtue of the status of the parties' agreement as a consent order. The court would have had no hesitation in exercising its inherent jurisdiction to extend time if the original order had been made after a contested hearing; the fact that this was a consent order made no difference.

The question whether the court is going to have jurisdiction to extend time will be a matter of construction of a case on its own particular facts. It is submitted that it will not always be apparent what defaults 'strike at the heart of [a] lump sum order'. It should be noted that it is irrelevant to the court's ability to interfere that the words 'liberty to apply' are inserted into the consent order.

A transfer of property order may not follow a settlement of property order made in respect of the same asset (*Carson* v *Carson* [1983] 1 All ER 478). The power to direct a sale of a property under the Matrimonial Causes Act 1973, s 24A may not be used to vary an existing property adjustment order (*Carson* v *Carson* [1983] 1 All ER 478; *Norman* v *Norman* [1983] 1 All ER 486; *Omielan* v *Omielan* [1996] 2 FLR 306). However, where a property adjustment order has been made ordering a property to be held on trust for sale with sale postponed until the youngest child of the family reaches the age of seventeen, the court may direct an earlier sale of the property under s 24A, even though it has no power to vary the substantive order, because it does have power to vary the working out of the effect of the order (*Thompson* v *Thompson* [1985] 2 All ER 243). Similarly, where, for example, a property is charged in favour of an occupying wife, an order for sale may be made under s 24A regardless of whether there was a liberty to apply provision in the original order. However, the discretion to make an order for sale will not be exercised if the consequence is the displacement of vested rights under the original order (*Taylor* v *Taylor* [1987] 1 FLR 142). Therefore, there is no power to postpone the sale of property beyond the period fixed in an original *Mesher* order (*Dinch* v *Dinch* [1987] 1 All ER 818) nor is it possible to apply under CCR Ord 13, r 4 to extend the time limit for the redemption of a charge under a property adjustment order (*Knibb* v *Knibb* [1987] 2 FLR 396; see further pp 201–203). The court has power to vary an order for sale made under s 24A by virtue of s 31(2)(*f*)—but not where the order created a settlement of property (see *Omielan*).

Section 31(5) contains an express prohibition on the making of a lump sum order or a property adjustment order on an application to vary a periodical payments or secured provision order except in the case of a lump sum order made in favour of a child. It was held in *Powys* v *Powys* [1971] 3 All ER 116 that the declared policy of the legislation should not be undermined or out-flanked by making, on an original application many years after decree and many years after the making of an order for periodical payments or secured provision, an order which could not be made on an application to vary. The purpose of the omission of lump sums from s 31 [other than as provided for by the Pensions Act 1995, s 166(3)] is to prevent two bites of the cherry, and to provide for certainty and a determination of the issues between the parties' (per Butler-Sloss LJ in *Masefield* v *Alexander* [1995] 1 FLR 100 at p 105). (This view was, however, disapproved of by the Court of Appeal in *Chaterjee* v *Chaterjee* [1976] 1 All ER 719). One means of circumventing the subsection in order to effect a clean break on a variation application is to accept an undertaking from the payer to pay a capital sum on payment of which the periodical payments order is discharged and the application for periodical payments then dismissed. This course, which can only be achieved by the consent of the payer, was approved though not adopted in *S* v *S* [1986] 3 All ER 566 (appealed not on this point [1987] 2 All ER 312) and *Boylan* v *Boylan* [1988] 1 FLR 282 (see further p 198). In *S* v *S* Waite J (as he then was) rejected the clean break figure put forward by H, and, in the course of his judgment which fixed a revised amount of maintenance for W, suggested that the appropriate clean break figure would be £400,000. The judge therefore gave liberty to H to apply to a registrar at any time within three months from the judgment for an order directing that, if H within 28 days paid W the sum of £400,000, W's periodical payments order would terminate three months after the date of payment of the said sum. In *Boylan*, Booth J was invited by counsel to indicate the appropriate clean break figure, but declined to do so until she had the benefit of detailed financial information and proper argument on quantum. The lesson from *Boylan* is clear: if arguing for a clean break, be equipped with the appropriate capitalisation figures in the way suggested on pp 110–115, below; the *Duxbury* figures contained in the FLBA's publication 'At A Glance', updated each year, and would be a good starting point). The Legal Aid Board's statutory charge will, however, attach to a capital sum paid in commutation or satisfaction of any and all of a payee's potential obligations by way of periodical payments (*Stewart* v *The Law Society* [1987] 1 FLR 223; *Watkinson* v *Legal Aid Board* [1991] 2 FLR 26). However, the potentially significant effect on a recipient's income support of a capitalised maintenance figure should be noted (*Bolstridge* v *Chief Adjudication Officer* [1993] Family Law, October 576).

Duckworth at p 334 of *Matrimonial Property & Finance* 5th ed (FT Law & Tax) highlights the co-relation of clean break and bankruptcy, with particular reference to the Insolvency Act 1986, s 339. He suggests that to this end it would assist if the arithmetical exercise adopted to capitalise the wife's periodical payments claim were set out in the recitals in circumstances where a trustee in bankruptcy might challenge a transaction at an undervalue.

In *Sandford* v *Sandford* [1986] 1 FLR 412, the wife applied for a variation of a periodical payments order, which was part of a consent order. The consent order, which followed the wife's application for a transfer of property and a periodical payments order (but not a lump sum order, a prayer for which was included in the petition), also contained a transfer of property order. When the application came before the registrar, he allowed the wife to amend it to include an application for a lump sum order. The wife was then awarded a lump sum of £50,000 and, upon the husband's failure to comply with this order, the registrar made a second transfer of property order in the wife's favour in satisfaction of the lump sum order. Ewbank J held (at first instance [1985] FLR 1056) that the original agreement embodied in the consent order had been a final settlement of the capital assets and it was no longer open to the wife to make a further application for a lump sum order. The registrar had therefore acted without jurisdiction in making both the second transfer of property and the lump sum order. It was held that this was not a case where the question of a lump sum had been left in abeyance. The fact that the wife had not previously applied for a lump sum order was not decisive. The decision of Ewbank J was upheld by the Court of Appeal. Oliver LJ commented (at 425):

> The instant case may be said to be an object-lesson in the care which ought to be, but is not always, taken in the preparation of consent orders. . . . The case does, however, underline once again the necessity which

should be clearly in the minds of solicitors and counsel alike to ensure that consent orders do truly embody beyond any equivocation what the parties are agreed upon, and should include any provisions which are consequential upon that agreement.

In order to avoid any possibility of a subsequent application for a non-variable order being made, applications for all such orders should be dismissed as part of the overall agreement, in the way discussed below, where no substantive order is made for any particular form of relief. It is also important to ensure that the wording of the order accurately reflects the understanding of the parties as to the terms of the agreement reached between them (*Dinch* v *Dinch* [1987] 1 All ER 818; *Peacock* v *Peacock* [1991] Fam Law 139).

- *Variable orders*

If the order is of a type capable of variation under s 31 (or if it is not intended to make any substantive order of a non-variable nature), it is necessary to dismiss the wife's claims as in *Mills* and *L* v *L*. Strictly speaking, only applications which have been made may be dismissed. A respondent who has not filed an answer should therefore be required to file notice in Form M11 (see Appendix 1 to the Family Proceedings Rules 1991) marked 'for dismissal purposes only' in relation to all applications to be dismissed. Similarly, care should be taken to ensure that the petition claims all the relief to be dismissed, as an application for leave to amend the petition (before decree) or for leave to file notice in Form M11 (before or after decree) cannot be entirely discounted. In the case of an application for periodical payments or secured periodical payments, it is necessary as well as dismissing the application to include in the order a direction that the applicant shall not be entitled to make any further application in relation to the marriage for an order under s 23(1)(*a*) or (*b*). This requirement for a fully effective clean break is to be found in the Matrimonial Causes Act 1973, s 25A(3). It is difficult to understand what purpose the additional direction serves; it can only be regarded as surplusage. It is submitted that the dismissal of an application for periodical payments (whether or not secured) without the requisite direction would not allow a wife to make a subsequent application for such relief. It was surely not Parliament's intention to derogate from the concept of the clean break as established in *Minton*. The authors are supported in this view by the data of Thorpe J as he then was in *Richardson* v *Richardson* (No 1) [1994] 1 FLR 286:

> to terminate rights immediately, all that is required is the order for dismissal, as the case law had clearly demonstrated since the decision in

Minton v *Minton*. What need therefore for the addition of the words 'with a direction that the applicant shall not be entitled to make any further application in relation to that marriage for an order under s 23(1)(*a*) or (*b*) above'? At present I can offer no confident answer to that question.

Lord Scarman's views on the wording of s 23(1) and (4) of the 1973 Act in *Minton* at 87 may be thought to be of some assistance:

> Thus, when the section is conferring jurisdiction in respect of children of the family, it expressly provides that orders may be made 'from time to time'. Had Parliament, when re-enacting s 1 of the 1958 Act, wished to overrule *L* v *L*, it could have added to subs (1) the words 'from time to time'. When Parliament wished to make it clear that no previous dismissal of an application or discharge or termination of an order could displace the court's powers to make maintenance orders in favour of children, it added, by subs (4) the words 'from time to time' to the words 'at any time thereafter' which it had used in subs (1). No plainer indication could be given of the intention of Parliament.
>
> For these reasons, I conclude that s 23(1) of the 1973 Act does not empower the court to make a second or subsequent maintenance order after an earlier application has been dismissed.

It is, of course, safe to adopt the wording of s 25A(3). Bush J went further in *H* v *H* [1988] 2 FLR 114 to indicate that no specific statutory authority was required to make a declaration that no further application be made under s 23(1)(*c*) or s 24.

It will be recalled that the order in *Minton* itself did not contain any formal dismissal of the wife's application. Such a situation should be avoided as should an order simply indicating that 'no order' has been made on an application. This latter type of order cannot be corrected under the slip rule. It may be possible for the respondent to the application to argue that it has the same effect at a dismissal of the application. It remains, however, needlessly ambiguous and should be avoided (*Carter* v *Carter* [1980] 1 All ER 827). A liberty to apply provision which is expressly or impliedly included in a consent order will not affect its finality. The purpose of such a provision is to give effect to the order and not to enable the substance of the order to be changed In *Masefield* v *Alexander*, Butler-Sloss LJ pointed out that even if there was provision in the consent order for liberty to apply, it begged the question whether there was jurisdiction for the court to interfere with the order; if there is otherwise no jurisdiction, the parties cannot give jurisdiction to the court (see p 179). A nominal order for periodical payments should not be included in an order where a complete clean break is intended (*Dunford* v *Dunford* [1980] 1 All ER 122) (see pp 96–101). An order may prospectively dismiss an application for periodical payments, for example, in payment of a lump sum or completion of the conveyance of the matrimonial home, and indeed this is a frequent way of ensuring a party's compliance with obligations contained in the order.

A 'postponed clean break' can be achieved by agreeing an order for periodical payments for a rehabilitative term under s 25A(2) of the 1973 Act, incorporating a direction under s 28(1A) that no application may be more under s 31 for an extension of the term specified in the order. It will, nonetheless, remain possible for the recipient of the periodical payments to apply for a variation as to quantum within the term of the order. Such a direction was described by Sir Stephen Brown P in *Waterman* v *Waterman* [1989] 1 FLR 380 as a 'Draconian prohibition' in a case involving the maintenance of a mother of a child aged five. Roch LJ in *N* v *N* [1993] 2 FLR 868 at 883B put it this way:

> It can be anticipated that it will be an exceptional case that an order for periodical payments will be limited to a term under s 28(1) where there is a child of the family who remains in the care and control of the party in whose favour the order for periodical payments is being made and who has yet to attain the age of eighteen years, and that it will only be in the most exceptional and unusual case that a direction under s 28(1A) will be made in such circumstances.

It should not therefore be added to a specific term order without careful consideration.

The authors have seen cases where, to encourage payment of the term maintenance, the *payee's* solicitors have so drafted the order that the s 28(1A) direction is only effective when the term order has been complied with.

If the practitioner does not insert a s 28(1A) direction in the order, there will be jurisdiction to enable the order to be extended. In *Richardson* v *Richardson* (No 1) [1994] 1 FLR 286, Thorpe J (as he then was) ruled that the wife was entitled to apply for an extension of her maintenance payments just before the end of the three year term which had been negotiated and contained in a consent order:

> The consent order had provided that H should pay periodical payments to W 'at the rate of £8,000 per annum payable monthly on the first day of each month commencing on 1 February 1988, such payments to cease with the payment due on 1 January 1991 and thereafter W's claims for periodical payments for herself be dismissed'. The consent order then went on to provide that 'upon compliance with the terms of this order any claim by either party for financial provision or property adjustment orders be dismissed and it is further ordered that neither party be at

liberty to claim against the estate of the other under the Inheritance (Provision for Family and Dependants) Act 1975'. On 18 December 1990, about fourteen days before the termination of the maintenance payments, W applied for a variation of the order to provide for an extension of the duration of the periodical payments. Thorpe J ruled that the outcome was 'finely balanced', but that the omission of the s 28(1A) direction was the crucial aspect of the case and that there was therefore jurisdiction to extend the maintenance term.

Thorpe J said at 293F:

> In practice the distinction as to whether an applicant is or is not to have the right to apply for an extension of the agreed finite term is often significant and the subject of hard negotiation.

The consent order litigated in *N* v *N* (above) illustrates just such a negotiation.

In *B* v *B* [1995] 1 FLR 9, Thorpe J (as he then was) allowed an application by a wife to extend maintenance beyond the seven year term provided in the consent order because:

(1) there was no s 28(1A) direction in the order, and

(2) despite an agreement between the parties that the wife would not apply for an extension, her legal advice at the time of the order had been so bad that, in view of the s 25 factors, she would be permitted to receive periodical payments extended to last for their joint lives. The case is authority that the *Camm* principles apply to consent orders just as they apply to separation agreements (and see p 32 *et seq*). If a direction under s 28(1A) is not made, an application to extend the term must be made, as in *Richardson* (No 1), prior to the end of the term, although the application may be determined after the expiration of the term (*T* v *T* (Financial Provision) [1988] 1 FLR 480). Although there is a mandatory duty imposed on every court by virtue of s 25A(2) to *consider* whether it would be appropriate to set a term to an order for periodical payments (*Suter* v *Suter and Jones* [1987] 2 FLR 232; *Whiting* v *Whiting* [1988] 2 FLR 189), there is not a presumption in favour of termination, as it is only a factor to be considered (*Barrett* v *Barrett* [1988] 2 FLR 516).

- *Inheritance (Provision for Family and Dependants) Act 1975, s 15*
In order to achieve a clean break which continues after the death of one party, the consent order should, pursuant to the Inheritance (Provision for Family and Dependants) Act 1975, s 15(1), order that neither party shall be entitled to apply on the death of the other for an order under s 2 of the 1975 Act. Such an order can be made without the consent of the other party. It is a requirement of s 15(1)

that the court must consider it just to make a s 15 order. In considering whether it is just to make an order, the court will normally be prepared to make an order as part of an overall clean break, but not usually where there is continuing periodic maintenance provision for the wife unless the unusual circumstances of the case warrant it (*H v H* [1988] 2 FLR 114). *Richardson* (No 1) was a case in which the husband had won the right in negotiation to obtain a dismissal of the wife's application against his estate under the Inheritance (Provision for Family and Dependants) Act 1975, whilst being under an obligation to pay maintenance to her. In the authors' experience, however, district judges will frequently object to making consent orders containing such a dismissal in cases where there are continuing maintenance obligations and no s 28(1A) direction. The court may also be reluctant to exclude the provisions of the Inheritance (Provision for Family and Dependants) Act 1975 where either or both parties are very elderly. It was suggested by the Court of Appeal in *Whiting* v *Whiting* [1988] 2 FLR 189 that in order to determine whether an order under s 15 of the 1975 Act would be just the court must have information as to the likely estate and claimants. It is submitted that the strict requirements of *Whiting* apply only to contested cases. Perhaps significantly, the statement of information for a consent order (Form M1 in Appendix 1 to the Family Proceedings Rules 1991) was not amended to reflect the requirements of *Whiting*.

Unless a husband has contracted out of his prospective liability under the 1975 Act in this way, his estate could face a further claim from his former wife even though a consent order has been made dismissing her claims against him during his lifetime. An attempt to limit the dismissal to capital or income claims only is unlikely to be effective, although it may have some evidential value as to the intentions of the parties. Even where the consent order does not contain an order under s 15 of the 1975 Act, the former wife may find that an unsuccessful application for financial provision out of the estate could place her at risk as to costs (*Re Fullard, deceased* [1981] 2 All ER 796).

Where it has not been possible to achieve a s 15 order, a testator may leave with his will a memorandum, which will be admissible as evidence under the Inheritance (Provision for Family and Dependants) Act 1975, s 21, explaining why no provision has been made for a (former) spouse which the court may then take into account under s 3 of the 1975 Act in the event of an application for reasonable financial provision from the estate.

(e) Interpretation by the courts
The burden of proof in establishing that a clean break has been effected lies on the person alleging a clean break (*Brown* v *Kirrage* (1980) 11 Fam Law 141). Where a consent order is silent as to a particular type of provision, the court will regard such a claim as outstanding, unless the order on its true construction was intended to put an end to the claims of either party (*Harrison* v *Harrison* (1983) 13 Fam Law 20; *Carson* v *Carson* [1983] 1 All ER 478; *Sandford* v *Sandford* [1986] 1 FLR 412). An order of the court is required; a statement made in open court is unsatisfactory (*Ross* v *Ross* [1950] 1 All ER 654; cf *Wright* v *Wright* [1970] 3 All ER 209). It should be made absolutely clear that a clean break is intended (*Empson* v *Empson* (1979) 10 Fam Law 209).

A spate of decisions relating to the clean break followed immediately in the wake of *Minton*. The majority of these concerned whether a clean break could be effected without the applicant's consent (*Dunford* v *Dunford* [1980] 1 All ER 122; *Carter* v *Carter* [1980] 1 All ER 827; *Dipper* v *Dipper* [1980] 2 All ER 722). In *Dipper*, it was held that the court had no power to dismiss an application for periodical payments, unless the applicant consented. This decision has now been overruled by s 25A of the 1973 Act, which imposes upon the court, when granting a decree of divorce or nullity, a duty to consider whether it would be appropriate to exercise its powers under ss 23(1)(*a*), (*b*) or (*c*), 24 or 24A so as to effect the clean break. The court has the power to dismiss the claim of one party for financial relief and at the same time make an order in respect of another party (*Thompson* v *Thompson* [1988] 2 FLR 170).

In *Jessel* v *Jessel* [1979] 3 All ER 645, it was held that the concept of the clean break did not apply where the wife accepted an agreed level of periodical payments 'until further order' and 'in settlement of all her claims to periodical payments', undertaking 'not to apply to increase the [husband's] liability'. Such an order was a continuing order capable of variation (or discharge or suspension) under s 31. The use of the words 'in settlement of her claims to periodical payments' did not in the circumstances make the order final. The power given to the court by s 31 to vary 'any provision' in the order included the wife's promise not to ask for more. However, clauses such as that used in *Jessel* may still be of some evidential value on the *Edgar* principle (see Chapter 2, p 30) when the court comes to decide what variation should be made. The reason why Thorpe J was prepared to allow the wife in *Richardson* (No 1) to extend the term of periodical payments, in spite of the wording of the consent order, and her apparent agreement not to do so, was the existence of minor children, failing which the wife might have been held to the *Edgar* principle.

A suitable form of wording which might be incorporated in a consent order by way of recital would be:

AND UPON the petitioner/respondent recording his/her intention not to seek variation of the [nominal order] for maintenance for himself/herself hereinafter appearing save in the event of severe need/for a period of —— years from the making of these orders.

We have seen how the Court of Appeal in *N* v *N* (above) disapproved of such an intention being recorded in a side letter where there were minor children of the family.

There were *obiter dicta* in *Jessel* (at 649 per Brown LJ and at 651 per Lane LJ; cf, however, at 647 per Lord Denning MR) which tended to suggest that the words 'in settlement of all her claims to periodical payments' might be caught by s 34 (see Chapter 2, p 28). It is submitted, however, that s 34 has no application to an agreement which is subsequently incorporated into a consent order (*Russell* v *Russell* [1956] 1 All ER 466; *L* v *L* [1961] 3 All ER 834). In any event, even if an agreement contains a provision which purports to 'restrict any right to apply to a court for an order containing financial arrangements' and is thereby pursuant to s 34(1)(*a*) void, the very fact that the provision is agreed will carry substantial weight with the court.

> Such provision is evidence of the states of mind and the intentions of the parties at the moment the agreed maintenance order was made, and could and should, therefore, be taken into account by a court hearing a variation application under s 31 (*N* v *N* [1993] 2 FLR 868 at 880G–H).

The rule in *Hyman*, which was the common law predecessor of s 34, is not inconsistent with the concept of the clean break established in *Minton*, as applied in *Jessel*. As Lord Scarman put it at 85:

> *Hyman* v *Hyman* was concerned only with the effect of an agreement which purported to oust the jurisdiction of the court. It is no authority as to the extent of the court's jurisdiction. That question must depend on the true construction of the statute conferring the jurisdiction.

The concept of the clean break was applied by the Privy Council in *De Lasala* v *De Lasala* [1979] 2 All ER 1146. This was an appeal from the Court of Appeal of Hong Kong where the legislation in respect of financial provision on divorce was in the same terms as the relevant English legislation. An attempt was, however, made to distinguish *Minton* on the basis that, when the original consent order was made on 23 May 1970 dismissing the wife's application for relief, the Hong Kong court did not have power to make a transfer of property or settlement of property order. This jurisdiction was conferred in 1972, but the Privy Council rejected the argument that the enlargement of the powers of the court conferred on it a brand new jurisdiction additional to and distinct from the previous jurisdiction which it had exercised when it dismissed the wife's application for financial provision. The fact that the court's powers were not the same at the date of the dismissal of the wife's original application as at the date of her fresh application (as was the case in *Minton*) did not mean that the court would exercise its new jurisdiction notwithstanding the fact that the court's previous jurisdiction had been exhausted. As Lord Diplock put it at 1154:

> In *Minton* v *Minton* the House of Lords decided that the policy of the English legislation, to which effect was given by the language which has been cited above, was to permit parties to a marriage that had irreparably broken down, to make a 'clean break' also as respects financial matters from which there could be no going back. The means provided for achieving this result were for the parties to agree on a once and for all financial settlement between them and to obtain the court's approval to it and an order of the court either of a once and for all type or dismissing the parties' claims to any court order against one another for financial relief. The House of Lords decision as to the policy and effect of the English legislation was not confined to the current 1973 Act, or to the Acts which were consolidated by it. It applied to all preceding Acts of Parliament dating back to 1958 in which similar wording had been used, as is shown by the House's express approval of *L* v *L*. In their Lordships' view the grant to the court of power in 1972 to make the two new kinds of orders did no more than enlarge the ways in which the court could exercise the jurisdiction it already had to order one spouse to make a once and for all financial provision for the other. The difference between a lump sum order which the court already had power to make and a property transfer order that it acquired power to make in 1972 is the difference between providing money and money's worth. The finality of the break effected by the consent order dismissing the wife's application for financial relief cannot in their Lordships' view be prejudiced by the courts having acquired at some later date a power to make once and for all orders for financial provision of kinds which were not available at the time that the 'final break' which the court then approved was made.

It was further held in *De Lasala* that a deed of arrangement and annexed trust deeds, upon which the consent order was based, did not constitute a subsisting 'maintenance agreement' within the meaning of s 35 (see Chapter 2, p 28) and therefore were not capable of variation under that section. Once the deed of arrangement and trust deeds had been made the subject of a consent order they derived their legal effect from the court order and not from the agreement of the parties. Where terms of the order remain executory, enforcement is by summons under the order pursuant to the liberty to apply provision rather than by action between the parties.

What can best be described as a 'delayed' clean break was achieved in *Brown* v *Brown* (1980) FLR 322:

> An agreement had been reached between H and W in May 1972. The agreement, which represented a clean break, had never been incorporated into a court order. In August 1976, W applied for periodical payments, a lump sum order and a transfer of property order, undertaking not to enforce the agreement of May 1972 if granted such relief. H restored for hearing a summons issued in 1974 for an order in the terms of the agreement backdated to decree nisi. The agreement of May 1972 was reached after the matrimonial legislation of 1970 but before the clarification of its effect given by the Court of Appeal in *Wachtel* in February 1973. The Court of Appeal in *Brown* upheld the decision of the court below to make an order in the terms of the agreement of May 1972 on the grounds that it had been entered into on the basis of what was good legal advice at the time and would have been approved by the court.

The moral of the story is clear: where a clean break is intended an order should be made sooner rather than later.

The statutory codification of the clean break by the Matrimonial and Family Proceedings Act 1984 led to popular expectations of the end of the 'wife's meal ticket for life'. An early example of judicial expression of this view is found in *Harmon* v *Glencross* [1986] 2 FLR 241, where Balcombe LJ indicated that a clean break is to be favoured 'wherever possible'. However, this does not create a presumption that periodical payments should be terminated as soon as possible, unless the wife can show some good reason to the contrary (*M* v *M* [1987] 2 FLR 1; *Barrett* v *Barrett* [1988] 2 FLR 516). What is 'undue hardship' is to be considered in relation to the standard of living previously enjoyed by the wife (*Boylan* v *Boylan* [1988] 1 FLR 282; *Hepburn* v *Hepburn* [1989] 1 FLR 373).

A substantial body of case law has built up since the introduction of s 25A on the application of the clean break principle in variation applications, in certain instances where the payee has commenced cohabitation after the making of the consent order. It has been argued (see *Walsh* [1989] Fam Law 158–59) that the jurisdiction of the court under the Matrimonial Causes Act 1973, s 31 is different from that under s 25A. It is suggested there that strictly there is no power to be found in s 31 to impose a clean break nor make a limited term order which is capable of extension on a variation application. Section 31(7) sets out the matters to which the court is to have regard on a variation application; the court is required to consider whether it is appropriate to make a limited term order which will in the opinion of the court be sufficient to enable the party in whose favour the order is made to adjust without undue hardship to the termination of the payments (s 31(7)(*a*)). However, the court is able to achieve the same effect under s 31 because s 31(1) contains a power to order an immediate discharge of a periodical payments order (thereby achieving the same effect as s 25A(3)) and s 31(10) enables the court to direct that a discharge order shall not take effect until a future date (thereby achieving the same effect as a s 28(1A) direction). In *Hepburn* v *Hepburn* [1989] 1 FLR 373 Butler-Sloss LJ derives the power to impose a clean break on a variation application from the power to make an immediate discharge order in s 31(1), whereas in *Whiting* v *Whiting* [1988] 2 FLR 189 the power to achieve a clean break on a variation application is treated as being implied in s 31(7). In *Richardson* v *Richardson* (No 2) [1994] 2 FLR 1051, Thorpe J made a direction pursuant to s 28(1A) in relation to the wife's application for an extension of her periodical payments order pursuant to s 31. As has been seen, this order was upheld by the Court of Appeal. The authors respectfully agree that the s 28(1A) direction can be imposed in the course of variation applications. It would appear there is no practical difference in this context between the jurisdictions exercised by the court in originating and variation applications.

Before reviewing the body of case law referred to above, it is worth reflecting on the extent to which these cases reflect any departure from the generally perceived ascendance of the clean break principle and the day-to-day practice of district judges sitting in the divorce county courts. One could be tempted at first glance to take the view that a substantial erosion of the clean break principle is in the course of taking place. However, it is submitted that these decisions must be set against the limited basis on which the Court of Appeal is entitled to intervene. In order to justify intervention, the Court of Appeal must be satisfied that the decision of the court below was plainly wrong (*Bellenden* v *Satterthwaite* [1948] 1 All ER 343; *G* v *G* [1985] FLR 894). In *Whiting*, all three judges felt that a clean break was appropriate. However, it was only Balcombe LJ who felt that the judge's decision was so plainly wrong as to justify the court's intervention. The available statistics bear out the fact that the majority of maintenance orders for a spouse are dismissed or made for a fixed term rather than continuing *ad infinitum*. In the county courts during the course of

1993, 10,082 applications were dismissed and 8,351 orders were made for a fixed term; continuing maintenance orders were made in 8,964 cases (Judicial Statistics Annual Report for 1993, Lord Chancellor's Department).

First in the line of cases was *Morris* v *Morris* [1985] FLR 1176, which is discussed on p 212. Then in *Ashley* v *Blackman* [1988] 2 FLR 278, Waite J had to consider in the case of parties of limited means the inter-relation of the mandatory consideration of the clean break objective in variation cases and the principle in *Barnes* v *Barnes* [1972] 3 All ER 872 that regard should not be had to the availability of state benefits, unless any maintenance order made would render a husband's income inadequate to meet his proper financial commitments. Waite J found that there was no legislative inconsistency between the two principles. Both should be borne in mind so that (at 284):

> The devious or the feckless husband will still be prevented from throwing his proper maintenance obligations upon the state. The genuine struggler, on the other hand, will be spared the burden of having to pay to his former spouse indefinitely the last few pounds that separate him from total penury. Between those two extremes there will be ample opportunity for flexible orders which give proper weight to both heads of policy, including in suitable cases a use of the phased or tapered termination process over a period of time which the amended version of s 31(7) of the 1973 Act appears to contemplate.

In the event, Waite J ordered on the variation application, which was the subject of the appeal before him, an immediate discharge of the wife's periodical payments.

Next came *Whiting*. There, a consent order had been made at the time of the divorce in 1975 for periodical payments in favour of the wife. When she had undergone training, the wife became financially independent and in 1979 a further consent order was made reducing her periodical payments to a nominal amount. The husband was made redundant in 1983 and subsequently applied, *inter alia*, for an order discharging the nominal periodical payments order under s 31(7). At the time of the application, the husband was aged fifty-three and earned £4,358 per annum, whereas the wife, who was aged forty-eight, earned £10,500 per annum. The husband, however, had greater capital resources than the wife, and had a higher pension expectation. The registrar dismissed the husband's application and, on appeal, the judge upheld his decision on the ground that the nominal periodical payments order should continue as a 'last backstop'. A majority of the Court of Appeal upheld the judge's decision.

It was held that the statutory obligation under s 31(7) did not impose upon the court an obligation to vary an order and impose a clean break, unless there were adequate reasons for doing so. In *Whiting*, it was conceded that the judge in the court below had considered s 31(7). Once the subsection had been considered, the discretion conferred was a very wide one and it could not be said that its exercise had been plainly wrong. Balcombe LJ (at 200) dissented from this view holding that to make mutual orders for periodical payments in nominal amounts just in case something should happen to either party was to negate entirely the principle of the clean break. Slade LJ added *obiter* (at 204) that the consideration of the clean break principle required by both ss 25A and 31(7) must be real and substantial and the easier course of declining to order a clean break might not in all cases be the right one. (The husband intended to pursue the appeal to the House of Lords, but, in the event, for costs reasons he did not do so.)

The favouring of the clean break by Balcombe LJ, and his specific approach in this case, has been the flavour of post-*Whiting* decisions. It won the endorsement of Thorpe J, for example, in *H* v *H* (Financial Provision) [1993] 2 FLR 35. This was a variation application, where the parties were both age fifty-nine, the wife was relatively affluent, and the husband far from so: the judge ruled that, in effect:

> enough was enough ... [it was] ... appropriate and right to apply a clean break solution to these parties at this stage of their lives in disposing of the applications ...

Thorpe J said that; although Balcombe LJ's judgment in Whiting was:

> a dissenting judgment, the statement of principle that it contains survives the difference of view on outcome. I am in no doubt that I should regard myself as properly directed by that passage.

The outcome in *Whiting* was applied by the Court of Appeal in *Hepburn*. In *Hepburn*, there was a divorce in 1980 after a ten-year marriage. A consent order was made giving the wife periodical payments of £6,500 per annum and a lump sum equal to half the value of the matrimonial home, with which she bought another house. During 1980, another man moved in with the wife. From that time, they lived together as man and wife and were involved in a number of business transactions together for which the wife advanced a substantial sum of money. In February 1987, the parties made cross-applications for a variation of the periodical payments order, the wife asking for them to be increased and the husband applying for them to be discharged because of the wife's cohabitation. The registrar discharged the wife's order and the judge on appeal substituted a nominal order. The Court of Appeal dismissed the husband's appeal against the nominal order concluding that the judge below had paid due regard to the Matrimonial Causes Act 1973, s 31(7) by taking into account, *inter alia*, the wife's cohabitation without equating it to remarriage. Butler-Sloss LJ did not share the view that nominal orders were a hangover from a previous period and undesirable. The Court of Appeal felt that a court should not pressurise a former wife to regularise her position with another man so that he would assume a husband's obligation towards her (for a more recent judicial pronouncement that cohabitation does not equate to marriage (whilst still being a factor to be taken into account) see *Atkinson* v *Atkinson* [1995] 2 FLR 356). The further question which exercised the court's mind was whether, applying the s 31(7) criteria, the wife had had sufficient time to adjust to the termination of her maintenance payments. It should again be stressed that both judges in *Hepburn* felt constrained to dismiss the appeal because they could not say that the judge in the court below was plainly wrong in the exercise of his discretion.

In *Fisher* v *Fisher* [1989] 1 FLR 423, the wife had a child by another man, from whom she was unable to obtain financial support for the child, shortly after the making of a consent order for periodical payments in favour of herself and a child of the marriage. Six years later, the wife applied to vary the periodical payments for herself and her son by increasing both to keep pace with inflation. The husband made a cross-application seeking the discharge or alternatively the reduction of the periodical payments to the wife on the basis of the clean break provisions introduced by the Matrimonial and Family Proceedings Act 1984. The registrar varied the original consent order by increasing the payments to the wife and her son and the husband's appeal from that order was dismissed. The Court of Appeal reaffirmed that the purpose of the 1984 amendments was to discourage in cases of marriage of short duration, particularly where no children were involved, orders for periodical payments which were colloquially known as 'meal tickets for life', and the court referred to the 'gradual but progressive effort on the part of the supported spouse'. But it dismissed the appeal, rejecting the husband's argument that under s 31(7) neither party was entitled to rely on any reduction of earning capacity which had occurred because of circumstances within that party's control, ie in the present case, the birth to the wife of another child. The Court of Appeal held that there was nothing in either s 25A or s 31(7) to restrict the wide-ranging discretion of the court so long as the considerations in the sections were given due weight. To ignore the existence of the wife's illegitimate child would be to fail to comply with the express requirement of s 31(7) to take into account all the circumstances.

Further examples of the interpretation of the courts of the clean break principle will be found in the following discussion of when a clean break may be suitable.

3 Suitability

(a) Advantages

A clean break between parties has become increasingly widely used as a means of resolving financial disputes, although the third party involvement of the Child Support Agency and the Department of Social Security, and their ability to pursue a husband despite the existence of a private agreement in a consent order reached with his wife may diminish the popularity of a clean break in some circumstances (see further pp 103–105) (see the Child Support Act 1991 and the Social Security Administration Act 1992 ss 100 and 107; in respect of the latter, refer, for instance, to p 201 of Duckworth, *Matrimonial Property and Finance* 5th ed (FT Law & Tax)).

Brandon J summarised the advantages of effecting a clean break where the wife has a subsisting maintenance entitlement in *Powys* v *Powys* [1971] 3 All ER 116, at 127 in this way:

> A lum sum payment [of a greater amount on the footing that it is in full and final settlement of all the wife's claims] might, in the long run be of advantage to both parties. From the wife's point of view it would enable her to plan her future on a firm basis with clearly defined capital resources of her own. It would also protect her entirely in the event of her remarriage, although potential gain to her in this respect would have to be taken into account, along with other factors, in arriving at the proper amount. From the husband's point of view, it might well be to his advantage to dispose finally, by a single capital payment, of all his obligations to the wife. In particular, he would be relieved of the need to face from time to time in the future further applications for variation by the wife, with all the trouble and costs necessarily involved in them.

A clean break therefore offers to a *wife* the prospect of economic independence free from the prospect of future variation applications and problems of enforcement. The wife must, however, consider the effect of the capital which she is to receive upon her eligibility for income support and the effect of the Legal Aid Board's statutory charge on the sum recovered (*Hanlon* v *The Law Society* [1980] 2 All ER 199; *Stewart* v *The Law Society* [1987] 1 FLR 223; *Watkinson* v *Legal Aid Board* [1991] 2 FLR 26 (see p 87)). Care must be taken that the lump sum to be paid to the wife is prudently invested and that the sum that she receives is sufficient to satisfy her financial requirements. The authors can vouch for the fact that there is no lack of banks, merchant banks and finance houses ready, willing and able to invest capital for a wife in such a situation. It is recommended practice, before settling on any clean break capital figure, to obtain the opinion of such an institution on a certain lump sum being likely to suffice for the payee's maintenance requirements; in our experience finance houses often consider that the presumptions set out in the *Duxbury* Tables in 'At A Glance' are unrealistic.

In variation applications wives have often prayed in aid of their applications that the capital which they received at the time of the first hearing has been unsuccessfully invested; this did not prove to be of much help to the appellants in, for instance, *N* v *N* (above) and *Richardson* (No 2) (above) (in both of which cases s 28(1A) directions were made).

Particular care is required where the amount of lump sum is dependent upon the sale price of the former matrimonial home or other property, especially during times of falling or uncertain property prices. Indeed this would be a prime example of when the solicitor should write to the client warning him or her of the problem inherent in such a calculation of the lump sum. It may be appropriate in such circumstances to provide for the wife to receive a specified lump sum or a percentage of the net proceeds of sale of the property, whichever is the greater (see eg *Hope-Smith* v *Hope-Smith* [1989] 2 FLR 56 discussed on p 152).

To the *husband*, a clean break offers certainty and, as to the wife, freedom from the prospect of variation applications. The husband must carefully consider the wife's prospect of remarriage and inquire of the wife's solicitors whether she had any present intention of remarriage (*Cook* v *Cook* [1988] 1 FLR 521); *Chaudhuri* v *Chaudhuri* [1992] 2 FLR 73 (where the former wife remarried some fourteen months after the consent order and the husband unsuccessfully applied for the consent order to be set aside) is a case in point. He must consider whether he is prepared to forego the limited tax relief obtainable on an order for periodical payments. He cannot ignore the effect on his own capital position of paying or raising the lump sum required to be paid to the wife, particularly should his circumstances deteriorate after the clean break has been effected.

In conclusion, both parties should be aware that unforeseen circumstances may arise following the making of the consent order which could fundamentally alter the basis upon which the order was made. Whether these circumstances justify a reconsideration of the original terms of the order will depend upon a number of factors laid down by the House of Lords in *Barder* v *Barder* [1987] 2 FLR 480. (See further Chapter 5, p 146.)

(b) Children
We have seen that the concept of the clean break should not be applied where there are children whose interests will be adversely affected. The court is specifically directed when exercising its powers as to ancillary relief to regard the first, but not the paramount, consideration as being the welfare of any minor children of the family (Matrimonial Causes Act 1973, s 25(1)). This is not to say that a clean break can never be effected where there are children. Indeed, in *Minton* there were four surviving children. It is rather that a father cannot achieve finality in relation to his obligations to his children. Lord Scarman put it in *Minton* (at 88) in this way:

> I would not deny the court power, where it thinks just, to achieve finality as between spouses (children are a different matter) unless compelled to do so by clear enactment.

When one speaks of children in the context of a clean break, there are two distinguishable situations. First, as will be seen, it may be appropriate for there to be a clean break as between the parties notwithstanding the existence of children. Secondly, whether or not spousal maintenance is a live issue, attempts may be made to limit the husband's liability for child maintenance to a nominal amount (for a specific period) by means of a recital by the wife recording her intention not to make any variation application. This cannot displace the court's power to make a subsequent order, but may be of limited evidential value. An agreement to limit child maintenance to a fixed sum is void as being contrary to public policy (*Bennett* v *Bennett* (1976) *The Times*, 24 March). The effectiveness of this second situation has been drastically curtailed by the Child Support Act 1991, by virtue of which, as has been seen in Chapter 5, a jurisdiction relating to child maintenance is largely vested in the Child Support Agency. It is impossible in such cases successfully to curtail a wife's or indeed a child's ability to apply for child maintenance.

Attention has already been drawn above on p 89 to the observations made by Lord Scarman in *Minton* at 87 emphasising that the court's powers in relation to children were exercisable under s 23(4) 'from time to time'. This wording indicates that no previous dismissal of an application or discharge of an order in respect of a child could displace the court's powers to make a subsequent order in favour of that child. No financial provision order and no order for transfer of property should, however, be made in favour of a child who has reached eighteen, save where the child was continuing to receive education or there were special circumstances to justify the making of the order (Matrimonial Causes Act 1973, s 29(1) and (3); see para 2(1) of Sched 1 to the Children Act 1989; *Kiely* v *Kiely* [1988] 1 FLR 248). There may, however, be particular circumstances where it is appropriate to order a lump sum for the benefit of children in effect as a substitute for periodical payments. However, this should only be done after due regard to the Matrimonial Causes Act 1973, s 25 (*Griffiths* v *Griffiths* [1985] Fam Law 88; *Kiely* v *Kiely*).

The cases which have been decided under Sched 1 to the Children Act 1989 have followed the principle set out in cases decided under the Matrimonial Causes Act 1973 that a lump sum should not, as a matter of principle, be paid as a 'windfall' to children under the age of eighteen (see, for example, *A* v *A* (A Minor: Financial Provision) [1994] 1 FLR 657 and *T* v *S* [1994] 2 FLR 883). In both cases, the court created trusts for the benefit of the children until they attained independence, whereupon the trust capital would revert to the settlor.

The authors consider that *Crozier* v *Crozier* [1994] 2 WLR 444 effectively puts the lid on the chances of success of any appeal out of time against an old consent order made on the basis of a 'clean break' relating to children. The Child Support Act 1991 was held not to constitute a 'new event' within the *Barder* principle (see p 159).

As to the future, clean break orders in the type of circumstances mentioned above where there is or is likely to be a reliance upon income support should be avoided. This is likely to lead to an increase in the making of *Mesher* orders or transfers with a charge-back in favour of a non-occupying spouse in either case with continuing maintenance. (This is ironic given the unpopularity of *Mesher* orders in the late 1980s, and the judicial concern expressed about 'chickens coming home to roost', when the former matrimonial home had to be sold on the children attaining the age of eighteen.) Indeed, this approach may become more prevalent in cases which do not involve income support. The Child Support Act 1991 has led to increases in the levels of child maintenance. If there has to be a clean break, consideration should be given to the possibility of a charge back in favour of the father to secure sums payable by him at the instigation of the Department of Social Security under either the 1991 or 1992 Act. (The authors have experience of consent orders containing such provisions which have been allowed by district judges since the introduction of the Child Support Act 1991.) The only alternative would appear to be to leave extant the husband's claim for a lump sum order, which would defeat the whole object of a clean break. We have seen how, in *Smith* v *McInerney* [1994] 2 FLR 1077, the court kept open the husband's claim for property adjustment for the express purpose of allowing the husband to recover such sums as he would have to pay pursuant to a Child Support Act assessment. Thorpe J was insistent that the property adjustment order could only be left open for the purpose of recovering the amount of the assessment—this was the limit of the claim that the husband would be able to make; it was therefore only a 'chink' in the clean break so far as the wife was concerned.

A clean break may be appropriate where the intention is to remove the cause of serious dispute between the parties, thus promoting the welfare of the children (*S* v *S* [1987] 1 FLR 71). Indeed, it has been said to be the duty of the courts in all cases to consider whether it is appropriate to make a clean break order even in cases where there are dependant children (*Suter* v *Suter and Jones* [1987] 2 FLR 232; *Waterman* v *Waterman* [1989] 1 FLR 380). Ewbank J in *C* v *C* (Financial Provision) [1989] 1 FLR 11 went so far as to say, in a case which involved one minor child 'I have to say in my judgment that for a young or middle-aged wife in possession of substantial capital the idea of periodical payments for life is largely obsolescent'. He dismissed the wife's maintenance claims at a time which coincided with her child's eighteenth birthday. Decisions predating the Matrimonial and Family Proceedings Act 1984 such as *Pearce* v *Pearce* (1980) 1 FLR 261 and *Moore* v *Moore* (1981) 11 Fam Law 109 now have to be read with the mandatory duty imposed by the Matrimonial Causes Act 1973, s 25A in mind.

At the top end of the financial spectrum, the Court of Appeal decided in *Preston* v *Preston* [1982] 1 All ER 41 (Brandon LJ dissenting at 56–57) that it was proper with the wife's consent to provide for the maintenance of the youngest child in the wife's lump sum order and not to make any separate order for periodical payments for him because of the very large resources which would be available to the wife under the lump sum order. Such an approach accorded with the parties' wish for a clean break. The husband would not be disentitled from having a say in the child's upbringing and education. The wife would still be entitled to seek periodical payments on the child's behalf in the event of financial catastrophe supervening. At the time when *Preston* was decided, a separate order for periodical payments for a child attracted substantial tax relief. This fact did not, however, override the desirability of avoiding further applications to the court or further negotiations regarding the child's maintenance. It is difficult to see the scope for this kind of order being made now in the light of the Child Support Act 1991.

(c) Insufficient resources
It has been held that there can be no clean break where the financial resources of the parties were insufficient. As Ormrod LJ put it in *Moore* v *Moore* (1981) 11 Fam Law 108, the practice of the court was to be realistic so as not to penalise the husband, but to ensure that his liabilities would be discharged. This can be seen as part of the view taken by the courts that a man should not be able to cast his financial obligations towards his family upon the state (and coincides with the Goverment's objectives in introducing the Child Support Act 1991). However, these remarks must now be read in the light of the objective found in the Matrimonial Causes Act 1973, s 25A to effect a clean break wherever appropriate.

In *Tandy* v *Tandy* (1986) CA Transcript No 929, Waite J reflected this shift in thinking:

> There will be circumstances in which fairness to one side demands, and to the other side permits, a severance of the maintenance tie in cases where no capital resources are available.

Waite J in *Ashley* v *Blackman* [1988] 2 FLR 278 (at 284) further expressed his views in the following way:

> No humane society could tolerate—even in the interests of saving its public purse—the prospect of a divorced couple of acutely limited means remaining manacled to each other indefinitely by the necessity to return at regular intervals to court for no other purpose than to thrash out at public expense the precise figure which one should pay the other ...

This view has been reinforced by that expressed by Ward J in the Court of Appeal in *Delaney* v *Delaney* [1990] 2 FLR 457, at 462:

> This court is entitled, as the authority of *Stockford* v *Stockford* [1982] 3 FLR 58 makes clear, to approach the case upon a basis that if, having regard to the reasonable financial commitments undertaken by the husband with due regard to the contribution properly made by the lady with whom he lives, there is unsufficient left properly and fully to maintain the former wife and children, then the court may have regard to the

fact that in proper cases social security benefits are available to the wife and children of the marriage; that having such regard, the court is enabled to avoid making orders which would be financially crippling to the husband. Benefits are available to this family of which the judge was not made aware, and I have come to the conclusion that the husband cannot reasonably be expected to contribute at all to the maintenance of his previous family without financially cripplng himself. In my judgment, it is far better that the spirit of effecting a clean break and starting with a fresh slate by implemented in this case, not by dismissing the claims of the wife and the children, but by acknowledging that now and it is likely, in the foreseeable future, he will not be able to honour the obligations he has recognised towards his children . . .

The shift in judicial thinking is reflected by the graphic words of Ward J, at 461:

> Whilst this court deprecates any notion that a former husband and extant father may slough off the tight skin of familial responsibility and may slither into and lose himself in the greener grass on the other side, nonetheless this court has proclaimed and will proclaim that it looks to the realities of the real world in which we live, and that among the realities of life is that there is a life after divorce.

Delaney was followed in *E* v *C* (Child Maintenance) [1990] 1 FLR 472, which was a husband's appeal against a child maintenance order. The judge held that the father, who was on benefit, had a new family and new resources, should not be the subject of a crippling order.

Indeed *C* v *C* (Financial Provision: Personal Damages) [1995] 2 FLR 171 illustrates how it may be to the advantage of a spouse who is in receipt of benefit to have a clean break imposed and the maintenance claims dismissed. In this case the court declined to make a periodical payments order in favour of the wife, and instead imposed a clean break, because the effect of any periodical payments order would have been to deprive her of the 'passport benefits' such as payment of council tax which she did not have to pay whilst she was in receipt of benefit.

(d) Short marriages

As has already been observed, the court's powers under s 25A are now such as to be able to impose a clean break in appropriate cases. Whilst the aim of this chapter is to consider circumstances in which a clean break may be the subject of a consent order, the power of the court to impose a clean break may well influence the order which is eventually agreed. The reduction of the time restriction for the presentation of a divorce petition from a discretionary bar within three years of marriage to an absolute bar within the first year of marriage has resulted in a greater number of petitions being issued in the very early stages of marriage. Such cases may be well suited to a clean break order being made, unless there are children or the wife is unable to work or there are any special features to the case. For example the age of the parties may make a clean break solution impracticable. If the wife is unable to work at the time of the divorce, a limited term maintenance order under s 25A(2) of the 1973 Act for a rehabilitative period (with or without a s 28(1A) direction) may be suitable, whilst the wife retrains or until a young child becomes of school age. In *Attar* v *Attar* (No 2) [1985] FLR 653, the wife, who had given up a good job on marriage, was awarded a lump sum amounting to two years' salary at the rate she was earning before marriage after a marriage of six months to enable her to readjust. In *Hedges* v *Hedges* [1991] 1 FLR 196, after a four and a half year marriage, the Court of Appeal dismissed an appeal against an order for periodical payments for a period of eighteen months. The order would enable her to adjust to the current situation and to allow her to find work of reasonable remuneration. A clean break would provide an incentive to the wife to make a new life for herself in her new surroundings and circumstances without causing her 'undue hardship'. A useful review of the case law on financial provision in the case of short marriages is to be found in Duckworth, *Matrimonial Property and Finance* 5th ed (FT Law & Tax), 256–262.

(e) Long separations
Another situation where a clean break may be suitable, whether imposed by the court under s 25A or under a consent order, is where parties have been separated for a lengthy period before the wife brings a claim for financial provision. In *Twiname* v *Twiname* [1992] 1 FLR 29, the wife applied for increased maintenance and a lump sum order twenty-eight years after the parties were divorced. The Court of Appeal held that there is no time limit preventing an application being made many years after the divorce. An indication was, however, given that a clean break would be appropriate in a case such as this. The case law where there has been a lapse of time in the bringing of the wife's application is reviewed in Duckworth, *Matrimonial Property and Finance* 5th ed (FT Law & Tax) 287–291.

(f) Need
The circumstances of the case may be such as to dictate that the needs of the wife in terms of accommodation are such that the only solution is to order an absolute transfer of the matrimonial home to her

on the basis of a clean break. *Seaton* v *Seaton* [1986] 2 FLR 398 is an example. The court should not, however, make orders which reflect unrealistically the expectations of a spouse's capacity for economic independence (*M* v *M* (Financial Provision) [1987] 2 FLR 1).

(g) Conduct
It will be unusual for conduct alone to form the basis of *agreeing* a clean break. However, approaching a consent order with the court's powers under s 25A in mind, a clean break may be suitable where the husband's/wife's conduct is such that it would be inequitable to disregard it (s 25(2)(*g*) of the 1973 Act) or gross and obvious under the *Wachtel* test. In *Evans* v *Evans* [1989] 1 FLR 351, for instance, the wife had hired someone to murder her husband. On the husband's s 31 application, the periodical payments payable to the wife were discharged. In *A* v *A* (Financial Provision: Conduct) [1995] 1 FLR 345, the husband had assaulted the wife with a knife and was reported to have made statements of intent to harm her. Thorpe J held that the assault constituted conduct which it would be inequitable to disregard; however, it was only one of the factors to be reflected in the s 25 exercise, but on the facts he ruled that there ought to be a full and final settlement and a clean break.

(h) Difficulties of enforcement
A clean break may be appropriate where enforcement is problematical because the husband has moved abroad (*Smith* v *Smith* [1970] 1 All ER 244; *Williams* v *Williams* [1971] 2 All ER 764; *Griffiths* v *Griffiths* [1974] 1 All ER 932). A similar course may be adopted if the husband has made it clear by his actions that he does not intend to pay the maintenance ordered by the court (*Moisi* v *Moisi* (1984) 5 Fam Law 26; *Bryant* v *Bryant* (1976) 120 SJ 165). Perhaps the more conventional course, however, would be to negotiate secured provision, where possible.

(i) Removal of bitterness
Although persisting acrimony between the parties is a relevant factor when considering the imposition of a clean break, it should not be a deciding factor in a case where it would not otherwise be appropriate for a clean break to be made (*Morris* v *Morris* [1985] FLR 1176; *C* v *C* [1989] 1 FLR 11, at 19). Where children are involved, see *S* v *S* [1987] 1 FLR 71 discussed on p 105.

Having said that, time and time again judges have buttressed their arguments in favour of clean breaks on the desirability of getting rid of the bitterness between parties. It is hardly surprising to read such sentiments expressed following litigation between parties. *P* v *P* (Financial Relief: Non-Disclosure) [1994] 2 FRL 381 is a case in point. Thorpe J (as he then was) commented:

> I am quite clear that it is important in this case to bring the litigation between the parties to a final conclusion at the earliest possible opportunity. It has been an expensive and no doubt painful experience for each, and I can see nothing of advantage to either in its extension, so the importance of ensuring that this hearing is in all senses a final hearing bears on my conclusions ... In relation to the application for an order under s 28 ... obviously giving weight to that consideration, I have reached the conclusion that the term order should be an order of absolute finite duration and that there should not be any application hereafter for its extension.

In *B* v *B* [1995] 2 FCR 813, Thorpe J (as he then was) referred to the bitterness between the parties and said that he would have wished to impose a clean break but was constrained by concern about the earning potential of the husband (a popular musician) which was substantial but unpredictable.

4 Calculation

It may be thought trite to observe that the calculation of the lump sum payable on a clean break must begin with a review of the provisions of the Matrimonial Causes Act 1973, s 25; the courts have, however, repeatedly said that this is the best approach. Where the parties have a clean break in mind, certain considerations may assume greater importance. The age of the wife will be a particularly important factor as is the duration of the marriage. It is vital to know of any present intention to remarry or cohabit, as specifically referred to in r 2.61 of the Family Proceedings Rules 1991, when making the necessary calculation (*Hendrix* v *Hendrix* (1981) unreported CA Transcript No 57). Cohabitation does not of itself, however, automatically disentitle the wife to receive maintenance. Much will depend upon the wife's financial dependence on her cohabitee (*Atkinson* v *Atkinson* [1988] 2 FLR 353; *Duxbury* v *Duxbury* [1987] 1 FLR 7; and *Atkinson* v *Atkinson* [1995] 2 FLR 356).

Before undertaking the task of calculating the capital lump sum payable on a clean break, the following factors should be borne in mind:

- Does the wife have any maintenance entitlement over and above a nominal order in any event? She may only be entitled to a nominal

order because of the present extent of her earnings. There may, therefore, be no liability in real terms on the part of the husband to maintain the wife, which has to be commuted into a lump sum. A negotiated settlement may, however, take account of possible future loss of employment by the wife or a deterioration in her health;
- There is no rule as such when calculating the lump sum payable on a clean break as to the proportion (eg one-half) of the available capital resources that the wife should receive (*Page* v *Page* (1981) 2 FLR 198, at 202 per Dunn LJ; and see *W* v *W* (Judicial Separation: Ancillary Relief) [1995] 2 FLR 259 where it was held that even after a long marriage, a half-and-half starting point would not be an appropriate starting point—the wife's advanced age meant that her reasonable needs could be provided for by a smaller sum). A purely arithmetical approach is wrong in principle and is no more than a useful check on the figure emerging from working through the considerations in the Matrimonial Causes Act 1973, s 25 (*Preston* v *Preston* [1982] 1 All ER 41, at 47 per Ormrod LJ; whose judgment in that and other seminal cases was respectfully highlighted by Thorpe LJ giving the leading judgment of the Court of Appeal in *Dart* v *Dart* (June 1996, as yet unreported), in which a wife's attempt to increase a lump sum award from £9m to over £100m was unsuccessful).
- The usual approach is to balance the wife's reasonable capital requirements against the husband's ability to pay (*Potter* v *Potter* [1982] 2 All ER 321). Consideration has to be given to the sources of the husband's income and capital and, in particular, of its realisability (*Bullock* v *Bullock* [1986] 1 FLR 372; *Potter* v *Potter* [1982] 2 All ER 321). It should also be borne in mind that the wife might be entitled to a larger sum than one merely covering her needs (*B* v *B* [1990] 1 FLR 20, at 25–26).
- The wife's reasonable capital requirements will depend upon the means of the parties and, to some extent, their previous lifestyle (*Page* v *Page* [1981] 2 FLR 198). Where the parties have very substantial assets, a 'plateau' can be reached as to the amount of lump sum that the wife can expect to receive regardless of the extent of the husband's wealth (*Thyssen-Bornemisza* v *Thyssen-Bornemisza* [1985] FLR 670; *Attar* v *Attar* (No 1) [1985] FLR 649). Indeed the view was put forward by Wilson J (who had vast experience of acting for parties of considerable financial means whilst he was at the Bar) that a wife would not get over £4m or £5m by way of lump sum settlement ([1994] Fam Law 504). This view, however, does have to be treated with a certain amount of caution. In *F* v *F* (Ancillary Relief:

Substantial Assets) [1995] 2 FLR 45, the wife achieved an overall settlement of over £9m; and all three judges in the Court of Appeal in *Dart* [1996] 2 FLR 286 left straws blowing in the wind despite rejecting the wife's appeal against a £9m capital order. For example, per Peter Gibson LJ:

> standing back and looking at the position overall, were I unconstrained by authority I would have to say that I regard an award of £9m to a good wife in a marriage of fourteen years and a good mother to the respondent's children out of the respondent's resources of £400m as on the low side.

Those doubts were shared by Butler-Sloss LJ:

> I wonder whether the courts may not have imposed too restrictive an interpretation upon the words of s 25 and given too great weight to reasonable requirements over other criteria set out in the section.

- The powers of the court ought not to be exercised for the benefit of adult children, by enabling the wife to set up a child in business (*S v S* (1980) *The Times*, 10 May) or to provide by will for a child or others who are perhaps unlikely to benefit under the husband's will or otherwise (*Page v Page*; *Preston v Preston*; *Thyssen-Bornemisza v Thyssen-Bornemisza*).
- Active participation by the wife either by working in the business or by providing finance, will greatly enhance her contribution to the welfare of the family under s 25(2)(f) and may lead to a substantial increase in the lump sum over and above her 'reasonable requirements'. This in effect, recognises that she has 'earned' a share in the total assets, and should be able to realise it and use it as she chooses (*S v S*, which was a farming case; *Preston v Preston*; *Gojkovic v Gojkovic* [1990] 1 FLR 140).
- The acceptance by the wife of a frugal standard of living throughout the marriage, enabling the husband to plough back into the business a large proportion of the profits and so develop it into a considerable enterprise, is a factor which can properly be reflected in the lump sum order (*S v S*; *Page v Page*; *Preston v Preston*; *Gojkovic v Gojkovic*).
- Advanced age may be an important factor in that the wife's fullest requirements may be provided for by a smaller capital lump sum (*Page v Page*; *Preston v Preston*; *W v W*). A clean break may, however, be unsuitable in cases where a spouse is known to suffer from a chronic illness (*M v M* (Property Adjustment: Impaired Life Expectancy) [1993] 2 FLR 723). The wife suffered from a brain tumour. Balcombe LJ commented that:

this is not, and never could have been, a clean break case, even as between the wife and the husband alone and without regard to the children. Because of the wife's health, and its affect on her income-earning capacity, she is always going to need the support of periodical payments from the husband.

- As in all ancillary relief claims, the wife must ensure on a clean break that she is adequately compensated for loss of widow's pension rights. If this is not possible because of a lack of resources, consideration should be given as to whether an order under the Inheritance (Provision for Family and Dependants) Act 1975, s 15 should be avoided so as to provide a 'backstop'.

The process of calculating the appropriate lump sum payable on a clean break begins by identifying two separate component elements: first, the capital award (obviously including purchase of accommodation) which the wife may receive on the basis of continuing maintenance and, secondly, the additional lump sum payable to compensate her for loss of future maintenance. Two methods of approach have been adopted to calculate this second element, each of which initially requires a calculation of the wife's continuing maintenance needs. The first approach is actuarial and is based upon the traditional assessment of damages for loss of future earnings in a personal injury claim or a widow's loss of dependency in a fatal accident claim. An appropriate multiplier can be applied by this process to the calculated maintenance figure to give the appropriate lump sum. Useful tables are to be found in Volume 2, Section G to Duckworth, *Matrimonial Property and Finance*, 5th ed (FT Law & Tax), which shows the appropriate multipliers to be used depending on whether or not a wife's prospects of remarriage are to be taken into account and allowing for varying discounts for accelerated payment. Volume 2, Section G, Table 4 of Duckworth shows multipliers which might be used in calculating a term periodical payments order for rehabilitative maintenance.

The second approach adopted has been the use of what has become known as the *Duxbury* calculation following the decision of the Court of Appeal in *Duxbury* v *Duxbury* [1987] 1 FLR 7. There, the amount of capitalised maintenance awarded to the wife was arrived at on the basis of accountancy evidence, which was unchallenged in the Court of Appeal. The background to the *Duxbury* calculation is described by Ward J in *B* v *B* [1990] 1 FLR 20, at 24:

> The calculation was conceived to address the observations of the Court of Appeal in *Preston* v *Preston* [1981] FLR 331. There the Court of Appeal pointed out firstly that the recipient of the lump sum is expected

to expend it, or so much of it as is intended to meet future income needs, by drawing both upon its capital as well as relying upon the income it can produce. Secondly, that help should be given to the court by accountants or investment consultants, or even by reference to annuity tables, to show the court how the lump sum could be thus applied. As a result of *Preston* the practice has grown up for accountants to devise a computer programme which can calculate the lump sum which, if invested on the assumptions as to life expectancy, rates of inflation, return on investments, growth of capital, incidence of income tax, will produce enough to meet the recipient's needs for her life. The first case in which this was done was the case of *Duxbury* v *Duxbury*.

Duxbury calculations have received some judicial criticism in *B* v *B* and in *Gojkovic* v *Gojkovic* [1990] 1 FLR 140. In *B* v *B*, Ward J observed that the calculation was a useful tool for the court's use but no more, subject always to the wide discretion conferred on the court by the Matrimonial Causes Act 1973, s 25. If it is accepted in this way, Ward J concluded that it is a very valuable help in many cases subject to limitations upon its use and restrictions upon its unblinkered application. The court must bear in mind, *inter alia*, the unpredictability of future events, the question whether or not it was proposed to buy an annuity with the proposed sum and the fact that the wife might be entitled to a larger sum than one simply covering her needs. In summary, the *Duxbury* calculation is a means to an end, not an end in itself. These views were echoed by the Court of Appeal in *Gojkovic*, where Butler-Sloss LJ commented at 144 that a *Duxbury* calculation cannot by itself provide the answer as to the sum to which the wife is entitled, though it produces a figure to which the judge is entitled to have regard in deciding what is the right answer. This view was indorsed in *Gojkovic* by Russell LJ at 148 where he commented that *Duxbury*, properly understood, provides no more than a useful guide, and should not be regarded as a case from which there emerges any binding principle. Purchas LJ commented in *Vicary* v *Vicary* [1992] 2 FLR 271 at 278B:

> whilst acknowledging that in the negotiation process . . . *Duxbury* calculations are obviously useful as guidelines, I must emphasise that there is a danger of such an approach achieving a status far beyond that which it ever had in the [*Duxbury*] case . . . it certainly should never be allowed to derogate in any way from the wide discretion of the court to take into account all the circumstances of the case as required in s 25 of the Act.

A useful discussion of the *Duxbury* calculation by its creator, Tim Lawrence, is to be found at [1990] Fam Law 12.

F v *F* (*Duxbury* Calculation: Rate of Return) [1996] 1 FLR 833 comments on the sophistication introduced by specialist accountants and lawyers into the calculations of *Duxbury* sums. In this as in other cases, accountants and counsel had been bitterly and expensively engaged in arguing about the appropriate rate of return to be used in calculating *Duxbury* sums. The husband argued for a 5 per cent income return; the wife argued for only a 3 per cent income return. Holman J imposed an 'industry standard' rate of 4.25 per cent, which will doubtless be adopted at least until interest rates vary dramatically from current 1996 rates. Whilst imposing the 4.25 per cent figure, the judge acknowledged that there may be exceptional circumstances justifying a departure from this figure, such as cases involving a wife going to live abroad and investing there; a wife who was so old and incapacitated that she could not reasonably be expected to give any management to her income-producing fund; and wives whose husbands' resources were so great that they could be expected to invest with freedom from all risk.

A useful two-page guide to the capitalisation of a wife's maintenance has been produced in 'At A Glance' published annually by the Family Law Bar Association. Its table of *Duxbury* calculations features at pp 22–23 of the 1996 edition. The figures should not be taken to be 'tablets in stone', but rather should be taken with a pinch of salt. As the notes to the calculations explain, all sorts of assumptions have been made about tax, income and inflation rates over the next few decades; indeed, the life expectancy column of the calculations reflects assumptions which are generally thought of by actuaries as out-of-date: the authors have been able to argue in court that a woman lives two years longer than the 'At A Glance' tables reflect!

A possible third approach—the annuity approach—is based upon how much is needed to purchase an index-linked annuity and will usually be supported by quotations from insurance companies. This approach, though it remains a possibility, is criticised by Ward J in *B* v *B*, at 26, as it is unlikely that wives in their middle years will invest a substantial lump sum in an annuity.

In *B* v *B*, at 26–27, Ward J declined to lay down any hard and fast rule as to the preferability of the *Duxbury* calculation over the actuarial approach. He emphasised that the court can take whatever reasonable calculation it is given and apply it either with precision or with the broad brush as may in the exercise of the s 25 discretion seem appropriate in each case.

Chapter 5

Consensus and the Child Support Act

1 Introduction

The Child Support Act 1991 ('the Act') has provoked controversy from the outset; that controversy shows no signs of abatement. Few have, however, sought to challenge the underlying aim of the Government in the Act, as expressed in the White Paper: 'Children Come First' (1990) (Cm 1264), that parents should meet their financial responsibilities towards their children or the subsidiary aim of creating a system which produces consistent and predictable results. Most of the adverse comment is related to the lack of flexibility of the formula applied to the calculation of maintenance assessments, (which the Government has taken steps to address in the reforming regulations of April 1995 including the Child Support and Income Support (Amendment) Regulations 1995 (SI 1995 No 1045)) and the departure direction procedure contained in the Act, ss 28A–28I (as inserted by the Child Support Act 1995 ('the 1995 Act'), s 1).

Traditionally, the negotiation of consent orders and agreements has been approached on a 'package' basis with child maintenance being but one element in the overall solution. The arrival of the Act has had a profound effect on this approach and has in many cases reduced the number of available solutions particularly where a clean break (or as 'clean' a break as is possible where children are involved) would previously have been envisaged.

The purpose of this chapter is not to provide a summary of the main provisions of the Act or even to offer an exhaustive commentary on its relationship with the continuing jurisdiction of the courts in relation to child maintenance. Instead, the following discussion looks at the interface between the Act and consent orders and agreements in the family jurisdiction.

2 Agreements relating to child maintenance

'Agreements about maintenance' are dealt with by s 9 of the Act (as amended by s 8 of the 1995 Act). A 'maintenance agreement' is defined in s 9(1) of the Act as any agreement for the making, or for securing the making, of periodical payments by way of maintenance (or in Scotland aliment) to or for the benefit of any child. This definition therefore includes an oral agreement as to child maintenance, although problems of enforceability may arise in connection with such an agreement. Further, it may be contrasted with the definition found in MCA 1973, s 34(2) and ss 4(10) and 8(5)(*a*) of the Act, which state that the agreement must be in writing.

It remains possible to enter into a maintenace agreement; s 9(2) of the Act provides that nothing in the Act is to be taken to prevent any person from entering into a maintenance agreement. However, the benefit of entering into such an agreement is limited in that the jurisdiction of the Child Support Agency cannot be ousted (except as explained below). Further, it must be constantly borne in mind that, under s 6 of the Act, a person claiming income support, family credit or disability working allowance may be required to authorise the recovery of child support maintenance under the Act. There is nothing novel in the notion that an agreement cannot oust the jurisdiction to claim child maintenance: MCA 1973, s 34(1) provides that a provision in a maintenance agreement purporting to restrict any right to apply to a court for an order containing financial arrangements is void. This provision is mirror-imaged by two subsections of s 9 of the Act designed to ensure that the jurisdiction of the Child Support Agency is not ousted by a maintenance agreement. First, s 9(3) of the Act provides that a maintenance agreement will not prevent any party to the agreement, or any other person, from applying for a maintenance assessment with respect to any child to or for whose benefit periodical payments are to be made or secured under the agreement. Secondly, s 9(4) of the Act goes on to provide that, where any agreement contains a provision which purports to restrict the right of any person to apply for a maintenance assessment, that provision is void. The implication is that such a provision would be severable and that the rest of the agreement may stand even though the offending clause is void. It is submitted that this provision is retrospective in that it applies to agreements entered into both before and after the coming into force of the Act (5 April 1993). In short, a party to a maintenance agreement may resile from it to the extent of applying for a maintenance assessment under the Act at any point (except as explained below). A person who claims one of the benefits mentioned above—perhaps some time after the agreement—may be compelled to do so, but only when required to do so by the Child Support Agency regardless of the existence of a written agreement.

By virtue of the new s 4(10) of the Act (brought in by s 18(1) of the 1995 Act), no application for an assessment may be made at any time pursuant to s 4 of the Act 'if there is in force a written maintenance agreement made before 5 April 1993, or a maintenance order', either of which oblige the absent parent to make maintenance payments in respect of a qualifying child. This is a fundamental change of emphasis, because it *prima facie* denies jurisdiction to the Agency in any case where there is a written maintenance agreement which pre-dates 5 April 1993 or a maintenance order (whenever made). It therefore goes much further than the regulations made under the Act which created a 'transitional period' during which the jurisdiction of the Agency would be excluded from certain cases. However, the full rigour of this statutory provision is tempered by the Child Support (Maintenance Arrangements and Jurisdiction) Regulations 1992 (SI 1992 No 2645), reg 9 (as inserted by the Child Support (Miscellaneous Amendments) (No 2) Regulations 1995 (SI 1995 No 3261)), which are discussed below on p 121–2. Nonetheless, the balance has now shifted so as to concentrate within the Agency's jurisdiction effectively only those cases which involved the receipt of benefit.

The Secretary of State is given power by s 18(5) of the 1995 Act to repeal by order any of the provisions in s 18 of the 1995 Act so that it is conceivable that there could be another *volte face* in the future so as to take these cases back within the Agency's jurisdiction.

MCA 1973, s 35 enables a party to a written maintenance agreement to apply to the court during the lives of the parties for its variation. Section 9(5) of the Act (which applies, as a result of s 4(10) of the Act, only to written maintenance agreements made on or after 5 April 1993 which have not been converted into court orders pursuant to s 8(5) of the Act) prevents only an application to insert a provision to pay child maintenance, where s 8 of the Act would oust the jurisdiction of the court. The reason for this is that s 9(6) of the Act modifies s 9(5) so as to omit the restriction on varying an agreement by increasing the amount payable where s 4(10) prevents the making of an application for a maintenance assessment, and no application has been made for a maintenance assessment under s 6, or such an application has been made but no maintenance assessment has been made in response to it. In the case of a written maintenance agreement made on or after 5 April 1993, it is therefore possible to make an application under MCA 1973, s 35 to vary the agreement by either increasing or decreasing the amount of the maintenance payable, but not by inserting a provision to pay child maintenance. That apart, a parent with the care of a child, who is a party to a written maintenance agreement made on or after 5 April 1993 and who seeks an increase in the amount of child maintenance, may either apply for a maintenance assessment under the Act or negotiate a new agreement. Such a new agreement may be dealt with by means of a supplemental deed or other form of agreement or may be converted into a court order under s 8(5) of the Act (see below). In the case of a written maintenance agreement made before 5 April 1993, it is possible to apply to the court for an increase in the maintenance payments (the Agency's jurisdiction having been excluded by virtue of s 4(10) of the 1991 Act). The appropriate way to vary a written maintenance agreement which was in place on 5 April 1993 is therefore either to make an application to the court under MCA 1973, s 35 or to convert the agreement into an order pursuant to s 8(5) of the Act and then apply to the court for a variation of that order or to negotiate a new agreement. Further, where an application for an order varying a written maintenance agreement was pending before the court on 5 April 1993, s 9(5)(*b*) of the Act (which would have prevented a court, in circumstances where s 8 would prevent it from making a child maintenance order, from increasing the amount payable under a provision in the agreement) does not apply before 7 April 1997 to any case which would have fallen within the now revoked para 5(2) of Part I of the Schedule to the Child Support Act 1991 (Commencement No 3 and Transitional Provisions) Order 1992 (SI 1992 No 2644) (as substituted) (s 18(9) of the 1995 Act).

3 Written agreements and consent orders

Section 8(1)–(3) (as amended by s 18(3) of the 1995 Act) sets out the basic exclusion of the jurisdiction of the court to make, vary or revive a child maintenance order where the Child Support Agency has jurisdiction. Section 8 goes on to provide for various situations in which the court is to retain a residual role. Despite the basic exclusion of the court's jurisdiction, parents are able not only—in a non-benefits case—to reach a maintenance agreement as discussed above under s 9 of the Act, but can have a written agreement converted into a court order. Section 8(5) of the Act provides that the Lord Chancellor, or in Scotland the Lord Advocate, may by order provide that, in such circumstances as may be specified by the order, the court

is not to be prevented from exercising any power which it has to make a child maintenance order if:
   (a) a written agreement (whether or not enforceable) provides for the making, or securing, by an absent parent of the child of periodical payments to or for the benefit of the child; and
   (b) the maintenance order which the court makes is, in all material respects, in the same terms as that agreement.

The appropriate order, which has been made, is the Child Maintenance (Written Agreements) Order 1993 (SI 1993 No 620), which came into force on 5 April 1993. Article 2 of the Order simply provides that s 8 of the Act is not to prevent a court from exercising any powers which it has to make a maintenance in relation to a child in any of the circumstances in which paras (a) and (b) of s 8(5) apply.

It will be noted that neither s 8(5) nor the Order defines what is meant in this context by a written agreement. Clearly, a formal written maintenance agreement or separation deed will suffice as would an exchange of solicitors' correspondence. Equally, it now appears to be the practice of most district judges to accept the recital of an agreement in the preamble to a consent order thereby enabling the practice of negotiated package orders to be perpetuated. The only fundamental requirement is that the order must be in all material respects in the same terms as the agreement. It should also be borne in mind that, regardless of whether the consent order contains terms other than those relating to child maintenance, the requirements of FPR, r 2.61 must be met.

It will also be noted that there is no restriction in this useful process of conversion to agreements entered into prior to the coming into force of the Act on 5 April 1993. Section 8(5) therefore remains an important part of the armoury of the family practitioner in a non-benefits case by permitting the conversion of an agreement (whether or not contemporaneous) into a court order. The practitioner will, therefore, wish to consider in such a case whether or not to oust the jurisdiction of the Agency by converting an agreement into a court order and giving exclusive jurisdiction to the court by virtue of s 4(10) of the Act (see p 118 and 121). One approach might be to agree a nominal maintenance order, which will then give the court the jurisdiction to vary.

It is perhaps fallacious to regard the conversion process as applying only to consent orders. Close scrutiny of the precise wording of s 8(5) of the Act demonstrates that it is open to the court to convert an existing written agreement after a contested hearing if the parties agree. Further, where there is no written agreement, it is open to a district judge hearing a contested ancillary relief application to invite the parties to agree at least child maintenance and to incorporate such an agreement into a written document which he can then convert as part of his overall order.

It was originally thought that s 8(5) would only be a temporary measure. It has, however, become clear that it is now viewed as a long-term measure available in non-benefits cases. The Secretary of State has no financial interest in bringing non-benefit maintenance cases within the jurisdiction of the Agency.

4 Old agreements and orders

The Child Support Act 1991 (Commencement No 3 and Transitional Provisions) Order 1992 (SI 1992 No 2644) Schedule Part I (as substituted by the Child Support Act 1991 (Commencement No 3 and Transitional Provisions) Amendment Order 1993 (SI 1993 No 966)) contained the original transitional provisions in relation to 'old' agreements and orders, which were in existence when the Act came into force on 5 April 1993. These transitional provisions were revoked by s 18(8) of the 1995 Act. The current position is now as follows:

(a) Pending applications

Where a notice of application in the appropriate form under the FPR—and not simply a prayer in a petition—has been filed at court before 5 April 1993, the applicant can choose whether to proceed with the application to the court or to apply to the Child Support Agency for an assessment. This is the effect of amending s 18(9) of the 1995 Act which preserves para 5(2) of the Schedule Part I of SI 1992 No 2645 (as amended), which related to applications pending as at 5 April 1993 for a maintenance order or an application for an order varying a written maintenance agreement. The court order will, however, have to be made before 7 April 1997.

(b) Old agreements and orders

Where there was a *written* agreement made before 5 April 1993 or court order (whenever made), the Agency has no jurisdiction (as explained above) by virtue of the new s 4(10) of the 1991 Act. This replaces what was known as the 'transitional period' during which only the court had jurisdiction to deal with cases which fell into this category. As indicated above, this fundamental change is tempered by the Child Support (Maintenance Arrangements and Jurisdiction) Regulations 1992 (SI 1992 No 2645), reg 9 (as inserted by the Child

Support (Miscellaneous Amendments) (No 2) Regulations 1995 (SI 1995 No 3261)). Regulation 9 provides that s 4(10) will not prevent an application being made for a maintenance assessment under s 4 after 22 January 1996, where a decision has been made by a relevant family court either that it has no power to vary or to enforce a maintenance order in a particular case. A maintenance order is so defined as to exclude a maintenance order which is mentioned in s 8(7) or (8) of the Act (an order for school or educational costs) (s 8(7)); or an order relating to a disabled child (s 8(8)) (s 18(6) of the 1995 Act).

It should be borne in mind that the court retains the jurisdiction under s 8(4) of the Act to *revoke* a child maintenance order. If such an order made before 5 April 1993 is revoked, the court then ceases to have the power in general terms to make a child maintenance order. If such an order is not revoked and there is no assessment under s 6 of the Act, the court retains the power to vary the order under MCA 1973, s 31. In *B v M* (Child Support: Revocation of Order) [1994] 1 FLR 342, it was held that, although an assessment under the Act was likely to produce a higher figure than would be achieved under the MCA 1973, it did not follow that an assessment under the Act was necessarily in the best interests of the child. It might be that other matters might follow which would outweigh such purely financial benefit and that the relevant factors had to be weighed up. In the generality of cases, the regime set out in the then applicable transitional provisions was the appropriate regime, that is, that the appropriate course would normally be that the parent with care should apply to the court for a variation of the existing order rather than applying for its revocation so as to permit an application to the Child Support Agency. The authors consider that weight has been given to this decision by the reforms brought in by s 18(1) of the 1995 Act in that the Government has thereby shown that it wishes the court rather than the Agency to have jurisdiction in such cases.

(c) Benefit recipients
Whether or not there is in existence an old written agreement or court order, a parent with care receiving any of the benefits referred to above cannot apply to the court for a variation, but must await the Agency's requirement that she authorise recovery under s 6 of the Act.

There are further transitional provisions introduced by Part III of the Child Support (Miscellaneous Amendments and Transitional Provisions) Regulations 1994 (SI 1994 No 227) which came into force on 7 April 1994, which deal with the situation where a maintenance order or written maintenance agreement was in force on 4 April 1993 and the absent parent is a member of a new family. The detailed provisions of these Regulations are outside the scope of this work.

5 Relationship between child maintenance assessments and agreements/court orders

Section 10 of the Act deals with the relationship between court orders and maintenance agreements (whether old or new) on the one hand and child maintenance assessments on the other. Section 10(1) provides that court orders of a prescribed kind will cease to have effect on the making of an assessment under the Act except insofar as they are modified. Such modifications, as explained below, permit an order to remain effective, for example, in relation to school fees or in relation to a non-qualifying child. The orders prescribed under s 10(1) are scheduled in the Child Support (Maintenance Arrangements and Jurisdiction) Regulations 1992 (SI 1992 No 2645), reg 3(1) (as amended by the Child Support and Income Support (Amendment) Regulations 1995 (SI 1995 No 1045), reg 27(1) and (2)) and consist of 23 statutory jurisdictions including, *inter alia*:

(*a*) Affiliation Proceedings Act 1957;
(*b*) Part II of the Matrimonial Causes Act 1973;
(*c*) The Domestic Proceedings and Magistrates' Courts Act 1978;
(*d*) Part III of the Matrimonial and Family Proceedings Act 1984;
(*e*) Family Law (Scotland) Act 1985; and
(*f*) Sched 1 to the Children Act 1989.

Regulation 3(2) of the Regulations provides that where, a maintenance assessment is made with respect to all of the children covered by a prescribed order or one or more but not all of the children involved and where the amount payable under the order to or for each child is separately specified, the order will, so far as it relates to the child or children with respect to whom the maintenance assessment has been made, cease to have effect two days after the assessment is complete (reg 3(5)). This principle does not operate where the order was made under s 8(7) (educational expenses) or (8) (where the child is disabled) of the Act (reg 3(3)).

There are mirror-image provisions in relation to maintenance agreements to be found in s 10(2) of the Act. Where there is an agreement of a prescribed kind (which is defined by reg 4(1) as a maintenance agreement within the definition found in s 9(1) of the Act), the relevant part of the agreement will become unenforceable from the effective date of the maintenance assessment under reg 4(2), where the assessment is made in circumstances parallel to those set out in reg 3(2) discussed above. The agreement may therefore be modified where it relates to a non-qualifying child. The agreement superseded by the assessment will remain unenforceable until such date as the child support officer no longer has jurisdiction to make a maintenance assessment (reg 4(3)).

6 A new approach

Despite the fact that ss 8(5) and 9 of the Act have preserved the private ordering of child maintenance in non-benefit cases, the rigid formulaic approach adopted by the Act will loom large in negotiations. The formula has become the one unalterable factor to be taken into account. There is no reason in essence why a parent with care should be prepared to accept by way of child support maintenance less than would be achieved under an Agency assessment (see, eg *E* v *C* (Child Maintenance) [1996] 1 FLR 472). Other factors may of course enter into the equation; a good deal of trust may remain between the parties and the wife may be anxious to secure an advantageous capital settlement. The absent parent will nonetheless wish to bear in mind the prospect of a future application to the Agency should the parent with care be obliged to claim benefit at some future date.

Another problem area is the interface between the jurisdictions of the court and the Agency. A consent order may fall to be negotiated or a contested application for ancillary relief may reach court at a time when the child support maintenance assessment is incomplete. Even if the assessment is complete, its factual basis may not be known in the absence of an appeal to the Child Support Appeal Tribunal. The problem is exacerbated by periodic changes in the child support legislation. This is amply demonstrated by the decision of Thorpe J in *Mawson* v *Mawson* [1994] 2 FLR 985. It was held that changes to the legislation which brought about a reduction in the maintenance assessment could not have been contemplated by the district judge, whose decision was appealed. The deficiency could not be dealt with by an order to the child since the court had no jurisdiction by virtue of s 8(3) of the Act and could only be made good by way of an order for periodical payments to the wife. The decision establishes that a legitimate ground for a variation of a wife's maintenance order is an alteration in the amount of an Agency assessment deriving from changes to the child support regime; this is of some significance especially in view of the important changes brought into effect by the Regulations made in April 1995.

The way in which the Act has brought about a new approach is perhaps best viewed from the twin standpoints of assessing the income requirements of the family as a whole and in terms of the erosion of the clean break principle:

(a) Family orders
The term 'family order' is intended to refer to an order made by consent under s 8(5) of the Act covering the needs of the family as a whole. It could equally apply to an order for maintenance pending suit for a parent with care, where the court is prepared to include in that order the income requirements of the children given that an Agency assessment has not been completed.

This approach affects both the calculation of spousal maintenance and the way in which it is expressed in the court order. Spousal maintenance will most likely now be viewed in terms of looking at the income requirements of the family as a whole, in the light of MCA 1973, s 25, but regarding child support maintenance assessed pursuant to the Act as a resource of the parent with care. In consequence of this approach, the overall levels of spousal maintenance are likely to decrease. The reader is referred to the precedents relating to appropriate clauses to be inserted in consent orders and touching on the Act in the Solicitors' Family Law Association's *Precedents for Consent Orders* (4th ed) (in particular Precedent 48 (*Segal* order) and Precedent 49 (*Connell* order)).

(b) The clean break
It had in the past been a common practice for the family home to be transferred to a wife in consideration of a dismissal of her claims for maintenance on the basis that little or no maintenance would be paid for the children. It was usually the expectation that the wife and children would receive income support and perhaps that the mortgage on the transferred family home would be similarly met. A consent order providing for this type of solution made before 5 April 1993 came under the scrutiny of Booth J in *Crozier* v *Crozier* [1994] 1 FLR 126. The husband applied to set aside or vary the consent order to recover his share in the family home relying upon the principle in *Barder* v *Barder* [1987] 2 FLR 480. Booth J emphasised the principle that parents could not achieve a clean break in respect of their children. Even before 5 April 1993, the Department of Social Security was empowered to seek recovery of its expenditure on benefit from a person liable for maintenance under the Social Security Administration Act 1992, ss 106–107. The essence of the distinction

between the 1991 Act and the 1992 Act, which consolidated the Social Security Act 1986, s 24, was that under the 1986 and 1992 Acts the justices were able to exercise judicial discretion, whereas no discretion existed under the 1991 Act. Booth J held that the fact that Parliament had chosen an administrative method outside the jurisdiction of the court for assessing child maintenance did not fundamentally alter the position as it was at the date of the consent order. There was therefore no new event in fact or in law sufficient to invalidate the basis of the consent order. The harshness of the decision in *Crozier* has been significantly ameliorated in two ways. First, Sched 3A has been added to the Child Support (Maintenance Assessment and Special Cases) Regulations 1992 (SI 1992 No 1815) by the Child Support and Income Support (Amendment) Regulations 1995 (SI 1995 No 1045), reg 57. The effect of the new Schedule is that, in appropriate cases, there must be taken into account in calculating the exempt income of the absent parent (or sometimes, the parent with care) an amount in respect of a 'qualifying transfer' of property. The intention is that the transferor will receive credit in child support terms for having bought off *child* periodical payments by a property adjustment or lump sum order or equivalent agreement. Secondly, an application may be made under s 28A of the Act for a departure direction in the circumstances set out in paras 3 and 4 of Part I of Sched 4B of the Act, which deal with property or capital transfers. The departure direction jurisdiction is at present only partly in force at the present time (Child Support Departure Direction (Anticipatory Application) Regulations 1996 (SI 1996 No 635)). It must, however, be stressed that in both situations the purpose of the transfer must have been to reduce the level of *child* maintenance and not for the sole purpose of compensating the parent with care for the loss of any right to claim periodical payments or capital for herself.

The problems exemplified by *Crozier* have to some degree led to an erosion of the clean break principle and in turn a revival in the popularity of *Mesher* orders with all their attendant problems. There will, nonetheless, still be situations in which an absent parent is insistent on a clean break solution. The parent with care may not at the time of negotiation of the consent order be in receipt of benefits and an element of trust and goodwill may still subsist between the parties. Before a clean break solution is adopted, it will be necessary to advise the absent parent of his potential liability under the Act should the parent with care be obliged to claim benefits. One possible solution, which offers only a measure of comfort, may be for the absent parent to secure his potential liability under either the Acts of 1991 or 1992 by means of a charge back on the family home to be transferred to the parent with care under the envisaged clean break consent order. A precedent for such a charge-back is reproduced at Appendix 6 by kind permission of the Solicitors' Family Law Association. Some measure of judicial support for the notion of a charge back is to be found in the decision of Thorpe J in *Smith* v *McInerney* [1994] 2 FLR 1077:

> H and W separated in 1990. Pursuant to a separation agreement, H transferred to W his half-share in the family home in consideration of which he was released from any future liability under the mortgage and from any future obligation to maintain either W or the three children. Despite this, H paid £200 per month to W for the benefit of the children until he was made redundant in July 1990. In 1993, H applied for a property adjustment order and a lump sum order. The district judge made an order that the family home be charged with payment to the husband of 35 per cent of the net value of the property with all other claims to be dismissed upon the execution of the charge. Thorpe J allowed W's appeal applying the principle in *Edgar* v *Edgar* [1980] 3 All ER 887 to the terms of the separation agreement. However, since W asserted her rights under the agreement, it followed that H too was entitled in full to the benefits for which he had contracted. H was entitled to the return of the monies he advanced prior to his redundancy by way of a lump sum order. Further, since W was likely to claim benefits in the near future, it was likely that H would be the subject of an assessment by the Agency. Thus, having already transferred his interest in the family home to W, H would in reality be paying twice to discharge the same obligation. Thorpe J therefore adjourned H's application for a property adjustment order generally 'for the single purpose of providing a means of pursuing a claim for indemnity if, and only if, the Child Support Agency extracts from him substantive periodical payments'.

Chapter 6

Challenging consent orders and agreements

1 Introduction

So far the reader's attention has been directed towards the parties' attempts to compose their differences and find a solution acceptable to them both with all the advantages that that will bring. What, however, will be the position where one party becomes disenchanted with the solution reached whether by agreement or order? One must first consider whether the circumstances giving rise to the need to challenge the agreement or order occurred before or after it was made. Ormrod LJ summarised the distinction between the variation jurisdiction and the power to set aside in *Robinson* v *Robinson* (Disclosure) [1983] 4 FLR 102, at 114 in this way:

> A distinction has to be drawn between the restrictions imposed by the Matrimonial Causes Act 1973 on varying lump sum orders or property adjustment orders which cannot be varied, and the power to set aside an order which has been obtained by fraud or mistake, or by material non-disclosure. The essence of the distinction is that the power to vary usually reflects changes of circumstances subsequent to the date of the order, whereas the power to set aside arises when there has been fraud, mistake or material non-disclosure as to the facts at the time the order was made.

The distinction drawn above has by no means been rigidly applied and variation has been used as a remedy in the case of a consent order invalidated by mistake (see p 133). Variation applications made in the normal circumstances connected with a subsequent change in circumstances are dealt with fully in Chapter 7. Equally, as will be seen a fresh action, rehearing or appeal may well be appropriate, where new events occur after the making of the consent order which invalidate the basis upon which it was made, relying on the rule established by the House of Lords in *Barder* v *Barder* [1987] 2 All ER 440.

Much of the state of confusion surrounding the challenging of consent orders was removed by the comprehensive lucidity of the judgment of Ward J in *B–T* v *B–T* [1990] 2 FLR 1. Since then there have been a number of important procedural reforms relating to this area of the law: Family Proceedings Rules r 8.1 coupled with the County Court Rules 1981 Ord 37 r 6 introduced new appeal procedures; a rehearing procedure for the county court is set out in Ord 37 r 1; and the appeal procedures set out in RSC Ord 59 have also been changed. Further guidance and procedural avenues are opened up by Thorpe J in *Re C* (Financial Provision: Leave to Appeal) [1993] 2 FLR 799, a case which perhaps raises more questions than answers and seems bound to spawn further case law; and by Bracewell J in *Benson* v *Benson (Deceased)* [1996] 1 FLR 692, which seeks to answer some of the questions posed by *Re C*. These procedural considerations are examined in detail at p 160 *et seq*.

Of the remedies discussed below, it will be seen that some relate to consent orders, some to agreements and some to both means of compromise. Fresh actions, appeals and rehearings have been treated under the single heading of *Setting Aside* to enable the reader to compare the available remedies and decide upon the appropriate procedure and because of the similarity in the grounds capable of supporting each remedy.

To anticipate the conclusion, the discernible trend of the courts since *Barder* has been to restrict the possibility of reopening financial matters. Case law has respected the public policy objective of finality of both agreements (to the extent that they can be regarded as 'final' before an order is made) and orders being brought to bear upon parties. The cases which we go on to describe show that whilst, on the one hand it is right that there is a jurisdiction to set orders aside, on the other hand it is difficult to get within the *Barder* criteria.

2 Setting aside

(a) Grounds

No exhaustive list can be drawn up as to the grounds on which a consent order or agreement may be set aside. As will be seen, the grounds themselves do overlap; frequently, the facts of an individual case will reveal the presence of more than one of the available grounds.

First, there are those cases in which there are 'new events' in the *Barder* sense. These may be, for example, the death of a party or the cohabitation of the parties with each other immediately following an order, and these events may or may not suffice to set an order aside. Secondly, there are those cases which involve a 'vitiating factor' (per Thorpe J in *Re C*) such as fraud or non-disclosure. It may be said of the cases that involve a vitiating factor that the basis of them all is the lack of true consent and it is submitted that further extensions of the available grounds will stem from this concept. Another way of categorising these two aspects according to contractual principles would be to adopt the rationale of Hale J in *Cornick* v *Cornick* [1994] 2 FLR 530. Here she referred to cases in which there were 'new events' in the *Barder* sense, which were more akin to the doctrine of frustration than to mistake. Secondly, there were cases where the court proceeded on a mistaken basis at the trial, which was so significant that had the court known the true facts it would have made a substantially different order.

Balcombe J in *Tommey* v *Tommey* [1982] 3 All ER 385 considered that the policy considerations governing the development of existing law as to the grounds upon which a matrimonial order can be set aside were twofold. He held at 392:

> In my judgment, this involves holding a balance between two important principles which are often expressed by the Latin phrases: *ubi jus ibi remedium* [the law should provide a remedy for wrongs] and *interest reipublicae ut sit finis litium* [it is in the interests of society that there should be some end to litigation].

Not all of the grounds discussed below extend to consent orders. The wide supervisory jurisdiction of the courts over agreements has already been discussed in Chapter 2, pp 29–40. Dr Ines Weyland in his excellent article *Maintenance Agreements and Consent Orders—A Legal Maze* [1985] Fam Law 110, at 112 analyses this jurisdiction by suggesting that one can distinguish between, on the one hand, situations where either there is no agreement at all or where the agreement is void and, on the other, voidable agreements. The former can be avoided by either party, whereas the latter by only one of them.

All matrimonial consent orders must reflect an underlying agreement. In *Huddersfield Banking Co Ltd* v *Henry Lister & Son Ltd* [1895–99] All ER Rep 868, it was held that a consent order could be impeached not only on the ground of fraud, but upon any grounds which invalidate the agreement it expresses in a formal way. However, the view was taken in *Tommey* v *Tommey* [1982] 3 All ER 385 that the contractual basis of matrimonial consent orders was to be disregarded and that they must be dealt with in the same way as non-consensual orders, except that a matrimonial consent order cannot be challenged on the ground that the court reached the wrong conclusion on the evidence before it, as there has been no adjudication by the court of first instance on the evidence (*Thwaite* v *Thwaite* [1981] 2 All ER 789, at 794). This departure from the general principle established in *Huddersfield Banking Co Ltd* v *Henry Lister & Son Ltd* means that a matrimonial consent order cannot be challenged on grounds sufficient to invalidate the underlying agreement, unless those grounds also suffice to invalidate a non-consensual order. Balcombe J in *Tommey* relied on the decisions in *De Lasala* v *De Lasala* [1979] 2 All ER 1146 and *Thwaite* v *Thwaite* [1981] 2 All ER 789, which clearly indicate that the legal effect of a consent order is derived from the order itself and not from the underlying agreement. A distinction is therefore to be drawn between matrimonial consent orders and those made in other types of litigation—a principle applied in *B* v *Miller & Co* [1996] 2 FLR 23. In this case it was held that such a consent order could not be equated with an order made following a contested hearing; the plaintiff's negligence action against the solicitors who acted for her in obtaining the order could not therefore be struck out as being a collateral attack on an order made by a court of competent jurisdiction

(i) Lack of consent
As indicated above, the grounds discussed below stem from this particular ground, which should therefore be treated at the outset. Lack of consent could of itself constitute a ground for challenging a consent order or agreement. *Parkes* v *Parkes* [1971] 3 All ER 870, discussed below is an example of how lack of real consent has been used to challenge a consent order.

Counsel has an implied authority to enter into a compromise on behalf of a client subject to any limitation imposed by his instructions. Any application to challenge a consent order on the basis that counsel has exceeded his instructions should normally be made before the order is perfected. An example of a misguided attempt by a party to challenge an order is *Re F(A Minor)* (Custody: Consent Order: Procedure) [1992] 1 FLR 561, where a father acting in person had contended that solicitors and counsel representing him acted without his authority and that he had not consented to the making of what was purportedly a consent order. The father was told that the appropriate procedure would have been for him to commence a fresh action to set the order aside rather than appealing what was purportedly a consent order. If counsel's instructions were expressly limited unbeknown to the other party and he nonetheless entered into a compromise for which he had no authority, the court may set aside the compromise and the order based on it, if grave injustice would be done by allowing the compromise to stand (*Marsden* v *Marsden* [1972] 2 All ER 1162).

In *Re R* (Contact: Consent Order) [1995] 1 FLR 123, a mother consented to an order unwillingly and only after comments made by the judge during a hearing and before she herself had given evidence. It was held by the Court of Appeal that, where a judge had by improper conduct at the trial prevented a party from putting his case properly, his judgment would be set aside on appeal and a retrial ordered. It followed that, if the improper conduct of a trial led to a settlement to which there was no true consent, the party aggrieved should appeal. The conduct of the judge should be reviewed by the appellate court rather than by the judge himself or another judge of co-ordinate jurisdiction. Exactly the same principle would of course apply to a financial relief application.

(ii) Mistake
Cornick, with its useful analysis of post-*Barder* cases (see p 46 below), shows that a mistake is one of the most significant aspects of appeals and applications to set aside.

Reference has already been made on p 13 as to how an agreement may be rendered void because of the *common* mistake of the parties, where both parties make the same mistake. On this basis a consent order or agreement may be challenged.

A *mutual* mistake, where the parties misunderstood each other, has also been established as an available ground. In *Parkes* v *Parkes* [1971] 3 All ER 870, the wife opposed the granting of a decree nisi of divorce based on five years' separation on the ground of grave financial or other hardship (now s 5 of the 1973 Act). An agreement was reached whereby the wife understood she was to receive periodical payments of £1,200 per annum clear. The husband, however, understood the agreement to be that he was to pay £1,200 per annum less tax. It was held that there was no real agreement, since one party thought it meant one thing and the other party another. The wife succeeded, both at first instance and on appeal, in her application that the decree nisi should not be made absolute.

The use of *unilateral* mistake, where only one of the parties is mistaken, requires caution as it is necessary to show that the other party knew or should have known of the mistake and that the mistake concerned the fundamental object of the agreement. The court may be more ready to intervene on the ground of unilateral mistake where an interlocutory order is involved (*Mullins* v *Howell* (1879) 11 Ch D 763). It is submitted that the test for determining whether the order in question is interlocutory or final is that propounded in *De Lasala* (at 1155). In *Wales* v *Wadham* [1977] 2 All ER 125, at 144–145, it was held that a unilateral mistake of fact would not constitute a ground for setting aside a consent order, as the husband was not mistaken as to the fundamental object of the agreement since the possibility of the wife's remarriage had been in his mind during negotiations (cf *Cook* v *Cook* [1988] 1 FLR 521: see p 138). A differing approach to unilateral mistake, where there exists only an agreement upon which a consent order has not yet been made, is to be found in the case of *Cross* v *Cross* (1983) 4 FLR 235, which is discussed in more detail on p 36 and p 140. It was held that an order for specific performance of such an agreement may be refused on the ground of mistake. 'A classic case of mistake'—unilateral mistake—was identified by Glidewell LJ in *Re M* (1990) *The Times*, 31 March, where a consent adoption order made in favour of a natural mother and her new husband was set aside because, unbeknown to the natural father, the mother was terminally ill at the time of the adoption order and died three months later.

In *Redmond* v *Redmond* [1986] 2 FLR 173, a consent order was made on the expressly recorded basis that the husband had no present intention of accepting voluntary redundancy. Two months later, the husband applied for voluntary redundancy and received a severance payment of £25,000. The wife applied for leave to appeal out of time and for the order to be set aside on the basis of fresh evidence, mistake, fraudulent misrepresentation and non-disclosure. Judge Stannard sitting in the Liverpool County Court found that the order should be set aside on the alternative ground that it was entered into in consequence of a mistake as to essential facts. These were that the husband had the physical capacity to follow his employment and that he was unlikely to receive a redundancy payment in the foreseeable future. Although the wife had indicated in her evidence that she did not believe the husband's assurances with regard to redundancy, the husband could not be heard to say that she was not genuinely mistaken. The husband's case was that he was subject to the same mistake and that on discovery of the true extent of his injuries resulting from a motor accident prior to the consent order he was compelled to accept redundancy. The judge held (at 184) that in these circumstances there was at least a unilateral mistake of fact on the part of the wife and, if the husband's evidence was true, there was a common mistake of fact which was shared by both parties.

Variation has been used as a means of remedying a mistake in a consent order which has arisen because its tax effect has been misunderstood (*B(GC)* v *B(BA)* [1970] 1 All ER 913 *sub nom Brister* v *Brister* [1970] 1 WLR 664). The use of variation in this way does, however, represent a departure from the general distinction drawn between setting aside the variation in *Robinson* referred to on p 89. Indeed, the Privy Council in *De Lasala* v *De Lasala* [1979] 2 All ER 1146 rejected the wife's claim that she was entitled to have a consent order set aside because she had been induced to agree to it by the bad legal advice she had received from her then legal advisers as to what her tax position would be. The Privy Council dealt with the submission (at 1155–1156) on the procedural basis that an application to set aside on the ground of mistake should be pursued by a fresh action.

The situation arising where there is a mistake in valuation of a matrimonial home or of a business which reveals a discrepancy between the valuation used in the proceedings and the sale price has been a fertile source of dispute between parties in the post-*Barder* cases. This is hardly surprising given the recession post-1988 and its effects on matrimonial assets. This is discussed on pp 152 *et seq.*

An omission in a consent order can be challenged by way of a fresh action on the ground of mistake, the issue being whether the registrar had been given the wrong material when making the consent order and not whether he had been wrong (*Harrison* v *Harrison* (1983) 13 Fam Law 20). It should be noted, however, that ignorance of relevant facts on the part of the court is not of itself a ground for impeaching a consent order (*Tommey* v *Tommey* [1982] 3 All ER 385, at 390).

(iii) Fraudulent misrepresentation

The clearest of grounds upon which to challenge a consent order or agreement is where there has been fraud or misrepresentation on the part of one spouse. This will frequently overlap with the ground of non-disclosure. No clearer basis of fraud could exist than where this is admitted by the party involved. This occurred in *Allsop* v *Allsop* (1980) 11 Fam Law 18 where the husband filed a further affidavit admitting fraudulent misrepresentation as to his assets. The consent order was set aside enabling the wife's application to be reheard. *De Lasala*, on the other hand, was a case of the opposite extreme where the Privy Council rejected the wife's allegations of fraud indicating (per Lord Diplock at 1156) that they were 'couched in terms that suggest that she is willing to wound and yet afraid to strike'.

The consent order in *Redmond* v *Redmond* [1986] 2 FLR 173, referred to above at p 133, was also set aside on the ground of fraudulent misrepresentation. The court expressed its views in this way (at 184):

> If, having regarding to my earlier findings, it is necessary for me to determine the issue of whether the husband did in fact intend at the date of the order to accept voluntary redundancy, and in that sense was guilty

of fraudulent misrepresentation, my conclusion is that at that date he had formed an intention to accept redundancy at the first available opportunity which afforded good prospects of avoiding the sharing of any redundancy payment with his wife. In *Wales* v *Wadham* [1977] 1 WLR 199, at p 211E, Tudor Evans J held that 'a statement of intention is not a representation of existing fact, unless the person making it does not honestly hold the intention he is expressing, in which case there is a misrepresentation of fact in relation to the state of that person's mind'. In this sense I find that there was a fraudulent misrepresentation by the husband which induced the wife to enter into the consent order, and for the reasons which I have already stated I exercise my discretion to set aside the order on this ground also.

(iv) Material non-disclosure
Non-disclosure will only operate as a basis for challenging a consent order or agreement where a duty existed to disclose the relevant information. The nature and extent of the duty to disclose has already been discussed in Chapter 3, section 5. So far as agreements are concerned, it will be recalled that there is no general duty of full and frank disclosure (*Wales* v *Wadham* [1977] 2 All ER 125; see p 14). For an agreement to be challenged on this ground, it must be established that the parties had accepted that the agreement had been arrived at on the basis that there had been full and frank disclosure (and often there will be a recital to this effect). There would appear to be a distinction to be drawn between agreements reached in the course of proceedings and those where no proceedings are pending eg a separate deed (see *Prow* v *Brown* (1982) 12 Fam Law 214 discussed below).

In the light of what is now the *locus classicus* of cases relating to material non-disclosure: the decision of the House of Lords in *Livesey* v *Jenkins* [1985] 1 All ER 106, what is *material* non-disclosure? Lord Brandon ended his opinion in *Livesey* v *Jenkins* with what he described as an 'emphatic word of warning' (at 119):

> It is not every failure of frank and full disclosure which would justify a court in setting aside an order of the kind concerned in this appeal. On the contrary, it will only be in cases when the absence of full and frank disclosure has led to the court making, either in contested proceedings or by consent, an order which is *substantially different* [authors' italics] from the order which it would have made if such disclosure had taken place that a case for setting aside can possibly be made good. Parties who apply to set aside orders on the ground of failure to disclose some relatively minor matter or matters, the disclosure of which would not have made any substantial difference to the order which the court would have made or approved, are likely to find their application being summarily dismissed, with costs against them, or, if they are legally aided, against the legal aid fund.

Two contrasting cases, which explain what the courts have previously considered to be a *substantial difference*, are *Robinson* v *Robinson* (Disclosure) (1983) FLR 102 and *Hill* v *Hill* [1984] Fam Law 83. In *Robinson*, the Court of Appeal found that there was a variation of many thousands of pounds between the disclosed value of the husband's wealth and its true value. Whilst intensive research might have revealed to the wife the husband's financial position, the order was set aside. The husband was criticised for obfuscating the true picture of his financial position by exchanging uninformative accounts. In *Hill*, on the other hand, the husband gave an accurate disclosure of his income and the value of the matrimonial home, the net sale proceeds of which were ordered to be divided equally between the husband and the wife. The husband also disclosed the existence of three endowment policies describing their surrender value as 'minimal'. The wife subsequently ascertained that as at the date of separation the surrender value of the policies was £979. The Court of Appeal did not regard these facts as proving material non-disclosure which would justify the order being set aside. Cumming-Bruce LJ had regard to the fact that it was possibly justifiable for the husband to describe the surrender value of the policies as minimal when compared to the value of the matrimonial home of £120,000. He indicated that the husband had given incomplete disclosure, the incompleteness was obvious and the wife's advisers, if they had wanted, could have discovered the accurate figures, but decided not to, before bringing the wife's application for financial provision before the court. Other examples of financial non-disclosure may be found in *Barber* v *Barber* [1987] Fam Law 125 and *Gurney* v *Gurney* (1989), unreported (see p 67).

What *types* of material non-disclosure will justify an appeal? It follows from the comments of Lord Brandon in *Livesey* v *Jenkins* (at 113) that the duty to make full and frank disclosure relates to 'all the circumstances of the case, including, *inter alia*, the particular matters' specified in s 25 of the 1973 Act that any attack upon a consent order on the ground of non-disclosure may be very broadly based subject to the word of warning referred to above. The decided cases, however, appear to fall into two groups: (*a*) where a party has failed to disclose his true financial position; and, (*b*) where a party has failed to disclose an intention to remarry. *Robinson* and *Hill* are examples of the former group.

The remarriage cases, in particular *Wales* v *Wadham* [1977] 2 All ER 125, must now be reviewed in the light of the decision in *Livesey* v *Jenkins* which is discussed in Chapter 3, section 5. In *Prow* v *Brown*

(1983) FLR 352, an agreement, which transferred the matrimonial home to the wife, was successfully challenged because she had failed to disclose her intention to remarry and the day following the transfer to her had conveyed the property to herself and her new husband. No consent order had been made, but the agreement was reached against the background of the wife having made an application for ancillary relief in divorce proceedings (cf the general position of agreements referred to on p 14). The husband applied to the court for rescission of the agreement and conveyance, but subsequently converted his application into one for ancillary relief under ss 23–25 of the 1973 Act. In *Toleman* v *Toleman* [1985] FLR 62, the husband was granted leave to appeal out of time against a consent order reached on the express basis indorsed on counsel's brief that the wife had no intention of remarriage or cohabitation on the ground that some three months after the date of the consent order the wife indicated that she intended to remarry. The court considered that the considerable change in the wife's intentions over a period of only three months justified a rehearing to investigate whether the basis of the consent order had disappeared because the wife had given the husband unjustified assurances as to her intentions at the date when the consent order was being negotiated. It is fundamental therefore to prove that the wife failed to disclose an intention to remarry, which existed at the time of the making of a consent order. The decision in *B–T* v *B–T* [1990] 2 FLR 1 is of greatest importance for its analysis of the procedural aspects of setting aside. The facts behind the decision, however, revolved around the failure by the wife to disclose until October 1986 a permanent relationship with another man which had commenced in late 1983 following the making of a consent order on 21 April 1986 after a door of the court settlement. The wife had had a child by the man involved in March 1986. The husband was unsuccessful in his attempt to set aside the consent order because the registrar had no jurisdiction to rehear the application which had not been brought in the proper form under CCR Ord 37. It is submitted that the result may well have been different had a fresh action been brought to set aside the consent order or an application been made for leave to appeal out of time. The decision is a striking example of the need to adopt the correct procedure when challenging a consent order. It is also worthwhile noting that no statement of information under r 2.61 of the Family Proceedings Rules 1991—which may or may not have avoided the whole sorry tale—was required because the consent order resulted from a door of the court compromise.

The current form of statement of information under r 2.61 should ensure that clear statements of the parties' intentions are made known to the court. If these statements are incorrect, the consent order may be challenged on the ground of fraud or misrepresentation. What, however, will be the position if the wife quite genuinely forms the intention to remarry *after* the consent order has been made? This matter was not decided by *Livesey* v *Jenkins*. However, in *Wells* v *Wells* decided on 18 June 1980 and reported at [1992] 2 FLR 66 (referred to in *Livesey* v *Jenkins*, at 119), the wife began to associate with another man whom she had known before (and whom she subsequently married) two months after an order for financial provision and property adjustment had been made in contested proceedings. Six months after the date of the order the husband was granted leave to appeal out of time against the order and, upon the substantive appeal being heard, it was held that the whole basis on which the original order had been made had been falsified by events occurring within about three months of the date of the order and that accordingly the order should be set aside and a different order substituted for it based on the true state of affairs. The decision in *Wells* was part of a line of authority which led to the emergence of the rule in *Barder* v *Barder* (see p 145). The rule may therefore be invoked where the intention to remarry is formed after the making of the consent order as a new event invalidating the basis upon which the order was made. However, as can be seen from the decision of the Court of Appeal in *Cook* v *Cook* [1988] 1 FLR 521, there must be a complete change of circumstances rather than a development in an already existing relationship of which the party seeking to set aside the consent order was already aware. *Cook* was a 'wife swop' case, where the wife had resumed a sexual relationship with the other husband involved with some degree of cohabitation in August 1986. On 15 December 1986, a consent order was made but the r 76A (now r 2.61) statement filed by the wife failed to disclose that relationship. Although the husband was given leave to appeal out of time, the substantive appeal was dismissed because the wife's failure to disclose the relationship constituted a change of circumstances which would not have made any substantial difference to the original consent order. (*Crozier* v *Crozier* [1994] 2 WLR 444 was another case where it was held that there was a development in an existing situation and there was therefore no 'new event' in the *Barder* sense).

Another case which involved a wife's remarriage was *Chaudhuri* v *Chaudhuri* [1992] 2 FLR 73. An order had been made in May 1988, the effect of which was to allow the wife to remain with the children in the former matrimonial home. The property was subject to a

CHALLENGING CONSENT ORDERS

charge in the husband's favour amounting to three-quarters of the net proceeds of sale of the property, the charge not to be realised without the wife's consent or until the older child ceased full-time education or until the death or remarriage of the wife or her permanent cohabitation with another man, whichever event should first occur. It was the central plank of the wife's case that she needed to stay in the property in order to provide a secure home for the children in a neighbourhood where she would have the support of friends. The house was transferred to her in July 1988. In June 1989 the wife's solicitors informed the husband that she intended to remarry and move to Chester. The husband then applied for leave to appeal out of time, the main ground being that the circumstances of the wife had changed fundamentally, so as to vitiate the basis on which the order had been made, and secondly on the basis that there had been a material non-disclosure by the wife, in that she had opened a joint bank account with another man (the person whom she married) before the appealed order and without informing the court. There was therefore an alleged non-disclosure of two kinds. The Court of Appeal dismissed the application for leave. It held that the husband had known of his wife's friendship with the other man at the time when the order had been made, and the non-disclosure was not of such significance as to justify leave to appeal out of time. Secondly, since the order appealed against contemplated in its very words the possibility of the wife's remarrying and the sale of the property, it could not be said that there had been a sufficient change in the circumstances underlying the basis of the order for the appeal to be likely to succeed. Furthermore, the time that had elapsed (fourteen months), although borderline, was too great. The decision in *Wells* (see p 138) was distinguished as in that case the change of circumstances was much more drastic.

Worlock v *Worlock* [1994] 2 FLR 689 was another case in which a challenge was made to a consent order upon the dual front of alleged non-disclosure and new event. It is analysed at page 159. It provides a good example of the Court of Appeal restricting the opportunities where a party is going to be able to rely on non-disclosure in any application to set aside, or on appeal.

Apart from the two groups identified above, non-disclosure can relate to a host of other factors. In *Thwaite* v *Thwaite* [1981] 2 All ER 789, the failure by the wife to disclose her intention to return to Australia led to the Court of Appeal upholding the decision to set aside a consent order under which a property in England was to be transferred to her to provide a home for herself and the children here.

As will be seen below, non-disclosure may be a reason for the court refusing to grant an order of specific performance (*Cross* v *Cross* (1983) FLR 235, where the wife had not disclosed that she had vacated the former matrimonial home, which was to be transferred to her, in order to live with her present husband).

After a consent order has been made, it is not open to a party to go on a 'fishing expedition' to find out whether there is material non-disclosure which might form a basis for challenging the order by delivering a questionnaire under the Family Proceedings Rules 1991, r 2.63 (*H* v *B* [1987] 1 All ER 766).

(v) Undue influence

There is no presumption that a husband has exercised undue influence over his wife (*Howes* v *Bishop* [1909] 2 KB 390; *McKenzie* v *Royal Bank of Canada* [1934] AC 468). The principle of undue influence was examined by the House of Lords in *Barclays Bank plc* v *O'Brien* [1994] 1 FLR 1, in which the court referred to 'an invalidating tendency' implicit in a relationship between husband and wife (and indeed in a relationship between cohabitees). In cases where the wife relies in all financial matters on her husband and simply does what he suggests, the presumption of undue influence of this type can be established solely from the proof of such trust and confidence without proof of actual undue influence. In the words of Browne-Wilkinson LJ:

> I accept that the risk of undue influence affecting a voluntary disposition by a wife in favour of a husband is greater than in the ordinary run of cases where no sexual or emotional ties affect the free exercise of the individual's will.

The onus of proof rests upon the party seeking to establish that undue influence was exerted. If undue influence is proved, transactions between spouses can be set aside in the same way as between other persons (*Bank of Montreal* v *Stuart* [1911] AC 120).

Undue influence has long been recognised as a ground for not upholding an agreement reached between husband and wife (see eg *Edgar* v *Edgar* [1980] 3 All ER 887, at 893–894; *Backhouse* v *Backhouse* [1978] 1 All ER 1158, at 1166 and *Evans* v *Evans* (1981) FLR 33). It is one of several factors which the court will bear in mind in deciding what weight is to be given to the agreement when a party applies to the court for an order for ancillary relief. The bearing of undue influence upon agreements is discussed in Chapter 2 in section 6.

However, Balcombe J held in *Tommey* v *Tommey* [1982] 3 All ER 385 that undue influence was not a good ground for setting aside a consent order. As indicated in the passage from his judgment above on p 130, Balcombe J was very much influenced by considerations of finality, by the fact that (at 392) 'it will be a rare case where undue influence can be shown to exist right up to the making of the order' and by difficulties of definition.

Balcombe J expressed these difficulties in this way (at 393):

> I have also been influenced by the consideration that fraud, in its strict legal sense, is a well-defined and understood concept. If fraud, as a ground for setting aside a matrimonial order, were extended to include undue influence, where should one draw the line? What about other forms of pressure or exploitation? The wife who is in receipt of legal aid and uses that fact as a bargaining counter with the husband who has to pay his own costs. Or the husband who accepts a disadvantageous financial settlement rather than risk his access to the children being disturbed. One can envisage endless possibilities of further litigation. In my judgment the policy of the law in this field should be to encourage finality and certainty, the 'clean break' as in *Minton* v *Minton* [1979] 1 All ER 79, [1979] AC 593, and to prefer that principle even if it means that the occasional 'hard case' will be without remedy.

The decision in *Tommey* has, however, been called into question by Lord Brandon in *Livesey* v *Jenkins* (at 116) where he commented:

> Balcombe J held, as a matter of law, that undue influence, even if proved, was not a good ground for setting aside a consent order. The question of the effect of undue influence in circumstances of this kind does not arise on this appeal, and, that being so, it would be undesirable to express even a provisional opinion on it. I think it right to say, however, that I am not persuaded that Balcombe J's decision on the question was necessarily correct.

The availability of undue influence as a ground to challenge a consent order remains, it is submitted, an open question. There was a flavour of undue influence, coupled with other matters, in *Camm* v *Camm* (see p 32). Indeed, Balcombe J himself in *Tommey* did indicate (at 392) that it would involve no great development of the existing law to hold that undue influence is a ground. As Lord Scarman warned in *National Westminster Bank plc* v *Morgan* [1985] AC 686 (at 709), 'there is no precisely defined law setting limits to the equitable jurisdiction of a court to relieve against undue influence'. This has to be set against the trend of the courts to uphold agreements and consent orders.

(vi) Unconscionable bargain

An agreement which is an unconscionable bargain may be set aside by the court. However, a matrimonial consent order reflecting such an agreement cannot be challenged on such a ground because of the principle established in *De Lasala* referred to above on p 131.

In *Cresswell* v *Potter* [1978] 1 WLR 255n, the wife, who did not obtain independent advice, conveyed to the husband her interest in the former matrimonial home, which had been vested in joint names, in consideration of an indemnity against her liability under the mortgage. The deed was set aside as an unconscionable bargain and the wife awarded half of the proceeds of sale.

Megarry J applied the three requirements laid down by Kay J in *Fry* v *Lane* (1888) 40 Ch D 312, at 322:

(*a*) purchase at a considerable undervalue;
(*b*) from a poor and ignorant man;
(*c*) the vendor having no independent advice.

The decision in *Cresswell* v *Potter* was referred to in *Backhouse* v *Backhouse* [1978] 1 All ER 1158 which is discussed on p 34. The facts of the two cases were similar, but in *Backhouse* the court proceeded to make orders for financial provision and property adjustment on the basis that the transfer by the wife had not been made. By contrast, in *Lyle* v *Lyle* (1972) 117 SJ 70, the wife's application to set aside an agreement, which benefited her considerably and upon which she had received legal advice and an explanation from the judge, failed. The defence of laches was fatal to the wife's claim in *Butlin-Sanders* v *Butlin* [1985] FLR 204 for rescission of a deed transferring her interest in the former matrimonial home to the husband without consideration on the grounds of misrepresentation and that the transaction had been an unconscionable bargain. The wife failed on the former ground; she also failed to establish that the transaction had been an unconscionable bargain as, unlike the wife in *Backhouse*, she had received advice from a solicitor to the effect that the transaction was contrary to her interests, but had chosen to proceed in the face of that advice.

Megarry J made it clear in *Cresswell* v *Potter* [1978] 1 WLR 255n at 257 that the requirements laid down in *Fry* v *Lane* (1880) 40 Ch D 312 were not intended to be exhaustive. Accordingly, it was found in *Watkin* v *Watson-Smith* (1986) *The Times*, 4 July; [1986] CLY 1282 that old age with accompanying diminution of capacity and judgment, together with a desire for a quick sale of a property, constituted a substitute for poverty and ignorance as one of the requirements for setting aside a sale at an undervalue as an unconscionable bargain.

(vii) Inequality of bargaining power

In *Lloyds Bank Ltd* v *Bundy* [1974] 3 All ER 757, at 763–765 Lord Denning MR summarised the various categories in which transactions could be set aside under the general heading of 'inequality of bargaining power', to which reference has already been made on p 34. These categories are very much reflected in the passage from the judgment of Ormrod LJ in *Edgar* quoted on p 30. Emphasis was placed on whether the inequality of bargaining power has been *exploited* so as to induce the other party to act to his or her detriment.

The general heading of 'inequality of bargaining power' has already been discussed in Chapter 2, section 6, in looking at the court's approach to agreements. It is not going to be very relevant in any consideration of consent orders, not least because of the r 2.61 procedure and the vetting role of the courts when making consent orders—one of the purposes of which is to 'sift out' cases in which there has been inequality of bargaining power. There is a useful critique of the so-called principle of 'inequality of bargaining power' at p 384 of *Treitel on Contract*, 9th ed (Sweet and Maxwell). Lord Denning was the only judge in the *Lloyds Bank Limited* v *Bundy* case to base his decision on this principle—the other members of the Court of Appeal based their decisions on the equitable doctrine of undue influence. The Privy Council in *Pao On* v *Lau Yiu Long* [1980] AC 614 rejected the argument that agreements were invalid if they were procured by 'an unfair use of a dominant legal position'. Furthermore the House of Lords has now held in *National Westminster Bank plc* v *Morgan* [1985] AC 686, at 708 that the doctrine of undue influence has been sufficiently developed not to need the support of a principle of inequality of bargaining power which by its formulation in the language of the law of contract is not appropriate to cover transactions of gift where there is no bargain. Lord Scarman went on to suggest that even in the field of contract it is questionable whether there is any need in the modern law to erect a general principle of relief against inequality of bargaining power. Cases therefore involving undue pressure by one party, bad legal advice or duress (see *Backhouse* v *Backhouse* [1978] 1 All ER 1158), which would previously have fallen under this general heading, may now have to be brought within one of the categories discussed above, eg undue influence or unconscionable bargain.

(viii) Fresh admissible evidence

RSC Ord 59, r 10(2) provides:

> The Court of Appeal shall have power to receive further evidence on questions of fact . . . but, in the case of an appeal from a judgment after

trial or hearing of any case or matter on the merits, no such further evidence (other than evidence as to matters which have occurred after the date of the trial or hearing) shall be admitted except on special grounds.

It is therefore only necessary to show special grounds where an application has been determined on its merits. This will not normally be the case with a consent order. The court does nonetheless retain a general discretion in the case of a consent order as to whether to admit the further evidence. But an important factor taken into account in exercising that discretion is the reason why the evidence was not adduced in the court below. Where it is necessary to show special grounds, three conditions must be satisfied (*Ladd* v *Marshall* [1954] 3 All ER 745; *Skone* v *Skone* [1971] 2 All ER 582; *Hughes* v *Singh* (1989) *The Times*, 21 April):

(*a*) It must be shown that the evidence could not have been obtained with reasonable diligence for use at the trial.
(*b*) The evidence must be such that, if given, it would probably have an important influence upon the result of the case, although it need not be decisive.
(*c*) The evidence must be such as is presumably to be believed, although it need not be incontrovertible.

In *Thwaite* v *Thwaite* [1981] 2 All ER 789, it was held that the court did have jurisdiction to hear an appeal from a consent order on the basis of fresh evidence that the wife did not intend to make a home for herself and the children in England. This was a non-disclosure case and indeed any such case will necessarily involve the need for fresh evidence subject to the restrictions referred to above. Another such case was *Redmond* v *Redmond* [1986] 2 FLR 173, where fresh evidence was admitted as an alternative basis of setting the order aside (see p 133). If the Court of Appeal is to be asked to give leave to adduce fresh evidence, it is important that that evidence is complete (*Rooker* v *Rooker* [1988] 1 FLR 219, at 223–224).

The admission of fresh evidence, however, as a ground for challenging a consent order, where there has been a change in circumstances '*subsequent* to' the date of a consent order, does run contrary to the general principle expressed in *Robinson* that such changes should normally be dealt with by way of a variation application. That the court exercises a tight control over the admission of fresh evidence is illustrated also by the principles exercised by the county court in its rehearing procedure set out in Ord 37 r 1. The note to that order in the *County Court Practice* (p 405, 1996 ed) indicates that it is essential that as a preliminary step a party asking for a new trial on the ground that new evidence has been discovered should show that there was no remissness on his part in adducing all possible evidence at the trial. It was decided in *Marsh v Marsh* [1993] 1 FLR 467 that the admission of further evidence on appeal was subject to the discretion of the judge hearing the appeal: see further p 170 below. The note goes on to quote the rule in *Ladd v Marshall*.

Not all orders, of course, are capable of variation. In such cases, RSC Ord 59, r 10(2) expressly provides for matters which have occurred after the date of the hearing. However, the discretion to admit such evidence must always be exercised sparingly with due regard to the need for finality in litigation (*Hughes v Singh* (1989) *The Times*, 21 April—see para 59/10/10 on p 1003 of the White Book (1996 ed)). Quite independently of this power, there has now emerged the rule in *Barder v Barder*, which was preceded by a line of authorities discussed below. It is interesting to note the Court of Appeal in *Penrose v Penrose* [1994] 2 FLR 621 drawing an analogy between the principles of *Ladd v Marshall* and the *Barder* rules. Balcombe LJ at 632G–H refers to the 'close analogy' between them and the common end—namely that 'it is in the general public interest that a decision once reached should be final, and that the grounds for upsetting it, certainly on new facts that come into existence after the date of the hearing, must be limited'.

(ix) The rule in Barder v Barder [1987] 2 All ER 440
- The facts

A consent order on a clean break basis was made in February 1985. Under the order, H was to transfer to W his interest in the former matrimonial home within twenty-eight days. In March 1985, before the order was implemented, W killed the two children of the family and committed suicide. W by will devised her estate to her mother. H applied under MCR 1977, r 124(1) and CCR Ord 13, r 4 for leave to appeal out of time against the consent order and the mother was given leave to intervene to oppose the application as W's sole personal representative. At first instance, H was granted leave to appeal, his appeal was allowed and the consent order set aside on the ground that it had been vitiated by a common mistake, namely, that for an appreciable time after the order W and the children would continue to live and benefit from it. The mother appealed to the Court of Appeal, which allowed her appeal. H appealed to the House of Lords, where the mother contended, *inter alia*, that W's death caused the suit to abate and that since the consent order made had been made on a clean break basis it could not be challenged. This contention was not accepted by the House of Lords, which allowed the appeal for this reason and because the four conditions referred to below for the granting of leave to appeal out of time were satisfied.

- The four conditions

The House of Lords held that leave to appeal out of time from an order for financial provision or property transfer made after divorce may be granted where the following four conditions are satisfied (per Lord Brandon, at 453):

(1) New events have occurred since the making of the order which invalidate the basis, or fundamental assumption, on which the order was made, so that, if leave to appeal out of time were to be given, the appeal would be certain, or very likely, to succeed. It will be noted that this condition contains two separate limbs: new events occurring after the making of the order may not be such that an appeal would be very likely to succeed (see *Thompson* v *Thompson* discussed on p 155).

(2) The new events should have occurred within a relatively short time of the order having been made. Lord Brandon indicated that the length of time could not be laid down precisely, but that he regarded it as extremely unlikely that it could be as much as a year, and that in most cases it would be no more than a few months. It should be noted that one year is not an inflexible period (see *Hope-Smith* v *Hope-Smith* [1989] 2 FLR 56: see p 152).

(3) The application for leave to appeal out of time should be made reasonably promptly in the circumstances of the case. (Cases such as *S* v *S* (Financial Provision) (Post-Divorce Cohabitation) [1994] 2 FLR 228 and *Heard* v *Heard* [1995] 1 FLR 970 have stretched this principle to the limits.)

(4) The grant of leave to appeal out of time should not prejudice third parties who have acquired, in good faith and for valuable consideration, interests in property which is the subject matter of the relevant order. (This fourth condition has hardly arisen in the cases which we go on to discuss.)

- Applications of the rule

Evidence of subsequent events was, it will be recalled, admitted in *Wells* v *Wells* [1992] 2 FLR 66 (see p 138).

The case of *Cornick* v *Cornick* is especially significant. In an erudite judgment, Hale J surveyed the post-*Barder* cases, drawing a distinction between cases where the equivalent of the contractual principle of frustration of contracts featured (in the shape of a *Barder*-type new event such as death of a party) and the alternative ground invalidating a consent order, namely mistake. The case also usefully set out the ways in which the courts have treated differences in valuation between the time of the court order and the time when it has been desired to review the order.

Cornick itself concerned the wife's appeal in May 1994 against an order made following a contested hearing in December 1992. The order had provided for the payment of a lump sum and periodical payments to the wife. The reason for her appeal out of time was a dramatic increase in the value of the husband's shareholdings following the date of the order. The effect of the 1992 order had been to give to the wife some 51 per cent of the total value of the couple's net assets. Following the rise in the price of the husband's shares, the net effect of the 1992 order gave the wife only 20 per cent of the total value. The wife maintained that the rise in the share price was a new event which would entitle the court to re-open the 1992 order. The wife's appeal was dismissed. The judge distinguished (at p 536E–H) between three possible causes of a difference in the value of assets between the date of the original hearing and the date of the review:

> (1) An asset which was taken into account and correctly valued at the date of the hearing changes value within a relatively short time owing to the natural processes of price fluctuation. The court should not then manipulate the power to grant leave to appeal out of time to provide a disguised power of variation which Parliament has quite obviously and deliberately declined to enact.
>
> (2) A wrong value was put on that asset at the hearing, which had it been known about at the time would have led to a different order. Provided that it is not the fault of the person alleging the mistake, it is open to the court to give leave for the matter to be re-opened. Although falling within the *Barder* principle, it is more akin to the misrepresentation or non-disclosure cases than to *Barder* itself.
>
> (3) Something unforeseen and unforeseeable has happened since the date of the hearing which has altered the value of the assets so dramatically as to bring about a substantial change in the balance of assets brought about by the order. Then, provided that the other three conditions are fulfilled, the *Barder* principle may apply. However, the circumstances in which this can happen are very few and far between. The case law, taken as a whole, does not suggest that natural processes of price fluctuation, whether in houses, shares or any other property, and however dramatic, fall within this principle.

So, in *Cornick*, because the shares had been correctly valued at the time of the hearing, the dramatic increase in their value could not constitute a 'new event' and the wife could not succeed in her appeal out of time.

Hale J provides further useful guidance, as follows:

> A price rise on this scale was not something which could with due diligence have been foreseen and put before the court on behalf of the wife at the [original] hearing. For the *Barder* principle to apply, it is a *sine qua non* that the event was unforeseen and unforeseeable. However the mere fact of such unforeseeability is not sufficient to turn something which would not otherwise be a *Barder* event into one. Yet that is in effect what is urged upon me now.

The judge went on (at 537F–G) to deal with the policy considerations as follows:

> There is also a 'floodgates' problem here, for although there are few couples with this sort of wealth, there are many couples whose wealth is bound up in assets which may well change value quite sharply within a relatively short period of time. It is a perennial problem and the court inevitably has to do the best it can on the material, including such prognostications as are relevant and available, at the time. Once the couple are divorced and their capital divided, they cannot normally expect to profit from, any more than they should expect to lose by, later changes in the other's fortune.

There is another interesting aspect of this decision which fettered the right to appeal out of time. The wife had obtained periodical payments in the original order. It was therefore possible for her to apply for a variation in the periodical payments and any voluntary capitalisation of her periodical payments would be based upon a survey of all the s 25 factors, including the husband's increased wealth.

Something rather similar happened in *Penrose v Penrose* [1994] 2 FLR 621, where the husband unsuccessfully appealed to the Court of Appeal against a High Court order. He alleged, *inter alia*, that a new event had occurred, in the shape of his tax liability being in the region of £400,000 and not £175,000 as had appeared to be the case at first instance. The Court of Appeal pointed out that the husband had at all times been in possession of the vital facts which would have established that the tax liability was the higher rather than the lower figure. This aspect of the decision is in line with what we have already seen about the court restricting a party's ability to rely on fresh evidence under the *Ladd* v *Marshall* principle.

Another relevant aspect of *Penrose* was that the appellate court still had jurisdiction to interfere with the order made by the court at first instance. The court of first instance had ordered that the husband should pay a lump sum by instalments, the second instalment of which had not been paid by the time of the appeal in the Court of Appeal. Balcombe LJ drew attention to the discretionary remedy of varying the second instalment payment. This was another reason why the appeal could not succeed.

We turn now to survey the developments in case law from 1983 onwards. The first of the cases, *Warren* v *Warren* [1983] FLR 529, involved an attempt to adduce fresh evidence as to property valuations. In this case, the wife was allowed to adduce further evidence as to the sale price of the matrimonial home at £92,500 against a valuation used in the proceedings of £52,000 in view of the substantial discrepancy between the two figures. Griffiths LJ, however, sounded this warning (at 537) to deal with the argument that reopening the valuation would open the floodgates to appeals to the Court of Appeal:

> In this case the discrepancy between the valuation and the subsequent sale price achieved was almost 100 per cent. By the very nature of things a valuation can only be an approximate estimate of the value of the property, and it will be very rare that, when the property is sold, it will achieve precisely the sum at which it was valued. The extraordinary discrepancy in this case must not be taken by the profession as any encouragement to bring appeals to this court wherever there is a difference between a valuation and the ultimate sale price.
>
> In *L* v *L* (1981) 11 Fam Law 57 Balcombe J expressed the view, albeit *obiter*, that he would not be prepared to reconsider a case where the discrepancy between the valuation and the sale price was £45,000 valuation and £52,000 sale price. If such a case came before me I should adopt precisely the same attitude as Balcombe J because that is the sort of margin of variation that will inevitably occur in many, many cases. As Sir Roger Ormrod said, this case is atypical because of the extraordinary discrepancy between the valuation and the sale price. It is for that reason only that this court allowed the further evidence of the sale price which enabled the figures to be re-examined.

Warren is one of the cases which was analysed by Hale J in *Cornick*. She saw the case as being one which involved a *Barder*-type new event (at 543D–E):

> A major reason for the discrepancy [between the value of the property at the hearing and its sale price eight months later] was that the husband had done a great deal of work to turn a virtually derelict house into a very desirable property. Whether or not the valuers had underestimated the value at the time of the trial, it is clear that the change was not attributable to normal fluctuations in house prices over the period.

The change could therefore be attributed 'largely to events taking place after the hearing rather than to underlying processes in train at the time'.

An attempt by a husband to reopen the valuation of the matrimonial home and adjoining farming land failed in *O'Dougherty* v *O'Dougherty* (1983) 4 FLR 407. In that instance, however, the husband had been aware at the time of the making of the consent order that the National Coal Board was seeking land in the area and that there was good reason to believe that the value which the Board would place upon the land at that time would be £26,000 as opposed to the valuation upon which the consent order was based of £8,000. Further, the husband had already had an appeal from the registrar's consent order dismissed.

A situation not too far distant from *Barder* on its facts arose in *Re Lane* [1986] 1 FLR 283. There a consent order had been made on a clean break basis under which *inter alia* the husband was to pay to the wife a lump sum and she was to transfer to him a property in Jersey, for which purpose she was to execute a power of attorney. The order was carried into effect, including the execution of the power of attorney, except for the transfer of the wife's interest in the Jersey property, which had not been completed at the time of the husband's death. The wife cancelled the power of attorney and went to live in the property. The executors of the husband's estate, *inter alia*, issued an application in the Family Division for a declaration that the consent order, insofar as it remained unperformed, was valid and enforceable against the wife notwithstanding the deceased's death. Sheldon J held that, whilst the power of the court to make a declaration was discretionary, the executors were entitled on the facts to the declaration sought unless there was some other supervening circumstances which should persuade the court to exercise its discretion in favour of the wife. A declaration was made in favour of the executors as the court was unable to find any merit in the wife's actions. The court could not readily subscribe to a state of affairs which would enable a party to reap the benefit of an earlier order—particularly an order made by consent—whilst successfully escaping its obligations.

Another case of unexpected death occurred in *Passmore* v *Gill* [1987] 1 FLR 441. A property adjustment order and periodical payments orders for the wife and a child were made by the registrar on 29 October 1984. On appeal on 21 December 1984, the judge increased the orders for periodical payments but left the property adjustment order unaltered. The wife died on 11 January 1985, at which time there was no appeal pending against either the original order or the variation order. The husband applied to the Court of Appeal for leave to appeal out of time against the variation order contending that it had been falsified by the wife's sudden death. The Court of Appeal allowed the appeal on the basis that if the registrar or the judge had known that the wife was to die in such a short space of time he would have made a property adjustment order less favourable to her because her need would have been quite different from that which was contemplated by the court when making the order. The Court of Appeal, in granting leave to appeal out of time and allowing the appeal, expressly applied *Wells* v *Wells*. Sir John Arnold P went on to comment (at 443):

> It is said, and I can see the sense of it, that this is a somewhat unexplored jurisdiction and, in particular, the limits to which it extends have not really been laid out. How long after the making of the order can the critical event cause the order to be reversed or reconsidered? How radical does the difference have to be between the assumed facts as they were at the date of the making of the order and those which come into existence by reason of the supervening events? None of those matters has been explored and nobody knows the exact limitations of this jurisdiction.

The limitations of the jurisdiction have now been delineated by the House of Lords' decision in *Barder* v *Barder*. An early attempt to apply the rule in *Barder* is to be found in the Court of Appeal's decision in *Rooker* v *Rooker* [1988] 1 FLR 219. The supervening event put before the court was the husband's alleged deliberate procrastination in the sale of a property, from the proceeds of which the wife was to receive £20,000 under a consent order. The consent order had been made on 8 May 1984, but the sale was not completed until 30 June 1986. The wife asked the Court of Appeal to increase the lump sum order. Her appeal, however, failed because the Court of Appeal took the view that the remedy for the wife was provided for within the terms of the consent order itself: she had, at all times, liberty to apply to the court which made the order to enforce it. This is another example of the principle of the court pointing to the terms of the appealed order in trying to prevent a re-opening of cases (a principle which we observed in commenting on *Cornick* and *Penrose* above).

An interesting example of the interaction of *Livesey* v *Jenkins* and the rule in *Barder* is to be found in *Cook* v *Cook* [1988] 1 FLR 521 (see p 138). It was alleged that the husband's discovery, shortly after the making of a consent order, of a resumption of a prior relationship by the wife constituted new events which invalidated the basis on which the original consent order was made. The Court of Appeal dismissed the appeal on the basis that, although there was a change of circumstances, the change would not have made a substantial difference (within the *Livesey* v *Jenkins* test) if the order were reopened.

The rule in *Barder* was successfully applied to the problems encountered with escalating property prices in *Hope-Smith* v *Hope-Smith* [1989] 2 FLR 56. In September 1985, the husband was ordered by the registrar to pay the wife a lump sum of £32,000 within twenty-eight days and that in default the matrimonial home was to be sold and the lump paid to the wife out of the net proceeds of sale. The husband appealed to the county court judge, who on 11 March 1986 dismissed the appeal and ordered the immediate sale of the home. The husband failed to comply with that order and the wife appealed to the Court of Appeal contending that the amount of the lump sum should be increased, having regard to the increase in property prices since the order was made, the home remaining unsold two and three-quarter years after the appeal before the county court judge. It was contended that supervening events had frustrated the order of the county court judge because the delay over and above that which he contemplated was of such proportions that it invalidated the basis upon which he arrived at his decision to the wife's detriment and the delay was wilfully induced by the husband's conduct and it was inequitable that he should benefit by it. Hollings J indicated that although the Court of Appeal was now concerned only with the appeal rather than with leave to appeal, he believed that the four *Barder* conditions should apply in deciding a substantive appeal. He held that a substantial increase in the property value, coupled with the husband's delay in selling the property, was sufficient to satisfy the first *Barder* condition and that, as no third party interests were involved, the fourth condition was also satisfied. His approach to the second *Barder* condition that the new events should have occurred within a relatively short time of the making of the order was to observe that the increase in value had accrued more or less gradually over the period of two and three-quarter years since the hearing below. Although the application for leave to appeal out of time was not made until 28 August 1987 (the third *Barder* condition), Hollings J took the view that the husband could not rely on any failure by the wife to satisfy the second or third conditions where such failure was due to the husbad's conduct. He held that the wife's failure to enforce the order before its basis was vitiated or to apply for leave to appeal earlier was entirely or very substantially due to the dilatory tactics of the husband. There were methods of enforcement built into the order of the registrar which were sought to be enforced by the judge. This enforcement was only frustrated by the husband's conduct, making the facts wholly different from those of *Rooker* v *Rooker*. In allowing the appeal, Hollings J went on to stress the desirability of expressing the wife's entitlement as a fraction of the net proceeds of sale. When commenting on this case in *Cornick*, Hale J reasoned (at 534H–535A) that 'it was clearly the husband's behaviour after the order that brought about the frustration of the judge's intentions rather than the fluctuation in prices alone'. The appeal court had therefore interfered with the order because the change, like that in *Warren*, could be attributed largely to an event taking place after the hearing rather than to underlying processes in train at the time—another *Barder*-type new event.

In *Edmonds* v *Edmonds* [1990] 2 FLR 202, the Court of Appeal found that the first *Barder* condition was not satisfied where there had been a sale at a price substantially in excess of the valuation figure adopted by the registrar, since the fact that the value of the property would almost certainly increase was known to all and was reflected in the terms of the original order. The decision in *Warren* could be distinguished on its facts. In particular, the husband failed to call valuation evidence. The husband could not seek to rely on the absence of expert evidence, since in none of the cases cited in *Barder* nor on the facts of *Barder* itself did the party applying for relief have the opportunity to avoid the false assumption.

A tragic unexpected death occurred in *Smith* v *Smith* [1991] 2 All ER 306. A registrar made a lump sum order in favour of the wife of £54,000 on a clean break basis. Six months later, the wife committed suicide, leaving her estate to her daughter. The husband applied for leave to appeal out of time against the registrar's order and the daughter was added as an intervener to the application. The judge granted the husband leave to appeal out of time and varied the registrar's order by requiring the estate to repay to the husband the lump sum except for the amount required to pay off the wife's debts and the costs of the estate. The daughter appealed to the Court of Appeal, by which time the husband had retired and was in indifferent health. The Court of Appeal held that, when applying the *Barder* principle, the court had to reconsider the matter afresh in the light of the facts known at the date of the reassessment and having regard to all the criteria in s 25(2) of the 1973 Act. Accordingly, the court should not restrict itself to considering the needs of the parties as then known but should also take into account matters such as recognition of a significant contribution to the marriage made by the deceased spouse if there were assets available to do so without acting to the unjust detriment of the other spouse. The ultimate destination of the deceased spouse's estate was an irrelevant consideration. On the facts, the Court of Appeal considered that the appropriate order was a lump sum of £25,000 to the wife. This was an obvious example of a *Barder*-type new event 'frustrating' the effect of the original order.

It is appropriate at this point to consider *Amey* v *Amey* [1992] 2 FLR 89. This also involved a *Barder*-type event, namely a death of one of the parties. In this case the wife died after the minutes of order were drawn up, but before the order was made. The husband had paid the wife £120,000 pursuant to the agreement, in return for a clean break (it being agreed between the parties that it was appropriate that there should be a roughly equal division of their capital assets). Following the wife's death, the husband tried to rescind the agreement on the basis that it was vitiated by a change in the fundamental assumption underlying it, ie by the wife's death. Scott Baker J held that the agreement stood or fell at common law and based upon principles of contract, as there was no statutory framework for the dispute (the minutes not having yet been made into an order). It was held that the *Barder* principles could apply to the law of contract and could therefore lead to a contract being frustrated. It was, however, essential to look at the terms of the particular contract between the parties; this was a case where the parties had negotiated a commercial settlement of matrimonial proceedings. It was not a case in which a husband was buying off a long term obligation to maintain the wife with a once and for all capital payment (at 96D):

> She had an earning capacity. He had not been paying periodical payments for her or otherwise maintaining her during the negotiations. This was a case where the parties were essentially dividing the capital in the light of the contributions that each had made, both financially and otherwise, to their business.

In the light of that, it could not be said that the death of the wife frustrated the purpose of the parties' agreement and the court would not intervene.

The case is a good illustration of the fact that a *Barder*-type new event will not necessarily invalidate an agreement or consent order. As was reasoned by Hale J at 533H, in *Cornick*, when commenting on this case, 'a party's death will not necessarily do this, if that person's continued good health was not the basis upon which the couple's assets were shared out between them'. The case of *Amey* therefore illustrates the principle that the courts will seek to preserve the 'status quo' of the finality produced by an agreement or consent order even when the *Barder*-type new event occurs.

The law applied in *Smith* v *Smith* was also applied in *Barber* v *Barber* [1993] 1 FLR 476. The wife in this case died less than three months after an order, following which the husband appealed. The Court of Appeal, allowing the appeal in part, held that the correct approach would be to start again from the beginning and consider what order should be made by the judge in the knowledge that the wife was to have only three months to live.

The Court of Appeal in *Thompson* v *Thompson* [1991] 2 FLR 530 gave some helpful guidelines on the first *Barder* condition. In *Thompson*, an order had been made after a contested hearing on the basis that the husband's business was worth £20,000. The wife had commissioned a valuation, yielding a figure of £45,000. However, the valuer who was at court was not called to give evidence as the valuer could not sustain his original valuation figure. Two weeks after the date of the order, the husband sold his business for £45,000. Mustill LJ made the following observations:

(*a*) The first *Barder* condition has two separate limbs. One first has to determine whether new events of the type mentioned in *Barder* exist and then look at the merits of an appeal.

(*b*) Differences in valuations expressed in percentage terms should be approached with caution:

> Here, we were naturally impressed in argument with the fact that the increase in the anticipated value of the business was proportionally large: in fact, 125 per cent. We believe that percentages should be used with caution, for it is easy to see that a modest-seeming percentage change in the figure for an asset or a liability may have a disproportionate practical effect on the order under appeal. Thus, if one posits that the principal asset of the former spouses is a house valued at £130,000, which is subject to a mortgage of £100,000 a rise of 30 per cent or fall of 23 per cent could wipe out or double the equity. We think it much better for the reviewing court, when considering questions of degree, to look in broad terms at the balance of the financial relationship created by the order under review, and then ask itself how this balance has been affected by the new state of affairs.

(*c*) The causation behind the new event is largely immaterial:

> First of all, counsel were disposed to agree, with two reservations, that the cause of the change in the balance of the relationship is immaterial. Thus, for example, it should make no difference whether something has happened to alter the evaluation of assets or liabilities or other factors already taken into account in the order originally made, or whether an

entirely new factor has come into play—such as the receipt of an unexpected legacy. Broadly speaking we concur, and add the words 'broadly speaking' only so as not to state an absolute rule in a field where the possible permutations of fact are so diverse.

Of these two qualifications, the first is that the change should not have been brought about by the conscious fault of the person who seeks to take advantage of it. We must emphasise that this must not be understood as a precise formulation of a principle which has not been in issue here. Merely to say that the applicant must not have brought the change on himself is not enough, for this would disqualify an applicant who had been ruined by an honest error of business judgment. But that some qualification of this kind must be imposed is, as it seems to us, just a matter of common sense.

The second qualification to the principle that the cause of the change in circumstances does not matter is that the cause has not been foreseen and taken into account when the order was made: for if it was, it cannot be 'new'.

It should be noted however that, even if an event is unforeseen and not taken into account in the original hearing, the event is not necessarily a *Barder* event (the rise in the share price in *Cornick* being a case in point).

(*d*) There are two distinguishable situations where the new events related to valuation:

We turn to a different aspect of the matter, arising where the change relied on is the ascertainment of the true value of an asset or liability after an order has been made on a mere estimate. Two situations must be distinguished: (i) where the change consists of a discovery that the estimate was unsound when made, and (ii) where a reasonable estimate has been falsified by subsequent events.

In situation '(i)' it seems that usually—we put it not higher than this because circumstances differ so greatly—the court must enquire whether the applicant was in some way responsible for the erroneous valuation. If he was, then he may well not be entitled to the indulgence of being allowed to appeal out of time. We take this to be the ground of the distinction drawn in *Edmonds* v *Edmonds*, above. So also if the applicant himself put forward a valuation which his opponent and the court were willing to adopt. But the mere fact that the valuation was agreed at the time when the order was made cannot be conclusive for or against an application to re-open it later, if the interests of justice so require.

Situation '(ii)' exists where a valuation reasonable when made, has afterwards become unexpectedly out of date. In our judgment it makes no difference how the valuation came into existence. If it was put forward by the applicant for leave to appeal or not; if it was challenged by him or not. The fact is that something new has happened.

CHALLENGING CONSENT ORDERS

It should be noted here that situation '(ii)' does not arise when there has been the normal fluctuation in property prices such as the first category of cases summarised by Hale J in *Cornick*.

(*e*) A word of warning:

> In making this order we wish to add our own endorsement, with as much emphasis as we can command, to the observation of Griffiths LJ in *Warren* v *Warren* already quoted: and to draw to the attention of those advising parties to matrimonial proceedings who might be tempted to try again, on appeal, with an argument that things have not turned out precisely as expected, to the severity of the requirements laid down by Lord Brandon. These advisers must be alert, and the Circuit Judges will be alert if they are not, to make sure that the courts are not swamped with meritless applications for leave to appeal out of time. Orders for ancillary relief are bound to be painted with a broad brush, often on the basis of estimates which by their nature must be speculative. Lord Brandon has shown that an order for a clean break is not *ipso facto* immune from review. At the same time the review should not be too readily granted, otherwise the whole basis of this essentially practical jurisdiction will be put out of joint.

As was said in *Cornick* at 535D–E:

> this case was clearly one where there had been a mistake at the hearing, such that had the court known the true facts then it would have made a different order, rather than one where later events had frustrated the court's intentions.

There was speculation following the decision in *Thompson* that the case had 'smashed' the 'floodgates' around *Barder*-type cases. The subsequent cases have shown that any such fear was unfounded. *Rundle* v *Rundle* [1992] 2 FLR 80 is a good example of how the floodgates have remained closed to prevent normal fluctuations in property values becoming *Barder*-type events. A wife's application for leave to appeal and to adduce further evidence was refused, and Purchas LJ observed (at 84 D–E and 85H–86A) that:

> all property adjustments orders and associated provisions must have an element of speculation built into them . . . Any order involving the sale of property must contemplate inevitable, if unpredictable, movements in the market. In this case, property values had been steadily falling . . . To allow this phenomenon to be, of itself, the basis of adducing fresh evidence on an appeal would be contrary to the principle that the discretion to allow it must be sparingly used and would deny the maxim that there should be some finality in litigation.

This case is therefore another example of the analogy between the sparingly-used discretion to admit fresh evidence and the rare grant of leave to appeal out of time.

A more recent example of a successful application for leave to appeal out of time based on a mistake relating to property values is *Heard* v *Heard* [1995] 1 FLR 970. The case was decided less than one month after *Cornick*, but there was no reference to *Cornick* in the judgment. The husband appealed to the Court of Appeal against the decision of the county court judge who had refused him leave to appeal against a district judge's decision in April 1992. The husband succeeded in the Court of Appeal, in essence because of a mistake as to the value of the former matrimonial home at the original hearing. The wife estimated at the hearing that the net equity of the former matrimonial home was £55,500. The district judge ordered that £16,000 of the proceeds of sale should be paid to the wife and the balance should be paid to the husband. On the figures which the district judge had, that left £39,500 for the husband. The Court of Appeal observed that the husband did not himself adduce valuation evidence and certainly did not challenge in any way the valuation evidence given on behalf of the wife; and the Court of Appeal speculated that he believed that the house would be worth at least as much as the value that had been estimated and he may even have thought that it was worth more. Unfortunately, the valuation of the property proved too wide of the mark. By May 1993 the best offer that the husband had received was £36,000, which would have left an equity in the house of £21,000, of which there would be £5,000 for him after payment of £16,000 to the wife. The Court of Appeal held that the discovery that the valuation was unsound, or alternatively the discovery that the house could not be sold at the price which had been assumed as its market price, did amount to 'new events' sufficient to satisfy the first *Barder* condition. The Court of Appeal in this case applied the decision in *Thompson*.

The decision that a mistake had been made at the original hearing was, in the circumstances of this case, not surprising. What is perhaps surprising, however, is that this case was held to fulfil the third of the *Barder* conditions, namely, that the application for leave to appeal out of time should be made reasonably promptly in the circumstances of the case. Indeed, Sir Thomas Bingham as he then was, giving the judgment of the court, indicated that the husband's delay in this case had caused him some concern, since plainly the matter had not been brought back before the court as promptly as one would have wished. The delay in this case, about fourteen months between the date of the original order and the application for leave to appeal out of time, was fairly significant and clearly troubled the judge. However, the then Master of the Rolls indicated that:

one notes that Lord Brandon required that the application for leave to appeal should be made reasonably promptly in the circumstances of the case. That use of words seems to me plainly to contemplate that account should be taken of the situation in which an individual finds himself and that no unreasonably inflexible rule of thumb should be applied.

The flexibility of this rule is well illustrated by *S* v *S* [1994] 2 FLR 228, in which a wife in September 1992 successfully applied for leave to appeal against a consent order which had been made in 1977. The wife had cohabited with the husband very soon after the consent order and decree absolute, and finally separated from him in 1993. The High Court judge, applying the *Barder* rules, adjudged that the cohabitation of the parties so soon after the consent order, coupled with their subsequent conduct, was a new event, and that in all the circumstances the applications to set aside and to obtain leave to appeal out of time were brought promptly after the parties' second, and final, decision to separate. Some commentators have suggested that this case is so exceptional that it has to be read on its own facts (and both judges in the Court of Appeal in *Hewitson* v *Hewitson* [1995] 1 FLR 245 expressed doubt about the decision), but it does demonstrate how the class of *Barder*-type new events cannot be closed, indeed the authors know of a case in which an applicant is alleging 'mistake' and asking for an order to be set aside on the basis that the applicant was 'incapable of rational thought' at the time that he consented to an order.

The previous edition of this book had foreshadowed the possibility of a party appealing out of time against a consent order on the basis of the introduction of the Child Support Act 1991. The case which duly settled the matter was *Crozier* v *Crozier* [1994] 2 WLR 444. The husband appealed out of time against a consent order dated February 1989, in which he had done his best to obtain a clean break in relation to the child of the family (by providing that the wife should have his share of the equity in the former matrimonial home). Booth J ruled that the enactment of the Child Support Act 1991 was not a new event—at the time that the parties had concluded the consent order, the state was empowered to seek the recovery of its expenditure on benefit from a person who was liable for maintenance under the then applicable legislation, (Social Security Act 1986, s 24). It is in this sense that the Child Support Act 1991 was merely 'a development from known facts' (quoting Hale J in *Cornick*).

Our survey of the post-*Barder* cases concludes with three cases which illustrate how the floodgates are being kept shut. In *Worlock* v *Worlock* [1994] 2 FLR 689, the wife founded her attack on a consent order upon allegations of non-disclosure by the husband and of a

Barder-type event. The facts of the case briefly were that a consent order was made in December 1984. In 1986 the husband's mother transferred to the husband her shares in a company which owned property which was actually worth about £3.5m even though the property was valued in the accounts at cost value, about £50,000. At the time of the hearing, the wife was aware that the husband had no current interest in the company but had the expectation of an eventual inheritance. The wife became aware of the true value of the company in 1988. Her application to set aside the 1984 order and for leave to appeal out of time was dismissed by the judge in chambers in 1990 and she went before the Court of Appeal on 29 January 1991 seeking leave to appeal against the order. The Court of Appeal held that, first, there had been no non-disclosure or misrepresentation by the husband at the time of the original order. In the President's words, (at 694F–G):

> the supervening event, if one may so term it, which is relied on in this case is, of course, the transfer of the shares . . . to the husband by his mother two years after the Registrar's order. But there is also the essential difference in this case that it is apparent that the essential facts were available to the wife and her advisers at the time of the Registrar's order. When I say 'the essential facts', I mean all the relevant information which it would be necessary for them to have in their possession to enable them to investigate and assess the complete position.

Neither judge in the Court of Appeal was in fact of the belief that the so-called 'new event' had occurred. It would be possible to slot this case into the *Wells* or *Crozier* category of a development from an existing situation or relationship: in this case, the husband's relationship with the mother and with the company of which he was a director, and the shares in which were advanced to him by his mother. In any event, two years was held to be far too late a period to come within the *Barder* rules.

Then there is the decision in *B* v *B* (Financial Provision: Leave to Appeal) [1994] 1 FLR 219. The husband was in this case seeking leave to appeal out of time against an order for financial provision made in favour of the wife over three years previously. He failed on most of the limbs of the *Barder* rules. The husband relied in his application on the diminution in the value of the former matrimonial home, a deterioration in his own financial situation, and the wife's improved financial situation upon her remarriage. The judge rejected the proposition that any of these were 'new events' falling within the *Barder*-type situation for the reasons which we have seen traced in the cases referred to above. There was no point of substance arising out of the fact that property values had declined; there was no substance in the contention that the deterioration in his financial position was so serious as to become a 'new event', and (at 222C) there was no substance in the reliance upon the wife's remarriage because this was a case in which

> the fact of that remarriage, even had it been before the court when the court decided the matter, would not have affected at all her entitlement to capital, and her being entitled to the share of the money which she had earned during the marriage by her efforts within it.

We have seen how judges will look at the way in which a party has the ability to exhaust the remedies inherent in the original order before being allowed to appeal; in this case (at 222F–G) the husband:

> was at all times able to elect to sell at any time when it began to appear that his fortunes were turning for the worse. He did not choose to do so. He cannot now complain of hardship which flows from a failure to exercise a choice which was given to him.
>
> The second requirement of Lord Brandon is that any supervening event should occur within a short time of the order being made, and none of them do ... None of these events appear to me to be so close to the making of the order as to justify this court, which, in its striving to do justice, has also to take into account the public interest in the finality of these orders.
>
> Finally the requirement is for the appeal to be made reasonably promptly in the circumstances of the case. There has been no prompt action by the husband.

This case is perhaps most notable for settling that the operative date in determining whether leave to appeal has been sought reasonably promptly was not the time at which the order came to be implemented, but the time at which the order was made.

In *Benson* v *Benson (Deceased)* [1996] 1 FLR 692, the relevant 'new event' was the tragic death of the wife. Shortly after the making of a consent order in December 1992, she was diagnosed as suffering from terminal cancer, from which she died in June 1993. The following month, a compromise was reached between the husband and the wife's estate whereby, *inter alia*, the estate would not enforce parts of the 1992 order.

The husband took a cautious approach by making a variety of applications to set aside the county court consent order: seeking leave to appeal out of time; issuing a writ in the Queen's Bench Division to set aside the consent order; making an application to set aside the original order; and seeking a review of the original order on the ground that it was still executory. The proceedings were consolidated and transferred to the Family Division of the High Court for determination.

It was held by Bracewell J that the death of the wife in June 1993 was a new event, but that the aspect that was fatal to the husband's application was the delay in the appeal, which was not prepared until September 1994, over a year after the death of the wife and a subsequent compromise between the husband and the wife's estate. The judge found that the reason for the delay was that the husband had been satisfied with the agreement reached in July 1993 (the agreement being clear and unambiguous, for good consideration, and reached when each side was fully advised) and the compromise would therefore not be disturbed.

Before departing from the consideration of the *Barder* rules, it is appropriate to draw attention to the different way in which the court treats consent orders on the one hand and agreements on the other. We have seen in our analysis of the cases how the courts tend to uphold consent orders. Agreements are of course less sacrosanct and Hoffmann LJ raised a powerful voice of complaint in the case of *Pounds* v *Pounds* [1994] 1 FLR 775 at p 791:

> It does not seem to me that the law is in an unsatisfactory state. There are in theory various possible answers to the problem. One might be that an agreement between the parties, at least where each has independent legal advice, is binding upon them subject only to the normal contractual remedies based on fraud, misrepresentation, undue influence etc . . . Another answer might be that when parties are negotiating with a view to an agreement which will be embodied in a consent order, everything should be treated as without prejudice negotiation until the order is actually made. . . . The result of the decision of this court in *Edgar* v *Edgar* and the cases which have followed it is that we have, as it seems to me, the worst of both worlds. The agreement may be held to be binding, but whether it will be can be determined only after litigation and may involve, as in this case, examining the quality of the advice which was given to the party who wishes to resile. It is then understandably a matter for surprise and resentment on the part of the other party that one should be able to repudiate an agreement on account of the inadequacy of one's own legal advisers over whom the other party had no control and of whose advice he had no knowledge . . . In our attempt to achieve finely-ground justice by attributing weight but not too much weight to the agreement of the parties, we have created uncertainty and, in this case, and no doubt others, added to the cost and pain of litigation.

(b) Procedure
(i) Available remedies

An appeal can obviously only be brought where a consent order as opposed to an agreement has been made. A consent order can also be challenged by a fresh action and, in certain circumstances, by applying for a rehearing. A party who wishes to challenge an agreement can apply to the court to have it set aside, as occurred in *Cresswell* v *Potter* [1978] 1 WLR 255n, although it may be more convenient to pursue an application for ancillary relief under ss 23–25 of the 1973 Act as discussed below.

The available procedures in the case of a consent order were summarised helpfully by Ward J (as he then was) in *B–T* v *B–T* [1990] 2 FLR 1, at 24 in tabular form. This summary was updated by Martyn Bennett at [1993] Fam Law 84–85, following the introduction of Family Proceedings Rules 1991. Since publication of that article, the decision of Thorpe J in *Re C* (Financial Provision: Leave to Appeal) [1993] 2 FLR 799 has been handed down and Bracewell J has considered the variety of remedies in *Benson* v *Benson (Deceased)* [1996] 1 FLR 692. The table is our own:

Type of order	Appeal	Fresh action	Rehearing under the Rules
1. County court district judge, by consent	No	Yes	Yes, apply to the district judge (CCR Ord 37 r 1(1))
2. High Court district judge, by consent	Yes	Yes	No
3. County court judge, by consent	Yes, but only with leave of the judge	Yes	Yes, apply to the judge (CCR Ord 37 r 1(1))
4. High Court judge, by consent	Yes	Yes	No
5. County court district judge, after contested hearing	Yes, without leave. Fresh evidence admissible (though within judge's discretion)	Yes	Yes, apply to the judge (CCR Ord 37 r 1(1))
6. High Court district judge, after contested hearing	ditto	Yes	No
7. County court judge after contested hearing	Yes, but with leave of judge or Court of Appeal. Need leave to admit fresh evidence	Yes	Yes, apply to judge (CCR Ord 37 r 1(1))
8. High Court judge	ditto	Yes	No

Ward J observed in *B–T* (at 6) that:
> The issue before me is in what form an aggrieved respondent should apply to set aside an order for ancillary relief on the grounds of material non-disclosure. Although this may seem to give rise to a question of quite sterile technicality, the point is one which troubles the profession and I am satisfied by counsel and by my inquiries of the Senior Registrar that some guidance as to the proper practice and procedure is necessary and would, therefore, be welcomed by all.

The judgment of Ward J in *B–T* provided an erudite and adroit guide around a procedural minefield. It presaged the procedural reforms made by the Family Proceedings Rules 1991 and held out the probability that there would be further developments in this area. Sure enough, and perhaps inevitably in view of the number of leading cases on these points since *B–T*, further valuable clarification and simplification of procedure has been highlighted, by Thorpe J in *Re C* (Financial Provision: Leave to Appeal) [1993] 2 FLR 799. The essence of the judgment, which drew on the starting point of *De Lasala* followed by Ormrod LJ in his dicta in *Robinson*, was as follows:

(1) If seeking to set an order aside because of a vitiating factor such as misrepresentation or non-disclosure, it is procedurally more convenient to proceed by way of fresh action rather than having to obtain leave to appeal. The rules do not provide that applications to set aside should be 'filtered' by the obtaining of leave.

(2) There is no reason why the application for a fresh action should not be made in the Family Division (and Bracewell J in *Benson* encouraged an application in that Division rather than in the Queen's Bench Division). Ward J (in *B–T*) had envisaged the fresh action being commenced in the Queen's Bench Division or in the Chancery Division leading to an order setting aside the impugned order only following which would it be possible to have the case transferred (by a procedurally difficult route) to the Family Division for a substantive order to be made on the true facts. Thorpe J surmised that an application for a fresh action could be made to the judge who made the impugned order. That judge would then be able not only to set the order aside, but to make a fresh order based on the new, or corrected, facts of the case. Therefore, it would be possible to proceed by way of summons or application before a district judge (who would transfer the case up to the High Court if the complexity of the case so merited).

(3) The advantage of so doing is to do away with the 'time' bar. There is no need to obtain leave because of the delay between the impugned

order and the fresh action. This renders rather redundant the other way of challenging an order, namely by way of rehearing in the county court pursuant to CCR Ord 37 r 1(1), where you would have to obtain leave to apply for a rehearing out of time.

(4) The advantage of the fresh action at first instance rather than going on appeal is that the Court of Appeal does not as a matter of practice re-investigate a case on oral evidence. As a matter of practicality therefore a case is better dealt with by a judge in the lower courts.

Thorpe J's judgment in *Re C* was relatively short and may conveniently be set out by way of illustration of the appropriate procedures. The wife was seeking to set aside various orders that had been made by district judges in the Principal Registry of the Family Division. The wife alleged that the husband had been guilty of misrepresentation and non-disclosure in the obtaining of those orders (and indeed succeeded in the substantive application decided by Thorpe J and reported as *C v C* (Financial Provision: Non-Disclosure) [1994] 2 FLR 272):

> The application is supported by an affidavit which sets out her case in specific detail and which exhibits 250 pages of corroborative evidence culled from various sources. It is enough to say that the affidavit discloses a strong *prima facie* case of fraudulent misrepresentation . . . For the purposes of the application for leave it is sufficient, in my judgment, for the applicant to show a clear *prima facie* case, a standard which this application has fully satisfied and accordingly I grant the application for leave.
>
> However, I question in my own mind whether the applicant's right to re-open prior orders obtained by fraud is subject to the filter of a leave application. The starting point for me is the speech of Lord Diplock in the case of *De Lasala* [1980] AC 546, where he said in the clearest terms: 'Where a party to an action seeks to challenge, on the ground that it was obtained by fraud or mistake, a judgment or order that finally disposes of the issues raised between the parties, the only ways of doing it that are open to him are by appeal from the judgment order to a higher court or by bringing a fresh action to set it aside'.
>
> That statement dictated the preparation of *Robinson v Robinson* [1983] FLR 102 which was ultimately decided in the Court of Appeal on 12 March 1982. In the case of *Robinson*, the wife sought to set aside earlier obtained orders for financial provision on the ground that the awards had been depressed by the husband's material non-disclosure. Her application was initiated on a belt and braces approach by an action in the Queen's Bench Division to set aside and by appeal to the Court of Appeal. Ultimately she proceeded by the appellate route.
>
> The hearing in the Court of Appeal was confined to the immediate question, were the orders vitiated by material non-disclosure. The

appellant succeeded in satisfying the Court of Appeal that they were, but the Court of Appeal was not then in a position to determine what orders would have been made had the respondent husband made proper disclosure and accordingly that second stage was the subject of further proceedings before a judge of the Division.

The submission to the Court of Appeal that this would be procedurally impractical succeeded and Ormrod LJ said specifically: 'From the point of view of convenience there is a lot to be said for proceedings of this kind taking place before a judge at first instance because there will usually be serious and often difficult issues to be determined before the power to set aside can be exercised. These can be determined more easily as a rule by a judge at first instance. Moreover he can go on to make the appropriate order, which we cannot do in this court. I think that these proceedings should normally be started before a judge at first instance, although there may be special circumstances which make it better to proceed by way of appeal'.

He does not there say explicitly the method by which proceedings should normally be started before a judge at first instance, *but I am in no doubt at all that his meaning was that they should be started by issue of summons* [authors' italics].

Manifestly the possibility of recommencing litigation at first instance by fresh writ was open on the decision of *De Lasala*, but what was submitted was that that was not appropriate in the Family Division, where proceedings are not commenced by writ but by originating summons or by simple summons in existing proceedings.

So, on the face of it, if orders made in ancillary relief by a judge of the Division may be reinvestigated by the issue of a summons, the same procedures should be available to orders made by a district judge sitting in the Registry. After all, the district judge has exactly the same statutory powers and responsibilities and it is a matter of practice whether a case is allocated to a district judge or to a judge of the Division for the purposes of a final hearing. But the decision of Mr Justice Ward in the case of *B–T* . . . led the applicant in this case not to issue a simple summons before the district judge who had made the last order in the case but to proceed by way of appeal, for which of course leave was required since it was years out of time. That decision is one which was preceded by a great deal of research by the judge and it is manifestly a very erudite judgment. But I think it is important that the facility established by the judgment of Ormrod LJ in *Robinson* v *Robinson* should not be eroded.

I am in no doubt at all that if an order made by a judge of the Division has been secured by some vitiating factor, then the aggrieved party can reopen the proceedings by the issue of a judge's summons for which no leave is required [authors' italics]. Taking fraud, since it is the most serious of the vitiating elements, it is manifest in my judgment that a litigant whose relief has been denied or depressed by fraud has an absolute right to bring the injustice to the judge at trial and should not be subjected to any sort of prior filter by way of application for leave. By analogy, if the order was obtained from a district judge, the aggrieved litigant should have the same right.

Obviously in practice these cases, if they are to be re-opened, become complex and difficult and usually involve an investigation not just of credit but also of integrity and, accordingly, are appropriately listed before a judge of the Division. So in practice if the order is made by the district judge, the re-investigation is likely to be before a judge of the Division. But that seems to me not to be of necessity in principle but something out of practicality and recognition of the practice that an issue that depends upon findings of credit and integrity is, ordinarily speaking, assigned to a judge of the Division.

The reason why I believe it is important to clarify and declare the simple procedure approved in *Robinson* is that re-investigation by writ action is inappropriate to this Division and unduly cumbersome. Secondly, the appellate process is plainly impractical if the order impugned is an order obtained from a judge of the High Court from whose decision an appeal climbs to an appellate division that does not have the facility to re-investigate on oral evidence.

Obviously, the right to re-open on an allegation of one of the vitiating elements is a right which might be abused in a field of litigation which is so influenced by human emotions. But in my experience these applications are comparatively rare and if the right is abused it will lead to penalty in costs.

The reasoning of Thorpe J was taken forward in *Benson* by Bracewell J. In her opinion, the litigant should choose whichever route of challenging the impugned order he considered most appropriate, as in her judgment (at p 698G): 'I do not consider that the choice of remedy and procedure affects the nature and extent of the issues to be determined'.

Further, in her opinion, and in disagreement with Thorpe J, it was *not* possible to make an application in the county court for a rehearing without first obtaining leave. She reasoned that a simple notice which is akin to a summons in the county court would not be appropriate under County Court Act 1994, s 76 since CCR Ord 37 r 1 already provides for a specific procedure.

The decision of the Court of Appeal in *Ritchie* v *Ritchie* [1996] 1 FLR 898 is relevant in this connection. Here the court held that CCR Ord 13 r 4(1) and (2) enabled a district judge in the county court to extend time. The decision in *Ritchie* related to an application to appeal out of time, but the decision in relation to extension of time applies to CCR Ord 37 r 1, and so the district judge has jurisdiction to extend the time for a rehearing under CCR Ord 13 r 4(1) and (2) beyond the fourteen days provided under CCR Ord 37 r 1. It was further held in *Ritchie* that, as a matter of practice in cases involving applications under *Barder*, such an application should be listed before a judge and not a district judge in view of the difficulty and/or complexity of the matter (per Bennett J at p 902, A–B).

There was a similar debate about the appropriate remedy in relation to an impugned order in *Crozier*. It was suggested to Booth J by the wife's counsel in that case that the husband should have proceeded by way of application for rehearing pursuant to CCR Ord 37 r 1 rather than by way of appeal. The judge surveyed the applicable rules and indicated that either alternative was available to the husband in the case, but was satisfied that the appeal procedure was appropriate for the case that she was trying. On analysis, the judge seemed to prefer the appeal route simply because it enables the issue, which was of some public importance, to be aired before an appellate court. Because the appeal was proceeding in the High Court, the judge was able to comment (at p 447F) that:

> there is no suggestion anywhere in the authorities that the court would apply a different approach on the basis of the procedure adopted so that the same principles would apply in either case [ie appeal and/or fresh actions].

It is worthy of note that the judge did not rule out the possibility of the *Barder*-type new events being dealt with under the rehearing/fresh action procedures. The decision is not therefore authority for the proposition that a *Barder*-type new event should be dealt with by appeal rather than by fresh action.

- Conclusion

In conclusion therefore the position seems to be as follows:
(1) The remedy imposed by the court in respect of any application arising out of a *Barder*-type complaint will be the same whatever route is chosen (whether application for rehearing or appeal out of time: *Crozier* and *Benson*).
(2) The advantage of a summons, highlighted by Thorpe J in *Re C*, is simply procedural rather than substantive (*Benson*): it enables an application to proceed without the prior filter of leave.
(3) However (*Benson*), it is not possible to make an application for a rehearing to the district judge in the county court outside the fourteen day period enjoined by CCR Ord 37 r 1, unless time has been extended.
(4) The district judge does have the power to extend time and to deal with an application under CCR Ord 37 r 1 outside the fourteen days period (*Ritchie*), but the point is academic as any *Barder*-type applica-

tion should normally be dealt with by a judge (*Ritchie*) and there will therefore be a transfer to the High Court.

Before dealing with the three remedies outlined in the table on page 163, we mention again the possibility of making application for variation. This should not be regarded as the normal procedure, but it does enable the court to vary the method of giving effect to an order (*B(GC)* v *B(BA)* [1970] 1 All ER 913 *sub nom Brister* v *Brister* [1970] 1 WLR 665 discussed on p 133; *De Lasala* v *De Lasala* [1979] 2 All ER 1146; *B–T* v *B–T*).

There follows a comparative analysis of the three remedies outlined in the procedural table set out on page 163, followed by an examination of the procedures relating to each remedy in turn.

(ii) Consent orders: which remedy?
- Is the choice of remedy governed by the ground alleged?

Here we are concerned with the availability rather than the preferability of a remedy according to the ground alleged. It is now clear from the cases of *B–T*, *Re C* and *Benson* that, with one restriction, any of the three procedures mentioned above may be used to set aside a consent order whatever the ground alleged. It is submitted this is the case in relation to an application made under the rule in *Barder* v *Barder*, although *Barder* is not expressly referred to in either *B–T* or in *Re C* (and the latter case specifically referred to setting aside based on vitiating factors rather than on *Barder*-type new events). The restriction relates to the availability of the right to apply for a rehearing under CCR Ord 37, r 1, which is discussed on pp 171 *et seq*. The reason why the grounds do not materially affect the choice of remedy is because in the matrimonial jurisdiction consent orders are to be treated in the same way as non-consensual orders on the principle established in *Thwaite* (see p 131) subject to the requirement in the case of a High Court order of obtaining leave to appeal under RSC Ord 59 r 1B(1)(*b*).

- Appeals

The vast majority of consent orders are made by district judges sitting in the divorce county courts. There is a difference of view among the commentators about whether and how it is possible to appeal against such an order. The authors of Rayden (16th ed) believe that it is possible (see, for instance, pp 1408 and 1446). The second edition of this book put forward the same view. However, both Bennett (*op cit*) and Duckworth in *Matrimonial Property and Finance*

5th ed (FT Law & Tax) p 340 think otherwise, and their view has been recently supported by Bracewell J in *Benson*. Family Proceedings Rules r 8.1(2) provides that (for appeal purposes) any order made on an application for ancillary relief shall be treated as a final order for the purposes of CCR Ord 37 r 6, by virtue of which, under CCR Ord 37 r 6(1) 'any party affected by a judgment or final order of the district judge may *except where he has consented to the terms thereof*, [authors' italics] appeal from the judgment order to the judge . . .' It seems therefore that it is impossible to appeal district judges' orders in the county court, but there is an easy if artificial remedy, namely for the order to be transferred to the High Court under MFPA s 39 so as to enable the procedure set out in RSC Ord 58 r 1 to be put into place—no leave is required for an appeal from a district judge sitting in the High Court to a judge (and this was the procedure adopted in *Benson*). The appeal proceeds by way of a rehearing as determined by the Court of Appeal in the case of *Marsh* v *Marsh* [1993] 2 All ER 794, the *ratio* of which is:

(1) The judge hearing an appeal from a district judge is free to substitute his own discretion for that of the district judge, even if adopting all his findings on the evidence before him. He is entitled to give such weight as he thinks fit to the manner in which the district judge exercises his discretion. The judge will not normally admit additional evidence, unless there is good reason so to do.

(2) The admission of further or oral evidence and the re-opening of matters already determined by the district judge are subject to the discretion of the judge hearing the appeal and he is entitled to admit such further evidence as he thinks fit and upon such terms as he considers appropriate. No party is entitled as of right to adduce such evidence and there is no unfettered right to begin entirely again *de novo* 'with a clean sheet'.

Fresh affidavits may be filed and oral evidence given. Leave to appeal out of time (see p 173) may be required, but is likely to be granted if the applicant's affidavit reveals a *prima facie* case of non-disclosure as was observed in commenting on the case of *Re C* above. In contrast, an appeal from a judge sitting in either the High Court or a divorce county court or the Court of Appeal is less desirable. As Ward J observed in *B–T* (at 25):

> Since leave is necessary, the issues the judge would have to consider in deciding whether or not to grant that leave could be better placed before him on an application for a rehearing if the power is or could be given to him. Two if not three stages (leave, appeal, new trial) could be compressed into one.

The strict conditions attaching to the Court of Appeal's power to receive fresh evidence have already been referred to on p 143. We have seen why Ormrod LJ made it clear in *Robinson* that, in the case of an appeal to the Court of Appeal on the grounds of fraud, mistake or material non-disclosure involving inevitably disputed issues of fact, the preferable course is to proceed by way of a fresh action.

- Fresh action by way of originating summons

It follows from what is said above in relation to appeals that (at least where the case has been transferred to the High Court (*pace Benson*) which is likely to have happened in any *Barder*-type case (*pace Ritchie*)) the appropriate procedure is likely to be by way of a fresh action.

It is submitted that the procedure envisaged by Thorpe J in *Re C* should be followed. A summons should be issued before the judge or the level of judge who tried the original matter or who made the consent order. The summons should be supported by a full affidavit setting out the reasons why the original order is impugned, and the relevant financial history of the marriage, together with the applicant's up-to-date disclosure. The applicant should then seek a directions appointment and an order should be made at that stage providing for the filing of affidavit evidence by the respondent in the application and, if appropriate, directions relating to questionnaires under FPR r 2.63, for valuations of properties and for a hearing date to be fixed when a certificate of readiness has been filed. We have seen how Thorpe J envisaged that a case may have to be transferred up to a different level of judge if the complexity so warrants. This procedure is preferable to the procedure envisaged by Ward J in the case of *B–T*, ie the issuing of an originating summons in the Queen's Bench Division.

- Rehearing

An application for a rehearing under CCR Ord 37, r 1 is only definitely available in respect of a consent order made by a circuit judge or district judge in a county court. It is analogous to the High Court summons procedure advocated by Thorpe J in *Re C*, but the remedy is likely to be rare as most *Barder*-type applications should be transferred to the High Court (*pace Ritchie*—see p 169 above).

The procedure provided by CCR Ord 37, r 1 may only be adopted when no error of the court at the hearing is alleged. The meaning of this limitation is fully considered by Ward J in *B–T* v *B–T* [1990] 2 FLR 1, at 16–24. Ward J concluded (at 23):

It should not be difficult to show that no error of the judge at the hearing could be alleged if he has endorsed a consent order.

[The authors respectfully disagree with the view put forward by Bennett (*op cit*) to the effect that if a district judge goes through the MCA 1973 s 33 exercise of approving the consent order on the basis of the FPR r 2.61 statements presented to him and, if that order is later challenged, an error of the court must thereby be alleged. The authors prefer the view of Ward J on this issue.]

> When the order has been opposed and the very issue has been in dispute, then the matter is more uncertain. To seek a rehearing simply because fresh evidence has become available is probably a matter for appeal. I am concerned with non-disclosure of material information which it was the duty of a party to place before the court. In that case it should be possible to construe Ord 37 widely enough to allow the rehearing in the county court even though there may be a right of appeal to the Court of Appeal. The substance, as opposed to the form of the allegation being made in such a case, ie the essential ground on which the rehearing is sought, is not that the court erred, in the sense that it made an incorrect selection of conflicting testimony or drew an erroneous inference therefrom, but that the court was misled by a party whose duty it was to give full and frank disclosure. It would not be open to that party then to allege that the court erred in reaching that conclusion.

Ward J commented that there is no corresponding provision in the High Court (in that no rules have been made under the Supreme Court Act 1981, s 17(2)) save for MCR 1977, r 54. This rule, which now appears in an amended form as FPR 1991, r 2.42 is irrelevant to the question of financial applications because it applies only to divorce causes. It is more restrictively interpreted than CCR Ord 37, r 1. It provides that in the Family Division an application for rehearing of a cause tried by a judge alone (whether in the High Court or a divorce county court) where no error of the court at the hearing is alleged must be made to the judge. The words 'no error of the court at the hearing' have been construed as intending to exclude from a rehearing all cases which would ordinarily go to the Court of Appeal.

Ward J suggested (at 23–24) that the extent of the rehearing jurisdiction might be reviewed so that a single procedure could be made available in both the High Court and the county courts.

Finally, it should be noted that a further procedural difficulty which one encounters under CCR Ord 37 r 1 applications relates to the admissibility of fresh evidence. It is clear that an applicant for a rehearing has to show that there was no remissness on his part in adducing all possible evidence at the original trial—see the note to the

CCR 1981, Ord 37 r 1 (*County Court Practice*, 1996 ed p 404) and the reference to the *Ladd* v *Marshall* conditions). It is suggested that future case law will show that similar evidential rules will be applied to fresh actions.

(iii) Appeals
- Where does the appeal lie?

The flow chart below sets out the structure of appeal procedure up to the Court of Appeal together with the relevant rules:

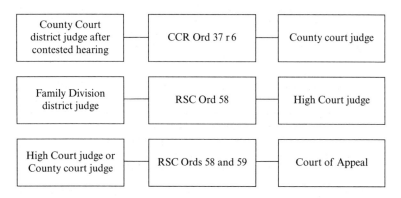

A detailed consideration of appeal procedure is outside the scope of this book and reference should be made, for example, to Butterworths Family Law Service, Division C, Chapter 7.

- Leave to appeal

A High Court order made by consent may only be appealed with the leave of the court making the order RSC Ord 59 r 1B(1)(*b*). It should be noted that leave to appeal to the Court of Appeal is required against an order for or relating to ancillary relief in matrimonial proceedings, including a property adjustment order, an order for the payment of a lump sum and any other order making or relating to financial provision whether of a capital or income nature (RSC Ord 59 r 1A(6)(*z*); and any interlocutory orders of the High Court or any other court (RSC Ord 59 r 1B(1)(*f*)).

- Leave to appeal out of time

An application to extend the time for appealing should be made in the first instance to the court below, unless the time has already expired when the application is made in which case it should be made to the Court of Appeal (RSC Ord 59, r 14(2)). In a county court, either the judge or district judge may extend the time for appealing CC Ord 13 r 4(1) and (2), as determined in the case of *Ritchie* v *Ritchie* [1996] 1 FLR 898).

It is entirely in the discretion of the court to grant or refuse an extension of time. The factors which are normally taken into account in deciding to grant an extension of time for serving a notice of appeal are:

(1) The length of the delay;
(2) The reasons for the delay;
(3) The chances of the appeal succeeding if time for appealing is extended; and
(4) The degree of prejudice to the potential respondent if the application is granted.

The leading case in this area is *C M Van Stillevoldt BV* v *El Carriers Inc* [1983] 1 WLR 297. There is a useful note on this at p 972 of the White Book (1996 ed) commenting on RSC Ord 59 r 4.

It is necessary for the party seeking leave to appeal out of time to show due diligence (*McC (RD)* v *McC (JA)* [1971] 2 All ER 1097 (three years' delay)). In *Harrison* v *Harrison* (1983) 13 Fam Law 20, leave to appeal out of time five years after a consent order had been made was refused not only on the ground of the long delay but also because Balcombe J thought that procedurally a fresh action was required. The Court of Appeal held, however, in *Johnson* v *Johnson* (1980) FLR 331 (notice of appeal six weeks out of time) that where no hardship is suffered it is always very doubtful whether the court should use time limits to deprive an aggrieved party from presenting an appeal out of time. The application related to an appeal from a district judge to a judge and may imply a rather looser test operating at that level. Leave should be granted where it would be a denial of justice for leave to be refused (*Williams* v *Williams* (1980) FLR 157 (notice of appeal one day out of time); *Jeavons* v *Jeavons* (1983) CA Transcript No 240 (leave to appeal given fifteen months after the registrar's order)). In *Barber* v *Barber* [1987] Fam Law 125, the Court of Appeal refused to leave to appeal out of time against a consent order after a delay of three years four months. A different view was taken by the Court of Appeal in *Passmore* v *Gill* [1987] 1 FLR 441, which is discussed more fully on p 150, where there had been a delay of just under six months.

When mounting an appeal based on a *Barder*-type new event, it is necessary to obtain leave to extend time for the appeal, and satisfy the

Van Stillevoldt tests as well as coming within the *Barder* rules. There will also, as previously shown, be the requirement to obtain leave for the appeal itself (unless you are appealing a county court district judge's judgment after a contested hearing). There are thus two hurdles to overcome, which is, as already explained, a good reason for opting for the fresh action or rehearing procedure rather than proceeding by way of appeal.

Two of the criteria for granting leave to appeal out of time established by the rule in *Barder* v *Barder* [1987] 2 FLR 480, discussed on p 145 *et seq*, relate to time, namely, that the new events should have occurred within a relatively short time, probably less than a year, of the original order being made and that the application for leave to appeal out of time should have been made promptly. In *Barder*, where the application for leave to appeal out of time was eventually successful before the House of Lords, the consent order had been made on 20 February 1985, the wife's suicide occurred on 25 March 1985 and application for leave to appeal out of time was made by the husband on 23 April 1985. It has, however, been shown in *Hope-Smith* v *Hope-Smith* [1989] 2 FLR 56 that the period of one year suggested in *Barder* is not inflexible.

In an application described as 'exceptional', leave to appeal out of time notwithstanding a lapse of four years was granted in *Ross* v *Ross* [1989] 2 FLR 257 because the order had not taken effect and neither party had acted on the order or been adversely affected in reliance on it.

Any application for leave to appeal to the Court of Appeal automatically includes an application for an extension of time for appealing, where such extension is necessary (RSC Ord 59 r 14(2)(*a*)). In addition to summarising in the notice the reasons for the delay, the applicant must also lodge with that notice an affidavit in support deposing to all the facts relied on in support of the application for an extension of time for appealing and giving a full account of and an explanation for the whole of the delay (refer to the useful note 59/14/18 on p 1023 of the *Supreme Court Practice*, 1996 ed).

(iv) Fresh action

The advantages of adopting this procedure and the procedure itself have already been commented upon on p 171. A county court has jurisdiction in proceedings for relief against fraud or mistake, where the amount involved does not exceed £30,000 (County Courts Act 1984, s 23(*g*)). The equity jurisdiction of the county courts is unaffected by the High Court and County Courts Jurisdiction Order 1991

(SI 1991 No 724). The jurisdictional limit of the county courts may in any event be exceeded by consent.

The cause of action to be pleaded will be based upon the grounds for challenging the consent order discussed above. In the case of an agreement, the claim will be for the rescission of the agreement and any conveyance entered into under the agreement (see eg *Cresswell* v *Potter* [1978] 1 WLR 255n) on the same grounds. A delay in bringing such an action may allow the defence of laches to be used successfully (*Butlin-Sanders* v *Butlin* [1985] FLR 204).

(v) Rehearing

An application for a rehearing under CCR Ord 37, r 1 is made to the circuit judge or district judge who made the original order. The application is made on notice stating the grounds of the application and must be served on the opposite party not more than fourteen days after the date of the order challenged and not less than seven days before the date of the rehearing (CCR Ord 37 r 1(5)). Inevitably, the applicant will have to seek leave to pursue the rehearing out of time in any case involving a *Barder*-type event.

3 Matrimonial Causes Act 1973, ss 23 and 24

It a party seeks to challenge an agreement, this may be done by making application under ss 23–24 of the 1973 Act, providing that that party has not lost this right by remarrying without making an application for ancillary relief (s 28(3) of the 1973 Act). It was precisely this course which was left open to the wife to pursue in *Sutton* v *Sutton* [1984] 1 All ER 168. It is a right which a party cannot contract out of, as s 35(6) makes expressly clear. The court must deal with the application by applying the provisions of s 25 of the 1973 Act, which will include having regard to the existence of any agreement as an important piece of conduct to be considered under s 25 (*Edgar* v *Edgar* [1980] 3 All ER 887—which has to be read subject to the amendments brought in by the MFPA 1984, as is clear from *N* v *N* [1993] 2 FLR 868). The court's approach to prior agreements has been considered already in detail in Chapter 2, section 6. Instances of an application for ancillary relief being used to challenge a prior agreement are to be found in *Prow* v *Brown* (1983) 4 FLR 352; *Cross* v *Cross* (1983) 4 FLR 235 and *Sabbagh* v *Sabbagh* [1985] FLR 29.

An application under ss 23–24 may also be an available remedy, where a consent order is set aside and an application for ancillary relief has been made in the proceedings by the applicant before his or her remarriage. This is in essence what happens in the *Re C* fresh application procedure outlined by Thorpe J. Such a course was taken in *Thwaite* v *Thwaite* [1981] 2 All ER 789 and *Camm* v *Camm* (1983) FLR 577. This latter decision is discussed in detail on p 22. In *Camm*, the court proceeded to deal with the wife's application for periodical payments there having been no previous express dismissal of the wife's application. The agreement included a term that there would be no other claim by either party on the basis of the assets disclosed. This agreement was incorporated into the orders made on decree nisi. The decision is therefore best explained by saying that Ormrod LJ, in the passage from his judgment quoted on p 32, did not feel that the wife should be bound by her agreement. If this were not the case, to allow the wife to proceed in such circumstances would run contrary to the principle of the clean break and in particular the comment by Lord Scarman in *Minton* (at 88) that:

> The difference between a dismissal of an application by consent on terms recited or referred to in the order, which the courts have recognised as effectual since 1940 (if not earlier), and an order whose terms incorporate the parties' agreement is a mere formality. The substance of the transaction in each case is a final settlement, as between the parties, approved by the court.

In *Atkinson* v *Atkinson* [1984] FLR 524, the registrar had made a consent order including orders for periodical payments and an order that the sale of the matrimonial home be postponed until the child of the family attained eighteen or completed full-time education and that upon sale the wife should receive not less than one half of the net proceeds. The Court of Appeal held that the registrar had not adjudicated upon the wife's claims for property adjustment and lump sum orders and so it was open to her to proceed with them. It was not, however, necessary for that part of the original consent order to be set aside.

It would be a matter of construction in each case as to whether an applicant can pursue an application under MCA 1973 ss 23 and 24, even in a *Barder*-type application. *S* v *S* (Financial Provision) [1994] 2 FLR 228 is a case in point. In this case, which we discussed at 159 above, an order had been made in 1977 which provided that the husband would continue to reside in the former matrimonial home until the daughter was eighteen, and then the property would be sold and the net proceeds divided equally. The order acknowledged that the provisions relating to capital were to be in full and final settlement of the parties' claims. It will be recalled that the wife returned to the property to cohabit with the husband in December 1977, and the order was treated by the parties as being of no effect. In April 1992, by which time the parties had decided to separate again, the wife made an application to set aside the consent order of 1977 and, in September 1992, she applied for leave to appeal against the order of 1977 out of time. Douglas Brown J mooted the possibility both during the proceedings and in his judgment that it might have been possible for the wife to have pursued an application for a lump sum rather than applying to set aside and appeal out of time (at 236 G–H):

> I raised with both Counsel during final speeches whether in fact the wife could even now make application for a lump sum provision on the basis that the earlier application had resulted in an order that had for many years been impossible of performance. The husband would not be able to defend such an application by saying that there had been a clean break order in full satisfaction because that order would only have taken effect and the wife be barred from fresh claims if either the order was still capable of performance or she had been paid out.

Although the point was not ruled on during the judgment, it is interesting to note that the possibility of the lump sum application being alive gave weight to the judge's decision in the case to give leave for the order to be challenged.

4 Liberty to apply

A liberty to apply provision will offer a party a limited means of resolving difficulties in the working out of a consent order. We have seen in the case of *Masefield* v *Alexander* that incorporating such a provision in an order does not give jurisdiction where jurisdiction does not exist. It is not a magic phrase which will give jurisdiction to the court regardless of the true legal position. Such a provision will be implied in some orders which are interlocutory (*Supreme Court Practice* 1996 Vol 2 para 4606). On the test laid down in *Guerrera* v *Guerrera* [1974] 3 All ER 460, this includes all orders made on ancillary relief applications. However, such a provision is sometimes expressly included in an order, for example a *Mesher* order, so as to specify the particular matters upon which the court envisages a further application being necessary. The desirability of such a clause was stressed in *Alonso* v *Alonso* (1974) 4 Fam Law 164 and *MH* v *MH* (1982) 3 FLR 429, at 434–435 so that the parties could come back to the court in the event of unforeseen or unexpected contingencies and so that an arrangement could be made to fit any new circumstances that have arisen. It is good practice to include the liberty to apply provision when drafting a consent order.

It should be stressed that the liberty to apply allows the order to be worked out and given effect to; the substance of the order cannot be changed nor does the clause provide a right to seek a variation (*Cristel* v *Cristel* [1951] 2 All ER 574; *Potts* v *Potts* (1976) 6 Fam Law 217; *Nikoloff* v *Nikoloff* (1977) 7 Fam Law 129; *Thwaite* v *Thwaite* [1981] 2 All ER 789). However, in *Abbott* v *Abbott* (1931) 47 TLR 207, it was held that after a consent order for alimony *pendente lite* the words 'liberty to apply' in the order gave the registrar power to review the order. On the other hand, a liberty to apply provision will not empower the court to order a variation prohibited by MCA 1973, s 31 (see p 204).

An order may be made under MCA 1973, s 24A irrespective of whether there is a liberty to apply provision in the original order. The court retains a discretion as to whether or not an order for sale under s 24A will be made. The discretion will not be exercised if the consequence is the displacement of rights vested under the original order (*Taylor* v *Taylor* [1987] 1 FLR 142). Therefore, in practice, s 24A will not be used to vary orders made under s 23 and s 24 in any way which is prohibited by s 31 of the Act. Section 24A is a procedural enactment limited to verifying and expanding the court's powers of implementation and enforcement, and confers no jurisdiction to vary any settlement created on the making of the original order—a s 24A order being a procedural 'gloss' (*Omielan* v *Omielan* [1996] 2 FLR 306).

The liberty to apply provision does not give the right to apply to the court without using the procedure under the Family Proceedings Rules 1991, r 10.9, except in special cases (*Practice Direction 4 March 1980* [1980] 1 All ER 1008).

5 Resist specific performance of an agreement

This possibility exists where an *agreement* has been entered into which is still executory. The position regarding an order which is still executory is discussed in *Thwaite* v *Thwaite* (1981) FLR 280, at 284H (per Ormrod LJ):

> Where the order is still executory, as in the present case, and one of the parties applies to the court to enforce the order, the court may refuse if, in the circumstances prevailing at the time of the application, it would be inequitable to do so: *Mullins* v *Howell* (1879) 11 Ch D 763 and *Purcell* v *F C Trigell Ltd* [1961] 1 QB 358 at pp 367 and 368. Where the consent order derives its legal effect from the contract, this is equivalent to refusing a decree of specific performance; where the legal effect derives from the order itself the court has jurisdiction over its own orders *per* Sir George Jessell MR in *Mullins* v *Howell* (1879) 11 Ch D 763 at p 766.

This should not be taken as an invitation to an aggrieved litigant to sit back and refuse to perform the obligation in the order, if the litigant's grievance is based on (for instance) the happening of a new *Barder*-type event, he or she should proceed promptly with the relevant application.

The source of the legal effect of a consent order made in the matrimonial jurisdiction is discussed on p 131. The remedy of an order for specific performance is discretionary and will therefore be refused by the court, if grounds exist for setting the agreement aside or if such an order would be highly unreasonable or cause an injustice or if it would be inequitable to enforce the agreement (*Cross* v *Cross* (1983) FLR 235). The facts of *Cross*, where an order of specific performance was refused, have already been discussed above on p 36. The refusal was based upon the wife's failure to disclose her change of circumstances and her future plans both before and after the agreement was reached. The court then dealt with the wife's alternative claim for a transfer of property order having regard to the agreement under the general heading of conduct under s 25 of the 1973 Act.

In *Sutton* v *Sutton* [1984] 1 All ER 168, the husband resisted the wife's action seeking an order for specific performance by contending that the oral agreement in question was not legally enforceable on four grounds:

(*a*) There was no memorandum or note of the agreement within the meaning of the Law of Property Act 1925, s 40. Whilst the court acknowledged that there was no memorandum or note, there had been a sufficient act of part performance on the wife's part in that her consent to the divorce was interrelated to the agreement. This ground would no longer be arguable (see p 14).

(*b*) There was no mutuality. It was held that although the husband could not enforce the wife's promise not to seek maintenance nor could he compel her to consent to the divorce, once she had performed her part of the bargain he could not then assert that there was no mutuality.

(*c*) The agreement was collusive. It was held that the agreement was not void on this ground as a divorce granted under s 1(2)(*d*) of the 1973 Act was necessarily collusive and public policy no longer validates a collusive agreement under the current legislation.

(*d*) The agreement purported to oust the jurisdiction of the court and it would accordingly be contrary to public policy to enforce it. The husband succeeded on this particular ground, as the court's jurisdiction under ss 23 and 24 of the 1973 Act could not be ousted by a private agreement between the parties. It remained open to the wife to pursue an application for a transfer of property order under s 24 of the 1973 Act.

This decision has been criticised by Peter Duckworth, in a published lecture given to the FLBA in May 1993, on the basis that the judge in the case was not referred to the Maintenance Agreements Act 1957, which (like its successors) abolished the common law principle of implied ouster at any rate in relation to written agreements. The Matrimonial Causes Act 1973 s 34 is of very similar effect to the Maintenance Agreements Act 1957; and we have seen how (in cases such as *N v N*) a party's agreement not to go back to the court for further financial relief (even when his or her financial claims have not been dismissed in the order) have, although void according to MCA 1973 s 34(1)(*a*), been upheld as an agreement by the court.

An interesting critique of this decision by Dr Ines Weyland is to be found at (1985) Fam Law 114–115.

For a discussion of *Harris (formerly Manahan) v Manahan* [1996] 4 All ER 454, an important case decided during the publication of this edition, see the addendum at p 257.

Chapter 7

Variation

Attention has already been drawn to the distinction commented upon by Ormrod LJ in *Robinson* v *Robinson (Disclosure)* (1983) FLR 102 (at 114) between, on the one hand, grounds which may invalidate an agreement or consent order where there has been fraud, mistake or material non-disclosure as to the facts at the time the agreement or order was made and, on the other, variations (as discussed in this chapter) where the concern is with subsequent changes in circumstances. The distinction is well summarised by Cazalet J when giving the leading judgment in *Garner* v *Garner* [1992] 1 FLR 573:

> Almost invariably, an application to vary an earlier periodical payments order will be brought on the basis that there has been some change in the circumstances since the original order was made; otherwise, except in exceptional circumstances, the application will, in effect, be an appeal. If an order is not appealed against, or is made by consent, then the presumption must be that the order was correct when made. If it was correct when made, there will usually be no justification for varying it unless there has been a material change in the circumstances. However, because of the impact of continuing inflation, because children grow older and cost more to support, and because, for example, the costs of living in its increase may hit one party harder than another, it will usually follow that, if time has passed, there will inevitably have been some changes in the circumstances, and in particular in the financial circumstances, of the parties concerned.

However, new events may also, subject to stringent conditions, be a ground for applying for leave to appeal out of time against a consent order (*Barder* v *Barder* [1987] 2 FLR 480: see pp 145 *et seq*).

The court will approach such changes according to the means adopted by the parties to regulate their circumstances: hence, for example, the distinction between ss 31 (which applies to variation of orders) and 35 (which applies to variation of agreements) of the 1973 Act (see *Simister* v *Simister* (No 2) [1987] 1 FLR 194, at 201).

1 Agreements

During the lives of the parties

(a) Variation of an agreement as a post-nuptial settlement under the Matrimonial Causes Act 1973, s 24(1)(c)

If proceedings for divorce, nullity or judicial separation are contemplated, an order may be made on or after the granting of the decree for the benefit of the parties or the children of the family varying any ante-nuptial or post-nuptial settlement (including a settlement made by will or codicil) made on the parties to the marriage. A maintenance agreement may constitute a post-nuptial settlement under s 24(1)(c) enabling a variation of settlement order to be made. An application for such an order (or a full application for ancillary relief under ss 22–24) may be the only means of achieving a variation, where the maintenance agreement does not fall within the definition contained in s 34(2) (and so cannot be varied under s 35) or the parties cannot agree a deed of variation. Where a party intends to pursue an application for maintenance as well as applying to vary a separation deed as a post-nuptial settlement, the two applications should ordinarily be heard together (*Jeffrey* v *Jeffrey* (No 2) [1952] P 122). A variation of settlement order under 24(1)(c) may be made notwithstanding that there are no children of the family (s 24(2)). The term 'settlement' has been given a wide meaning by the courts (see eg *Brown* v *Brown* [1959] 2 All ER 266; *Radziej* v *Radziej* [1968] 3 All ER 624. For a useful discussion on the subject, refer to pp 258 *et seq* of Jackson's *Matrimonial Finance and Taxation*, 6th ed (Butterworths).

The most recent and authoritative consideration of the meaning of 'settlement' for the purposes of MCA s 24 is to be found in *Brooks* v *Brooks* [1995] 2 FLR 13 at 19B and D per Lord Nicholls LJ:

> Broadly stated, the disposition must be one that makes some form of continuing provision for both or either of the parties to a marriage, with or without provision for their children. Conversely, a disposition which confers an immediate, absolute interest in an item of property does not constitute a settlement of that property ... The authorities have consistently given a wide meaning to settlement in this context, and they have spelled out no precise limitation.

The procedure on applying for a variation of settlement order is the normal procedure when applying for a property adjustment order. The court's approach to the application will be first to consider the welfare of any children and secondly not to interfere with the post-nuptial settlement more than necessary for the purposes of s 25 (*E* v *E* (Financial Provision) [1990] 2 FLR 233.

An agreement between the parties may conceivably be in place after decree absolute (rather than as usual pursuant to an order). It will not of course be possible to apply for relief under s 24 if the application under s 24 was dismissed in an order made on the divorce.

(b) Application for ancillary relief under the Matrimonial Causes Act 1973, ss 22–24

A party seeking a variation may make a full application to the court for ancillary relief in the same way as a party who is dissatisfied with a pre-existing agreement (see pp 176–178), where proceedings have been commenced and such a course remains open to the applicant. By this course, the applicant is not restricting the application to one under s 24(1)(c), which varies the agreement, but is invoking the court's full powers under ss 22–24 so as to override the agreement. The manner in which the court will approach such applications has already been discussed on pp 29 *et seq* and pp 176–178. The agreement will be considered as an important part of conduct under s 25. It will, however, be noted that s 35(6) contains an express saving enabling a party to proceed under ss 22–24 rather than under s 35. However, Waite J held in *Simister* v *Simister* (No 2) [1987] 1 FLR 194, at 201 that a party must first establish that a case has arisen for the intervention of the court under s 35 before being entitled to any relief at all, whether by way of ancillary relief or by way of variation of a subsisting agreement. The function of s 35(6) is, as Waite J held at 202, to ensure that the variation jurisdiction under s 35 remains subservient to other jurisdictions and in particular to that of granting ancillary relief in general terms. Once the jurisdiction to vary has been established, there are no limits to the court's powers. Accordingly, in *Simister*, the power of revocation in s 35(2)(b)(i) was used to revoke all the income provisions of the maintenance agreement benefiting the wife and substituting for them an order for periodical payments under s 23 of the 1973 Act, which would enable future variations to be achieved more readily under s 31 of the 1973 Act than under the cumbersome procedures of s 35. (See also *Orton* v *Orton* (1959) 109 Sol Jo 50 and p 36.)

(c) Alteration of agreements during the lives of the parties under the Matrimonial Causes Act 1973, s 35

(i) The types of agreements which may be varied

An agreement may be varied by the High Court (in an application transferred to it), a divorce county court and, subject to limitations, a magistrates' court under the Matrimonial Causes Act 1973, s 35, if it falls within the definition of a 'maintenance agreement' contained in s 34(2) set out on p 28. The definition is in every sense wide: no particular form is required save that the agreement should be in writing. A letter may suffice (*MH* v *MH* (1982) 3 FLR 429, at 433). Each of the parties must be either domiciled or resident in England and Wales at the date of the application to the court (s 35(1)).

The agreement must be subsisting (s 35(1)). In *Pace* v *Doe* [1977] 1 All ER 176, the husband agreed, *inter alia*, to pay the mortgage instalments on the home occupied by the wife and to pay maintenance for her. The wife remarried, thereby terminating her right to maintenance. She applied to the court to vary the agreement by altering the capital provision in the agreement. At the time of the hearing, the husband was no longer making the mortgage repayments. The court rejected the husband's argument that the only subsisting provisions related to the children and held that the relevant date for determining whether the agreement was subsisting was the making of the application to the court at which time the husband was still making the mortgage repayments under the agreement which benefited the wife. There will be no subsisting maintenance agreement if the terms of the agreement have subsequently been incorporated into a consent order (*De Lasala* v *De Lasala* [1979] 2 All ER 1146 applied in *Thwaite* v *Thwaite* [1981] 2 All ER 789; see p 131). It is submitted that *D* v *D* (1974) 5 Fam Law 61 may now be wrongly decided in that it appears that the agreement had been approved by the court. It was held that the court did have jurisdiction to entertain the application to vary the agreement relating to the transfer of the matrimonial home under s 35, although on the facts a variation was not justified.

It was held by the Court of Appeal in *Kent-Jones* v *Kent* (1985) (unreported CA Transcript No 373) that a maintenance agreement was no longer subsisting by reason of the wife's remarriage. The subsistence of the agreement cannot depend upon an estoppel arising out of an assurance given that a pension would be paid notwithstanding remarriage; this ignores the fact that remarriage involves a change of status and is not merely a contract.

(ii) Requirements justifying a variation

Before the court's powers under s 35 can be exercised, it is necessary to satisfy the court that the conditions set out in s 35(2) have been satisfied. Section 35(2) provides that variation may be made by a court if it is satisfied:

(*a*) that by reason of a change in the circumstances in the light of which any financial arrangements contained in the agreement were made or, as the case may be, financial arrangements were omitted from it (including a change foreseen by the parties when making the agreement), the agreement should be altered so as to make different, or, as the case may be, so as to contain, financial arrangements, or

(b) that the agreement does not contain proper financial arrangements with respect to any child of the family.

It will be noted in particular that a change in circumstances includes a change *foreseen* by the parties at the time of the making of the agreement and that it is sufficient alone to show that the agreement does not contain proper financial arrangements for a child of the family irrespective of any change in circumstances. The test in deciding whether there has been 'a change in the circumstances in the light of which financial arrangements were made' is that regard must be had to the circumstances which the parties had in mind as reasonable people in determining whether there had been a relevant change (*Gorman* v *Gorman* [1964] 3 All ER 739). The court will only be prepared to vary an agreement when injustice is caused by a change in certain circumstances (*K* v *K* [1961] 2 All ER 266; *Gorman* v *Gorman* [1964] 3 All ER 739—in which it was held that a case for varying the agreement was not made out because, *inter alia*, a wife for whose maintenance no provision had been made in the agreement was not debarred from instituting proceedings against her husband for his wilful neglect to provide reasonable maintenance for her (now MCA 1973, s 27)). A voluntary reduction of income will not constitute a change in circumstances sufficient to satisfy the court (*Ratcliffe* v *Ratcliffe* [1962] 3 All ER 993). The test is more restrictive than under s 31 (*Simister* v *Simister* (No 2) [1987] 1 FLR 194, at 200). The only relevant question is whether the agreement works unequitably today (*Simister*, at 202).

(iii) The court's powers

Once the jurisdiction to vary has been established, the court's powers are wide. They are set out in s 35(2) where it is provided that the court may order alterations in the agreement:

(i) by varying or revoking any financial arrangements contained in it, or
(ii) by inserting in it financial arrangements for the benefit of one of the parties to the agreement or of a child of the family,
as may appear to that court to be just having regard to all the circumstances, including, if relevant, the matters mentioned in s 25(4) above; and the agreement shall have effect thereafter as if any alteration made by the order had been made by agreement between the parties and for valuable consideration.

The interaction of the court's powers under s 35 and ss 23–24 has already been reviewed on pp 184.

As has been seen on p 28, the meaning of 'financial arrangements' itself is, under s 34(2), very wide and can encompass not only maintenance and capital but matters such as the occupation of the matrimonial home. For the reasons mentioned below, the court is more likely to be asked to vary or insert a maintenance term in an agreement. The court has power to backdate such a variation prior to the date of the application to the court (*Warden* v *Warden* [1981] 3 All ER 193). However, whatever the court's jurisdiction may be, tax relief cannot also be backdated (*Morley-Clarke* v *Jones* [1985] 3 WLR 749, CA; [1986] 1 WLR 978, HL (petition for leave to appeal dismissed).

A more problematical area is where the wife wishes the court to vary or insert a term as to capital provision in the agreement. There is no doubt that on a literal construction of the section such an application would be possible, even if such an approach is diametrically opposed to the regime imposed upon the variation of a court order under s 31(5) (see p 83). Reverting to *Pace* v *Doe*, the wife's application for capital provision by way of variation of the agreement failed, even though the court had jurisdiction to entertain her application, because she had remarried. The question was left open as to whether the court had jurisdiction to insert a lump sum into a subsisting agreement by reason of a change of circumstances where there was no remarriage. Despite the fact that it had previously been held in *Furneaux* v *Furneaux* (1974) 118 SJ 204 that the court had no power to insert a provision for a lump sum or property adjustment, it is submitted that this open question has now been resolved by Waite J in *Simister*, at 202–203, where he found that once the jurisdiction to vary is established it has no limits. It may well be, however, that the court will be reluctant to exercise its discretion to insert capital provision. As Waite J graphically put it at 203:

> I appreciate that an order in this form will leave the maintenance agreement still standing like a partially demolished building with its income floors all gutted and only its capital facade intact and perhaps possessing no more than an historical interest. I was minded at first, for that reason, to revoke the maintenance agreement in its entirety. On balance, however, I can see no harm in allowing its remaining provisions, obsolete though they may be, to stand, if only for the sake of the record and as a reminder to the parties of their past dealings should an overall capital settlement of the wife's financial claims ever become possible.

Waite J may have had in mind capitalisation of the wife's continuing claims for maintenance, it being certainly clear that the previous capital provision for the wife under the maintenance agreement would be a relevant factor in any such future proceedings.

The powers of a magistrates' court are limited by s 35(3). Both the parties to the agreement must be resident in England and Wales and at least one of the parties must be resident within the commission area for which the court is appointed. The only orders which a magistrates' court can then make are:

- in a case where the agreement includes no provision for periodical payments by either of the parties, an order inserting provision for the making by one of the parties of periodical payments for the maintenance of the other party or for the maintenance of any child of the family;
- in a case where the agreement includes provision for the making by one of the parties of periodical payments, an order increasing or reducing the rate of, or terminating, any of those payments.

The curious feature of s 35(3) is that if an agreement contains provision for the payment by the husband of periodical payments for a child, a magistrates' court has no power to alter the agreement by inserting a provision for the payment of periodical payments for the wife (or vice versa).

Provisions relating to child maintenance must of course now be viewed in the light of the Child Support Act 1991; the specific interrelation between the Act and MCA 1973, s 35 is discussed on pp 118–119.

The duration of maintenance provision which may be inserted in an agreement on an application under s 35 is governed by s 35(4) and (5). Unsecured maintenance may not extend beyond the death of either of the parties to the agreement or the remarriage of the payee. Secured maintenance may not extend beyond the death or remarriage of the payee (s 35(4)). Child maintenance is subject to the normal limits contained in s 29(2) and (3), (s 35(5)). There is no express power in s 35 to remit arrears on an application for a variation of an agreement.

(iv) Procedure

Orders under s 35 may be made either by the High Court (in an application transferred to it), a divorce county court or a magistrates' court. Subject to the qualifications mentioned above in relation to a magistrates' court, each of the parties must either be domiciled or resident in England and Wales. An application to the magistrates' court is by way of complaint and summons (Magistrates' Courts

Rules 1981, r 105). If the application is not made to a magistrates' court, it must be made to any divorce county court following the Family Proceedings Rules 1991, rr 3.2 and 3.5. The application is by originating application supported by an affidavit from the applicant exhibiting a copy of the maintenance agreement and verifying the originating application in Form M21. The application is served in the same manner as a petition together with a notice in Form M20 with Form M6 (Acknowledgment of Service) attached (see Appendix 1 to the Family Proceedings Rules 1991). The respondent must send an acknowledgment of service to reach the court within eight days after service inclusive of the day of service. The respondent must file, within fourteen days after the time for acknowledging service, an affidavit with a copy for service by the court on the applicant, containing full particulars of his property and income and setting out any grounds on which he intends to contest the application. The case will proceed in the orthodox way, with requests for information made, if appropriate, pursuant to FPR 1991 r 2.63, and with directions appointments as appropriate to prepare the case for a final hearing, which will usually take place before a district judge. The case may be transferred, in the usual way, from the county court to the High Court or between courts pursuant to FPR r 10.10, and CCR Ord 48 r 9.

(d) Alteration of maintenance agreements for children during the lives of the parties under the Children Act 1989, Sched 1, para 10 (formerly the Family Law Reform Act 1987, s 15)

This topic has to be read subject to the provisions of the Child Support Act 1991, explained in Chapter 5. The powers of the court, which we now go on to discuss, are therefore going to be relevant, *inter alia*, where:

(1) the Child Support Act does not apply to the facts of a particular case; or

(2) the court, rather than the Child Support Agency, has jurisdiction over a matter.

Section 15 came into force on 1 April 1989 and enables the court to alter certain subsisting maintenance agreements in respect of a child. Section 15 was replaced by Sched 1, para 10 without any material alteration with effect from 14 October 1991. Paragraph 10(1) defines a 'maintenance agreement' as:

> any agreement in writing made with respect to a child, whether before or after the commencement of this paragraph—
> > (a) is or was made between the father and the mother of the child; and

(b) contains provision with respect to the making or securing of payments, or the disposition or use of any property, for the maintenance or education of the child.

Such provisions are referred to as 'financial arrangements'.

Where each of the parties to the agreement is either domiciled or resident in England and Wales, either party may apply to the High Court, a county court or a magistrates' court for an order under para 10. A magistrates' court, however, only has jurisdiction if both the parties to the agreement are resident in England and Wales and at least one of the parties is resident in the commission area for which the court is appointed (para 10(6)). The only orders which a magistrates' court may make under para 10 are:

(*a*) in a case where the agreement contains no provision for periodical payments by either of the parties, an order inserting provision for the making by one of the parties of periodical payments for the maintenance of the child;

(*b*) in a case where the agreement includes provision for the making by one of the parties of periodical payments, an order increasing or reducing the rate of, or terminating, any of those payments (para 10(6)).

The court may alter the agreement by varying or revoking any financial arrangements in it as may appear to be just having regard to all the circumstances if it is satisfied either:

(1) that, by reason of a change in the circumstances in the light of which any financial arrangements contained in the agreement were made (including a change foreseen by the parties when making the agreement), the agreement should be altered so as to make different financial arrangements; or

(2) that the agreement does not contain proper financial arrangements with respect to the child (para 10(3)).

When altered by order, the agreement has effect as if any alteration had been made by agreement between the parties and for valuable consideration (para 10(4)).

By para 10(5), the duration of the term of periodical payments under an agreement as altered by an order is governed by the Children Act 1989, Sched 1, para 3(1) and (2). Strictly, this will only apply to an inserted provision or the additional element of an altered provision. However, the High Court or a county court could revoke the original maintenance provision and substitute an inserted provision, the duration of which would then be governed by para 3.

Nothing in para 10 affects any power of a court before which any proceedings between the parties to a maintenance agreement are brought under any other enactment (eg the Matrimonial Causes Act 1973, s 35) to make an order containing financial arrangements or any right of either party to apply for such an order in such proceedings (para 10(7)).

The procedure in the High Court and the county court is contained in FPR 1991, r 4.4. An application to a magistrates' court is in accordance with the Family Proceedings Courts (Children Act 1989) Rules 1991, r 4.

Paragraph 10 broadly follows the regime of s 35 of the 1973 Act, but will, for example, enable an affiliation agreement or a cohabitation contract between unmarried parents in respect of an illegitimate child to be altered by the court. It is submitted that the powers of the court under para 10(3) are wide enough to enable the High Court or a county court to insert provision for a lump sum in an agreement. This view is supported by the wording of para 10(6) which, whilst restricting the powers of magistrates' courts, does enable a provision for periodical payments to be *inserted*. It is also consistent with the approach adopted to s 35 by Waite J in *Simister* (see p 184).

After the death of one party

(a) Alteration of agreements after the death of one party under s 36
   (i) The court's powers

If a maintenance agreement, again as defined by s 34(2), provides for the continuation of payments after the death of one of the parties and that party dies domiciled in England and Wales, the surviving party or the personal representatives of the deceased party may apply under s 36 to the High Court or a county court (which need not necessarily be a divorce county court) for an order under s 35. A county court has jurisdiction by virtue of s 36(3) to entertain an application under s 36, if it would have jurisdiction to determine an application for an order under the Inheritance (Provision for Family and Dependants) Act 1975, s 2. By art 2 of the High Court and County Courts Jurisdiction Order 1991 (SI 1991 No 724) the jurisdiction of a county court under this section is unlimited. A magistrates' court has no jurisdiction.

Except with the permission of the court, no application may be made after the end of the period of six months from the date on which representation in regard to the estate of the deceased is first taken out (s 36(2)). Regard should be had to s 31(9) applied by s 36(6) on the question of when representation was first taken out. A standing search of the Central Probate Registry will ensure that notice is received when a grant of representation has been taken out (*Practice*

Direction [1975] 3 All ER 403). The personal representatives of the deceased are protected from liability by s 36(5) for having distributed any part of the estate after the expiration of the six-month period referred to above on the ground that they ought to have taken into account the possibility that a court might permit an application to be made under s 36 by the surviving party after the six-month period.

If a maintenance agreement is altered by the court under s 36, the alteration is treated as if it had been made immediately before the deceased's death by agreement between the parties and for valuable consideration (s 36(4)).

(ii) Procedure

The procedure is governed by FPR 1991, rr 3.3, 3.4 and 3.5. In the High Court proceedings are issued in the Family Division out of the Principal Registry of any district registry by originating summons in Form M22 (FPR 1991, Appendix 1) supported by an affidavit from the applicant exhibiting a copy of the agreement and an official copy of the grant of representation and of every testamentary document admitted to proof. The contents of the affidavit in support are set out in FPR 1991, r 3.3(2). An acknowledgment of service in Form 6 and a copy of the affidavit in support are annexed to the service copy of the summons (FPR 1991, r 2.6(6) applied by r 3.5(2). The summons is served in the same manner as a petition (FPR 1991, r 3.5(2)). A respondent must send an acknowledgment of service to reach the court within eight days after service inclusive of the day of service. A respondent must file an affidavit in answer with a copy for service by the court on the applicant within fourteen days after time limited for giving notice of intention to defend. This is not a mandatory requirement in the case of a respondent who is not a personal representative (FPR 1991, r 3.4(4) and (6)). The contents of the affidavit to be filed by a respondent who is a personal representative are set out in r 3.4(4).

Where a county court has jurisdiction, application should be made by originating application in Form M 22, which is a dual purpose form for use in both the High Court and county courts. The procedure in both courts is governed by FPR 1991. Certain parts of the CCR 1981 are, however, expressly applied by FPR 1991, r 3.3(3) and r 3.4(3). The county court in which proceedings must be commenced is governed by CCR Ord 48, r 3(1) applied by FPR 1991, r 3.3(3) ie, the court for the district in which the deceased resided. The application may be heard by a district judge or the application may be transferred to the High Court in which event the district judge should direct whether the application is to be assigned to the Chancery

Division or the Family Division (CCR Ord 48, rr 7 and 9 applied by FPR 1991, r 3.3(3)).

(b) Alteration of maintenance agreements for children after the death of one party under the Children Act 1989, Sched 1, para 11 (formerly the Family Law Reform Act 1987, s 16)

Section 16 came into force on 1 April 1989. It was replaced by Sched 1, para 11 without any material alteration with effect from 14 October 1991. By it, where one of the parties to a maintenance agreement, as defined by para 10(1) of Sched 1 to the 1989 Act (see p 189), has died and the agreement provides for the continuation of payments for the maintenance of a child after the death of one of the parties, the surviving party or the personal representatives of the deceased may apply to the High Court or a county court for an order under para 11. The deceased must have died domiciled in England and Wales. A magistrates' court has no jurisdiction (para 11(1)). A county court has unlimited jurisdiction (para 11(5)).

The application cannot be made after the end of a period of six months from the date on which representation regarding the deceased's estate was first taken out, unless the court's permission is obtained (para 11(3)). In this context, a grant limited to settled land or to trust property is left out of account and a grant limited to real estate or to personal estate is similarly left out of account unless a grant limited to the remainder of the estate has previously been made or is made at the same time (para 11(4)).

If the agreement is altered under para 11, the effect of the alteration is as if it has been made immediately before the deceased's death by agreement between the parties and for valuable consideration (para 11(27)).

Protection for personal representatives is provided by para 11(6).

The procedure is as stated on p 191 in relation to para 10. The purpose of para 11, which follows the regime of s 36 of the 1973 Act, is to enable, for example, the mother of an illegitimate child to apply to the court to vary an affiliation agreement after the father's death.

(c) Inheritance (Provision for Family and Dependants) Act 1975, ss 17 and 18

(i) Section 17

Where an application is made to the court (ie the High Court or a county court if the value of net estate as defined by s 25(1) of the 1975 Act does not exceed £30,000) for an order under s 2 of the 1975 Act by a person who was at the deceased's death entitled to payments from the deceased under a maintenance agreement which provided for their continuation after the deceased's death, the court has power in the proceedings under s 2 to vary or revoke the maintenance agreement on the application of either the payee or the personal representatives of the deceased (s 17(1)).

'Maintenance agreement' is defined more liberally than in s 34(2) of the 1973 Act. In particular, the agreement need not be in writing. Section 17(4) defines a 'maintenance agreement' for the purposes of s 17 of the 1975 Act as:

> any agreement made, whether in writing or not and whether before or after the commencement of this Act, by the deceased with any person with whom he entered into a marriage, being an agreement which contained provisions governing the rights and liabilities towards one another when living separately of the parties to the marriage (whether or not the marriage has been dissolved or annulled) in respect of the making or securing of payments or the disposition or use of any property, including such rights and liabilities with respect to the maintenance or education of any child, whether or not a child of the deceased or a person who was treated by the deceased as a child of the family in relation to that marriage.

The court is directed by s 17(2) when exercising its powers under the section to have regard to all the circumstances of the case, including any order which the court proposes to make under s 2 or s 5 of the Act and any change (whether resulting from the death of the deceased or otherwise) in any of the circumstances in the light of which the agreement was made. If a maintenance agreement is varied under s 17, the variation takes effect as if it had been made immediately before the death of the deceased by agreement between the parties and for valuable consideration (s 17(3)).

(ii) Section 18

If a maintenance agreement within the meaning of s 34(2) of the 1973 Act provides for the continuation of payments after the death of one of the parties and an application is made under s 36 for the alteration of the agreement, the court has power under s 18(1)(*b*) of the 1975 Act to direct that the application under s 36 shall be deemed to have been accompanied by an application for an order under s 2 of the 1975 Act. In this event, the court has power in the proceedings under s 36 to make any order which it would have power to make under s 2 of the 1975 Act (s 18(2)). However, where an order has been made under s 15(1) of the 1975 Act that a party shall not be entitled on the death of the other to apply for an order under s 2 of the 1975 Act, the court cannot override this order by making a direction under s 18(1)(*b*) (s 18(3)).

2 Consent orders

(a) When and how may an order be varied?
(i) Introduction
In discussing the concept of the clean break in Chapter 4, section 2, it has been seen that only certain types of orders for ancillary relief are capable of variation under s 31 of the 1973 Act. Subject to these limitations and to s 28(1A) which is discussed below, a consent order may be varied in exactly the same way as a non-consensual order (*Gregory* v *Wainwright* (1984) 14 Fam Law 86).

The orders which may be varied are referred to in s 31(2) and are set out below:
- maintenance pending suit;
- interim maintenance. It is submitted that this term is intended to embrace an interim order for periodical payments and is not confined to an order made under s 27(5);
- periodical payments;
- secured periodical payments;
- instalment provisions in a lump sum order;
- deferred lump sum orders relating to pension and made under MCA s 25B(4) of s 25C (which may be varied until the death of either party—see further pp 83–84 above).
- settlement of property order or variation of settlement order (where made on a decree of judicial separation and when there is a subsequent application for rescission of that decree or for dissolution of the marriage);
- order for sale under s 24A(1) (see *Omielan* v *Omielan* [1996] 2 FLR 306; see p 179)

If the order in question is incapable of variation under s 31, the court will still have no jurisdiction to vary it even if the order was made prior to the 1973 Act (*Whitfield* v *Whitfield* [1985] FLR 955, Hollis J; not appealed on this point [1986] 1 FLR 99, CA).

The court's power under s 31, in relation to the orders to which the section applies under s 31(2), are not only to vary, but to discharge, suspend temporarily or to revive such suspension. Only a continuing order of one of the types set out in s 31(2) may be varied. This may include a nominal maintenance order made in favour of a party (cf where orders falling within s 31(2) have been dismissed to achieve a clean break; see pp 88 *et seq*.

(ii) Term orders

An order for periodical payments which has been framed as a limited term order subject to a direction made under s 28(1A) cannot be varied under s 31 by extending the term of the order but only as to the amount of maintenance payable under the order during the original term. A term maintenance order for a wife looking after a minor child, coupled with a s 28(1A) direction, will be very rare: such a scenario was disapproved by the Court of Appeal in *Waterman* v *Waterman* [1989] 1 FLR 380 (where the s 28(1A) direction was removed on appeal) and in *N* v *N* [1993] 2 FLR 868; see p 90. An example of a case where a court deemed it appropriate to extend the wife's maintenance for a term expiring on the youngest child's eighteenth birthday, coupled with a s 28(1A) direction, is *C* v *C* [1989] 1 FLR 11, which involved a very rich wife.

If a term order contains no such direction, the recipient may apply to the court to vary the order by extending its term. Whether a wife will succeed in so doing depends on the judicial consideration of all the circumstances of the case. Thus, in the case of *Sandford* v *Sandford* [1986] 1 FLR 412, the court extended the term because it considered that otherwise the wife would suffer undue hardship. We have seen (p 97) that the wife in *Richardson* v *Richardson* (No 2) [1994] 2 FLR 1051 succeeded in extending her maintenance for three years (albeit with the imposition of a s 28(1A) direction preventing any subsequent extension. An application for an extension of the term must be made prior to the expiration of the original term (*T* v *T* [1988] 1 FLR 480). This is so even if the words 'or further order' are included in the original maintenance order, as such an expression is to be construed as meaning 'or further order in the meantime'.

That the court will extend the wife's term order for maintenance based on a combination of the circumstances of the case is well illustrated by the case of *B* v *B* (Consent Order: Variation) [1995] 1 FLR 9. The decision is especially illuminating in the light of the fact that the wife had at the time of the original order agreed not to apply to extend the maintenance, which was to run for a fixed period of seven years. However, no s 28(1A) direction was included in the order, the causes of which were discussed on p 91. Her claims under the Inheritance (Provision for Family and Dependants) Act 1975 were dismissed in the order. Thorpe J agreed with the proposition that the wife's agreement not to apply to extend the term of the order was conduct which had to be taken into account by him under the *Edgar* principle. The decision is therefore authority, along with *N* v *N*, that the *Edgar* principle applies to variation as well as to original applications. The court recited the history of the marriage and of the negotiations leading up to the original order; and the particular circumstances, which enabled the judge to follow *Camm* (see p 32) and allow the wife to step outside her agreement, were the facts that she suffered from psychological problems at the time of the original negotiations and had received exceptionally poor legal advice (on which the judge was able to pronounce having read her solicitors' file). The husband had been able to put forward the 'millionaire's defence' and not particularise his financial position. The periodical payments order was therefore extended to last during the joint lives of the parties, with the wife's maintenance set at such a level as to enable her to 'make provision immediately from this day forward by insurance or otherwise to secure her against the possibility, which is more than theoretical, that there will be a lengthy period of survivorship during which she will have nothing but her state pension and what she can extract from her capital'.

(iii) Arrears

The court has power under s 31(2A) when varying any of the four types of order mentioned above for periodic maintenance to remit any arrears due under the order wholly or in part. There is no such power to remit arrears of maintenance due under an agreement.

(iv) Section 31(5)

Attention has already been drawn on p 86 to the prohibition contained in s 31(5) on a property adjustment order being made on an application for a variation of a periodical payments or secured periodical payments order (whether in favour of a party or a child) and on a lump sum order being made on such an application (except in favour of a child). The way in which the court has interpreted this subsection can be seen in the cases of *Powys* and *Chaterjee*, which are again referred to on p 86. The reluctance of the courts in general to allow an *original* application for a property adjustment order or a lump sum order made years after the original decree to circumvent the policy of the legislation can also be seen in eg *Williams* v *Williams* [1971] 2 All ER 764 (retroactive effect of the Matrimonial Proceedings and Property Act 1970: property adjustment order made); *Jones* v *Jones* [1971] 3 All ER 1201 (lump sum justified because of substantial increase in the husband's wealth, but not awarded due to voluntary transfer of matrimonial home); *Ladbrooke* v *Ladbrooke* (1977) 7 Fam Law 213 (no further capital provision ordered beyond original consent order); *Sandford* v *Sandford* [1986] 1

FLR 412 (registrar wrong to grant leave to amend an application for variation of a periodical payments order to include a claim for a lump sum order: see further p 87; *Dinch* v *Dinch* [1987] 1 All ER 818; qv). In some instances, the applicant may face the additional procedural hurdle of having to obtain leave before making an original application under the Family Proceedings Rules 1991, r 2.53(2). It was noted on p 108 that the Court of Appeal in *Twiname* allowed an application for a lump sum to be made some twenty-eight years after the parties were divorced, whilst indicating that a clean break would be appropriate in such a case.

Another attempt to overcome the prohibition in s 31(5) has been by appealing out of time (see *Nikoloff* v *Nikoloff* (1977) *The Times*, 28 March charge in favour of husband not extinguished despite subsequent conviction for manslaughter) and, generally, those cases alleging *Barder*-type new events which are reviewed on pp 146 *et seq*.

The prohibition in s 31(5) does not prevent the court accepting an undertaking to pay a specified lump sum or transfer a property on the basis that upon payment the recipient's order for periodical payments will be dismissed. This course does not involve a lump sum order or property adjustment order and must involve the payer's consent (*S* v *S* [1987] 1 FLR 71; [1987] 2 All ER 312 and [1987] 2 FLR 342n, CA (not overruled on this point); *Boylan* v *Boylan* [1988] 1 FLR 282; *Peacock* v *Peacock* [1991] 1 FLR 324). This practice accords with the rationale behind the substituted s 31(7), namely, that there should be a possibility of achieving a clean break after a period sufficient to enable the maintained spouse to adjust providing that the welfare of any minor child of the family has been given primacy. In *S* v *S*, the court varied the periodical payments order in favour of the wife and the youngest child with liberty to the husband to apply to the registrar within three months for an order directing that, if he should pay to the wife a specified sum within twenty-eight days, the periodical payments order in favour of the wife would terminate three months after payment.

There have been loud cries for reform emerging from the legal profession, the Lord Chancellor's Department and from the judiciary, suggesting that it should be possible on a variation application to impose a clean break by way of forced capitalisation of a periodical payments order. To quote from the last paragraph of Hale J's judgment in *Cornick* v *Cornick* [1994] 2 FLR 530, where the wife sought unsuccessfully to appeal out of time in a case where her periodical payments were continuing (at 538G):

It is quite clear what the exactly appropriate remedy would be in this case: it would be the power to order a lump sum in partial or total replacement for the periodical payments order. That is expressly excluded by s 31(5) of the 1973 Act, yet it is difficult to see how it could possibly conflict with the principle that there should only be one capital settlement. The Law Commission (in its report on 'The Ground for Divorce' (Law Com no 207, 1990)) has already recommended that such a power become available and this is referred to in the Government's recent Green Paper, 'Looking to the Future—Mediation and the Ground for Divorce' (1993) (Cm 2424). It would be open to the parties to compromise the wife's application for an increase in her periodical payments by the payment of a lump sum, but it is not for this court to seek to provide by an indirect route that which Parliament has not yet provided.

The remedy is at hand—cl 16(7) of Sched 8 to the Family Law Act provides that the court may order a lump sum payment on a variation application.

Yet a further attempt to circumvent s 31(5), where there has been undervaluation and/or delay, has been to seek an order for interest. In *L v L* (1980) *The Times*, 13 November, Balcombe, J (as he then was) dismissed the husband's application for a variation of the lump sum order, where the property had upon sale realised more than an agreed valuation, on the ground of lack of jurisdiction. Balcombe, J observed that, even had there been jurisdiction, he would have dismissed the application because all the advantages of using an agreed valuation would be lost if the parties were able to come back and say that the circumstances had changed because of an undervaluation. The husband was, however, awarded interest from three months from the date of the order to the date of sale. The order in question in *L v L* was an order of the High Court and therefore interest could be awarded under the Judgments Act 1838. County court lump sum orders over £5,000 made on or after 1 July 1991 now automatically carry interest (see p 74). A provision for interest cannot be *inserted* in a lump sum order for less than £5,000 made by a county court. In such a situation, interest may only be awarded under the original order until the date specified for payment. Interest thereafter where there is default may be dealt with by a further instalment of the lump sum order *Burrows* v *Burrows* (1981) *The Times*, 10 March; s 23(6) of the 1973 Act; Salter (1989) *Law Society's Gazette*, 5 July 20. This article was quoted by Ewbank J in *L v L* (Lump Sum: Interest) [1994] 2 FLR 234 as indicating that there was ambiguity as to whether a judge had the power subsequent to a lump sum order to award interest on the lump sum pursuant to s 23(6) of the 1973 Act. It was held that in fact there was no ambiguity and that there is no power for a court to order the payment of interest retrospectively. The case therefore exposes a serious lacuna for the unwary draftsman of consent orders.

In *L* v *L*, a wife agreed in a consent order to transfer her interest in the matrimonial home to her husband, and he agreed to pay a lump sum to her within fourteen days of the sale of a commercial property owned by him. The consent order dismissed her claims for periodical payments. Upon the husband's failure to sell the commercial property and pay the lump sum, the wife applied for enforcement of the order and a district judge directed the husband to implement the payment of the lump sum by 1 September 1993, some two years after the consent order had been made in May 1991. Payment was not made on that date, and the wife made a further application contending that the district judge should have directed that interest be payable from a much earlier date and an order was then made retrospectively awarding interest on the lump sum to the wife. The husband successfully appealed against this order. Ewbank J, on the appeal, quoted from Hansard and the Lord Chancellor's explanation which showed beyond doubt that if interest is going to be awarded then the appropriate direction should be given on the making of the substantive order (at 326E–F):

> It often happens, particularly when the court is trying to bring about what is now called a clean break on the dissolution of marriage, that an order is made for one party to pay the other a lump sum by way of maintenance. If the capital is already available, there is no problem, of course. But often it cannot be paid immediately but only by instalments or by payments out of the proceeds of sale of the home or both.
>
> In this case, it would assist the court if an order could be made for the lump sum to carry interest at a rate fixed by the court from the date of making the order down to the date of payment and this clause [s 23(6)] so provides.

The decision holds out a number of lessons, which should be applied in the drafting of consent orders:
(1) Provide in the order for a lump sum to be paid by a certain date so as to enable interest to run from that date pursuant to the automatic interest provisions quoted above. There was no such direction in this case.
(2) It is best, for the avoidance of doubt, to provide specifically for interest to run on any part of the lump sum not paid over, pursuant to s 23(6).
(3) The wife's solicitors allowed an order to be made the effect of which was to dismiss the wife's claims for financial relief upon the

making of the order; it is much better practice to keep the claims open until the other party's obligations have been fulfilled (see p 74–75).

(4) The wife's transfer of her interest in the matrimonial home to her husband was not linked, as it could and should have been, to the husband's payment of the lump sum.

The lacuna is addressed in Sched 2 to the Family Law Act, which provides, under the prospective s 22A(7) and (8), for the court to be able to make interest provision at any time after the lump sum order has been made.

(v) Variation by extension of time

In *Gregory* v *Wainwright* [1984] Fam Law 86, the wife was ordered, *inter alia*, to transfer her interest in the former matrimonial home to the husband who was to pay to her a lump sum of £10,000. There were default provisions by way of an open market sale in the event of the transfer to the husband not proceeding, although the precise form of order is not clear from the report. The husband did not complete within the stipulated period and the wife took the view that the husband had lost his chance to obtain the property and that she was entitled to sell it on the open market. The husband applied to the court to extend the time provided for by the original consent order and the wife applied for an order that the husband should hand over all documents which were required to effect the sale. At first instance, both applications were decided in favour of the wife. On appeal, Sheldon J held that the court's power as to the extension of time was to be found in RSC Ord 3, r 5(1) and CCR Ord 13, r 4(1). It was held that the court would be slow to make any order which would have the effect of undermining the policies of the Matrimonial Causes Act 1973 as to the variation of property adjustment orders, but that the order sought by the husband would not have that effect. The husband was not asking for the order to be altered in relation to any substantial term but for a slight extension of time with which to complete it.

A similar problem came before the Court of Appeal in *Knibb* v *Knibb* [1987] 2 FLR 396 where the leading judgment was given by Sheldon J, although *Gregory* v *Wainwright* does not appear to have been cited in *Knibb*. In *Knibb*, the wife was given the option to redeem a charge in favour of the husband securing 40 per cent of the net value of the former matrimonial home and operable on specified events by paying £3,500 to the husband within four months of the date of the order. The wife did not redeem the charge in time and applied for an extension of time. Referring to CCR Ord 13, r 4, Sheldon J held:

In my judgment, that is a procedural provision and no more, relating to an act in the proceedings, or a step in the action in question. It does not empower the court to vary the terms of a duly constituted property adjustment order, particularly what may be (and in this instance was) a vital term as to the time within which an option may be exercised, still less so if to do so would be to subvert the clear intention and effect of s 31 of the 1973 Act. (at 398)

Sheldon J went on to indicate that the situation could not be saved by having recourse to CCR Ord 22, r 10, which gives the court power to vary the dates for payment of money due under a 'judgment or order made for the payment of money', as the type of order in question could not be described as a 'judgment or order made for the payment of money'.

This problem was not resolved by the Court of Appeal in *Potter* v *Potter* [1990] 2 FLR 27. The consent order there was in a form commonly found under which the wife agreed to pay the husband a lump sum of £6,000 by 31 May 1988 upon payment of which the husband was to transfer all his interest in the former matrimonial home to the wife. The wife was unable to complete by the specified date and the husband took the point that he was not obliged to transfer his interest to the wife as the time limit for payment of the lump sum had expired and the court had no power under s 31 to extend the time limit. The wife applied for an order that the transfer to her should be executed by the registrar. The main question arising on the appeal was whether the husband's obligation to transfer his interest to the wife was conditional upon payment by her of the lump sum by the specified date so that if, for whatever cause, the wife failed to pay the lump sum before that date, the husband never became subject to the obligation to make the transfer. The Court of Appeal held that on the true construction of the order the respective obligations of the husband and the wife had been intended to be mutual. Although payment by the wife of the lump sum was a condition precedent for the coming into existence of the husband's obligation to transfer his interest to the wife, it was not necessary for that purpose for the lump sum to be paid before the specified date. The facts were treated as being analogous to a normal conveyancing transaction. The date in the order gave the wife a period of grace within which to raise the money, after which the husband was entitled to enforce the order. Non-payment by the wife put her in breach of the order, but it did not discharge her obligation. Since the two obligations were co-extensive, neither was the husband's obligation to hand over a transfer upon payment of the lump sum discharged.

In view of the construction put upon the order in question in *Potter*, the Court of Appeal did not consider it necessary to consider whether the court had power to extend the time for payment of the lump sum. Balcombe LJ does hint in *Potter* (at 32) that the only way out of the difficulty is to say that the court has power to extend time where the provision as to time does not go to the main or substantive part of the order. In this way, *Gregory* v *Wainwright* and *Knibb*, which are distinguishable on their facts, are reconcilable. In *Gregory* v *Wainwright* the short extension of time granted did not amount to a variation of a substantive part of the order, whereas in *Knibb* the court considered that the extension sought would have constituted just that.

A full analysis of the above cases by Rodger Hayward Smith QC is to be found at [1989] Fam Law 443, where it is suggested that the problem would be surmountable by the inclusion in the lump sum order of a liberty to apply provision as to extension of time for payment.

Another solution to the problem encountered in *Knibb* might have been for the wife to apply under the liberty to apply provision to redeem the charge for what the court assessed to be the correct amount (*Popat* v *Popat* [1991] 2 FLR 163; see p 142).

A lot of light has been shed on the above decisions by *Masefield* v *Alexander* (Lump Sum: Extension of Time) [1995] 1 FLR 100, on which we commented in detail on p 84. It seems that time will be extended so long as the delay does not strike at the heart of the order and so long as time is not made of the essence. The court has the inherent jurisdiction to extend time; it is a discretion which the court has no difficulty in exercising in relation to orders made after contested hearings and therefore by analogy is a discretion available in relation to consent orders.

(vi) Variation of the instalment provisions in a lump sum order
The instalment provisions in a lump sum order may be amended by varying the dates or amounts of the instalments. This does not, however, mean that the court has power to make an interim lump sum order (*Bolsom* v *Bolsom* (1983) FLR 21; the interim capital orders described in *Barry* v *Barry* [1992] 2 FLR 233 and *F* v *F* [1995] 2 FLR 45 are not classified as interim lump sum orders made pursuant to statute, but as orders made by the court under its inherent jurisdiction). An interesting example of the use of this power is to be found in the Court of Appeal's decision in *Tilley* v *Tilley* (1979) 10 Fam Law 89. A consent order was made vesting a shop and the family home in

the wife and providing for a lump sum to be paid by her to the husband of £4,000 within three months and a further £3,500 to be paid over a period of six years. The order also contained a nominal periodical payments in favour of the children of £0.05 per year as he was unemployed. The shop failed and was sold by the wife. She then applied for a variation of the consent order so that she should not have to pay the instalment of £3,500 on the basis that this could not be done without selling the home and so rendering herself and the children homeless. The Court of Appeal varied the instalment provisions by providing that there should be no further payment to the husband. If, however, there were any application for periodical payments or lump sum for the children, any court faced with such an application ought to take into consideration the sum of £3,500 which in effect the husband had contributed towards the maintenance of the children.

Tilley was quoted with approval by the Court of Appeal in *Penrose v Penrose* [1994] 2 FLR 621. We have seen (on p 148) that here the husband applied out of time for leave to appeal against an order, based partly on the allegedly impaired financial position on which he relied at the appeal in seeking to avoid having to make a lump sum payment due under an outstanding instalment. There are two points to take away from the dicta of Balcombe LJ in Penrose, namely that:

(1) the variation jurisdiction under section 31(2)(d) 'is a jurisdiction to be exercised with caution'; and
(2) the variation application should be the first port of call for an aggrieved applicant, as if it is available it will disincline the court from giving leave to appeal out of time. 'Even if I had been of the view that there were *prima facie* grounds of appeal, which I am not, I would have hesitated to grant leave where another more effective and simpler remedy exists' (Lord Balcombe LJ at 634 D–F, supported in this respect by Nourse LJ at 636 C–D).

(vii) Liberty to apply

Such a provision does enable the court to give effect to the spirit and construction of the original order as a matter of working it out, but not to order a variation prohibited by s 31 (*Thompson v Thompson* [1985] 2 All ER 243 ('or further order' meant that the court was able to give immediate effect to the execution of a trust for sale in a *Mesher* order); cf *Dinch v Dinch* [1987] 1 All ER 818 (no power to postpone sale beyond the original period contained in a *Mesher* order); cf *Popat v Popat* [1991] 2 FLR 163 (charge back redeemable at any time in the absence of a clause restricting the right of redemption): see further p 203). It does not give jurisdiction, where jurisdiction does not exist (*Masefield* v *Alexander* (p 84); and see *N* v *N* (Valuation: Charge Back Order) [1996] 1 FLR 361.

(viii) Effective date of variation
Subsection 10 was added to s 31 by the Matrimonial and Family Proceedings Act 1984, s 6, and provides that, subject to the overriding factors governing the duration of continuing financial provision orders contained in s 28(1) and (2), the court has power to direct that the variation or discharge of an order for periodical payments or secured periodical payments shall not take effect until the expiration of such period as is specified in the order. It may be convenient for the parties to be able to delay the date on which a variation takes effect, particularly where a clean break is to be achieved. An order may be *backdated* beyond the date of the variation application to the date of the original order. However, any such backdating will not alter the taxation consequences (if any, having regard to the Finance Act 1988) of the original order in relation to payments already made (*MacDonald* v *MacDonald* [1963] 2 All ER 857; *Morley-Clarke* v *Jones* [1985] 3 WLR 749, CA; [1986] 1 WLR 978, HL (petition for leave to appeal dismissed)). Backdating for more than a comparatively short period is to be regarded as the exception rather than the rule and should not be used to provide the payee with a substantial capital sum (*S* v *S* [1987] 2 All ER 312, CA).

(ix) Secured provision
Where the person liable to make payments under a secured periodical payments order has died, an application for variation of the order and any order made under s 24A(1) requiring the proceeds of sale of property to be used for securing those payments may be made by the person entitled to payment or by the personal representatives of the deceased. No such application may be made, however, except with the permission of the court, after the end of the period of six months from the date when representation to the estate was first taken out (s 31(6)). The personal representatives are protected from liability under s 31(8) in the same way as under s 36(5). The time when representation is first taken out is defined in s 31(9).

(x) Undertakings relating to variation applications.
It has already been seen on p 40 that a consent order capable of variation under s 31 may still be varied notwithstanding an undertaking

from the wife not to apply for an increase (*Jessel* v *Jessel* [1979] 3 All ER 645). However, a clause of the type set out on p 94 may in practical terms for the reasons discussed on p 30 limit the wife's right to seek a variation. In *Beighton* v *Beighton* (1974) 4 Fam Law 119, it was held that it would be wrong to construe the consent order as a final order constituting a binding agreement which estopped the wife from exercising her right to apply for an increase in maintenance if there had been a material change in circumstances. The reader is referred to the authors' comments on *N* v *N*, *Richardson* v *Richardson* (No 1 and No 2), and *B* v *B* (Consent Order: Variation) above (pp 90–91).

A party is not under any general duty to reveal a change in circumstances which may lead to a variation (*Hayfield* v *Hayfield* [1951] 1 All ER 598). A consent order may, however, suitably contain an undertaking to the court to notify the other party of any change in remuneration or other specified circumstances; this principle was judicially approved, for instance, in *Barrett* v *Barrett* [1988] 2 FLR 516.

(b) Principles governing the exercise of the court's powers
(i) Introduction
Section 31 directs the court in exercising its powers under the section to have regard to:

> all the circumstances of the case, first consideration being given to the welfare while a minor of any child of the family who has not attained the age of eighteen, and the circumstances of the case shall include any change in any of the matters to which the court was required to have regard when making the order to which the application relates, and:
> (a) in the case of a periodical payments or secured periodical payments order made on or after the grant of a decree of divorce or nullity of marriage, the court shall consider whether in all the circumstances and after having regard to any such change it would be appropriate to vary the order so that payments under the order are required to be made or secured only for such further period as will in the opinion of the court be sufficient to enable the party in whose favour the order was made to adjust without undue hardship to the termination of those payments;
> (b) in a case where the party against whom the order was made has died, the circumstances of the case shall also include the changed circumstances resulting from his or her death.

The principles indicated above are contained in the s 31(7) substituted by the Matrimonial and Family Proceedings Act 1984, s 6. This provision can be seen as part of the policy of the 1984 Act to promote the concept of the clean break. Because of this, Professor

Cretney has suggested that cases decided before the 1984 Act should be treated with reserve. Where the application is for a consent variation order, the court need only have regard to the information prescribed by the Family Proceedings Rules 1991, r 2.61.

(ii) What is the correct starting point?
Does the approach which the court should adopt differ according to whether the original order was made by consent or after a full inquiry into the financial position of both parties? Must the original order be the starting point or can maintenance be fixed *de novo* on a variation application? The view formerly taken was that the original order must be regarded as the starting point whether it was made by consent or after full inquiry. Exceptions to this general principle were in the case of consent orders where a husband had failed to make a full and frank disclosure of his assets and the wife had been prejudiced by this failure or where one party had not been independently and competently advised before consenting to an order (*Foster* v *Foster* [1964] 3 All ER 541; *Payne* v *Payne* [1968] 1 All ER 1113; *Wilkins* v *Wilkins* [1969] 2 All ER 463 (in particular at 468 D–E)). It has, however, now been clearly established by the Court of Appeal in *Lewis* v *Lewis* [1977] 3 All ER 992 and *Garner* v *Garner* [1992] 1 FLR 573 that the court is not confined when considering a variation application to looking at changes in the means of the parties which have occurred since the original order was made. The court can regard the assessment of maintenance as being at large and consider all the circumstances *de novo*, although the court will want to know whether there were any special factors which came into play in the original order (by way of example, a wife's maintenance being fixed partly by reference to the investment income that she would receive on a proportion of her lump sum payment not used for the purchase of a property). The Court of Appeal in *Garner* and *Lewis* rejected the restricted approach suggested in *Foster*, based upon earlier legislation, that the correct approach was to start from the original order and see what changes had taken place since that order was made and then make adjustments roughly in proportion to those changes, if that were possible.

Ormrod LJ in *Lewis* formed this view having regard to the different wording of s 31(7) (as it then was), which as has been seen effectively requires the court to have regard to changes in any of the matters mentioned in s 25. Ormrod LJ commented (at 994–995):

> I am bound to say that it has always seemed to me, with respect, that the powers of variation, which were given by statute to this court in a series of enactments going right back to 1857, have been, if anything,

progressively enlarged and that the intention of Parliament is that, in handling these family matters where money is concerned, the court should have as unfettered a discretion as possible to deal with the situation as it is when the matter comes before it. I am sure it is not the intention of Parliament in any way to trammel the discretion by any kind of technical reasoning or technical grounds.

The current approach of looking at the matter in accordance with s 31(7) afresh applies equally to consent orders and orders made after a full inquiry (*Gregory* v *Wainwright* [1984] Fam Law 96). Whilst there is no actual requirement under s 31(7) to prove a material change in circumstances, the court's approach will generally be, once a change in circumstances subsequent to the original order has been proved, to proceed to fix the level of maintenance *de novo* on the basis of the means of the parties at the time of the hearing of the variation application.

Giving the leading judgment in *Garner*, Cazalet J surveyed the leading decisions on variation referred to above and gave some very useful lessons to be applied in advising on the appropriateness or otherwise of a variation application as well as illuminating the court's approach on any such application (at 581D–582B):

> By the Matrimonial and Family Proceedings Act 1984 there has been... a new substituted subs (7) of s 31. This requires the court, in having regard to all the circumstances of the case, to give first consideration to the welfare, while a minor, of any child of the family. This requirement of primacy being given to the welfare of the child re-emphasises the court's powers to step outside any actual changes which may have occurred and look at the totality of the circumstances, without being confined solely or essentially to matters of change...
>
> Following *Lewis* v *Lewis*, by which decision this court is bound, a court on the hearing of an application to vary is fully entitled to look at all the relevant matters set out in s 25 of the Matrimonial Causes Act 1973. On occasions, the court may be slow to accede to an application to vary a consent order; not least because the parties' solicitors might otherwise be deterred from either seeking to negotiate such a provision or to achieve finality. Another factor which may influence a court will be the time that has passed since the original order was made. If any application consequent on an order is brought very soon after that order has been made, the court, in normal circumstances, is likely to attach more weight to the earlier order than if it had been made some years previously. Likewise the court would expect to pay full regard to any special terms agreed between the parties at the time the original order was made—as, for example, when endorsements on briefs or contemporaneous correspondence shows that an agreed order has, for some particular reason, been set at an artificially low figure. Shortly stated the court must decide what weight it should attach to the original order and all the sur-

rounding circumstances. However, once an application to vary is before it, the court is fully entitled to make an order considering all the circumstances afresh, paying such regard to the old order as may be thought appropriate.

In *Cornick* v *Cornick* (No 2) [1995] 2 FLR 490 the husband appealed to the Court of Appeal against an order for variation of the periodical payments made by him to her from £20,000 to £35,000 per annum. Counsel for the husband argued in the appeal that a court dealing with an application for the variation of periodical payments was constrained by the 'budgetary approach' of concentrating simply upon the stated needs of a payee, which therefore restricted the broad s 25 exercise; the barrister further submitted that if the court supported an approach which differed from the 'budgetary approach', it would have a serious effect upon the administration of the practice and settlement of financial relief applications throughout the country; and that *Boylan* v *Boylan* and *Primavera* v *Primavera* were wrongly decided. The Court of Appeal rejected the submissions, restating the authority of *Boylan* and *Primavera*; in a variation application the court is not blinkered by concentration on only one of the circumstances (in the present case, the wife's stated needs) but has to survey the totality of the relevant circumstances and, in *Cornick*, the vastly increased wealth of the husband since the date of the original maintenance order was a relevant factor. We have seen from *Crozier* (see p 159), however, that changes in legislation subsequent to a consent order can frustrate a party's intentions and leave him with no effective opportunity to vary or set aside.

An exception to this general principle is where the original order was made on an erroneous basis.

In *Smethurst* v *Smethurst* [1977] 3 All ER 1110, it was held that jurisdiction to vary existed as the registrar had made a mistake in the original order in assessing the husband's ability to pay. Similarly, in *B (GC)* v *B (BA)* [1970] 1 All ER 913 *sub nom Brister* v *Brister* [1970] 1 WLR 664, a variation order was made because the tax effect of the original order had been misunderstood by the husband's solicitor. In *Clothier* v *Clothier* (1980), unreported, CA Transcript No 392, the order was varied for the express purpose of making it tax effective.

The court is not restricted to considering the circumstances existing at the date of the hearing, but can have regard to evidence of a change which is to occur in the near future in order to avoid a further variation application within a short period (*Furlong-Taylor* v *Furlong-Taylor* (1982) 13 Fam Law 143). This principle emerges readily from the fact that under s 25 the court is required to have regard to a range of matters which may arise 'in the foreseeable future'.

(iii) Estoppel

There are, however, cases where the circumstances surrounding the making of the original order are such as to create a potential estoppel in relation to a future variation application. Examples of the guidelines given by the court which operate in this way can be seen in *B (MAL)* v *B (NE)* [1968] 1 WLR 1109 (where the husband consented to a maintenance order in favour of the wife in consideration of the wife waiving a claim in bankruptcy under the agreement: the husband was thereby estopped from setting the consent maintenance order aside) and *Bateman* v *Bateman* [1979] 2 WLR 377 (where a maintenance order was made in favour of the wife for £1,000 per annum: such order not to be varied if she found gainful employment) cf *Beighton* v *Beighton* (1974) 4 Fam Law 119 (see p 206). A further example of such estoppel may be found in the artificial apportionment of maintenance orders in favour of children for tax purposes. This practice was commonplace before the changes brought about by the Finance Act 1988 (see p 23). Variation applications continue to come before the courts in relation to 'existing obligations' under the Act where the global maintenance payable to a wife and children under a consent order has been so apportioned as to take full advantage of all available personal allowances. There will frequently have been a side letter between the parties' solicitors indicating the actual level of maintenance payable to each party named in the order for the purposes of subsequent variation applications. In this way, all other factors apart, when the wife's maintenance terminates on remarriage, that part of her maintenance payable under the order for the children may also terminate or, when the order in favour of one of the children expires, the wife may be entitled to an upward variation in her own maintenance to reflect that part of her maintenance included in a child's order. It is submitted that the 'estoppel' ground arises out of, rather than being distinct from, the 'special terms' referred to in the passage from Cazalet J's judgment in *Garner*, quoted above.

(iv) Children

Reference should be made to Chapter 5, 'Consensus and the Child Support Act'. Section 31(7) specifically directs the court in having regard to all the circumstances of the case to give first consideration to the welfare while a minor of any child of the family who has not attained the age of eighteen. The conduct of the parties should not be taken into account in considering maintenance for children; there should therefore be no discount by reason of a lack of access. The principle will apply even if anything paid by the father would simply reduce the family's income support (*Foot* v *Foot* [1986] Fam Law 13). Giving first consideration to the welfare of the minor children will usually involve a father paying something more than a nominal amount, even if he is in strained financial circumstances (*Roots* v *Roots* [1987] Fam Law 397).

(v) The circumstances of the case
The reference in s 31(7) to 'any change in any of the matters to which the court was required to have regard when making the order to which the application relates' dictates that, (as we have seen on p 207) when exercising its jurisdiction on a variation application, the court must consider the guidelines set out in s 25. Conduct since the date of the original order may as part of s 25 be relevant on a variation application (*J (HD)* v *J (AM)* [1980] 1 All ER 156; *Kyte* v *Kyte* [1988] Fam 145; *Evans* v *Evans* [1989] 1 FLR 351; *K* v *K* [1990] Fam Law 19), but not in relation to children's maintenance (*Foot* v *Foot* [1986] Fam Law 13). A wife's inheritance since the original order, and her financial mismanagement, will fall to be considered (*Primavera* v *Primavera* [1992] 1 FLR 16, where both an inheritance and alleged financial mismanagement were held to be irrelevant in the special circumstances of the wealth of the husband, who had put forward a millionaire's defence). Cohabitation and the cohabitee's earning capacity may also be relevant (*MH* v *MH* [1982] 3 FLR 429; *Duxbury* v *Duxbury* [1987] 1 FLR 7; *Atkinson* v *Atkinson* [1988] 2 FLR 353; *Hepburn* v *Hepburn* [1989] 1 FLR 373), as may be a husband's responsibility towards his cohabitee and his children by her (*Roberts* v *Roberts* [1969] 3 All ER 479; *Delaney* v *Delaney* [1990] 2 FLR 457). As to the relevance of remarriage, see eg *Bellenden* v *Bellenden* [1948] 1 All ER 343; *Grainger* v *Grainger* [1954] 2 All ER 665; *Cowie* v *Cowie* [1983] Fam Law 250 and *Ashley* v *Blackman* 1988 2 FLR 278. The fact that the wife has by her thrift managed to collect some savings will not normally be a reason for a variation on the husband's application (*Sansom* v *Sansom* [1966] 2 All ER 396).

(vi) Is a clean break achievable?
The underlying philosophy of the substituted s 31(7) is that of the clean break wherever this is achievable. An early reported decision after the 1984 Act came into operation, where the Court of Appeal was invited to consider the clean break provisions in the substitute

s 31(7)(*a*), was *Morris* v *Morris* [1985] FLR 1176. At first instance, the judge had varied the periodical payments order so as to make it terminate either on the husband having no further employment with tied accommodation or on his attaining the age of sixty-five. The marriage had lasted for twenty-four years. The purpose of the judge in fixing a termination date so as to bring to an end an acrimonious dispute between the parties was described by the Court of Appeal as an incorrect use of the clean break provisions. The Court of Appeal held that insufficient attention had been given to whether the wife could adjust without undue hardship to the termination of the periodical payments. May LJ, however, went further by indicating that in applying the clean break provisions the distinction was to be drawn between the making of a first order after a decree and an application to vary an original order. The authors respectfully submit however that there is no difference in this respect between the originating and variation applications, and May LJ's indication has not been followed in the subsequent decisions in variation applications discussed on pp 98 *et seq*.

The court will determine the quantum of maintenance to which the wife is entitled by reference to all the circumstances of the case and will then proceed to consider her position and the hardship, if any, that she would suffer were the periodical payments to be terminated. In this context, 'undue hardship' should not be given a narrow construction as referring solely to the needs of the wife. It will be relevant to this issue that the wife was the former spouse of a man of substantial wealth. In appropriate circumstances, it is by that standard that her reasonable requirements should be judged and an assessment made as to whether or not she would suffer 'undue hardship' on the termination of the payments (*Boylan* v *Boylan* [1988] 1 FLR 282, at 287 and 289; this has become known as the '*Boylan* principle' and was quoted, with approval, by two of the three judges in the Court of Appeal in the case of *Primavera*).

(vii) Automatic variations

The court may make an order which provides for automatic variation. It is submitted that such an order will only be made by consent. In *Sharp* v *Sharp* [1984] FLR 752, the order provided for the wife's maintenance to increase annually by the same percentage as the increase in the husband's pay. Automatic variations of this type might in the case of child maintenance be linked to a child's birthday or be index-linked in some way eg to the retail prices index. Such a clause cannot, however, oust the jurisdiction of the court to vary the order in a different way. It is however possible to recite the parties' agreement that the automatic increase provided for in the body of the order is intended by them to be a 'once and for all' settlement of any variation applications that may be made in the future and, although such a recital cannot oust the jurisdiction of the court to vary the order in a different way, it will be a 'special term' to which the court will have particular regard in any future variation application.

(c) Procedure

A variation application falls within the definition of an application for ancillary relief under FPR 1991, r 1.2(1). Application should therefore be made by notice in Form M11 (FPR 1991, r 2.53(3)) or in Form A where the pilot scheme is in place [1996] 2 FLR 368. The rules relating to an application for ancillary relief (FPR 1991, rr 2.53–2.68) apply largely to a variation application. In particular, an interim order may be made on a variation application (FPR 1991, r 2.64(2)). Where a variation order is itself made by consent the statement of information required by FPR 1991, r 2.61 is sufficiently complied with if it includes only the information in respect of the net income of each party and of any minor child of the family (FPR 1991, r 2.61(2)). An affidavit in support of the variation application does now have to be filed at the same time as the notice in Form M11 (FPR 1991, r 2.58(2)). It should be noted that the affidavit must contain full particulars of property and income and state the facts relied on in support of the application; it is therefore impossible for a party to argue, by inference from the fact that a r 2.61 statement relating to a consent variation application need contain only particulars of the parties' *income*, that the affidavit should contain income particulars only. As has been explained above, the court has to have regard to all the circumstances of a case in a variation application.

3 Agreements made rules of court

The question of whether an agreement which had been made a rule of court could be varied was one of the matters which fell to be considered by Wood J in *MH* v *MH* (1982) 3 FLR 429. Various types of provision had been made for the wife under a deed of separation which was made a rule of court. The husband applied for a variation of the deed under s 35 of the 1973 Act. It was held that the deed had ceased to be a subsisting maintenance agreement capable of variation under s 35, when it was made a rule of court, applying the decision in *De Lasala* v *De Lasala* [1979] 2 All ER 1146. Wood J seems to have regarded the deed as a 'once-for-all' settlement incapable of variation under s 31, as was the case in *De Lasala*, whereas in *MH* the deed did contain certain provisions for the continuing maintenance of the wife and children. It is submitted that the question as to whether such continuing provisions may be varied by the court remains unresolved.

4 Undertakings

The stress laid by Lord Brandon on the use of undertakings as part of the correct method of formulating consent orders in *Livesey* v *Jenkins* [1985] 1 All ER 106, at 118–119 gives rise to the need to consider how such undertakings may be varied. Such undertakings will most usually relate to matters which the court has no power to order eg payment of the mortgage and other outgoings relating to the property or the taking out and discharge of premiums on an insurance policy. Some undertakings may be analogous to continuing maintenance or make capital provision or be of a hybrid nature outside the framework of ss 23–24 of the 1973 Act, this being the very reason why they had been formulated as undertakings.

In *Whitfield* v *Whitfield* [1985] FLR 955; not appealed on this point [1986] 1 FLR 99, it was held by Hollis J that a settlement of property which had been agreed and incorporated into an order by way of undertakings could not be varied under s 31. The point was made that the order had superseded the underlying agreement, which follows the view expressed in *De Lasala* that consent orders derive their effect from the order of the court rather than the underlying agreement. An undertaking incorporated in a consent order may not therefore be varied under s 35 as a subsisting maintenance agreement.

It would appear therefore that an undertaking incorporated in an order will only be capable of variation if it is analogous to a type of court order which is itself capable of variation. An undertaking making capital provision as in *Whitfield* would not be capable of variation, but it is submitted that an undertaking of an income nature, such as the payment of the outgoings on the former matrimonial home, may be capable of variation. This view is consistent with the approach adopted by the courts as to the enforceability of undertakings indicated above on p 8 and p 71.

Chapter 8

Enforcement

The purpose of this chapter is to contrast the means by which agreements and consent orders may be enforced, whilst looking briefly at how agreements which have been made recitals, rules of court and undertakings given to the court fit into the enforcement process. It is not possible in a work of this size to examine the procedural aspects of enforcement in detail: reference should be made to eg Chapter 14 of Salter, Jeavons and Ayrton, *Humphreys' Family Proceedings 18th* ed (FT Law and Tax) or Chapter 13 of Duckworth, *Matrimonial Property and Finance* 5th ed (FT Law & Tax). Similarly, for a full treatment of emergency remedies aimed at the protection of family property such as s 37 of the 1973 Act, Anton Piller orders and Mareva injunctions, the reader is referred to Chapter 3 of Fricker and others, *Family Courts Emergency Remedies and Procedures* 2nd ed (Family Law).

The essence of the distinction between the enforcement of a maintenance agreement and a court order was neatly drawn by Lord Diplock in *De Lasala* v *De Lasala* [1979] 2 All ER 1146, at 1155:

> The [Hong Kong] ordinance and the corresponding English legislation recognise two separate ways in which financial provision may lawfully be made for parties to a marriage which has been dissolved. One is by a maintenance agreement entered into between the parties without the intervention of the court; the other is by one party obtaining a court order against the other for periodical payments or for once and for all financial provision. In the event of default, a maintenance agreement is enforceable by action; a court order is enforceable by judgment summons... Financial arrangements that are agreed on between the parties for the purpose of receiving the approval and being made the subject of a consent order by the court, once they have been the subject of the court order no longer depend upon the agreement of the parties as the source from which their legal effect is derived. Their legal effect is derived from the court order; and the method of enforcing such of their

provisions as continue to be executory . . . is not by action but by summons under the court order pursuant to the liberty to apply, reserved in the . . . consent order.

1 Agreements

It must first be considered whether the agreement is enforceable. In Chapter 2, it has been seen that agreements may be rendered unenforceable for a variety of reasons. If, however, the agreement is enforceable, either party may sue on it and, after obtaining judgment, seek any of the contractual enforcement remedies available in the court's armoury. The court does not have a discretion to remit arrears when dealing with an agreement, as is the case under s 32(2) of the 1973 Act in the case of a consent order nor is there any restriction on enforcing arrears which are more than a year old other than the normal contractual limitation period of six years. Bankruptcy proceedings may be based on arrears of maintenance of over £750 due under an agreement, which are a provable debt. However, proceedings may not be brought in respect of either arrears or future payments of maintenance after the commencement of the bankruptcy, as the husband's liability is discharged by his bankruptcy, whether or not the wife has elected to prove (*Victor* v *Victor* [1911–13] All ER Rep 959; *McQuiban* v *McQuiban* [1913] P 208).

What enforcement action may be taken in relation to, for example, property matters in an agreement which remain executory? This area has already been touched upon in Chapter 6 in the context of looking at the remedies open to a spouse who is dissatisfied with the agreement reached. It is open to either party to apply to the court for an order for specific performance, a discretionary remedy which may be refused if grounds exist for setting the agreement aside or if the making of an order would be highly unreasonable or cause an injustice (*Cross* v *Cross* (1983) 4 FLR 235). An order for specific performance was also sought in *Sutton* v *Sutton* [1984] 1 All ER 168, which has already been discussed on p 180. Where the agreement concerns the matrimonial home, it must be in writing in order to be enforceable (Law of Property (Miscellaneous Provisions) Act 1989, s 2: see p 14).

2 Consent orders

Instead of seeking to go behind the consent order by use of the remedies discussed in Chapter 6, a party will more normally wish to affirm the order and, where necessary, enforce its terms. Enforcement of a consent order is simpler than enforcement of an agreement, insofar as immediate enforcement action can be taken. The means of enforcement which is to be used will depend upon (*a*) the nature of the order to be enforced and (*b*) whether the proceedings are pending in the High Court or a divorce county court.

The procedures outlined here have been extended by the Maintenance Enforcement Act 1991. When making a maintenance order, or in related proceedings for its variation or revocation, the court may order payment to be made by standing order or some similar method ('a method of payment order') (MEA 1991, s 1(4) and (5)). Additionally, a defaulting party may be ordered to open a bank account for this purpose (MEA 1991, s 1(6)). There is now no longer any need to show default on the part of the debtor before an attachment of earnings order is made (MEA 1991, s 1(4)(*b*); AEA 1971, s 3(3A)). These powers are only exercisable in relation to a 'qualifying periodical maintenance order' (MEA 1991, s 1(2) and (10)).

It should also be borne in mind that the Child Support Agency can take on the collection of certain orders made under CSA 1991, s 8, ie 'top-up orders' (s 8(6)), 'school fees orders' (s 8(7)) and orders relating to disabled children (s 8(8)). Further, the Child Support Agency can also take over responsibility for the collection and enforcement of spousal maintenance where child support maintenance is also being collected and enforced.

3 Enforcement procedures

If the payer's whereabouts are unknown, the procedure for the disclosure of addresses by government departments may prove useful (*Practice Direction 13 February 1989* [1989] 1 FLR 307). If known or when known, an oral examination of the payer is a useful way of determining which means of enforcement is most appropriate (RSC Ord 48; CCR Ord 25, r 3 and FPR r 7.1(5)). Before any enforcement proceedings may be issued, an affidavit is required verifying the amount due under the order and showing how that amount is arrived at (FPR 1991, r 7.1(1)). Arrears of maintenance under a consent order may not be enforced without the leave of the court if the arrears became due more than twelve months before the enforcement proceedings were begun (s 32 of the 1973 Act). Leave may be refused or granted subject to such restrictions and conditions (including conditions as to allowing of time for payment or payment by instalments) as the court thinks proper or alternatively the arrears may be remitted wholly or in part (s 32(2)). The general rule of practice, which can, however, be departed from in unusual circumstances, is that arrears will not be enforced if more than a year old; the onus of persuading the court to act contrary to this general rule is on the party applying for enforcement (*Ross* v *Pearson* [1976] 1 All ER 790; *Russell* v *Russell* [1986] 1 FLR 465; *Bernstein* v *O'Neill* [1989] 2 FLR 1; *H* v *H* (Financial Provision) [1993] 2 FLR 35).

Care must always be taken to balance the cost of enforcement proceedings against the likely achievable benefit. In *Clark* v *Clark* [1989] 1 FLR 174; *Clark* v *Clark (No 2)* [1991] 1 FLR 179, the costs of sequestration proceedings, to which the sequestered monies must first be applied, exceeded the arrears of maintenance.

The flowchart on p 219 summarises the enforcement procedures available in each court in relation to particular types of orders.

Any obligation arising under an order made in family or domestic proceedings is not provable in bankruptcy (Insolvency Rules 1986, r 12.3). This rule covers maintenance arrears, any balance due under a lump sum order and outstanding costs. There are *obiter dicta* of Ewbank J in *Woodley* v *Woodley* [1992] 2 FLR 417, CA to suggest that the rule might be *ultra vires* the Insolvency Act 1986. However, the point was not fully argued and no concluded view expressed (at 423A). Balcombe LJ subsequently expressed the view in *Woodley* v *Woodley* (No 2) [1993] 2 FLR 477, CA at 485 that he was satisfied that the rule was *intra vires*. It should be borne in mind that the Insolvency Rules 1986, r 12.3 changed the pre-existing position under which orders for periodical payments were not provable in bankruptcy (*James* v *James* [1963] 2 All ER 465), whereas an order for a lump sum was provable (*Curtis* v *Curtis* [1969] 2 All ER 207). Subsequent discharge from bankruptcy does not release the bankrupt from obligations arising under orders in family proceedings, unless the court otherwise directs (Insolvency Act 1986, s 281(5)(*b*)). A maintenance creditor is entitled to participate in an individual voluntary arrangement under the Insolvency Act 1986 Part VIII both in respect of arrears of maintenance and costs (even though untaxed) (*Re Bradley-Hole* [1995] 4 All ER 865).

If a consent order remains executory, the court may as a matter of discretion refuse to enforce the order if grounds exist for setting it aside. *Thwaite* v *Thwaite* [1981] 2 All ER 789 is an example:

> A consent order was made that H would transfer his interest in a jointly owned property in England to W upon her undertaking to return from Australia to England with the three children and live in the property. On these terms, W's other applications for ancillary relief were to be

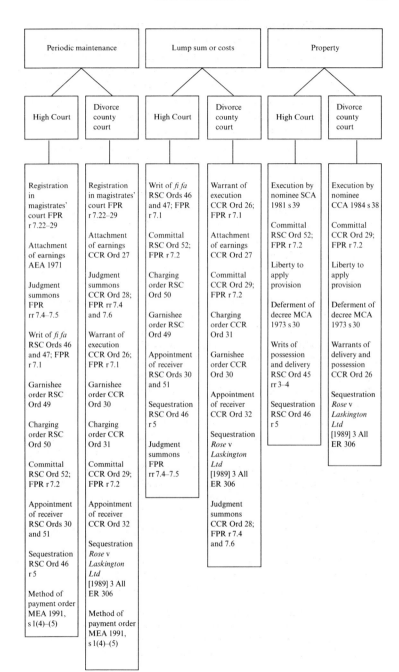

dismissed from the date of the conveyance. W returned to England but before completion of the conveyance removed the children from the jurisdiction and returned to Australia. H declined to complete the conveyance. The Court of Appeal held that the court had jurisdiction to refuse to enforce the consent order on the ground that effectively W had failed to honour her undertaking to return the children to England and it would be unjust in the circumstances to compel H to transfer his interest in the property to W. The court also had jurisdiction to make a fresh order for ancillary relief, since the dismissal of W's claims had not come into effect because the conveyance had not been executed and consequently W's application was still before the court.

A liberty to apply provision reserved in a consent order may be used as a method of enforcement insofar as its provisions remain executory, as Lord Diplock commented in *De Lasala* (at 1155). As has been seen on p 178, such a provision does have uses to deal with 'unforeseen or unexpected contingencies' (per Buckley LJ in *Alonso* v *Alonso* (1974) 4 Fam Law 164). The application should follow the Family Proceedings Rules 1991, r 10.9. Where a consent order, which remains executory, contains a provision for liberty to apply as to the implementation of the order, the proper course in the case of default is to enforce the order promptly rather than to attempt to treat the default as a supervening event justifying a variation of the consent order on the *Barder* principle (*Rooker* v *Rooker* [1988] 1 FLR 219).

The position may also remain executory because a party has resiled from an agreement to incorporate agreed terms into a consent order. In these circumstances, an application should be made to the court for the party who has resiled from the agreement to show cause why the agreed terms should not be made an order of the court (*Dean* v *Dean* [1978] 3 All ER 758).

4 Recitals incorporated in a consent order

Where a court order consists in part of recitals in the preamble to the order and in part orders, the contractual provisions only recited may be enforced as though they had been orders of the court (*Atkinson* v *Castan* (1991) *The Times*, 17 April, CA). It has been held that this principle is applicable in the Family Division, although the recital was not reproduced in the order section and although it was not the subject of an undertaking (*H* v *H* [1993] 2 FLR 35 at 37G, Thorpe J).

5 Agreements made rules of court

For the purposes of enforcement, an agreement which has been made a rule of court should be treated as a court order (*Green* v *Rozen*

[1955] 2 All ER 797; *Pasley* v *Pasley* (1964) 108 SJ 383; *Herbert* v *Herbert* (1978) 122 SJ 826). As Wood J commented in *MH* v *MH* (1982) 3 FLR 429, at 433:

> It will be remembered that this separation agreement was made a rule of court and, therefore, an order of the court for the purposes of enforcement.

6 Undertakings

The stress laid by Lord Brandon on the use of undertakings in consent orders in *Livesey* v *Jenkins* [1985] 1 All ER 106 has already been commented upon at p 8 and p 71. So far as the matter of enforcement of undertakings is concerned, Lord Brandon commented at 119 that 'such undertakings are, needless to say, enforceable as effectively as direct orders'.

Indeed, *Thwaite* is an example of the court's approach to undertakings given to the court (see p 218). A further example is to be found in *Gandolfo* v *Gandolfo* [1980] 1 All ER 833, where an undertaking by a husband to pay school fees was enforced by a garnishee order on his bank account. There is no need to convert the undertaking into an order (*Gandolfo* v *Gandolfo* (above)).

An undertaking in a consent order is enforceable by committal under a judgment summons depending on the terms of the undertaking (*Symmons* v *Symmons* [1993] 1 FLR 317). However, the undertaking must on its proper construction be seen as the equivalent of 'an order for periodical or other payments made, or having effect as if made, under Part II [of MCA 1973]' (AJA 1970, ss 11(*b*), 28(1) and Sched 8, para 2A). Thus, an undertaking to pay a monthly supplement and to pay school fees was treated as an integral and indivisible part of the court's order enforceable by way of judgment summons (*Symmons* v *Symmons* (above)). An undertaking in a consent order to discharge capital gains tax has also been treated as enforceable by way of a judgment summons (*M* v *M* (Enforcement: Judgment Summons) [1993] Fam Law 469).

Appendix 1

Pre-marital contract[1]

Date: _____ 19____
Parties: (1) _____ of _____ ('Mr _____')
        (2) _____ of _____ ('[Miss/Mrs] _____')

(1) This Deed is made in contemplation of the intended marriage of Mr _____ and [Miss/Mrs] _____ [on _____ 19___] ('the marriage')
(2) The parties wish by this Deed to enter into an agreement recording their wishes and intentions regarding their finances and property
(3) The parties intend that this Deed shall be legally binding upon them
(4) This Deed is intended to be binding upon the heirs and personal representatives of the parties
(5) Each party has received independent legal advice prior to the execution of this Deed

Now this Deed witnesses

1 This Deed shall become operative upon the parties' celebrating a valid ceremony of marriage whether on _____ 19____ or at a later date PROVIDED ALWAYS that should the marriage not be celebrated within _____ months of _____ 19____ this Deed shall be deemed to be discharged unless revived by a supplemental deed executed by both parties

2 All assets held by the parties in their respective names prior to the marriage shall remain in their respective absolute beneficial ownership following the marriage

3 All assets acquired during the marriage by either of the parties by way of gift or inheritance shall remain in their respective absolute beneficial ownership

4 All chattels purchased for not more than £_____ during the marriage by either of the parties or by them jointly shall be deemed to be in joint ownership and upon the death of either party shall accrue to the survivor

5   All chattels purchased for more than £_____ during the marriage by either of the parties or by them jointly shall belong to them in the shares in which the purchase monies were contributed and no presumption of advancement shall apply

6   The matrimonial home at _____ will be vested in the sole name of Mr _____ and notwithstanding any contribution which [Miss/Mrs] _____ may make directly or indirectly towards the purchase, maintenance or improvement of the said property she has and will acquire no beneficial interest in the said property

7   Mr _____ and [Miss/Mrs] _____ agree to indemnify each other and their respective estates in respect of all debts and liabilities incurred by the other

8   In the event of the dissolution of the marriage or the separation of the parties neither shall make any financial claim of any kind upon the other without prejudice to the right of either party to make such a claim in respect of any child of the marriage[2]

9   In the event of the death of either party,[3] then the survivor will be entitled to the following:
   (a) all personal chattels (as defined by the Administration of Estates Act 1925, s 55(1)(x)) of the deceased excluding those chattels specifically bequeathed by will
   (b) [Miss/Mrs] _____ shall have the right to occupy the property rent free until her subsequent death or remarriage but subject to payment by her of all outgoings in respect of the property and [Miss/Mrs] _____ shall further be responsible for keeping the property in good repair and condition and insured to the full value against loss or damage by fire, theft or other unusual risks[4]
   (c) the surviving party shall be entitled to receive the income from the estate of the deceased party for life or until earlier remarriage

10   The parties agree to make wills incorporating the terms of clause 9 of this Deed.

11   Any variation of this Deed shall only be effective if recorded in a supplemental Deed executed by both parties

IN WITNESS[5] the parties have set their hands and seals the day and year first before written

SIGNED SEALED AND DELIVERED by
the said _____
in the presence of:

SIGNED SEALED AND DELIVERED by
the said _____
in the presence of:

Notes

1. The deed attempts to adopt a modern style of drafting, which is more comprehensible to the lay client.
2. See pp 103 *et seq*.
3. As an alternative, clause 9 may be amended so that both parties agree not to make any claim on the estate of the other.
4. This subclause could also make provision for the acquisition of an alternative property on similar terms.
5. See p 12–13.

Appendix 2

Cohabitation contract[1]

Date: _____ 19___
Parties: (1) _____ of _____ ('the First Party')
        (2) _____ of _____ ('the Second Party')
(1) The parties [intend to live together]/[have lived together since _____ 19___]
(2) The parties wish by this Deed to enter into an agreement which they intend to be legally binding upon them during and after the relationship as to their respective rights and duties towards each other and any[2] children of the relationship
(3) The parties now live at _____ ('the Home') which is vested in the sole name of the [First Party]/[Second Party][3]
(4) Each party has received independent legal advice prior to the execution of this Deed

Now this Deed witnesses

1   All property owned by the First Party in her own right before the parties began to live together as set out in the First Part of the Schedule to this Deed and all property owned by the Second Party in his own right before the parties began to live together as set out in the Second Part of the Schedule to this Deed will remain their separate property

2   Any property owned jointly by the parties before they began to live together as set out in the Third Part of the Schedule to this Deed will remain their joint property and upon sale the proceeds will belong to them in equal shares[4]

3   All property acquired by the parties for their joint use after they began to live together will be jointly owned and upon sale the proceeds will belong to them in equal shares[5]

4   All property acquired by either party for that party's sole use after they began to live together will remain the separate property of that party[5]

5 The Home will remain the sole property of the [First Party]/[Second Party] notwithstanding any contribution by the [First Party]/[Second Party] to the purchase, maintenance or improvement of the Home but subject to the right of the [First Party]/[Second Party] until the termination of this Deed to use, enjoy and occupy the property

6 The parties will discharge the outgoings of the Home [excluding _____, which shall be the sole responsibility of the [First Party]/[Second Party]] and the costs of maintaining [and educating] any children of the relationship [equally]/[in proportion to their respective gross incomes] [as to ____% by the First Party and as to ____% by the Second Party]

7 Both parties will maintain separate bank current accounts and the monies in each such account will belong to the party in whose name it is

8 The monies held in any joint bank current account will belong to both parties equally in the event of such an account being opened

9 If at any time either party is not in full-time employment because of pregnancy, child birth or caring for any children of the relationship, half [or as appropriate] of the net amount earned by the other party shall belong to the party not in employment [for _____ months][6]

10 This Deed shall be terminated upon whichever of the following events shall first occur
    (a) the death of either party[7]
    (b) the marriage of the parties to each other
    (c) a court order varying the terms of this Deed[8]
    (d) _____ months' written notice of termination given by either party to the other whereupon clauses 11 and 12 of this Deed shall apply
    (e) the parties having ceased to live together for a period of _____ months whereupon clauses 11 and 12 of this Deed shall apply

11 Upon the termination of this Deed under clause 11(d) and (e) all property which by virtue of clauses 2 and 3 of this Deed is joint property shall be sold in the absence of any contrary agreement and the net proceeds of sale be divided [equally]/[or as appropriate][9] save that the party having the right of occupation of the Home under clause 5 of this Deed shall where such party has the responsibility for the care of any children of the relationship have a right to continue in occupation for a period of _____ months following the termination of this Deed;

12 Upon the termination of this Deed under clause 11(d) or (e) [the First Party]/[the Second Party]/[both parties] will continue to maintain any children of the relationship and will contribute one-_____ of [her]/[his]/[their respective] net income[s] after deduction of income tax and national insurance [or as appropriate] in respect of each child until they respectively attain the age of seventeen years or complete his or her full-time education (whichever shall be the later)

13 In the event of any dispute arising during the subsistence of or upon the termination of this Deed such dispute will be referred to [*Mediation Service*] without prejudice to the right of either party thereafter to refer the matter to the court for adjudication

14 Any variation of this Deed shall only be effective if recorded by a supplemental deed executed by both parties

15 The costs of and incidental to this Deed shall be borne by the parties equally [*or as appropriate*]

IN WITNESS[10] the parties have set their hands and seals the day and year first before written

SCHEDULE

Part 1
[*Property of First Party prior to cohabitation*]

Part 2
[*Property of Second Party prior to cohabitation*]

Part 3
[*Joint property prior to cohabitation*]

SIGNED SEALED AND DELIVERED by }
the said _____
in the presence of:

SIGNED SEALED AND DELIVERED by }
the said _____
in the presence of:

Notes

[1] The agreement adopts a modern style of drafting, which it is hoped will be better understood by the lay client. Clause 1 and the Schedule may be suitably amended to allow either party simply to retain all property owned prior to cohabitation excluding, if required, any scheduled items.

[2] If there are already any children of the relationship or of either of the parties, they should be named in an additional recital.

[3] The precedent assumes that the non-owning party is not to acquire any beneficial interest in the home. If this is not the case, an additional recital should refer to a declaration of trust (see p 19) and the operative part of the deed deal with matters such as mortgage repayments, repairs and improvements.

[4] Exceptions to this general principle may be dealt with in a separate part of the Schedule.

[5] Precise definitions of 'joint use' and 'sole use' to suit the individual circumstances by reference to particular types of assets are required.

[6] Alternatively, there can be a transfer of responsibility for outgoings referred to in clause 6.
[7] Cohabitees should be made aware of the importance of making wills in appropriate terms.
[8] Eg under the Children Act 1989, Sched 1, para 10.
[9] Where the home is jointly owned or held in trust for the parties jointly, the deed should provide that where there are children of the relationship no sale will occur for a specified period.
[10] See pp 12–13.

Appendix 3

Reconciliation agreement[1]

Date: _____ 19___
Parties: (1) _____ of _____ ('the husband')
        (2) _____ of _____ ('the wife')
(1) The husband and the wife were married on _____ 19___,
(2) Differences arose between the husband and wife as a result of which they separated on _____ 19___
(3) The husband and the wife have effected a reconciliation and have agreed to live together from _____ 19___
(4) The husband and the wife have agreed that should they again separate for a period in excess of _____ [weeks/months] [in aggregate] the terms of this Deed shall take effect

Now this Deed witnesses

1 The husband and the wife will live separate and apart and free from the marital control (if any) of the other

2 Neither the husband nor the wife shall annoy or interfere with the other or his or her relations, friends or acquaintances

3 The husband and the wife agree that neither will have any claim of any kind upon the property or money of the other or their respective estates[2]

4 At the expiration of two years from the date of separation, the wife will present to an appropriate court a divorce petition under the Matrimonial Causes Act 1973, s 1(2)(*d*) to which the husband will consent[3]

5 The husband and the wife agree that in the said divorce proceedings the court will be invited to dismiss all claims which each may have against the other for ancillary relief with a direction that neither party shall be entitled in relation to the marriage to make any further application under the Matrimonial Causes Act 1973, s 23(1)(*a*) or (*b*) and to order that neither party shall be entitled on the death of the other to apply for an order under the Inheritance (Provision for Family and Dependants) Act 1975, s 2[3]

6 The costs of and incidental to this Deed shall be borne by the husband and the wife equally

IN WITNESS[4] the parties have set their hands and seals the day and year first before written

SIGNED SEALED AND DELIVERED by }
the said _____
in the presence of:

SIGNED SEALED AND DELIVERED by }
the said _____
in the presence of:

Notes

[1] The agreement adopts a modern style of drafting, which it is hoped will be better understood by the lay client.
[2] The agreement pre-supposes that the parties' finances were agreed at the time of the original separation and that all that is required upon any future separation is a clean break without further distribution.
[3] It may be appropriate to omit clauses 4 and 5 where reference to a future divorce might prejudice the success of the attempted reconciliation.
[4] See pp 12–13.

Appendix 4

Separation deed[1]

Date: _____ 19____
Parties: (1) _____ of _____ ('the husband')
 (2) _____ of _____ ('the wife')
(1) The husband and the wife were married on _____ 19____ and have two children, namely, _____ (born _____) and _____ (born _____)
(2) The husband and the wife have lived separate and apart since _____ 19____

Now this Deed witnesses:

1 The husband and the wife will continue to live separate and apart and free from the marital control (if any) of the other

2 Neither the husband nor the wife shall annoy or interfere with the other or his or her relations, friends or acquaintances

3 At the expiration of two years from the date of separation, the wife will issue out of the _____ County Court a divorce petition under the Matrimonial Causes Act 1973, s 1(2)(*d*) to which the husband will consent. The wife will bear her own costs of and incidental to the said petition

4 The husband will pay to the wife from the date of this Deed the sum of £_____ per month for her maintenance until whichever of the terminating events in clause 7 first occurs

5 The husband will pay to the wife from the date of this deed for the benefit of each of the said children the sum of £_____ per month until each child ceases full-time education [*or as appropriate*][2]

6 The husband will allow the wife and the children to occupy the property known as _____ and will discharge the mortgage repayments and _____ in respect of the property

7 The maintenance payable under clause 4 of this Deed shall terminate upon whichever of the following events shall first occur:

(a) the death of either the husband or the wife
(b) the cohabitation of the wife with another man [for a period of more than _____ months]
(c) a court order varying the terms of this Deed
(d) a court order made in favour of the wife for maintenance pending suit, periodical payments or secured periodical payments
(e) the dissolution or annulment of the marriage or the judicial separation of the husband and the wife

8 The said children shall reside with the wife and have contact with the husband[3]

9 Any variation of this Deed shall only be effective if recorded by a supplemental deed executed by both parties

10 The costs of and incidental to this Deed shall be borne by the husband and the wife equally

IN WITNESS[4] the parties have set their hands and seals the day and year first before written

SIGNED SEALED AND DELIVERED by
the said _____
in the presence of:

SIGNED SEALED AND DELIVERED by
the said _____
in the presence of:

Notes

[1] The deed attempts to adopt a modern style of drafting, which is more comprehensible to the lay client. See pp 22–26 in Chapter 2 for other provisions which may suitably be included in a separation deed. A fuller form of Separation Deed is to be found in *Precedents for Agreements between Husband and Wife* (SFLA).

[2] As to the taxation position, see pp 23–24; as to the status of the deed under the Child Support Acts 1991 and 1995, see pp 117 *et seq.*

[3] Some definition of contact may be appropriate, eg whether staying access is intended and as to holidays.

[4] See pp 12–13.

Appendix 5

Draft consent order

No of Matter ____ (D) ____

IN THE _____ COUNTY COURT
[IN THE DIVORCE REGISTRY]
BETWEEN
                   [*Wife*]   Petitioner
                   and
                   [*Husband*]   Respondent

DRAFT CONSENT ORDER[1]

UPON the Petitioner and the Respondent agreeing that the provisions of this order are accepted in full and final satisfaction of all financial claims and claims in respect of any property whatsoever which either may be entitled to bring against the other [in any jurisdiction] howsoever arising [other than in respect of chattels][2]

AND UPON the Petitioner and the Respondent agreeing that the contents of the former matrimonial home _____ shall remain the absolute property of the party in whose possession they now are

AND UPON the parties agreeing that the Petitioner will not seek a variation of the order for periodical payments for herself hereinafter appearing for a period of at least [two] years from the making of this order save in the event of the Petitioner becoming unintentionally unemployed[3]

AND UPON the Respondent undertaking to the court to discharge the parties' joint overdraft with _____ Bank plc within twenty-eight days of the date of this order[4]

AND UPON the Respondent undertaking to the court promptly to discharge for the benefit of the Petitioner from the date of this order until completion of the transfer referred to in paragraph 2 of this order

    (a) all mortgage interest due in respect of the mortgage in favour of the _____ Building Society secured on the former matrimonial home _____; and

(b) the premiums in respect of the collateral endowment policy numbered _____ effected with _____ Assurance Company plc; and

(c) the gas, electricity and telephone accounts, the house and contents insurance premiums, the council tax and water rates on the said property

AND UPON the Petitioner undertaking to the court to assign within twenty-eight days from the date of this order to the Respondent her interest in the life assurance policy numbered _____ effected with _____ Insurance Company plc

BY CONSENT IT IS ORDERED THAT

1 The Respondent do pay or cause to be paid to the Petitioner a lump sum calculated as follows:
(a) £2,000 payable within three months of the date of final decree herein AND IT IS DIRECTED that interest shall be payable on the said lump sum by the Respondent at the rate applicable for the time being to a High Court judgment debt from the date of this order until the date on which the said lump sum falls due for payment and in default of payment as aforesaid by way of a further instalment of the said lump sum order from the date on which the said lump sum falls due for payment until the date of payment to the Petitioner[5]
(b) £20,000 payable on 1st August 2010 AND IT IS DIRECTED pursuant to the Matrimonial Causes Act 1973 section 25B(4) that this sum be paid by X & Co [*Trustees of the Respondent's Pension Scheme*] on behalf of the Respondent to the Petitioner.

2 The Respondent do transfer to the Petitioner within twenty-eight days of the date of final decree herein at his expense all his legal and beneficial interest in the property _____ registered at H M Land Registry under title number _____ subject to the mortgage secured thereon in favour of _____ Building Society

3 As from _____, the Respondent do pay or cause to be paid to the Petitioner maintenance pending suit until the date of final decree and thereafter periodical payments at the rate of £_____ per annum payable monthly in advance during their joint lives until _____ 19___ or until the Petitioner's earlier remarriage or further order whereupon the Petitioner's claims for periodical payments and secured periodical payments do stand dismissed and the Petitioner shall not be entitled to make any further application under the Matrimonial Causes Act 1973, s 23(1)(*a*) or (*b*) AND IT IS DIRECTED pursuant to the Matrimonial Causes Act, s 28(1A) that the Petitioner shall not be entitled to apply for an extension of the term of the above order[6]

4 As from _____, the Respondent do pay or cause to be paid periodical payments to the Petitioner for the benefit of the child of the family,

DRAFT CONSENT ORDER 235

_____ (born _____), until he shall attain the age of seventeen years or cease full-time education (whichever shall be the later) or further order at the rate of £_____ per annum payable monthly in advance[7]

5 The rate of periodical payments ordered under paragraph 4 of this order shall be varied automatically with effect from the payment due on _____ in each year commencing on _____ by the percentage by which the Retail Prices Index shall have changed between the date fifteen months prior to the variation and the date three months prior thereto. It is recorded that the Retail Prices Index at _____ was _____ [8]

6 The Respondent's applications for maintenance pending suit, periodical payments and secured periodical payments do stand dismissed and the Respondent shall not be entitled to make any further application in relation to the marriage under the Matrimonial Causes Act 1973, s 23(1)(*a*) or (*b*) and, save as aforesaid, the applications by each party for lump sum and property adjustment orders do stand dismissed

7 It is certified for the purposes of the Civil Legal Aid (General) Regulations 1989 [that the lump sum of £X has been ordered to be paid to enable the Petitioner/Respondent to purchase a home for himself/herself (or his/her dependants)] [that the property (*address*) has been preserved/recovered for the Petitioner/Respondent for use as a home for himself/herself (or his/her dependants)].[9]

8 There be no order for costs insofar as this application and the negotiations ancillary thereto are concerned save that the costs of the Petitioner be taxed in accordance with the Civil Legal Aid (General) Regulations 1989, reg 107

9 Liberty to apply as to the implementation and timing of the terms of this order[10]

DATED the _____ day of _____ 19____

(Signed) ....   (Signed) ....
    Petitioner   Solicitors for the Petitioner

(Signed) ....   (Signed) ....
    Respondent   Solicitors for the Respondent

Notes

[1] This draft order is not intended as anything other than a precedent incorporating provisions commonly encountered in practice and providing a suggested format. It is based by kind permission on the *Precedents for Consent Orders* (4th ed) of the Solicitors' Family Law Association. Details of how to obtain the full SFLA precedents are to be found on p 77.

[2] This introductory recital contains a capital clean break agreement, which would require amendment if a complete mutual clean break had been agreed. The recital does not have the effect of dismissing claims: formal orders are required in the operative part of the minute.

3. This provision is of dubious enforceability but is of some evidential value. It is dealt with by way of agreement rather than undertaking to the court to oust its own jurisdiction. The court may have regard to such an agreement as a matter of conduct under the Matrimonial Causes Act 1973, s 31(7) (see *Edgar* v *Edgar* [1980] 3 All ER 887).
4. This provision cannot be dealt with by way of an order: see p 71.
5. As to interest on lump sum orders, see p 74.
6. The periodical payments will be payable in arrears unless stipulated to be payable in advance.

    The term of the periodical payments order will be extendable unless the court makes a direction as here under the Matrimonial Causes Act 1973, s 28(1A) (see p 90).
7. For the jurisdiction to make orders for child maintenance where the parties agree, see pp 119–121. For the tax reasons mentioned on p 23, express the maintenance as payable to the spouse on behalf of the child.
8. If the RPI figures fifteen months before the date of variation was (x) and three months before was (y), then multiply the old maintenance by (y) and divide by (x) to give the new maintenance. Current RPI figures can be obtained by telephoning 0171 270 6364 or from the Employment Gazette (HMSO).
9. See *Practice Direction 19 August 1991* [1991] 3 All ER 896 and p 76.
10. See p 178.

Appendix 6

Property adjustment order with Child Support Act charge back[1]

The [Petitioner/Respondent] shall within _____ days [from the date of this order] [*if decree absolute already made*]/[after the date of final decree herein] transfer to the [Respondent/Petitioner] all [his/her] legal and beneficial interest in the property _____ [registered at H M Land Registry under title number _____ [*assuming registered land*]] subject to the mortgage secured thereon in favour of _____ [*if appropriate*] on condition that as from the date of the said transfer the said property do stand charged by way of legal charge as security for the payment to the [Petitioner/Respondent] of such sum [not to exceed £____] as shall represent the aggregate of any sums from time to time payable by the [Petitioner/Respondent] after _____ 19___ in respect of the maintenance of the child[ren] of the family _____ [*names of children*] under the Matrimonial Causes Act 1973, the Domestic Proceedings and Magistrates' Courts Act 1978, the Children Act 1989, Sched 1, the Social Security Administration Act 1992, ss 106–108, and/or the Child Support Act 1991 [such charge [not] to carry interest] [[such charge]/[and] to be in the form annexed hereto]

PROVIDED ALWAYS that such charge shall not become exercisable [and shall not carry interest] until:
   (a) the [youngest] surviving [of the] child[ren] of the family shall attain the age of eighteen years or complete [his/her] full-time [secondary/undergraduate/post-graduate] education [*or as appropriate*], whichever shall be the later; or
   (b) the death of the [Respondent/Petitioner]; or
   (c) the remarriage or cohabitation of the [Respondent/Petitioner]; or
   (d) the voluntary vacation of the said property for a period in excess of ____ by the [Respondent/Petitioner];

whichever shall first occur or further order of the court [provided that in any event the said legal charge shall not be exercisable without the leave of the court while any child of the family [in occupation of the said property] is still a minor or of full age but receiving full-time education].

The term 'gross proceeds of sale' referred to above shall mean the open market value of the property with vacant possession between willing seller and purchaser at the date of redemption of the said legal charge or, if the said property is to be sold, on completion of the sale of the property the gross sale price [including any consideration paid for fixtures and fittings[*as is appropriate*]]. The open market value of the property as between willing seller and purchaser as at the date of redemption of the said legal charge shall in default of agreement between the Petitioner and the Respondent be determined by a chartered surveyor appointed on the application of either party by the President for the time being of the Royal Institution of Chartered Surveyors who shall act as an expert and not as an arbitrator and whose costs shall be borne equally by the Petitioner and the Respondent [*or as appropriate*].

Note

[1] This precedent is produced by kind permission of the Solicitors' Family Law Association from the fourth edition of the Association's *Precedents for Consent Orders*. Details of how to obtain the full SFLA Precedents are to be found on p 77. Reference should be made to the footnotes to precedents 45 and 46 of the SFLA Precedents. Some judicial support for a charge back of this type is to be found in *Smith* v *McInerny* [1994] 2 FLR 1077 (see p 127).

Appendix 7

Application to make a rule of court into a consent order

No of Matter ____ (D) ____

IN THE _____ COUNTY COURT
[IN THE DIVORCE REGISTRY]
BETWEEN

                                                                            Petitioner

and

                                                                            Respondent

TAKE NOTICE that the Petitioner intends to apply to the court for an order that [paragraphs 1 and 2 of] the Rule of Court dated _____ 19____ now be made an order of this Honourable Court [and there be no order as to costs of and incidental to this application]

The application will be heard by the District Judge in Chambers at _____ [at Room _____, the Divorce Registry, Somerset House, Strand, London, WC2R 1LP]

on _____ day, the _____ day of _____ 19____, at ____ o'clock

DATED this _____ day of _____ 19____

We consent to an order in the above terms

(*Signed*) ....
Solicitors for the Respondent ....
of ....
....

                      (*Signed*) ....
                      Solicitors for the Petitioner ....
                      of ....
                      ....

Note

The Rule of Court must specifically state which terms are to be incorporated into a consent order at the appropriate time (see p 43 *et seq*).

Appendix 8

Affidavit in support of application for leave to appeal out of time

Filed on behalf of the Petitioner
Deponent: Petitioner
Affidavit No 2
Sworn this 23rd day of April 1996
Three Exhibits

[IN THE PRINCIPAL REGISTRY OF THE FAMILY DIVISION]
[IN THE BARCHESTER COUNTY COURT]   **[NO 123 OF 1996] [1996 D 1234]**

BETWEEN:

ABC

Petitioner

– and –

DEF

Respondent

AFFIDAVIT OF ABC

I, ABC of 7 Grange Road, St David's, West Glamorgan, Wales MAKE OATH and say as follows:

1   I make this affidavit in support of my application for leave to appeal out of time against a consent order made in the [Principal Registry of the Family Division] [Barchester County Court] by District Judge G made on 18 November 1995 (which order I refer to during the course of this affidavit as 'the Consent Order').

2   By paragraph 2 of the Consent Order, the former matrimonial home 7 Grange Road, St David's, West Glamorgan, Wales ('the property') was to be sold as soon as possible at the best possible price, and the net proceeds of sale were to be divided between the Respondent and me on the basis that:

2.1 the Respondent was to receive £45,000 with which to purchase a property for himself; and

2.2 I was to receive the balance of the net sale proceeds.

3 There is now produced, shown to me and marked 'ABC1' a letter sent by the Respondent's solicitors to my solicitors dated 14 September 1995, which, on page two, reproduces the calculations showing that it was expected that I would receive about £51,000 from the net sale proceeds of the property, worked out as follows (quoting from the letter):

	£
'The sale price of 7 Grange Road (based upon our client's estimate of its present worth, ie what he paid for the property four years ago)	100,000
Less Estate Agents' and legal costs on sale, say	4,000
Expected net sale proceeds	96,000
Less payment to our client from the proceeds	45,000
Balance left over for the Petitioner to enable her to purchase a property for herself and the children in the area	51,000'

4 In paragraph two on page three of the same letter, the Respondent's solicitors explained that the Respondent required £45,000 to purchase a property for himself in the area, and I could be accommodated by use of the £51,000 left over from the net sale proceeds. I had no cause to quarrel with those figures, because I recollected that we had indeed paid £100,000 for the property and I was willing to accept the Respondent's estimate of its present worth. He used to work as an estate agent and is more versed in these matters than I am.

5 I now refer to the Respondent's rule 2.61 statement dated 16 November 1995. He stated on page one of the statement that the property was worth in the region of £100,000. On page two of the statement his solicitors recorded that it had been calculated in the course of negotiations that I would be able to purchase a property for myself and the children in the area using the balance of the net sale proceeds, which were expected to be about £50,000.

6 The rule 2.61 statement also refers to the Respondent's other capital assets, together amounting to £50,000. The Respondent has other funds which he can use in the purchase of accommodation for himself. As I will go on to explain, I do not.

7 I refer to page one of the rule 2.61 statement signed by me on 17 November 1995, on which I stated that the former matrimonial home had been estimated by the Respondent to be worth about £100,000; and, on page two, to my disclosure that I would be purchasing a property for myself and the three children of the family using the net sale proceeds less the fixed sum payment to the Respondent, and that I expected to be able to purchase a property in the area for about £50,000.

8 My rule 2.61 statement shows that as at 17 November 1995 I had £217.42 in my current account at H Bank, that I owned chattels at the property, but

that I had no other capital assets. It also records the fact that I have no net income; I then depended, and still depend, on the maintenance payments paid to me by the Respondent. He has since the date of the Consent Order paid maintenance in the sum of £J in accordance with paragraph K of the Consent Order.

9 It came to my notice during December 1995 that the Respondent was spending a significant amount of time at a house owned by Miss L. Over Christmas 1995, the Respondent told me that she was his girlfriend, but that it was 'nothing serious'. I have reason to believe that the Respondent has been staying overnight with her for an average period of five nights per week since 1 January 1996, and I put the Respondent to proof of his relationship with her and the bona fides of the disclosure in his rule 2.61 statement to the effect that he had no intention to remarry or to cohabit. I reserve the right to develop this aspect of the case if I need to do so.

10 The Consent Order having been made on 18 November 1995, the Respondent and I agreed to appoint Messrs M & Co, the Agents who sold the property to us, as the Agents acting in the sale of the property. It was coming up to Christmas, which is a traditionally quiet time for house sales, and not much interest was shown in the property immediately after it was put on the market, but the Agents assured me that it would attract interest 'in the New Year'.

11 Following the General Election in January 1996, the new Secretary of State for Transport announced in Parliament on 14 January 1996 that an extension to the M4 was planned which would stretch into the heartland of Wales. The detailed plans published since then show that the motorway would in fact be extended to within 200 yards of the former matrimonial home. This has been a catastrophic development for me. The Agents immediately informed me that the property could not realistically be expected to sell for the asking price of £99,500, and they recommended some reduction in the price. They told me that they were also marketing number 47 Grange Road, which is a very similar property to the former matrimonial home, and that they were recommending that both we and the owners of 47 Grange Road should reduce the marketing price of our properties from £99,500 to £75,000.

12 There is no prospect of me receiving any kind of recompense from the Government as a result of the motorway extension. There is now produced, shown to me and marked 'ABC2' a copy of the Department of Transport's letter to me dated 16 January 1996 confirming that I will receive no compensation.

13 I immediately caused my solicitors to write to the Respondent's solicitors, informing them of the Estate Agents' opinion that the marketing price should be reduced to £77,500, and pointing out that the effect of such a reduction in the marketing price was that I would receive not the £51,000, which was expected as a result of the Consent Order, but instead in the region of £35,000, calculated as follows: _____. There is now produced, shown to me and marked 'ABC3' a bundle of the correspondence to which I go on to refer in the course of this Affidavit. My solicitors did not receive a reply to their letter (page 1 of 'ABC3') until 7 March

1996. The Respondent's solicitors' reply is at page two of the bundle. The letter was unsympathetic, suggesting that 'time will tell' and that I should go to other agents to obtain a second opinion on the marketing price.

14   I duly approached Messrs N and Messrs P, two other Estate Agents' firms in the area, on 9 March 1996, and they both put the property's worth at less than £75,000. Their opinions were recorded in the letters which feature at pages ____ and ____ of 'ABC3'. It can be seen from the letter sent by Messrs N that they were marketing a property in the same road as mine in the sum of £69,500, and that no interest had been shown in that property for the last five weeks.

15   My solicitors wrote to the Respondent's solicitors again on 11 March 1996 (page ____ of 'ABC3'), enclosing copies of the letters sent by N and P, and reporting on the lack of progress in the sale. As at that date there had been no interest shown in the property.

16   The Respondent's solicitors replied to their letter on 15 April 1996 (page 00 of 'ABC3'). The letter was again evasive, and suggested that I should continue to 'test the market'.

17   I commissioned a formal valuation of the property by Chartered Surveyors, Messrs V, dated 20 April 1996, a copy of which is now produced, shown to me and marked 'ABC4'. It indicates that the property is worth in the region of £60,000.

18   Our Estate Agents, having obtained no interest in the property at all, are now suggesting that it should be marketed at £60,000 (see page 00 of 'ABC3'). That is the price which they suggested for the marketing of 47 Grange Road, which was sold in that sum on 20 March 1996.

19   My solicitors then wrote to the Respondent's solicitors on 21 April 1996 (page 00 of 'ABC3') enclosing a copy of the Estate Agents' valuation of 20 April 1996 and pointing out that if the property was sold at that price, the effect would be that I would receive only £12,600, calculated as follows:

20   At pp 00 of 'ABC3' are copies of the Particulars of Sale of all the properties in this area currently on the market at less than £50,000. It can be seen that there are no properties at all which are being marketed for less than £20,000. The cheapest property on the market in this area is being marketed at £30,000, and that is a one-bedroom flat. I will have to arrange for the accommodation of myself and the three children of the family, and therefore £30,000 is going to be insufficient for our purposes.

21   By contrast the Respondent has the other capital to which he referred in his rule 2.61 statement. I put him to proof in his Affidavit in reply to this Affidavit of his up-to-date financial position. In my respectful submission he does not need to receive as much as £45,000 from the sale proceeds of the former matrimonial home.

22   I refer to paragraphs 000–00 of the first Affidavit which I filed in these proceedings sworn on _____, which relate to the history of the

AFFIDAVIT IN SUPPORT OF APPLICATION FOR LEAVE TO APPEAL OUT OF TIME

marriage, and the financial contributions made by me. In my respectful submission it would be fair for me to receive, at the very least, all of the net proceeds of sale of the property, as I will need every penny gained from the sale of the property to purchase a property for myself and the children.

SWORN this 23rd day of April 1996

Before me,

Solicitor/Commissioner for Oaths

Notes

1. This is a classic *Thompson* v *Thompson* and *Heard* v *Heard* situation (see p 155–159).
2. The affidavit should set out precisely what steps were taken, and when, in the marketing of the property and communication of the developments to the Respondent's solicitors, together with their responses.
3. It is vital to show that all four *Barder* limbs are satisfied by the application (see p 145 *et seq*).

Appendix 9

Application to show cause why an order should not be made in agreed terms

[IN THE PRINCIPAL REGISTRY OF THE FAMILY DIVISION]
[IN THE BARCHESTER COUNTY COURT]

No of Matter: _____ D _____

Between:

GHQ

Petitioner

and

KLM

Respondent

TAKE NOTICE that the Respondent intends to apply to the District Judge in Chambers at the [Principal Registry, Somerset House, London WC2] [Barchester County Court] on the _____ day of _____ 19___, at ____ o'clock for an order that:

1 An order be made by consent in the terms of the Minutes of Order contained in exhibit 'KLM1' to the Respondent's Affidavit of _____.

2 The Petitioner do pay the costs of this application.

The probable length of the hearing of this application is 60 minutes.

(Signed) ....
Solicitors for the Respondent
of

Counsel will not be appearing on behalf of the applicant.

Dated this _____ day of _____ 1996.

                L & Co
              Solicitors for the Respondent

To the Petitioner
c/o her Solicitors
Messrs M & Co

Appendix 10

Affidavit in support of an application to show cause why an order should not be made in agreed terms

> Filed on behalf of the Respondent
> Deponent: Respondent
> Affidavit No 2
> Sworn this 5th day of May 1996
> Two Exhibits

[IN THE PRINCIPAL REGISTRY OF THE FAMILY DIVISION]
[IN THE BARCHESTER COUNTY COURT]   No. _____ D

BETWEEN:

GHQ

Petitioner

– and –

KLM

Respondent

AFFIDAVIT OF KLM

I, KLM, of 10 Acacia Avenue, Oxford, MAKE OATH and say as follows.

1 I, the above named Respondent, make this affidavit in support of my application that an order should be made in the terms agreed between my solicitors, Messrs L & Co, and the Petitioner's former solicitors, Messrs M & Co. These terms are contained in the Minutes of Order, a copy of which is now produced, shown to me and marked 'KLM1'.

2 [*Assuming that this is the first affidavit in the suit dealing with financial matters, set out a summary of the history of the marriage and of the Respondent's financial circumstances in the normal way. If affidavits have*

AFFIDAVIT IN SUPPORT OF APPLICATION TO SHOW CAUSE 249

already been filed, simply refer to the financial circumstances already recited in the previous affidavit and bring the disclosure up to date].

3   Having initiated the proceedings, the Petitioner has been reluctant to finalise matters. It was only after considerable correspondence from my solicitors that the Petitioner was willing to apply for a decree nisi. She eventually did so, and a decree nisi was pronounced on _____. The Petitioner failed to apply for the decree absolute and I therefore made an application for this to be granted. The decree absolute was made on _____. I refer to my affidavit, sworn on _____, which sets out a history of the Petitioner's delay in the suit.

4   Through my solicitors, agreement was reached in open correspondence in the terms of the Minutes of Order. There is now produced and shown to me and marked 'KLM2' a bundle containing the copy correspondence passing between Messrs L & Co and Messrs M & Co in respect of the agreement, which culminated in Messrs M & Co sending to Messrs L & Co the draft Minutes of Order in the terms exhibited in 'KLM1'. The draft Minutes of Order were signed by my solicitors on 1 January 1996 and were returned to the Petitioner's solicitors. It was agreed that the Petitioner and her solicitors would sign the Minutes of Order and lodge them at court. Indeed, I performed part of the agreement by giving instructions for the preparation of the transfer of the former matrimonial home into the Petitioner's name pursuant to paragraph 000 of the Minutes.

5   My solicitors were informed by Messrs M & Co at the beginning of March 1996 that they were no longer instructed on behalf of the Petitioner and that she would be consulting Messrs N & Co. My solicitors wrote to that firm on 5 April 1996 inviting them to sign and return the Minutes of Order. However, to date, my solicitors still have not received a substantive response and I am therefore forced to make this application to resolve matters which were initiated by me by application in Form M11 on 1 June 1995 and have dragged on for nearly 12 months.

6   Now that the decree nisi has been made absolute, I wish to have a resolution of the financial matters so that I can continue my life and remove the needless stress and anxiety which this unresolved litigation is causing. I have made every effort to be reasonable and have promptly met all the needs and demands of the Petitioner through my solicitors. The Petitioner has at all times consulted legal advisers. I understood this matter had been resolved at the beginning of _____. Since then, considerable additional costs have been incurred by me due to the Petitioner refusing to conclude this matter.

7   I ask the court to make an order in the agreed terms and an order that the Petitioner do pay the costs which I have incurred unnecessarily since the date of the agreement.

APPENDIX 10

Sworn at ....
the 5 day of May 1996 ....
Before me, ...

Solicitor/Commissioner for Oaths

Appendix 11

Family Proceedings Rules 1991, r 2.61 (as amended)

2.61 (1) Subject to paragraphs (2) and (3), there shall be lodged with every application for a consent order under any of sections 23, 24 or 24A of the Act of 1973 two copies of a draft of the order in the terms sought, one of which shall be indorsed with a statement signed by the respondent to the application signifying his agreement, and a statement of information (which may be made in more than one document) which shall include—
- (a) the duration of the marriage, the age of each party and of any minor or dependent child of the family;
- (b) an estimate in summary form of the approximate amount or value of the capital resources and net income of each party and of any minor child of the family;
- (c) what arrangements are intended for the accommodation of each of the parties and any minor child of the family;
- (d) whether either party has remarried or has any present intention to marry or to cohabit with another person;
- (e) where the order imposes any requirement on the trustees or managers of a pension scheme by virtue of section 25B or 25C of the Act of 1973, a statement confirming that those trustees or managers have been served with notice of the application and that no objection to such an order has been made by them within 14 days from such service;
- (f) where the terms of the order provide for a transfer of property, a statement confirming that any mortgagee of that property has been served with notice of the application and that no objection to such a transfer has been made by the mortgagee within 14 days from such service; and
- (g) any other especially significant matters.

(2) Where an application is made for a consent order varying an order for periodical payments paragraph (1) shall be sufficiently complied with if the statement of information required to be lodged with the application includes only the information in respect of net income mentioned in paragraph (1)(b) (and, where appropriate, a statement under paragraph (1)(dd)),

and an application for a consent order for interim periodical payments pending the determination of an application for ancillary relief may be made in like manner.

(3) Where all or any of the parties attend the hearing of an application for financial relief the court may dispense with the lodging of a statement of information in accordance with paragraph (1) and give directions for the information which would otherwise be required to be given in such a manner as it sees fit.

Appendix 12

Statement of information pursuant to the Family Proceedings Rules 1991, r 2.61 (Appendix 1, Form M1)

In the _____ **County Court**

No of matter _____

Between _____ Petitioner

and _____ Respondent

Statement of information for a consent order

Duration of marriage:

Ages of parties

Petitioner _____ Respondent _____
Minor (i.e. under the age of 18) or dependent children)

___ ___ ___ ___ ___

Note
If the application is only for an order for interim periodical payments or variation of an order for periodical payments then only the information required under "net income" need be given.

Summary of means

Give as the date of the statement the approximate amount or value of capital resources and net income of petitioner and respondent, and, where relevant, of minor children of the family. State also the net equity in any property concerned and the effect of its proposed distribution.

	Capital resources (less any unpaid mortgage or charge)	Net Income
Petitioner		
Respondent		
Children		

Where the parties are to live
Give details of what arrangements are intended for the accommodation of each of the parties and any minor child(ren) of the family.

Marital plans
Please tick box

Petitioner	Respondent	
☐	☐	has no present intention to marry or co-habit
☐	☐	has remarried
☐	☐	intends to marry
☐	☐	intends to cohabit with another person

To be answered by the applicant where the terms of the order provide for a transfer of property.

Notice to mortgagee
Has any and every mortgagee of the property been served with notice of the application?

Yes ☐ No ☐

Has any objection to such a transfer been made by any mortgagee within 14 days from the date of service?

Yes ☐ No ☐

Other information
Give details of any other especially significant matters.

Signatures

Signed _____ Signed _____
(Solicitor for) Petitioner   (Solicitor for) Respondent

Date _____   Date _____

(* Form M1 now requires a positive indication of the absence of any intention to marry or cohabit cf *Practice Direction 17 February 1986* [1986] 1 **FLR** 337.)

Addendum

The decision in *Harris (formerly Manahan) v Manahan*

In the case of *Harris (formerly Manahan) v Manahan* [1996] 4 All Er 454 a wife appealed to the Court of Appeal against the judge's dismissal of her application to set aside a consent order made by the district judge in ancillary relief proceedings. The basis of the appeal was that she had been badly advised by the solicitor who represented her at the time of the making of the original consent order; she had also sued her solicitors for negligence. This was the first case in which the Court has had to determine whether a consent order can be set aside by reason of bad advice given by a solicitor. On the facts of the case Ward LJ giving the judgment of the Court dismissed the appeal.

The principal reason given for the dismissal of the appeal is that 'only in the most exceptional case of the cruellest injustice will the public interest in the finality of litigation be put aside', and this was not such a case (p 437b–c). The formulation of this principle suggests a raising of the threshold by the Court of Appeal and may be a pointer to the way in which courts will deal with attempts to set aside consent orders in the future.

The advice given by the solicitors in this case seemed plainly to the Court of Appeal to fall within the category of bad advice, and it is difficult to envisage circumstances in which bad legal advice will ever suffice to enable a consent order to be set aside.

Bad legal advice is one of those circumstances which will be taken into consideration by the Court as part of the s 25 overview (p 469j–470a).

Ward LJ made the following points *obiter*:

(i) He thought that it was arguable that an appeal does lie against a district judge's order in the county court (*Benson* was not cited in argument). Until the point is determined *per curiam*, it will be good practice to request transfer of a case from the county court to the High Court (from which there is no doubt that an appeal will lie).

(ii) The rehearing procedure runs parallel to the appeal procedure and will ordinarily be available to challenge a consent order, as it is difficult to imagine how the court could have been in error in the making of a consent order.

(iii) There is some doubt about the *re C* procedure advocated by Thorpe J (as he then was) and taken in this case: 'Where the rules sufficiently provide the remedy, as they do, I see no justification for importing ad hoc procedures' (p 465j–466a). Until the point is decided *per curiam*, the safest procedure would be where possible to use the blunderbuss approach adopted in *Benson* by combining all possible remedies—appeal, rehearing, and application in the suit.

(iv) The family Proceedings Rules Committee could usefully look again at r 8.1 of the FPR.

It is evident that this area is ripe for review.

Index

Affidavits—
  agreed terms, to show cause why article should not be made in, App 10
  appealing out of time, App 8
  consent orders, 54
  enforcement, 217
Agreement—
  advantages, 1
  alteration, 15
  capacity, 13
  challenging, *see* Challenging orders and agreements
  circumstances, change in, 35–7
  classification, 14–22
  cohabitation contracts, *see* Cohabitation
  consent, 13
  consideration, 12–13
  contractual requirements, 12–14
  "dead letter", 26
  deed, by, 14
  discharge, *see* Discharge of agreement
  disclosure, 14
  Edgar v Edgar, 30–4
  encouragement for, 2
  enforcement, *see* Enforcement
  full and frank disclosure, 14
  future separation, 16
  inadequate knowledge, 35–6
  incorporation, 39
  intention to create legal relationship, 12
  lack of formality, 12
  letters, exchange of, 12
  maintenance, *see* Maintenance Agreement
  mediated, 21–2

Agreement—*contd*
  mistake, 13
  object, lawful, 13
  oral, 14–15, 28
  part performance, 14
  pre-marital contracts, 20–1
  public policy, 13
  purpose, 7
  reasonableness, 39
  reasons for using, 1–2
  reconciliation, 16
  requirements, 12–14
  rules of court, made, *see* Rule of court, agreement made
  separation, *see* separation agreement
  uberrima fides, 14
  undue pressure, 34–5
  uses, 7–8
  void, 13
  voidable, 13
  wife-swopping, 13
  written, 14–15
Alteration of agreement, 15
Ancillary relief—
  application, 9, 15, 59
  covenant not to apply for, 24–5
  jurisdiction of court, 39
Appeal—
  availability, 162, 169–70
  Barder type event, 174–5
  criteria for leave, 175
  discretion of court to grant extension, 174
  due diligence, 174
  exceptional cases, 175
  extension of time, 174
  flow chart, 173
  fresh evidence, 170–1

INDEX

Appeal—*contd*
  further evidence, 170
  jurisdiction, 169
  leave to, 173
  methods, 169–70
  out of time, leave to appeal, 173–174, App 8
  procedure, 163
  re-hearing, by, 170
  refusal of leave, 174
  structure of procedure, 173
  whom to, 173
Arrears—
  enforcement, 216, 217–18
  variation, 197

BALM, 3
Bankruptcy, 218
  discharge of agreement, 27
Barder rules, *see* Setting aside
Bargaining power, inequality of, 143
Booth Report—
  ancillary relief claims, 9
  conciliation, 9
  publication, 8
  recommendations, 8–9
  terms of reference, 8
Bristol Family Courts Conciliation Service, 3
British Association of Lawyer Mediators (BALM), 3
Burden of proof—
  clean break, 93

Calderbank offer, 4–6
Capacity—
  agreement, 13
Capital gains tax, 7
Capitalisation figures—
  clean break, 87, 113–15
Challenging orders and agreements—
  appeal, *see* Appeal
  Barder rules, *see* Setting aside
  confusion surrounding, 129
  executory agreements, 179–80
  fresh action, *see* Fresh action
  generally, 128–9
  liberty to apply provisions, 178–9
  MCA 1973 ss. 23 and 24, 176–8
  procedure, available remedies, 162–9
  reasons for, 128
  setting aside, *see* Setting aside
  specific performance, 179–81

Child support—
  agreements about maintenance, 117–19
  benefit recipients, 122–3
  charge back, App 6
  clean break, 125–7
  controversy over, 116
  conversion of agreement into order, 119–21
  criticism of system, 116
  disabled children, 217
  exclusion of jurisdiction, 119–21
  family order, 125
  formula, 124
  maintenance assessment—
    agreements, relationship with, 123–4
    court orders, relationship with, 123–4
    effect, 29
  maintenence agreements, 117–19
  new approach, 124–7
  non-benfit cases, 119–21
  old agreements, 121–3
  pending applications, 121
  pre- 5 April 1993 agreements, 118, 121–2
  post–5 April 1993 agreements, 119
  reform of, 124–7
  revocation of order, 122
  school fees orders, 217
  top-up orders, 217
  transitional period, 121–2
  White Paper, 116
  written agreements and, 119–21
Child Support Agency—
  clean break settlements, 101
  courts and, 124, 189
  enforcement by, 217
  spousal maintenance collection, 217
Children—
  child support, *see* Child support
  clean break, 81–2, 103–6
  cohabiting parents, 19–20
  contact, 25
  disabled, 217
  parental responsibility agreement, 20
  residence, 25
  separation agreement, 25
Circumstances, change in, 35–7
Clean break—
  absence of consent, 93–4

Clean break—*contd*
  additional lump sum, 113
  adult children, 112
  advantages, 101–3
  age, 112–13
  annuity approach, 115
  approach to calculation, 111
  basis, 81–2
  bitterness, removal of, 109–10
  burden of proof, 93
  businesses, 112
  calculation, 110–15
  capitalisation figures, 87, 113–15
  child support, 125–7
  Child Support Agency and, 101
  children—
    adult, 112
    appropriate uses of clean break, 105–6
    payments for, 82
    welfare of, 81, 103–5
  classic case, 82
  codification, statutory, 96
  concept, 80 *et seq*
  conduct, 109
  consent, 93–4
  consideration of termination of financial dependancy, 82
  courts' interpretation, 93–101
  cpaital award, 113
  defeating, 83
  delayed, 96
  difficulties of enforcement, 109
  Duxbury figures, 87, 102, 113–15
  effecting, 83–101
  enforcement, 109
  extension of time, 84–5
  family provision, 82, 91–2
  final orders, 83
  financial, 82
  financial dependancy, considering terminating, 82
  forseeability test, 84
  historical background, 6–7
  husband, advantages to, 102
  imposition, 81
  income support, 101–2
  insufficient resources, 106–7
  interpretation by courts, 93–101
  investment of lump sum, 102
  limiting term of order, 81
  long seperations, 108
  lump sum order, deferred, 83–4

Clean break—*contd*
  maintenance agreement, meaning of, 95–6
  mandatory duty on court, 81
  Martin order, 83
  meaning, 6, 82–3
  Mesher order, 83
  methods of effecting, 83–101
  Minton decision, 78
  modern common law, 80
  needs, 108–9
  nominal order, 83
  nominal periodical payments order, 98–9
  non-variable orders, 83–8
  one-sided, 83
  origins, 78–80
  pensions, 84, 113
  postponed, 83, 90–1
  power to impose, 81
  principle, 6
  proportion of capital resources, 111
  reasonable capital requirements of wife, 111–12
  recitals, 94
  remarriage and, 102
  removal of bitterness, 109–10
  resources of parties, 106–7
  sale of property postponed, 86
  short marriages, 107–8
  standard of living, 112
  state benefits, 98
  statistics, 97–8
  statutory charge, 87
  statutory recognition, 79–80
  subsequent application to court, 83, 88
  suitability, 101–10
  transfer of property order, 85–6
  types, 82–3
  uses, 101
  uses of term, 82
  variable orders, 88–91
  variation application, 86, 97–101
  widow's pension rights, 113
  wife, advantages for, 101–2
Code of Practice—
  erosion of principle, 97–8
  mediation, 3
Coercion—
  cohabitation contracts, 17
Cohabitation—
  contracts—
    certainty, 20

INDEX

Cohabitation—*contd*
  contracts— *contd*
    children, provisions as to, 19–20
    coercion, 17
    consideration, 19
    content, 19
    discretion of court, 20
    diversity, 18
    divorce proceedings, party to, 20
    drafting, 18
    duress, 17
    enforcement, 17
    essential elements, 18
    form, 18
    generally, 16–17
    home, 19
    intention to create legal
      relationship, 17, 18
    marriage and, 18
    personal property, 19
    possible, 18
    precedent, App 2
    professional negligence, 19
    public policy, 17, 18
    purpose, 18
    status, 17–18
    subject matter, 19
    support obligation, 19
    terms, 19
    validity, 17
    void, 18
  family provision, 18
  public policy, 17, 18
  resumption—
    agreement, 16
    conditions, 16
    discharge of agreement on, 26
  social attitudes, 18
Collusion—
  absence of, 2
  bar to divorce, 41
  defend, agreement not to, 16
Conciliation—
  Booth Report, 9
  Bristol Family Courts Conciliation
    Service, 3
  establishment of national service, 9
  mediation distinguished, 2
  National Family Conciliation Service,
    9
Condonation, 2
Conduct—
  Edgar v Edgar, 30–4
Connivance, 2

Consent—
  setting aside ground, 131–2
Consent orders—
  advantages, 1, 8
  affidavits, 54
  agreements and, 7–8
  application—
    certificate, 53
    fee, 60
    information on, 51–8
    maintenence pending suit, 52–3
    notice of application, 60
    petitioner's, 59, 60
    respondent's application, 59–60
  approval of court, 41–3
  certificate, 53
  challenging, *see* Challenging orders
    and agreements
  construction, 67–9
  copies of draft, 56
  court approval, 41–3
  court inquiries, 61–3
  criticisms, 49
  decree nisi, subject to pronouncement,
    59
  development, 6
  direction from Family Division, 50
  disclosure, *see* Disclosure duty
  dispensation with statement of
    information, 55, 57, 60
  door of court, agreement reached at,
    60
  draft, App 5
  drafting, *see* Drafting order
  enforcement, *see* Enforcement
  estimate in summary form, 55–6
  evolution, 48–9
  family provision, 56
  faulty completion of statement, 58
  fee, 60
  form of statement of information, 57
  hearing, order agreed during, 55
  historical background, 48–9
  importance, 2
  information on application, 51–8
  inquiry by court, 61–3
  interest, 74
  judicial intervention, 61–3
  lodging documents, 59
  maintenance pending suit, 52–3
  minutes of order, 56, 57
  notice of application, 60
  petitioner's application, 59, 60
  post-statement changes, 55

INDEX

Consent orders—*contd*
  procedure, 58–60
  property orders, 54
  purpose, 70
  reasons for using, 1–2
  relief already sought, requirement, 74
  remarry, intention to, 54
  respondent's application, 59–60
  service, certification of, 53
  shipshod completion of statement, 58
  side letters, 60–1
  significant matters, attention drawn to, 56
  statement of information, 53–6
    copies of draft order, 56
    dispensation, 55, 57, 60
    estimate in summary form, 55–6
    faulty completion, 58
    form of, 57
    hearing, order agreed during, 55
    importance, 57–8
    minutes of order, 56, 57
    post-statement changes, 55
    precedent, App 12
    shipshod completion, 58
    significant matters, attention drawn to, 56
  statutory recognition, 2, 49, 51
  subsidiary terms, 60–1
  supervisory jurisdiction, 61–3
  tax considerations, 58–9
  timing of agreement, 59
  Tomlin order, 48
Consideration—
  agreement, 12–13
  cohabitation contract, 19
Contact for children, 25
Contract—
  cohabitation, *see* Cohabitation
Contracting out—
  disclosure duty, 66
Costs—
  drafting order, 76
  separation agreement, 26
Covenant not to apply for ancillary relief, 24–5

"Dead letter" agreements, 26
Decree absolute—
  delayed for breach of agreement, 38
Decree nisi—
  consent orders subject to, 59
  drafting consent orders, 73
  Deed, agreement by, 14

Defend, agreement not to, 16
Desertion, 16, 27
Disabled children, 217
Discharge of agreement—
  affirmation of validity, 27
  agreement, by, 26
  bankrputcy, 27
  breach, by, 26–7
  "dead letter" agreements, 26
  law, operation of, 27
  maintenence non-payment, 26–7
  non-payment of maintenance, 26–7
  operation of law, 27
  repudiation, 26
  resumption of cohabitation, 26
Disclosure duty—
  application of duty, 66
  compliance with r.2.61, 65
  contested proceedings, 66
  continuation of duty, 66
  contracting out, 66
  court, duty owed to, 66–7
  duration, 65–6
  existence, 64–5
  general nature, 65
  material non-disclosure, 63–4, 135–40
  nature, 65
  non-contested proceedings, 66
  origins of, 64–5
  party, duty owed to other, 66–7
  questionnaire procedure, 66
  setting aside order, 63–4
  to whom owed, 66–7
Dispensation with statement of information, 55, 57
Divorce—
  one year bar, 7
  reform of law, 10–11
Dominant position, exploitation of, 34–5
Drafting order—
  advantages of well-drawn order, 69
  approaches to, 68–9
  "BY CONSENT", marked, 70
  capacity for enforcement, 75
  commencement of order, 73
  completeness, 74–5
  construction of order, 67–9, 70–1
  costs, 76
  court making order, 71–2
  dates, 74
  decree nisi pronouncement, 73
  duplications, 73
  enforcement, 75

Drafting order—*contd*
  family provision, 75
  good practice, 70–7
  guidelines, 70–7
  House of Lords' view, 67–8
  interest, 74
  judicial warnings, 69
  "liberty to apply", 76
  mechanisms for enforcement, 75–6
  notice of acting, 76–7
  periodical payments, 75
  precedents, 77, App 5
  precision in, 74–5
  purpose of order, 70
  recitals, 72
  relief already sought, requirement, 74
  strict settlements, 75
  term in correct part of order, 72–3
Due diligence—
  appeal, 174
Duress—
  cohabitation contracts, 17
Duty to negotiate, 4–6
Duxbury figures, 87, 102, 113–15

Edgar v Edgar, 30–4
Emergency remedies, 215
Enforcement—
  agreement—
    arrears, 216
    capacity to be enforced, 216
    consent order enforcement
      distinguished, 215–16
    discretion of court, 216
    executory property matters, 216
    matrimonial home agreements, 216
    reasons for, 216
    specific performance, 216
  clean break, 109
  consent orders—
    affirmation of order, 216–17
    agreement enforcement
      distinguished, 215–16
    bank account opened, 217
    Child Support Agency and, 217
    payment methods, 217
    procedures, 217
    recitals, 220
    undertakings, 221
  costs, 218
  drafting order, 75
  emergency remedies, 215
  generally, 8, 215–16

Enforcement—*contd*
  procedures—
    affidavit, 217
    arrears of maintenance, 217–18
    bankruptcy, 218
    costs, 218
    executory consent order, 218–19
    flowchart, 219
    oral examination, 217
    unknown whereabouts, 217
  recitals, 220
  rule of court, agreement made,
    220–1
  undertakings, 221
Estimate in summary form—
  consent orders, 55–6
  financial resources estimate, 55–6
Estoppel—
  variation, 210

Family Court—
  unified, proposals for, 11
Family Law Bar Association (FLBA)
Family Mediators' Association (FMA),
  3
Family order, 125
Family provision—
  clean break, 82, 91–2
  cohabitation, 18
  consent orders, 56
  drafting order, 75
  variation and, 193–5
Fianncial arrangements—
  definition, 28
  statutory definition, 28
Finer Committee, 1
FLBA, 3
FMA *see* Family Mediators' Association
Fraudulent misrepresentation—
  setting aside, 134–5
Fresh action—
  advantage, 165, 175–6
  amounts involved, 175–6
  availability, 162–3
  B-T procedure, 171
  generally, 128
  jurisdictional limits, 176
  originating summons, by way of, 171
  pleadings, 176
    delays, 176
  procedure, 163, 171, 175
Fresh admissible evidence—
  setting aside, 143–5

INDEX

Full and frank disclosure—
  agreement, 14

Historical background—
  agreement, 2–7
  clean break, 6–7
  consent order, 2–7, 48–9
  mediation, 3
Hyman v Hyman, rule in—
  child support, 29
  decision, 27–8
  facts of case, 27–8
  financial arrangement, 28
  interpretation by courts, 29–30
  maintenance agreement, 28
  statutory provisions, 28

Income support—
  clean break, 101–2
Income tax, 8
Indemnity, 24–5
Inequality of bargaining power, 143
Inheritance *see* Family provision
Inheritance tax, 59
Inquiry by court—
  consent orders, 61–3
Instalment provisions—
  variation, 203–4
Intention to create legal relationship—
  agreement, 12
  cohabitation contracts, 17, 18
Interest, 74

Judicial separation, 7

Law Commission Report, 10
Law reform, 9–11
Legal advice, 32–4
Legal aid—
  statutory charge, 6, 87
"Liberty to apply", 178–9
  drafting order, 76
  variation, 204–5
Lump sum—
  calculation, 110–15
  clean break, *see* Clean break
Lump sum payments—
  rule of court, agreement made, 44

Magistrates' court orders, 188
Maintenance—
  agreement, *see* Maintenance agreement, 15–16

Maintenance—*contd*
  child support, *see* Child support
  income tax, 8
  non-payment, 26–7
  tax relief, 7–8, 14–15
Maintenance agreement—
  ancillary relief, covenant not to apply for, 24–5
  child support, 117–19
  construction, 22–6
  content, 22–6
  covenant not to apply for ancillary relief, 24–5
  definition, 15, 28
  discharge, *see* Discharge of agreement
  extent of obligations, 24
  future proceedings, 23
  Hyman v Hyman, rule in, *see Hyman v Hyman*, rule in
  incorporation, 39
  indemnity, 24–5
  meaning, 15–16
  non-molestation clause, 22–3
  property, 25
  reasonableness, 39
  recitals, 22
  separation agreement distinguished, 15–16
  statutory definition, 15, 28
  tax relief, 23–4
  taxation, 26
  variation, *see* Variation
  will, agreement to leave by, 26
Maintenance pending suit—
  consent orders, 52–3
Martin order, 83
Material non-disclosure—
  setting aside, 135–40
Mediation—
  agreement resulting from, 21–2
  British Association of Lawyer Mediators (BALM), 3
  Code of Practice, 3
  conciliation distinguished, 2
  court-based, 3
  Family Law Bar Association (FLBA), 3
  Family Mediators' Association (FMA), 3
  growth of movement, 2
  historical background, 3
  UK College of Mediation, 3
Mesher order, 83, 126

Minutes of order, 56, 57
Misrepresentation, 134–5
Mistake—
 agreement, 13
 setting aside, 132–4

NAFMCS *see* National Association of Family Mediation and Conciliation Services
National Association of Family Mediation and Conciliation Services (NAFMCS), 3
National Family Conciliation Council (NFCC), 2–3
National Family Conciliation Service, 9
NFCC *see* National Family Conciliation Council
Non-molestation clause—
 separation agreement, 22–3
Non-variable orders—
 clean break, 83–8

Omissions—
 setting aside, 134
Oral agreement, 14–15, 28

Parental responsibility agreement, 20
Part performance, 14
Payment methods, 217
Pensions—
 clean break, 84, 113
Periodical payments—
 drafting order, 75
 nominal, 98–9
 rule of court, agreement made, 44
 secured order, 197–8
 variation, 197–8
Post-nuptial settlement, 183–4
Postponed clean break, 83, 90–1
Pre-marital contracts—
 20–21, App 1
Procedure—
 consent orders, 58–60
 setting aside, *see* Setting aside
Property—
 maintenance agreement, 25
 separation agreement, 25
Property adjustment orders—
 child support and, App 6
 rule of court, agreement made, 44
Public policy—
 agreement, 13
 cohabitation contracts, 17, 18

Public policy—*contd*
 future separation, 16

Questionnaire procedure, 66

Re-hearing—
 application, 171, 176
 availability, 171
 Barder type event, 176
 difficulties with, 172–3
 error of court at hearing, 172
 extent of jurisdiction, 172
 procedure, 171–2, 176
Recitals—
 agreement, 22
 clean break, 94
 consent orders, 72
 function, 72
 historical, 22
 introductory, 72
 narrative, 22
Reconciliation agreement—
 16, App 3
Reform of law, 9–11
Relevant law—
 separation agreement, 26
Residence of children, 25
Restriction of rights, *see Hyman v Hyman*, rule in
Resumption of cohabitation, *see* Cohabitation
Rule of court, agreement made—
 advantages, 45, 46–7
 application, App 7
 capital gains tax disposals, 47
 consent, 44
 documents, 45
 early stage, made at, 44
 effect, 46
 enforcement, 220–1
 estoppel, 44
 jurisdiction, 43–4
 lump sum payments, 44
 "normal rule", 47–8
 periodical payments, 44
 procedural requirements, 45
 property adjustment orders, 44
 protection, as, 47
 slip rule, 44
 special procedure, 45–6
 tax considerations, 58–9
 terms of agreement, 45
 use of procedure, 44–5

INDEX

Rule of court, agreement made— *contd*
  variation, 213–14

School fees orders, 217
Separation agreement—
  ancillary relief, covenent not to apply for, 24–5
  breach of obligation, 38–9
  children, 25
  circumstances, change in, 35–7
  construction, 22–6
  contact for children, 25
  content, 22–6
  costs, 26
  covenant not to apply for ancillary relief, 24–5
  deed, App 4
  discharge, *see* Discharge of agreement
  dominant position exploited, 34–5
  future proceedings, 23
  inadequate knowledge, 35–7
  incorporation, 39
  indemnity, 24–5
  live apart, agreement to, 22
  maintenance agreement distinguished, 15–16
  meaning, 15–16
  non-molestation clause, 22–3
  precedent, App, 4
  property, 25
  recitals, 22
  relevant law, 26
  residence of children, 25
  resonableness, 39
  taxation, 26
  undue influence, 34–5
  variation, *See* Variation
  will, agreement to leave by, 26
Setting aside—
  Barder rules—
    applications of rule, 146–56
    approach to, 155–6
    causation, 155–6
    caution in, 157
    clean break orders, 150
    conditions, 146
    effect of event, 154–5
    evidence, 146
    facts of case, 145–6
    floodgates argument, 157–60
    frustration, 147, 154
    generally, 129, 130
    increasing property prices, 152–4

Setting aside— *contd*
  Barder rules— *contd*
    knowledge of death, 15
    limitations of jurisdiction, 151
    Livesey v Jenkins and, 151–2
    mistake, 147
    out of time, leave to, 157–9
    policy considerations, 148
    property prices, 152–3
    qualification to principle, 156
    reopening valuation, 149–50
    status quo preservation, 154–5
    substance of case, 160–1
    unexpected death, 150–1, 153–4
    valuation differences, 147–8, 156–7
  bargaining power, inequality of, 143
  consent, 131–2
  fraudulent misrepresentation, 134–5
  fresh admissible evidence, 143–5
  generally, 129–30
  grounds, 129 *et seq*
  inequality of bargaining power, 143
  lack of consent, 131–2
  litigation, 131
  material non-disclosure, 135–40
  matrimonial consent orders, 130–1
  misrepresentation, 134–5
  mistake, 132–4
  omissions, 134
  policy considerations, 130
  procedure—
    available remedies, 162–9
    Barder type complaint, 168
    choice of route, 167, 169
    clarification of law, 164
    extension of time, 167–9
    fresh action, 164
    leave, obtaining, 167
    limitation, 168
    misrepresentation, 165–7
    normal, 169
    reform of law, 164
    summary, 163
    time bar, 164–5
  supervisory jurisdiction of courts, 130
  unconscionable bargain, 142
  undue influence, 140–1
  vitiating factor, 130
Side letters—
  consent orders, 60–1
Specific performance, 179–81, 216
Statement of information, *see* Consent orders

INDEX

Statutory charge, 6, 87
Strict settlements—
 drafting order, 75

Taxation—
 maintenance agreement, 26
 separation agreement, 26
Tomlin order, 48
Top-up orders, 217
Transfer of property order—
 clean break, 85–6

UK College of Mediation, 3
Unconscionable bargain—
 setting aside, 142
Undertakings, 40
 enforcement, 221
 variation, 205–6, 214
Undue influence—
 breakdown of marriage, 34–5
 pre-marital contracts, 21
 setting aside, 140–1

Variable orders—
 clean break, 88–91
Variation—
 agreements—
  capital provisions, 187–8
  children, maintenance agreements for, 189–91
  court's powers, 186–8
  during lives of parties, 183–91
  family provision, 193–5
  justification, 185–6
  lives of parties, during, 183–91
  magistrates' powers, 188
  MCA 1973, application under, 184–5
  post-nuptial settlement, 183–4
  procedure, 188–9
  requirements justifying, 185–6
 arrears, 197
 automatic, 212–13
 children, maintenance agreements for, 189–91
  consent orders, 210–11
  death of one party, after, 191–5
 consent orders—
  afresh, looking, 207–8
  arrears, 197
  automatic, 212–13
  budgetary approach, 209
  change in circumstances, 206

Variation— *contd*
 consent orders— *contd*
  children, 210–11
  circumstances of case, 211
  clean break promoted, 206, 211–12
  date of variation, 205
  effective date, 205
  erroneous basis of original order, 209
  estoppel, 210
  extension of time, by, 201–3
  extent of powers, 195
  forseeable future, 209–10
  full inquiry, after, 207
  future changes, 209–10
  incapacity, 195
  instalment provisions, 203–4
  interest, order for, 199–201
  liberty to apply, 204–5
  methods, 195
  "millionaire's defence", 197
  mistakes in original order, 209
  non-disclosure, 207
  orders, 195
  original order, 207
  periodical payments order, 197–8
  principles governing court's powers, 206–10
  procedure, 213
  reform proposals, 198–9
  secured periodical payments order, 197–8
  secured provision, 205
  starting point, 207–10
  term orders, 196–7
  time extension, by, 201–3
  undertakings, 205–6
 court's powers, 186–8
 death of one party, after, 191–5
 during lives of parties, 183–91
 estoppel, 210
 family provision, 193–5
 generally, 182
 instalment provisions, 203–4
 interest, order for, 199–201
 justification, 185–6
 liberty to apply, 204–5
 lives of parties, during, agreement, 183–91
 magistrates' powers, 188
 MCA 1973, application under, 184–5
 "millionaire's defence", 197

INDEX

Variation—*contd*
  periodical payments order, 197–8
  post-nuptial settlement, 183–4
  principles governing court's powers, 206–10
  procedure, 188–9
  reform proposals, 198–9
  requirements justifying, 185–6
  rules of court, agreements made, 213–14
  secured periodical payments order, 197–8
  term orders, 196–7

Variation—*contd*
  undertakings, 205–6, 214
Void—
  agreement, 13
  cohabitation contract, 18
Voidable agreement, 13

Widow's pension rights—
  clean break, 113
Wife-swopping agreement, 13
Will, agreement to leave by, 26
Written agreement—
  14, *see also* Agreement